Writing the Revolution

In Germany, the concept of "1968" is enduring and synonymous with the German Student Movement, and is viewed, variously, as a fundamental liberalization, a myth, a second foundation, or an irritation. The movement's aims—radical re-imagination of the political and economic order and social hierarchy—have been understood as requiring a "long march." While the movement has been judged at best a "successful failure," cultural elites continue to engage in the construction of 1968. Ingo Cornils's book argues that writing about 1968 in Germany is no longer about the historical events or the specific objectives of a bygone counterculture, but is instead a moral touchstone, a marker of social group identity meant to keep alive (or at bay) a utopian agenda that continues to fire the imagination. The book demonstrates that the representation of 1968 as a "foundational myth" suits the needs of a number of surprisingly heterogeneous groups, and that even attempts to deconstruct the myth strengthen it. Cornils brings together for the first time the historical, literary, and media representations of the movement, showing the motivation behind and effect of almost five decades of writing about 1968. In so doing, Cornils challenges the way 1968 has been instrumentalized: as a powerful imaginary that has colonized every aspect of life in Germany, and as symbolic capital in cultural and political debates.

Studies in German Literature, Linguistics, and Culture

Writing the Revolution

The Construction of "1968" in Germany

Ingo Cornils

CAMDEN HOUSE
Rochester, New York

Copyright © 2016 Ingo Cornils

All Rights Reserved. Except as permitted under current legislation, no part of this work may be photocopied, stored in a retrieval system, published, performed in public, adapted, broadcast, transmitted, recorded, or reproduced in any form or by any means, without the prior permission of the copyright owner.

First published 2016 by Camden House
Reprinted in paperback 2020

Camden House is an imprint of Boydell & Brewer Inc.
668 Mt. Hope Avenue, Rochester, NY 14620, USA
www.camden-house.com
and of Boydell & Brewer Limited
PO Box 9, Woodbridge, Suffolk IP12 3DF, UK
www.boydellandbrewer.com

Paperback ISBN-13: 978-1-64014-071-4
Paperback ISBN-10: 1-64014-071-9
Hardcover ISBN-13: 978-1-57113-954-2
Hardcover ISBN-10: 1-57113-954-0

Library of Congress Cataloging-in-Publication Data

Names: Cornils, Ingo, author.
Title: Writing the revolution : the construction of "1968" in Germany / Ingo Cornils.
Other titles: Construction of "1968" in Germany
Description: Rochester, New York : Camden House, [2016] | Series: Studies in German literature, linguistics, and culture | Includes bibliographical references and index.
Identifiers: LCCN 2016010607| ISBN 9781571139542 (hardcover : alk. paper) | ISBN 1571139540 (hardcover : alk. paper)
Subjects: LCSH: Nineteen sixty-eight, A.D. | Germany (West)—Politics and government—20th century—Historiography. | Protest movements—Germany (West) | Opposition (Political science)—Germany (West) | Authoritarianism--Germany (West)—History. | Counterculture—Germany (West)—History. | Popular culture—Germany (West)—History. | Student movements—Germany (West)—History.
Classification: LCC DD260.4 .C66 2016 | DDC 943.087/6—dc23 LC record available at https://lccn.loc.gov/2016010607

For Liza and Max

Contents

Preface to the Paperback Edition	ix
Acknowledgments	xi
Introduction	1
1: Heroes and Martyrs	16
2: Chroniclers and Interpreters	38
3: Critics and Renegades	73
4: Tale Spinners and Poets	94
5: Women of the Revolution	140
6: "1968" and the Media	151
7: "1968" and the Arts	175
8: *Zaungäste*	186
9: Not Dark Yet: The 68ers at Seventy	195
10: Romantic Relapse or Modern Myth?	210
Conclusion	222
Notes	229
Bibliography	267
Index	303

Preface to the Paperback Edition

THIS BOOK IS NOT ABOUT the events of a bygone era but rather about the edifice that has been constructed on top of these events by academics, writers, and the media. While the generation of 68ers is retiring from the limelight, their erstwhile disruption, their belief in the possibility and necessity of fundamental change, is endlessly reexamined, amplified, mythologized, and instrumentalized. This book demonstrates that the unity of thought, feeling, and action, the clarity of purpose associated with the cypher "1968,"[1] has become a holy grail and a black hole, an obsession for a cultural elite of intellectuals, writers, and opinion makers. It shows how the resultant myth of "1968" has entered the imagination of the many through the writings of the few, and continues to determine cultural production and political decision-making. This process cannot go on indefinitely—decisions have to be made whether Germany can integrate the memory of "1968" into its political culture, either by accepting the tenets of the movement as a moral touchstone or by rejecting them as romantic relapse. This is not just important for insider debates in the German media, academia, or literature but also for Germany's political and cultural identity. The construction of "1968" into a "magic moment" both unassailable and unattainable has dominated debates for over five decades, and arguably affected the country's ability to play its part on the global stage. By revealing the discourse on "1968" as largely constructed, my research will enable readers to see this process more clearly.

This book takes a conscious stand vis-à-vis one of the key debates about the legacy of "1968." I argue that there is a clear difference between the idealistic aspirations of a broad movement of young people rebelling against what they perceived to be an authoritarian political system, and the subsequent violent actions of a few.[2] In spite of many attempts to make all 68ers responsible for the terrorism of the Red Army Faction in the 1970s, the fact remains that the German student movement had run its course by the time the RAF was founded. The book is also unapologetic about its insistence on the continuing relevance of "1968" for political and cultural discourses in Germany. In spite of predictions that public and academic interest in the era would diminish, the fact is that the media, academics, and literary authors continue to engage with the movement and its legacy. Indeed, as the chart accompanying my bibliography shows, publications on the German "1968" show no signs of drying up.

One of the intriguing results of the conference "Memories of 1968: International Perspectives" that I co-organized in Leeds back in 2008 was that the events of that tumultuous period are remembered very differently in France, Italy, the United Kingdom, the United States, Mexico, and China.[3] The afterlives of "1968" at national level range from state-sponsored amnesia, through abhorrence and embarrassment, to celebration and state-sponsored remembrance. But "1968" isn't just about memories. As the historicization of the era gathers momentum, we must realize that what we remember, what makes it into our history books, is an artificial construct, the sum total of five decades worth of debates, representations, myths, and projections, but, above all, incessant writing. This construct is immensely political, given that many of the radical questions the students posed are still waiting for an answer: Is there an alternative to the commodification of every aspect of our lives, the politics of strength, the rituals of exploitation, inequality, and prejudice? And if so, will we find the political will to radically change the status quo?

NB: Unless otherwise indicated, translations of German sources into English are my own.

Acknowledgments

This project has had a long gestation period, and thanks are due to the School of Languages, Cultures and Societies as well as the Faculty of Arts at the University of Leeds for the granting of research leave and the opportunity to attend conferences and visit archives. I would like to thank past and present colleagues for their support: Margaret Atack, Michael Beddow, Paul Cooke, Syd Donald, Helen Finch, Frank Finlay, Chris Homewood, Claire Honess, Alan O'Leary, Stephan Petzold, Ingrid Sharp, Max Silverman, Stuart Taberner, and Sarah Waters. Equally, several cohorts of students who attended my seminar "The German Student Movement" have given me valuable insights. Hans Kundnani (London/Berlin) and Timothy S. Brown (Northeastern University, Boston) kindly came to Leeds to present their research on 1968. Beyond Leeds, I am grateful to Gerrit-Jan Berendse at Cardiff University and Detlef Siegfried at the University of Copenhagen, as well as Martin Klimke and colleagues at the International Centre for Protest Research in Heidelberg and Zurich, for many stimulating discussions. Various publishers have given me the opportunity to preview key publications in the field that have inspired me to organize my own thoughts. Mike Collins was the first to read the manuscript in its entirety and provided a much needed outside perspective. Adam Roberts helped to compile the index. The two anonymous readers of this book made many helpful suggestions, and Jim Walker, the editorial director of Camden House, has supported the project at every stage. Last but not least, my sincere thanks go to Wolfgang Kraushaar at the Hamburg Institute for Social Research for his insights and his unflagging enthusiasm for "the year that changed everything."

IC
Leeds/Cardiff, July 2016

Introduction

Few events in the second half of the twentieth century have been as influential (or, according to a different viewpoint, overhyped) as the global cultural revolutions of the late 1960s. Mark Kurlansky declared that "1968 rocked the world," while, for West Germany, Wolfgang Kraushaar declared that "1968" was "the year that changed everything."[1] The German "1968," one should note, signifies the German student movement, the constituent and most active part of the Außerparlamentarische Opposition (APO, Extraparliamentary Opposition) that emerged in response to the formation of the grand coalition between the conservative and social democratic parties in 1966. It lasted just three years in West Germany (mirroring the duration of the grand coalition), with a "hot phase" from June 1967 to the autumn of 1968. In this brief period, a student was shot dead by a policeman at a demonstration against the visit of the Shah of Persia in West Berlin and students mobilized against the monopoly of the Springer press, organized an international conference on the Vietnam War, and sought to prevent the introduction of new *Notstandsgesetze* (emergency laws). Following the assassination attempt on the student leader Rudi Dutschke and the subsequent *Osterunruhen* (Easter riots), the passing of the emergency laws, and the Warsaw Pact invasion in Czechoslovakia in August 1968, the movement fell apart. As such, it differs in duration and intensity from the shorter French "May" or the longer "sixties" (which include the Civil Rights Movement, the Free Speech Movement and the "Summer of Love") in the United States. But while "1968" has different connotations in countries of the Western world, the similarities with and interrelations between these protest movements are so strong that the events are now often regarded as the first global rebellion.[2]

Despite these similarities, the West German student movement arguably has a unique composition and afterlife. Termed by its intellectual leaders as "antiauthoritarian," it challenged authoritarian structures and practices, initially at universities, but increasingly in every institution from family to schools and factories. Conceived as fundamental critique against a system widely perceived by the left-wing activists at the time as representing the unreconstructed forces that had led to Fascism and World War II, the West German version of "1968" was burdened with more complex issues to rebel against and a greater ideological challenge than in other Western countries. Because of this, and its inconclusive legacy as "successful failure" (a compromise verdict often heard in the 1990s that allowed both sides to claim victory),[3] "1968" was never laid to rest in West Germany and continues to define several discourses in unified Germany. Thus, whether people debate the boundaries and identities of generational cohorts, the role of the intellectual, the legacy of politically motivated violence (from the Third Reich to the Red Army Faction), the power of social movements (e.g., the green and peace movements), the position of women in society, the power and limits of historiography (e.g., the positing of a "red decade" or the relative merits of the old Federal Republic of Germany and the German Democratic Republic), the merits of education reforms in schools and universities, the relationship between political protest and "cultural revolution," or the rise of transnational protest movements (e.g., the Arab Spring or the Occupy movement), "1968" provides a baseline for comment.

Several attempts have been made to consign "1968" to the past. "1968 is history" was the provocative title political scientist Claus Leggewie chose for his article in a special issue of the respected journal *Aus Parlament und Zeitgeschichte* (Politics and Contemporary History) on the "68er generation."[4] Ingrid Gilcher-Holtey's conference volume *1968: Vom Ereignis zum Gegenstand der Geschichtswissenschaft* (From Event to Object of Historical Science, 1998) had a similar message: apart from the obvious point about the passing of time, the authors argued that "1968" should be wrested from the control of the *Zeitzeugen* (contemporary witnesses) and given over to proper scrutiny by the professionals.[5]

These attempts have until now been fought off successfully by the 68ers themselves who are unwilling to lose control over the interpretation of their formative years. Not that the 68ers were ever united in how they see their own past. A number of former activists have broken ranks and turned to the "dark side," either as editor in chief of a conservative newspaper (Thomas Schmid) or in highly critical broadsides against their youthful escapades. "Unsere kleine Kulturrevolution" (our little cultural revolution) was the telling subtitle of Gerd Koenen's influential reflection on what he termed the "red decade" between 1967 and 1977,[6] while Götz Aly's autobiographical polemic *Unser Kampf* (Our Struggle, 2008) signaled not only the provocative thesis that the 68ers were not so different from their Nazi-fathers but that, in his view, it was *their* struggle, and not something they would give others permission to judge.[7]

The image of "1968" has never been static. Fresh revelations continue to challenge our understanding of the era. One example for this is the discovery in 2009 that the policeman who shot innocent bystander Benno Ohnesorg at a demonstration in West Berlin on June 2, 1967, was a Stasi informer. Given that this shooting was the catalyst for the "hot phase" of the German student movement, politically galvanized a generation, and provided the excuse for a minority of radical students to go underground and set up terrorist organizations such as the Bewegung 2. Juni (Movement June 2) and the Rote Armee Fraktion (Red Army Faction, or RAF), the news caused consternation among the followers of the "continuity thesis" who had staunchly believed that underneath its democratic facade, West Germany was a fascist state that would never tolerate an interruption to the accumulation of wealth by those in power. The fact that the West German policeman who pulled the trigger had been working for the East German Stasi brought down this theory with a bang.

Another example is the previously widely held belief that the German student movement was antinationalist, antifascist and antiauthoritarian. We now know that none of these assumptions were entirely correct. Rudi Dutschke's comrades Bernd Rabehl and Horst Mahler turned into exponents of far right German nationalism in later life. Antifascist did not mean pro-Semitic, as Wolfgang Kraushaar showed in his excellent *Die Bombe im jüdischen Gemeindehaus* (The Bomb in the Jewish Community Center, 2005). Indeed, there is evidence of a continuity of anti-Semitic positions from the Nazis to some 68ers. Finally, the contradiction between the autocratic alpha-male leaders in the Sozialistischer Deutscher Studentenbund (SDS, Socialist German Student League)[8] and their antiauthoritarian slogans was obvious not only to the Frankfurter Weiberrat (Council of Frankfurt Women) and the subsequent German women's movement (see chapter 5) but also to the members of the notorious Kommune I (Commune I) who continued to intrigue the public with their antics after they had been ousted by their SDS comrades in May 1967.

In spite of all these corrections to our "official" image of "1968," in spite of an unending barrage of criticism, ridicule, and media interest, and in spite of repeated attempts to link the idealism of the 68ers with the terror of the Red Army Faction, "1968" has become an integral part of German political and cultural history. This was not always the case. In fact, until Germany's Federal President Richard von Weizsäcker declared in 1990 that the movement had ultimately strengthened democratic engagement,[9] it was considered a failure by its sympathizers and a lucky escape for the democratic state by its opponents (see chapters 2 and 3). Yet today, "1968" features in the permanent exhibition in the Haus der Geschichte (House of History) in Bonn and in the Deutsches Historisches Museum (German Historical Museum) in Berlin. This "normalization," however, has been a rocky road.

One reason for the contested meaning of "1968" in Germany is that it serves as an ideal political battleground. In January 2001, Bettina Röhl, daughter of journalist-turned-terrorist Ulrike Meinhof, posted an accusation on her website stating that Joschka Fischer, then foreign minister and vice-chancellor of the Federal Republic of Germany, had committed serious crimes as a militant "sponti" during and in the aftermath of the German student movement. He was accused of beating up a policeman at a demonstration and, more seriously, of supporting terrorists.[10] The timing of these "revelations" was crucial: the CDU (Christian Democratic Union) opposition hoped to deflect public attention from their own party finance scandal, and put the red–green coalition government under pressure. The ensuing debate—held publicly and with surprising ferocity—brought all the old antagonists into the ring again. The majority of the population looked on in mild amusement, and wished Fischer to remain in office,[11] seeing him as a man who had learned from his experiences and accepting that his "historical baggage" was actually a positive attribute in Germany's bland political landscape.

As to the "serious debate" about the alleged catastrophic impact of the German student movement on German society, as attempted in the heated debate in the Bundestag on January 17, 2001, it did not yield anything new. Not only had the campaign of the CDU run out of steam—Angela Merkel's demand in the Bundestag that left-of-center politicians associated with "1968" should once and for all renounce their 68 past was generally considered ill-informed and hypocritical by political commentators. Ms. Röhl's publisher dropped her planned biography of Fischer, and an attempt to put him on trial for perjury was seen as an obvious ploy motivated by party-political interests. What was termed by German weekly *Die Zeit* as a "dritte Vergangenheitsbewältigung" (a third collective effort to come to terms with Germany's past) never really took place, not because there was nothing to come to terms with (Fischer did apologize for his violent acts and stressed that he had moved away from militant action by the midseventies) but because the "1968" had become a convenient object for political point-scoring.

The furor caused by the "Fischer scandal" is long gone. And yet, while the political dominance of the 68er generation and their red–green "project" came to an end in 2005, clearing the way for Angela Merkel to become chancellor, the 68ers stubbornly claim that history has proved them right: they argue that without "1968" Germany would not have turned into a tolerant and civil society where a woman could become chancellor and a gay man the mayor of the capital, Berlin.

A second reason for the rocky road to normalization is that "1968" has become a battleground over what constitutes the "correct" memory. For many Germans, "1968" is part of their formative past, the cherished or reviled object of memory, hotly contested by those who have living memories of, or a vested interest in, the era. Some feel that its utopian promise has not been fulfilled, while others believe that one must get rid of the utopian ideas to return to moral certainties that had existed before. Recent debates have contributed to a memorialization of "1968," which places precedence on the lived experience of these events through a plethora of personal testimonies, autobiographies, and partisan accounts. Former activists may wish to relive their days of glory or atone for what they now perceive as the sins of their youth. In any event, "1968" is alive in many people's memory, though these memories differ widely. "1968" has thus become an arena for what Anne Fuchs, Mary Cosgrove, and Georg Grote have termed "memory contests," where former activists and observers are often pitted against one another and different interpretations of the movement itself clash: "Memory contests are highly dynamic public engagements with the past that are triggered by an event that is perceived as a massive disturbance of a community's self-understanding."[12]

A third reason for the difficulties with "1968" is that it has become a bone of contention between different generations. There is a strong feeling that the 68ers have overstayed their welcome, dominating the limelight for too long while less glamorous generations, such as the "Generation Golf" or the generation that regards the Berlin Republic as its political and spiritual *Heimat* (home), have not received enough recognition for their own achievements. This perception is well founded. While the 68ers never had much influence in the worlds of business, finance, and manufacturing, they managed, on their "Long March through the institutions" (initiated by student leader Rudi Dutschke when it became clear that provocation and protests in the street were ineffective), to gain positions of influence in universities, schools, media, cultural industries, public administration, and NGOs. All of these have high visibility and impact. One example would be *Das Philosophische Quartett* (The Philosophical Quartet), a late-night television program aimed at the cultural elite that aired between 2002 and 2012. Fronting the program were Peter Sloterdijk and Rüdiger Safranski, both former 68ers.

It should come as no surprise, therefore, that there is no consensus as to what the effects of "1968" were and how we should interpret them. This may seem odd given that the *Wirtschaftswunder* (economic miracle) of the 1950s and the *Ostpolitik* of the 1970s have been consigned to the history books without much resistance. Yet Germany's "1968" appears to be impervious to the corrosion of time and inhabits a central place in Germany's collective consciousness entirely out of sync with its immediate political impact.

Even the most ardent supporters of the 68ers would agree that the aims of the German student movement (i.e., the short term goals of stopping the grand coalition parties to use their absolute majority to pass the so-called emergency laws; breaking up the monopoly of the Springer press; and forcing the United States to end their bombing campaign in Vietnam; as well as the long term goals of overthrowing the political order in West Germany and establishing a form of grassroots socialism) were not achieved. They would contend, though, that its medium and long-term cultural and social impact had a fundamental and positive effect on German society. Critics of the 68ers are scathing about such a benign political and social legacy and argue that if the 68ers had any positive cultural impact at all, it was unintended. It is this ambiguous verdict of a "successful failure" (with "success" and "failure" situated on different interpretive levels) and the tension between the opposing camps that drive the continued interest in "1968."

Seen by some as a watershed in the postwar history of West Germany that swept away the cobwebs of postwar restoration in a "Fundamentalliberalisierung" (fundamental liberalization),[13] and by others as ground zero for the country's moral decline, the era's legacy had become fiercely contested even before it attracted renewed interest when the 68er generation belatedly seized political power in Germany in 1998. The red–green coalition government came to an end in 2005, but the continuing production of journalistic, academic, and literary writings about the German student movement, together with the fact that many of the radical questions posed by the students remain "a thorn in the side" (Oskar Negt) of the Berlin Republic, ensure that the (contested) legacy and (constructed) myth of the 68ers still influence a host of debates and discourses in Germany.

For if "1968" is history, then history can and will be constructed. Perhaps this is not what Rudi Dutschke, the charismatic figurehead of the German student movement, intended when he pronounced, "Geschichte ist machbar" (We can make history), but the effect may well be the same. There is also no doubt as to the continuing attraction of "1968." In terms of identifying a political position, it is still a useful label for the media (e.g., when describing the mindset of the founders of *Charlie Hebdo*). "1968" is also lucrative. In the 2008 anniversary year no publisher could afford not to have at least one title on "1968" in its program, and the fiftieth anniversary may well see a similar flurry of activity. The media continue to feed the hunger for sensationalist titillation but also the curiosity of younger generations who want to know what all the fuss was about. In addition, nostalgia for a more innocent, yet also (allegedly) more exciting era drives the construction, as well as a desire to hang on to a utopian dream that the world needs to be different. And while the Federal Agency for Civic Education, leading German historians, and intellectuals collaborate to create to a semiofficial picture of "1968," grassroots networks, countercultural activists and micropublishers continue to challenge this appropriation "from above," arguing that "their" era has been taken over by the establishment.

Albrecht von Lucke correctly observes that "1968" has experienced several booms over the decades, during which the term was filled with completely different meanings and interpretations. The reason for this, he argues, has to do with the continuing struggles for cultural hegemony in Germany, the fight over who gets to define one of the key events of Germany's postwar history. He identifies three distinct phases: A first period lasting from 1967 to 1977, when the notion of the 68ers as a political generation was first established. The creation of this specific generational cohort led to a view that the history of "1968" was also the history of the 68ers, which in turn led to an "us and them" mentality. The term "68er" became either a positively charged badge of honor accepted by former activists or a derogatory term when used by their opponents.

Following the hardening of the battle lines during the confrontation between state and left-wing terrorists known as *Deutscher Herbst* (German Autumn), a second phase covers almost thirty years, from 1978 to 2005. In this period, the history of "1968" and the 68ers was read as a *deutscher Familienroman* (German family novel), with the focus of public interest very much on their political potential, most significantly the "red–green project." Since the demise of the red–green coalition government in 2005, we find ourselves in a third phase, which is less concerned about the future of the 68ers than about the rehabilitation of the bourgeois (the self-interested citizen as opposed to the *citoyen*, the public-spirited citizen). Von Lucke's argument culminates in the suggestion that the creation of the political generation of "the 68ers" is an ongoing process that involves both a measurable sociological process and an element of fiction.

It is the role of the "Generationsstifter und -erzähler" (founders and storytellers of a generation)[14] and how they go about their self-appointed project, which will be at the core of this study. For, as von Lucke points out, these tale spinners not only help to construct a generation but something much larger: the myth of a generation. The process of constructing "1968," as I shall argue in the following chapters, is achieved by a relatively small number of individuals, and via distinct yet closely related activities that mythicize, historicize, vilify, aestheticize, theorize, sensationalize, dramatize, and glorify the era. Together, these activities form a *Gesamtzusammenhang*: a complex discourse in the public sphere with a shared set of references, images, and ideas.

Susan McManus argues that in spite of the loss of faith in the grand narratives of our time, any political identity depends on "the imaginative moment, with its production of critical and perhaps even unruly and disruptive knowledges [. . .], and the moments of (re-)founding, (re-)ordering, and (re-)coding of the political."[15] This tallies with Ernst Bloch's insistence that reality is forever unfinished, and Herbert Marcuse's insight that dealing with an unrealized past necessarily constitutes the imperative to action.[16] In other words, in writing about the "successful failure," all those contributing to the construction of "1968" bring it that little bit closer to becoming a reality in our consciousness.

In turn, the continued effort of "writing" is a constituent element of the construction process. Its practice holds a central space in the mind of former activists and their sworn enemies—renegades, conservative intellectuals, and media pundits. It is their preferred mode of communication, their medium to organize their thoughts. For disappointed revolutionary selves, the written page is a refuge in the face of sobering reality, and an opportunity to keep alive "the spirit of 68." For others, it is their medium of choice to attack, denunciate, or ridicule the 68ers. By common consent, books, articles, and newspapers serve as the battleground, reflecting by and large the generational experiences and media preferences of the 68er generation. Even though television features, interviews, and, increasingly, new media are employed by both sides, the serious debates over the merits, impact, and unfinished business of the movement continue to be found in print: the battles are fought *am Schreibtisch* (at and from the writing desk).

The literary representation of "1968" is a particularly interesting case in point here, and certainly not restricted to Germany (see chapter 4). Fiction plays a vital, though often overlooked, role in the construction of "1968" in Germany. The writers "controlling the story" follow Gramsci's theory of passive revolution. I will read their sustained efforts to influence the debate in the light of a programmatic "political re-education" (Hans Magnus Enzensberger, 1968; Henning Marmulla, 2011) and an "aesthetics of resistance" (Peter Weiss, 1975ff.). While literary scholars (e.g., Ralf Schnell, Andrew Plowman) and critics have identified a distinct subgenre of semiautobiographical texts set in, or against the backdrop of, the German student movement, and literary histories generally feature key representations of the movement, there has been hardly any mention of these texts and their potential impact on the broader public in the political debate over the legacy of "1968." This is a major gap in current research that this study aims to fill. Major names in German literature (Günter Grass, Peter Schneider, Uwe Timm, Friedrich Christian Delius) have produced well-known texts—not only in the aftermath of 1968 but also over the last four decades. I will demonstrate that these and many less well-known texts not only help to shape what Germans believe about the movement but imbue "1968" with a utopian aura, an offer of identification, and a continuing obligation to act.

The secondary literature on "1968" in Germany is vast, and keeps on growing. Nick Thomas, who wrote the first serious history of the era in English, commented with surprise that bookshops in Germany had dedicated shelves and sections for the 68er movement.[17] On the fortieth anniversary in 2008, Timothy Garton Ash observed ironically that more ink has flowed recalling that year than did blood from the guillotines of Paris after 1789.[18] Years of writing about "1968" have created a myth, a cypher, and a caesura, according Wolfgang Kraushaar, Germany's foremost scholar on 1968.[19] "1968 ist eine Jahreszahl, in der sich das Imaginäre eingenistet hat" (1968 is a year that has become a breeding ground for the imagination) observed the German writer Hans Magnus Enzensberger.[20] In addition, the collapse of communism has created a market thirsty for the era's idealism and utopian dream. This is more than nostalgia: as long as the 68ers live, they will try and maintain the hegemony over the interpretation of their defining moment, while those who are challenging the "myth of 68" are simply adding to it.

Clearly, to construct an "imaginary" that has lasted well over forty years requires more than just a few activists-turned-writers telling their tale of sound and fury. In the case of writing about "1968" in Germany, we can observe a snowball effect: the revolutionary zeal of a handful of writers became decoupled from their object: the original story of the revolt of a few thousand young students was soon supplemented by sex, drugs, and rock and roll, an ideal mixture luridly presented in the pages of West Germany's most popular publication for students, *konkret*. Its editor Klaus Rainer Röhl and its chief columnist Ulrike Meinhof enjoyed financial support from the GDR to subvert the critical youth of the West and make them more favorably disposed toward (centralized) socialism, but the main impact of the magazine was to broaden the appeal of the student movement through association with the cultural and sexual revolution of the time, a trend that was soon followed by the West German mainstream media from *Der Spiegel* to *Bild* (see chapter 6).

A similar phenomenon can be observed in the academic study of "1968." While the nature of events, the continuing activity of political student groups after the demise of the German student movement, and the emergence of new social movements all ensured a broad awareness of events and their impact, initial research was limited to former activists-turned-academics who offered seminars on the political and social agenda of the movement. With the first literary representations of "1968," lecturers sympathetic to the aims and objectives of the movement began to run seminars roughly from the mid-1970s, though mainly at "progressive" universities such as Bremen and Hamburg.[21]

It is interesting to note that historical research into "1968" was initially carried out by former activists who had built up their own private archives. "Serious" historical research into "1968" at "traditional" universities is a relatively new phenomenon, and mainly carried out by a new generation of scholars. The reasons for this renewed and sustained interest are less clear and will be explored in chapter 2—as the era recedes it becomes the object of historicization, especially by *Zeitgeschichtler* (historians of recent history). At the same time, there is something intrinsically fascinating about the revolt of a young intellectual elite, particularly if one suspects that they had an impact on the course of history, political parties, and attitudes and aspirations of a larger proportion of the population. But even this explanation doesn't seem to go far enough—"1968" has now been subjected to such an intense scrutiny by historians of every persuasion, sociologists, political scientists and cultural studies scholars that there is literally no aspect that hasn't been explored, be it art, literature, design, education, ideology, language, fashion, music, art, forms of cohabitation, sexual behavior, protest forms, the biographical details of key protagonists, transnational connections or local manifestations, not to mention the movement's pre- and posthistory. What is missing in all this activity is an element of self-reflection: Why do researchers choose to work in this field, and what is the wider impact of their work?

Obviously, all this research needs to be funded, and it is interesting to observe that the federal government, as well as the European Union, political parties, universities, unions, large cities and local communities, private research institutes and media organizations have generously supported research projects in recent years. There is a paradox in this clustering of academic interest: on the one hand, it signals that "1968," despite its short duration and relatively small number of activists, is of great significance to the overall course of German history. On the other hand, the controversial nature of "1968" and the activists' failure to achieve any of their key objectives suggest that in order to maintain a research focus in this area, one requires a—perhaps unconscious—sympathy for and identification with these very objectives. This may simply be nostalgia for a moment of youthful exuberance on the part of former activists who have become historians of their own past, but there are, as I will demonstrate, more complex motivations at work, in particular where the younger generation of researchers who were often born after 1968 is concerned. This question is particularly important as it reveals the gap between the Humboldtian ideal and the *Wissenschaftskritik* (critique of science) demanded by the students whose very acts are now the object of allegedly "disinterested" research.

Just as the interest in 1968 had its boom years, writing about "1968" had its own peaks of output. Wolfgang Kraushaar has identified "Publikationsschübe" (surges of publication) that roughly align with the major anniversaries of the events: initially 1977 (at that time, 1967 was seen as the more significant year in the German context), then 1988, 1993, 1998, 2001 (following revelations about Foreign Minister Joschka Fischer's past as a militant street fighter) and most recently 2008.[22] On each occasion, media and academic interest and participation increased, with the 2008 anniversary the most productive in terms of academic articles, books, and online dossiers by every major newspaper. We can see a greater interest in "1968" by historians and sociologists starting roughly around 1988, and a more robust response from critics of the 68ers from around the time of German unification in 1990. Literary representations of "1968" in Germany tended to be less linked to anniversary years in the past, though 2008 saw a flurry of new fictions set in or against the background of 1968.

As the events recede into the past, "1968" has taken on a new significance as a "watershed" in German history. It has become part of Germany's collective memory, even though its position is still ill-defined.

Etienne Francois and Hagen Schulze count it among their "deutsche Erinnerungsorte" (places of memory),[23] and even the Springer publishing group, once locked in a bitter battle with the students, proudly acknowledges "1968" as part of its history. Most Germans understand cultural references to "1968," be it on the occasion of a referendum to rename a street in Berlin "Rudi-Dutschke-Straße," or former communard Rainer Langhans participating in the German version of the television show *I'm a Celebrity ... Get Me Out of Here!* At the same time, in spite of its integration into popular awareness at the surface level, there remain deep-seated suspicions among old and new conservatives about the 68ers, and worries about the impact of the lack of "1968" in East Germany for the cohesion of unified Germany.

In contrast to Kristin Ross's *May 68 in France and Its Afterlives* (2002) or Luisa Passerini's oral history project on 1968 in Italy (1996ff.), this book has a different agenda, going beyond the changing positions of former 68ers and intellectuals. Writing about "1968," in its German context, is no longer about the objectives of a bygone countercultural movement but rather about a moral touchstone, a unique marker of social groups, and an identity construct. The representation of 1968 as a "foundational myth" suits a number of surprisingly heterogeneous groups, and even the myth's deconstruction strengthens it. By delineating this process, understanding the interwoven patterns of self-reflection, self-stylization, spin, media exploitation, historicization, and memorialization, as well as juxtaposing the writings of former activists, historians, novelists, and journalists, this book demonstrates the constructedness of one of the key debates in German postwar history. Moreover, given the transnational nature of "1968," it will encourage further research on the complex interactions of historical, literary, and media representations of social movements in other countries.

Approaches and Theoretical Considerations

This study is motivated by the desire to understand and analyze the processes by which "1968" has been created in the German public imagination. The irony that by writing about the "myth of 1968" one is also adding to it is certainly not lost on the author. Unlike anthropologists, historians, political scientists, and sociologists often have a blind spot when it comes to the impact of their work on the object of their studies. In the case of the construction of "1968," only few scholars put themselves into the equation. On the other hand, the 68ers were nothing if not obsessed with the written word, and as such it seems appropriate that we look at the way factual, journalistic, and fictional texts combine to construct "1968" in a manner that goes far beyond the original events. This approach, essentially a "thick description" that incorporates and juxtaposes mythological, historiographical, literary, and media discourses, is the most appropriate to untangle the myriad of influences and interdependencies that contribute to the construction of "1968" in Germany.

The process of social construction of reality, as Peter Berger and Thomas Luckmann pointed out back in 1966, depends on continued maintenance and reaffirmation. If this process is sustained over generations, the meaning of what is being constructed changes in dialectical interaction with society.[24] John R. Searle added that it required a sense of collectivity, an alignment between individuals and groups in intention and action.[25] Dave Elder-Vass recently expanded our understanding of the process, pointing out that anything that is socially constructed can also be constructed differently. If we think differently about "1968," then the construction of it changes. But, according to Elder-Vass, a social construct is not simply a set of accepted beliefs of a social group—it transcends the individual and simultaneously constrains him or her:

> Contemporary culture may thus depend on the documentary archive, but it is not enough for an idea to be decodable from a text for it to be part of a culture. [. . .] it is only those ideas that are also collectively endorsed that shape our practices, rituals, and institutions.[26]

In her introduction to a recent special theme issue of *Seminar: A Journal of Germanic Studies* entitled "Questioning the RAF: The Politics of Culture," Karin Bauer, focusing on the much more clearly defined field of the Red Army Faction, faced issues similar to those that this book seeks to explore: namely "mass-mediated visual and narrative constructions" and "overlapping discourses" that "function as a projection screen for the collective imagination," with a topic that in turn functions "as a medium for the public staging of memory and history."[27]

Like its sensational and traumatic offshoot, the German student movement has become an object of two processes of remembrance: historicization and memorialization. It is nearing the moment when, according to Jan Assmann's theory of cultural memory, it will recede into the archives, mythology, and history books, but for the time being, it remains highly contested and "alive." Building on the work of Assmann,[28] Harald Welzer has defined the term "communicative memory" as denoting a social practice of communal remembering of real and fictive elements of life stories, constantly brought up to date.[29]

Welzer differentiates between three factors that contribute to the construction of the past: the past that is narrated, the present in which a group remembers its past, and the future into which the past is projected to ensure the coherence of the group. Given that the passage of time changes the makeup of the group, each instance of remembrance brings new aspects and a new constellation of group members. This in turn changes the nature of the past, and only those elements of the past that are revisited intellectually and emotionally remain active. For the purposes of this book it is important to note that Welzer sees any permanent change of memory happening through small adjustments, both individual and collective. Moreover, the communicative quality of its memory forms part of the story:

> If it is true that memory is the event plus the recollection of its memory, then communicative acts are [. . .] themselves part of an interactive story. In this sense, the communicative memory always exists within forms of reactivating the past, which in this process never remains what it once was. (235)[30]

The fortieth anniversary of "1968" showed that the era can no longer escape historicization. However, historians, writers, former activists, and the media have been unable to reach consensus on its real meaning and ultimate position in the German collective consciousness. "1968" remains a political battleground and a bone of contention between generations. In contrast to the memory of the GDR, which has been subject to a number of "official" memory projects like the Enquete-Kommission "Aufarbeitung von Geschichte und Folgen der SED-Diktatur in Deutschland" (the parliamentary commission to work through and evaluate the history and legacy of the dictatorship in East Germany)[31] and the Stasi Records Agency,[32] there has been no agreed process to come to terms with its memory. "1968" affects a generation that has until now been unable to release it from very public and divisive memory contests, insisting as they do that it represents "unfinished business." Now that the 68er generation has reached retirement age and with the fiftieth anniversary in sight, we are approaching the point when communicative memory turns into cultural memory.

As Aleida Assmann has pointed out recently, with the aging of the 68ers their generational link to the events becomes more tenuous, and their role as "Zeitzeugen" and "bridges"[33] between an increasingly strange past and our present will come to an end. As subsequent generations take responsibility for their memories and assert their power of interpretation, these will also provide their own specific approach to memorialization, for example in terms of the increasing use of digital media.[34] Responding to recent criticism of the conceptualization of cultural memory, she stresses that there is no direct connection between individual and collective memory. She sees the latter as constructed history,

> which provides a frame for personal memories, so that individuals can recognize themselves and their own experiences in it, and feel part of this history. The collective memory is thus twice representative: as part of a past that is considered vital, and of individual experiences. (17)

This "never-ending process" produces group or collective memories of differing degrees of stability, reach, and binding power. The consequences for the memories of "1968" are stark: "only that which is exhibited in museums, represented in monuments or conveyed in school books has the chance to be transmitted to following generations" (17). Key for the transmission are the seven *P*s: professors, priests, pastors, PR specialists, press, poets, and politicians. Their role, according to Aleida Assmann, is to construct "useable pasts" that enable people to come to terms with the burden of the past and at the same time formulate collective goals for the future. These "symbolic constructs" are vital for the orientation of the collective, but they need to be treated with care: "construct does not equal construct: there are memory horizons that are aggressive, as well as productive ones; those that further violence and those that have a civilizing effect" (22).

Aleida Assmann sees "1968" as "the focus point of numerous and by no means uniform memories" but reminds us of the role the 68er generation itself played in internalizing and externalizing memory. They stand accused by their critics of an emotional approach, for saying they were different compared to their parents when in fact they simply stylized themselves as victims of "the system," but they were also the "driving force behind German memory culture" (61) by challenging the collective silence of the Nazi generation. The critical potential of memory studies, she concludes, lies in its ability to explore the destructive as well as the healing aspects of memory constructs (209).

Chapter Overview

Chapter 1 presents some of the "heroes and martyrs" of the 68er movement, and how their portrayal has changed over the last four decades. Chapter 2 turns the spotlight on the chroniclers of the German 68ers, the historians, sociologists, and political scientists, some of them former activists while others were not even born in 1968. Chapter 3 explores the effect renegades and vociferous critics of the movement have had on the continuing debate on the legacy of "1968" in Germany. Chapter 4 focuses on German writers who have continued to add to the narrative of 68 by returning to the era in their works over several decades (Peter Schneider, Uwe Timm, Erasmus Schöfer, Friedrich Christian Delius, Jochen Schimmang). Chapter 5 explores the role played by women for and in the construction of "1968," while chapters 6 and 7 analyze the role of the media and the arts in the public construction of "1968." Chapter 8 looks at the curious case of the *Zaungäste*, individuals who either were not old enough or were prevented from actively participating in the events of "1968," but as *teilnehmende Beobachter* (participating observers) have made significant contributions to the debate. Chapter 9 picks up from chapter 4 and explores the most recent literary texts on 1968, texts that focus on the aging of this generation and their uncertain legacy. Chapter 10 offers various motives for the continuing interest in "1968" in Germany and explores a number of *Erklärungsmodelle* (explanatory paradigms) that link the continuing interest in the era with deep-seated German cultural traditions. My conclusion reflects on the fact that relatively few actors manage to keep "1968" in the collective German consciousness and answers the question to what extent the construction of "1968" today is a defiant act to reanimate the past, and to what extent it is an attempt to change the future.

1: Heroes and Martyrs

A NY NARRATIVE OF "1968" in Germany has to include a number of individuals who gained notoriety through their words and actions. Some of them died young, becoming martyrs for the cause. Others carried on and became "voices" of their generation. These familiar "faces" help historians, writers, and the media to tell the story, no matter whether they depict "1968" in its entirety or represent just a small aspect. Much has been written about them, and, in some cases, they have written or are still writing about "1968" themselves. In the following, we will meet some of these "marked individuals," and begin to understand how the construction of "1968" works.

Benno Ohnesorg

Benno Ohnesorg was a most unlikely figure to feature as martyr and catalyst of the hot phase of the German student movement. Ohnesorg was a quiet, introspective mature student, who was attending a demonstration against the state visit of the Shah of Persia on the evening of June 2, 1967 when he was shot in the head by plain-clothes policeman Karl-Heinz Kurras. While the police and West Berlin's press initially claimed that a policeman had been hurt, and that the students had only themselves to blame, the students painstakingly assembled the facts. However, in the subsequent trial, Kurras was acquitted while Fritz Teufel, a member of Kommune I, was remanded in custody for his alleged role as ringleader during the demonstration. This obvious miscarriage of justice was one of the reasons that politicized, energized, and radicalized students who until that moment had not become engaged in the demonstrations and Extraparliamentary Opposition. The Socialist German Student League quickly put itself at the front of the emerging protest movement. On the morning of June 3, 1967, with a curfew outlawing demonstrations anywhere in West Berlin, SDS leader Rudi Dutschke and his comrades organized protests at the Dahlem campus of the Freie Universität Berlin, brandishing banners with slogans like "Heute Ohnesorg, morgen wir" (Today it's Ohnesorg, tomorrow it's all of us). suggesting that the killing had been politically motivated, that students had now become the target for the authorities and could be hunted down at will.

This moment, which gained further poignancy when it became known in 2009 that Kurras had been working for the East German Stasi, can be understood as ground zero for the construction of "1968" in Germany. Without it, there would not have been the rapid growth of the protest movement, the escalation of violence, or the far-reaching repercussions for West German political culture that saw thousands of young people lose their faith in the integrity of the young West German parliamentary democracy. Ohnesorg became a martyr for the movement when the SDS, with the support from the GDR authorities, turned the transport of his coffin to his hometown Hannover into a media spectacle. A convoy of cars was allowed to cross GDR territory without being subjected to the usual petty controls, and, following the funeral, the SDS quickly organized a conference in Hannover—Organisation und Bedingungen des Widerstands (Organization of and conditions for resistance)—to discuss further steps. The discussions were characterized by an impotent rage over what happened, but there was also a growing awareness during the debate that the conflict between protesters and authorities had reached a new quality and that whatever was decided would have long-lasting consequences.[1]

The prominent sociologist Jürgen Habermas famously challenged the radical students of the SDS, especially their chief ideologist Rudi Dutschke, to come clean about how they planned to continue their protests. He felt that in the heat of the debate, Dutschke and his comrades were advocating a strategy of open rebellion, which would set the protesters squarely against the democratically legitimized executive and the police, and as such speculated on the loss of life that would ensue in order to fan the flames of the rebellion. While Dutschke believed that the Federal Republic was in a prerevolutionary phase, Habermas suggested that the students were blind to the reality that they were only a small minority, playing with fire. Their "escalation strategy" was, according to Habermas, tantamount to "left-wing fascism."

A chance picture taken at the scene of the shooting by the photographer Jürgen Henschel illustrated the new reality of the confrontation between the students and the organs of the state. Even today it is as central to Germany's collective memory as the pictures of the naked Vietnamese girl running away from her burning village or the street execution of a suspected Vietcong are to the Vietnam War. The photograph shows the dying Ohnesorg lying on the ground, with an elegantly dressed young woman holding his head, looking beseechingly to onlookers. The image, widely circulated at the time, continued to remind students of the atrocity committed, and that this could have been the unfortunate fate of any of them.

Benno Ohnesorg's journey from innocent bystander to martyr can be followed in detail through the wealth of literature that has accumulated over the decades. Crucial to the early phase was the investigation of the events by students of the Freie Universität who documented what had really happened on that fateful evening. Their report concentrated on the testimony of participants and observers. Only through a concerted effort by the students, intellectuals, and the liberal press did an alternative interpretation of the shooting become more broadly accepted: Ohnesorg acquired a second life not as a person, but as a symbol of (police) state repression.[2]

Siegward Lönnendonker, Bernd Rabehl, and Jochen Staadt, who have repeatedly written about the events over the past decades, are very clear in their verdict: "The 2 June 1967, in the history of the student protest movement in West Berlin and the Federal Republic, is the turning point, the moment when the rebellion began."[3] Uwe Wesel, at the time a young law professor at the FU, remembers how his sympathies lay with the students: the students had to be in the right if the reaction to their protest was so brutal that one of them was killed.[4] Even the cultural avant-garde voiced their concern: in an open letter to the influential weekly news magazine *Der Spiegel*, West Berlin writers, artists, gallery owners, and publishers accused the conservative Springer press, the police, the mayor, and the chief of police of aiding and abetting action leading to grievous bodily harm and manslaughter, and demanded a parliamentary inquiry.[5] This letter was signed by Hans-Christoph Buch as well as high-profile names like Günter Grass, Hans Werner Richter, Hans Magnus Enzensberger, Wolfdietrich Schnurre, and Reinhard Lettau.

While there is no doubt that the shooting of Benno Ohnesorg was a significant event that marked the end of the nonviolent phase of the conflict between students and the authorities, there is no discernible awareness in the public debates that this assessment is entirely constructed. I will return to the historical construction of the events into a kind of "foundational myth"[6] in the next chapter, but for now flag up one aspect of the process that has received little attention in the political and historiographical discourse on "1968," namely the literary representation of this moment. In Uwe Timm's novel *Heißer Sommer* (Hot Summer, 1974), the shooting becomes the turning point in the political awakening of student Ullrich Krause in Munich. He learns about the shooting over the radio:

> Berlin. On the occasion of the visit of the Shah there have been violent confrontations between demonstrators and the police in front of the Opera House. One student was killed [. . .]
> Ullrich jumped out of his bed and turned off the radio. He went to the open window.
> These pigs, he thought, and then, full of rage: do we live in Persia?[7]

Timm describes how Ullrich reads more details in the newspaper, and his reaction to the photos of the dying Ohnesorg and baton-wielding policemen. The student feels a great rage and joins a spontaneous demonstration. The marchers are losing their reserved attitude, everyone can talk to everyone. We learn that Ohnesorg's death had set in motion a complex emotional development in Ullrich:

> In addition to his anger and rage, he suddenly sensed something like joy in him [...], a joy which he tried to suppress as it seemed inappropriate to him. And then, this vague uneasiness, which he had discovered in himself, since that night when he had first heard about the death of Benno Ohnesorg, an uneasiness that had grown day by day. He felt this uneasiness in the others as well, here at the hot assembly point. It was only when the demonstration began to take shape that the uneasiness receded.[8]

What Timm attempts in this passage is an early example of the construction of "1968"—highly complex and individual journeys of development are described in great detail and transformed into a collective experience: the diffuse feeling of "Unruhe" (uneasiness, repeated four times), the growing awareness among the students that they needed to do something, even though it was unclear what that might be; a sense of joy, an almost forbidden emotion, of having found purpose and meaning in collective protest, which, in Ullrich's case, had until then been blocked by his sense of alienation from friends, family, girlfriend, university, and state. These emotions and developing thoughts are full of contradictions and almost impossible to convey in nonfictional accounts. They are also intended to justify the students' reaction to the shooting: the other side started it, so the students were justified in using "counterviolence."

Most of the literary representations of the German student movement from the 1970s describe Benno Ohnesorg's death as a caesura, a moment after which nothing was the same for the students.[9] They stress the initial confusion and lack of verbalization, the aimless rage, but also beginning thought processes. As a "turning point," though, the events remained strangely underdramatized until Leander Scholz's novel *Rosenfest* (Celebration of Roses, 2001).

Rosenfest is a literary road movie, depicting Gudrun Ensslin and Andreas Baader as heroic lovers on the run. They are placed right at the scene of the shooting of Benno Ohnesorg, thus connecting the founding members of the Red Army Faction firmly with "1968." Cutting scenes in the style of an American crime show, Scholz breaks through the "silence" of the texts dating from the seventies, turning the dramatic situation in front of the Berlin opera house into an orgy of violence:

> Andreas, holding his hands behind his head under the shouted orders of the police, saw Gudrun out of the corner of his eye. She shook her long hair, and kicked out at those around her, which served only to tighten her human manacles. Her wrists were twisted

by the muscles of strangers, tendons pulled and her hands turned into motionless lumps under the pressure of her attackers.

"Andreas," she screamed, twisting her neck out of the chokehold, "they want to break me!"

At this moment, with the attention of the police focused on Gudrun, one of the putative leaders of the protest managed to escape. With a thin mustache and red shirt, feet in sandals without socks as most boys wore them, he crawled away from the confusion of strong police bodies and ran as fast as his sandals allowed, when a policeman who had until then waved his weapon in front of Gudrun's face pointed at the troublemaker and trumpeted: "I am going to get that swine."

Even before Benno could straighten up to run, a 7.65 millimeter bullet penetrated above his right ear, plowed through his brain, and opened his skull so that one could see deep inside.[10]

Such a graphic and physical depiction of events creates the impression of an unscrupulous police machinery, which treats students the same way as Hitler's henchmen treated the Jews three decades before (the students who are caught are put into the "hole"[11]). From this perspective, Ensslin's and Baader's reaction is only logical:

"Fascists"—Gudrun wants to spit into the faces of the gawping onlookers. This is not our fault, no, Andreas thinks. From now on, you carry the full responsibility for all that happens, Andreas thinks, the full responsibility.[12]

Rosenfest constructs a simple message: the other side started it. Not the students, but the police, the state, the "establishment," the "system" are responsible for all the violence that was to come. This is the message and, for the reader, the explanation for the trail of violence the pair leave behind them: the arson attack in April 1968 on two Frankfurt department stores becomes an act of revenge for Ohnesorg,[13] the subsequent terrorist "actions" a legitimate answer for the police violence that had been so shockingly in evidence on June 2, 1967.

Scholz invests the shooting of Ohnesorg with enormous significance. Born in 1969, after the demise of the student movement, this author has the advantage of not having to battle personal experiences and memories. He can fantasize freely, mix elements anew, and inculcate his protagonists with ideas and thoughts that the students at the time definitively did not have. In a postscript Scholz cites the American writer and cultural critic Don DeLillo: "Fiction is not about changing names," perhaps in a veiled attempt to justify a writer's right to reinvent reality. Written from a distance, the novel connects a constructed past with appropriate "hooks" to lead the reader to the scene of the shooting. The irony is that the student Ohnesorg is simply a background figure for Scholz's Bonnie and Clyde story. Neither Ensslin, an SDS member, nor the apolitical Baader see Ohnesorg as "one of them"—he simply provides them with an excuse for the release of their latent violent fantasies.

In his autobiographical text *Der Freund und der Fremde* (The Friend and the Stranger, 2005),[14] Uwe Timm examined his own memories of Benno Ohnesorg. Both had met at the Braunschweig-Kolleg in 1961, a college that allowed gifted mature students to gain their entrance qualifications for university. Timm had never before publically discussed that he had been a close friend of Ohnesorg. Following on from his previous "memory project," the celebrated *Am Beispiel meines Bruders* (My Brother, for Example, 2003; in English as *In My Brother's Shadow*, 2005), Timm finally found a suitable literary form that allowed him not only to compose a requiem for his friend but to rediscover and confront his former self which was profoundly affected by his friend's death.[15]

The narrative—part autobiography and part documentary—starts with an image that casts Benno Ohnesorg in the pose of the medieval German poet Walter von der Vogelweide. Timm's first memory of meeting the stranger, sitting on a wall by a river and writing poems, is obviously stylized and serves to underline their mutual love for literature and a desire, on Timm's part, to flesh out Ohnesorg's somewhat two-dimensional personality. Timm recalls how they read to each other their first literary attempts and how, six years later, when he heard of Ohnesorg's death on the radio in Paris, he abandoned his PhD project to join the revolt, thus turning the personal into the political.

The events are mediated through remembered telephone conversations and photographs, especially the photograph that would become a representation of one of the key moments of the German student movement.[16] Timm reminds the reader of the details of the image, while reconstructing his own reactions:

> A few days later I saw his picture in a magazine, and seeing him again like this came as a shock. He is lying in the street, immediately recognizable—his face, his hair, his hands, his long, thin arms and legs. He is lying on the asphalt, dressed in khaki trousers, a long-sleeved shirt, his arm outstretched, his hand open and relaxed, his eyes closed, as if he was sleeping. Next to him kneels a young woman in a black dress or cape. The woman might have come from the opera, was my thought, perhaps a doctor. She looks up, as if she wants to ask something or give an instruction, and supports, a gentle gesture, his head by the back of his neck. One can clearly see the blood on his head and on the ground. In this black-and-white it could have been a frame from the film Orphee by Cocteau, that was my first thought when I looked at the photograph, this transformation. It was one of his favorite films. (11–12)

Timm wanted to write about his friend at the time but felt unable in his shock and anger to find the right words, with every sentence "acquiring an aggressive, abstract tone—a tone that had never been his" (11). Almost forty years later, Timm found that personal voice, which reflects his friend's gentle personality and outlook:

> We, reading Jean-Paul Sartre in those days, were convinced that—as paradoxical as it may sound—one is damned to be free; and yet this very freedom offers the choice to turn into someone different from what one has been turned into, and what one has made oneself into. (56)

The focus of their intense discussions about aesthetics, art, literature, and a new way of thinking was Albert Camus's *L'Etranger* (The Stranger, 1942), a book which promoted an attitude that they vowed to adopt in their own lives: to shun conventions and always to maintain an inner distance. However, it is exactly this pose of existentialist "distance" that turned Timm into a stranger to his friend and prompted him not to go to University in West Berlin with him but to move to Munich and establish himself on his own. Forty years on, he realized that he may have made a mistake when he cut himself free of the friendship with Ohnesorg: "*The dead remind us of the things we failed to do, our mistakes, our wrongdoings. They are our ghosts.*" (78, italics in original.)

This is not to say that Timm has become one of the many former activists who today distance themselves from their former utopian ideals. In fact, he still maintains the necessity of the protest. But the movement, Timm suggests, didn't start as a collective uprising—it was based on the emotional response of individuals to events, on their aesthetic and moral revolt against the establishment. Following his own "Erinnerungspfad" (memory path, 127), Timm visits the woman on the picture, the "Engelsgestalt" (figure of an angel, 119) who herself has become a reluctant part of history (see chapter 5). It was her act of kindness and solidarity, her human response to the inhuman act, that "saved" the moment from turning into the ugly murder that it represented at face value. By giving the dying Ohnesorg his dignity, easing his parting, this woman has become an essential element of the moment.

Inevitably, the book turns into an essay on the significance and power of myths: of the ancient Orpheus myth or the modern myth of the 68ers, of which Timm's friend has become a significant part. For the death of Benno Ohnesorg has become a "moment" in time: one that is invested with a special significance. For a minority it provided the excuse to turn terrorist. For a majority it has become a key date to be commemorated. It is endlessly revisited by historians and novelists, and used by the media as shorthand for a generational narrative and experience. And yet, while Timm accords himself the role of Orpheus who can bring back the dead, he does not only add to the myth but also deconstructs it, reminding his readers that Benno Ohnesorg was a real person who became the unlikely hero in a struggle for a better world with better beings in it. By recalling the aesthetic aspirations and moral foundations of the movement, Timm recaptures its essence and provides a corrective to his friend's memory.

Rudi Dutschke

Every movement needs its leaders, even when the activists themselves resist providing them for the delectation of the public. *Occupy* wasn't the first that tried and failed to do without leaders. While West Germany's Extraparliamentary Opposition of the late 1960s never formed an organized front, the most active parts engaged with, and were in turn courted, criticized, or vilified by press, radio, and television. The media took a particular interest in the exploits of the students in West Berlin who, ironically, maintained that as an antiauthoritarian movement they did not believe in having leaders. And yet, as the students' initial protests against encrusted structures at the Freie Universität expanded to target press monopoly and former Nazis in positions of power in government and in the legal and education system, as well as West Germany's unquestioning support for the American involvement in Vietnam, leading faces and organizers naturally emerged. The most recognizable was Rudi Dutschke, whose "journey" from charismatic voice of the rebellion via public enemy number one to tragic hero provides an instructive case study for the construction of "1968" in Germany. Dutschke embodied that curious mixture of ideological zeal and antiauthoritarian practice, romantic idealism and fashionable jargon that distinguished the German student movement. As "chief ideologist" of the SDS in West Berlin, he led students out of the universities and into the streets. As the victim of an attempted assassination on April 11, 1968, he became an icon of the revolt to the present day.

Dutschke was a revolutionary star; the cultural and intellectual elite wanted to talk to him. To counter the Springer press, which had singled him out as *roter Rädelsführer Rudi* (red rebel rouser Rudi) and identified him as public enemy number one, he embarked on a series of interviews with the liberal press, radio, and television. The most significant of these was broadcast on December 3, 1967, on national television. His interviewer introduced the 27-year-old Dutschke as the spokesperson of a small minority of young people, "revolutionaries in a time when one cannot believe in revolutions anymore."[17] Dutschke countered that one could very well believe in revolutions, that it was capitalism that kept people in an unconscious state. He argued that change was a question of will, that people had the opportunity to revolutionize society. Provocative actions by students would stir them from their unconscious state and inspire them to "create their own history." The interview can be seen as a serious attempt by a well-known journalist and commentator to understand the West German student movement and diffuse tensions. It certainly was a personal triumph for Dutschke, who had managed to convey to a national audience the seriousness of the students. It also demonstrated that the movement could present itself seriously, willing to engage in rational debate.

This image contrasts sharply with that adorning the title page of *Der Spiegel* a week later, on December 11, 1967. The cover shows Dutschke as an unshaven fanatic, screaming, with eyes blazing. The article begins:

> The revolution wears a sweater, roughly knitted, with a violent pattern. Colored stripes over chest and biceps signal the contrariness of the rebel. The sleeves are pushed up in a "let's do it"—manner. The upper body moves back and forth, in time with his speech. His fist, with thumb held up, lies clenched on the table, his lower arms seem to grasp space, as befitting the choreography of a workers' song.[18]

The reader gets an impression of Dutschke as a dangerous caged animal, ready to resort to violence and, as the article suggests, very likely controlled by sinister forces. The article acknowledges Dutschke's charisma, but the overall verdict is the same as in the Springer press: Dutschke has no majority, because the majority does not want change.

The students had difficulty learning to use the media to their advantage. While the movement needed the media to spread its message, the focus on Dutschke as high-profile rebel brought serious distortions. Michael Ruetz, then a young photographer in West Berlin following the activities of the Extraparliamentary Opposition, accuses *Der Spiegel* of fueling the hatred against Dutschke. Instead of showing him as a human being, the magazine chose to portray him as a fanatic:

> At the time the media was making Dutschke out to be the reincarnation of not just Hitler, but all of history's monsters. By substituting Hitler with Dutschke, they hoped to stimulate at least a posthumous opposition to the Nazis. [. . .] Only after he had been turned into a monster, could open season be declared on him.[19]

It is ironic that Ruetz's own pictures of the APO and Dutschke in particular have since become the main visual reference for the contemporary reader—and are regularly used both by *Der Spiegel* and the Springer press. These pictures, showing Dutschke with a megaphone at a rally, pushing against police barriers or captivating an audience in a packed main auditorium, convey a sense of great intensity, but never fanaticism. They also suggest that—at least in Ruetz's viewfinder—Dutschke was the leading figure of the movement, a view shared by the *New York Times,* which named him, shortly after the assassination attempt, not only the most charismatic of the student rebels but the most charismatic of all West German politicians.

Dutschke's long-term impact on West German society is still highly contested. The Springer press, predictably, sees him as the intellectual pied piper who caught the media attention while the "true" representatives of the time (who stayed on the sidelines) were largely ignored. But they have a vested interest in downplaying his significance, since the Springer press was and is held largely responsible for his attempted assassination (see chapter 6).

Even though the student movement failed in its immediate objectives, Dutschke is not associated with its failure. Instead, he has become the object of hero worship. This has less to do with his ideas of radical socialism than with his significance as a symbol of the revolt. His closest friends and associates have written numerous books about him, thus keeping interest in Dutschke alive and contributing to a modern myth. In the following, I shall demonstrate the process of construction with examples from biographies, newspaper articles, and fiction published over four decades.

One of the motors behind the campaign to keep Rudi Dutschke in the public consciousness is his friend Jürgen Miermeister. Following Dutschke's death in December 1979, Miermeister started to publish selections of Dutschke's speeches and writings that, by this time, had almost been forgotten (e.g., his speech at the International Vietnam Congress from February 1968). The intention behind his project, as stated in the postscript to *Rudi Dutschke: Geschichte ist machbar* (Rudi Dutschke: History Is Doable, 1980) was to inform younger readers about the revolt and its consequences, and to serve those who were part of it as a constructive aide-mémoire. Furthermore, in the context of the fragmentation of the Left following the traumatic experiences of the *German Autumn,* the book was to remind former activists that they had all started from the same point.[20] Together with Dutschke's widow Gretchen Dutschke-Klotz and Professor Hellmut Gollwitzer, a friend of the family, Miermeister followed up with a further volume of speeches, writings, and excerpts from Dutschke's diaries to counter the then prevalent image of Dutschke as a public enemy and promoter of violence. Movingly, it contains Erich Fried's poem *Nicht jeder ist ersetzbar* (Not Everyone Is Replaceable, 1980), which was read at his funeral.[21] In 1983, in the context of the "geistig moralische Wende" (the moral revival)[22] announced by the conservative chancellor Helmut Kohl, Miermeister and some of his friends compiled another volume about the "roots and traces" of a very different awakening. In his introduction, the series editor Freimut Duwe cites Miermeister in pensive mood:

As such, the revolt is trauma and dream, history and present. Even before the death of some of their "fathers" (Bloch, Marcuse, Sartre), many of the sons and daughters died, in the USA, in Western Europe, in many countries of the world. The revolt, the dreams, plans and utopias cannot be killed. This is no comfort for the mourners. But perhaps a glimmer of hope for the next attempt.[23]

The volume is notable for its inclusion of interviews with Rudi Dutschke about plans to expropriate the West German media tycoon Axel Springer, and the transcript of a 90 minute televised discussion with Dutschke, Daniel Cohn-Bendit, Kurt Sontheimer, and Matthias Walden, but perhaps even more so for a number of photographs that show Dutschke as family man and friend. It is worth remembering that before online newspaper archives and YouTube became available, the general public did not have easy access to past articles or programs and were dependent on the decisions of editors in press and broadcasting or their own memories.

Two biographies of Dutschke followed in quick succession: Ulrich Chaussy's *Die drei Leben des Rudi Dutschke* (The Three Lives of Rudi Dutschke, 1993) and Jürgen Miermeister's in 1986.[24] While Miermeister stuck to the facts and could draw on the wealth of sources from his three edited volumes, Chaussy, then a young journalist, was particularly fascinated by Dutschke's "third life" following the attempted assassination. The student leader's slow physical recovery, his odyssey in search of safe haven from Italy to Ireland to the United Kingdom and finally to Denmark, and especially his involvement with the new citizens' initiatives and the emerging movement against the building of nuclear power plants in Whyl and Brokdorf in 1977 provided new insights into his character and, more importantly, an inspiration for his biographer. But even journalists are not safe from becoming enraptured. In a postscript to the 1993 edition, Chaussy admitted:

> Everywhere I went I encountered the view that the shots at Dutschke had been meant for the entire movement. Often I could feel that this entire complex was associated with feelings of guilt. Thus, the charisma already present before Dutschke was shot was given extra emphasis. I was caught up in this sense of rapture.[25]

In 1996 two more biographies were published in Germany, by his wife Gretchen and again by Jürgen Miermeister.[26] While Gretchen Dutschke focused on her husband's role as leader who was held back by petty rivalries in the SDS, Miermeister now compared him to the philosopher Ernst Bloch and described him as "a chosen one, a charismatic leader, a prophet of the new age [. . .], a new, modern, militant messiah."[27]

In the liberal press meanwhile, Rudi Dutschke emerged as the "intellectual and moral heart of the revolt"—readers were invited to imagine what could have been if he had not been shot.[28] There no longer was any need to be too critical about him. This, along with a nagging feeling among 68ers that Rudi Dutschke had received those bullets on behalf of the whole movement, may explain why so many were willing to go along with the sanitized version. Dutschke had been "rehabilitated"; the public perception of him had changed from sinister revolutionary to moral icon. This did him no justice but was perhaps a natural by-product of the fall of communism.

In the new millennium, Dutschke's constructed image faced some challenges. The first was the publication of most, if not all, of his diaries by his widow Gretchen Dutschke-Klotz.[29] While the blurb claimed that with his death a political gap had opened that could not be closed, the banality of some of the entries and a disturbing naivety started to cast doubt on the "chosen one." More serious was the first academic study of Rudi Dutschke by Michaela Karl.[30] Her analysis of the "Personifizierung der Bewegung" (the personification of the movement, 514) explained some of the reasons for Dutschke's alleged charisma, but it was her discussion of Dutschke's stance on the use of violence that began to seriously damage his reputation as a pacifist. In the post 9/11 context, Bernd Rabehl, his former friend and comrade, admitted that the Red Army Faction had emerged from the core of the SDS and the APO, and that Dutschke had a lot to do with the concept of the "urban guerilla."[31] In recent years, Rudi Dutschke has continued to divide the German public, with the renaming of a part of the Kochstrasse in Berlin into Rudi-Dutschke-Straße a case in point.[32] Nevertheless, emotions do not run as high as before. Following the broadcast of a semidocumentary biopic of Dutschke on ZDF, even the *Bild-Zeitung* was moved to ask "what's the deal with the left-wing hero of the 68ers?"[33] and, in 2012, Helmut Reinicke's sentimental look back on Dutschke's commitment to libertarian communism met with a benign reception.[34]

In fiction, Rudi Dutschke has emerged both as a martyr for the cause and as a catalyst for action. In *Heißer Sommer*, Uwe Timm describes the effect of the assassination attempt on his protagonist Ullrich Krause as "a bolt from heaven"; confusion reigns before students, believing that the vicious campaign by the Springer newspapers is responsible for the assassination attempt, converge on the Springer-Hochhaus (Springer high-rise) in Hamburg, where a spontaneous demonstration turns violent as protesters try to stop the delivery of the *Bild-Zeitung*. Jochen Schimmang's protagonist Murnau in *Der schöne Vogel Phönix* (The Beautiful Bird Phoenix, 1979) is in the Bundeswehr when he hears the news. He immediately understands why the students blame Springer: "The connection was immediately clear to us, there was no point to talk about it."[35]

Twenty years later, Erasmus Schöfer's novel *Ein Frühling irrer Hoffnung* (A Spring of Crazy Hope, 2001) employs a dual perspective (juxtaposed in two columns on the same page) to describe on the one hand the riots following the attempted assassination and on the other the contradictory sense of losing one's bearings and finding them again in the physical reaction of collective protest. The assassination attempt is described in the chapter "Der Revolutionär Dutschke hinterlässt seine Schuhe und Zehntausenden passen sie" (The Revolutionary Rudi Dutschke Leaves Behind a Pair of Shoes, and They Fit Tens of Thousands), from the perspective of both Dutschke and his wife Gretchen. The novel's protagonists, the left-wing historian Viktor Bliss, his wife Lena, and a visiting friend, unionist Manfred, are initially shocked and incredulous but immediately know what to do: "There wasn't anything else to say."[36]

The year 2001 also saw the publication of Uwe Timm's novel *Rot* (Red, 2001), in which the author returns to the traumatic moment when the student movement lost its leader. The protagonist Thomas Linde, a funeral orator who was once active in the movement and now leads a comfortable life, is confronted with the imperative of his youth when a former comrade dies and bequeaths on him a box of explosives and a plan to blow up the victory column in Berlin. In a series of orations, Linde reflects on the loss of his youth, the course of history, and the widespread view, in the newly confident and materialistic Berlin Republic, that 68ers are well meaning but hopeless idealists:

> Should I say, honored mourners, that we have gathered today to inter someone who had blown a fuse? The typical fanatic—you might remember the pictures of this student revolutionary—Rudi Dutschke, a cartoonist had drawn him, standing on his head and looking at the world upside down. And the way this guy looked: fanatical, frightening, with piercing eyes, with this home-knitted jumper, worn-out shoes which, when a boy who cherished law and order had shot him in the head, immediately came off his feet. We need to imagine someone like Dutschke when we lay to rest this cuckoo guy, cheap jacket, threadbare trousers, one of these people refusing to consume.[37]

With his striking "detective novel" *Das magische Jahr* (The Magic Year, 2008), Rob Alef provides a satirical view of what might have happened had the 68ers won. In this alternative world, "things had shifted, and everything had changed" (29) in 1968. The crucial divergence from real events is that the great student leader Richard Dubinski (a thinly disguised Rudi Dutschke) was shot dead by the assassin. As a consequence, he is revered as a patriotic hero and martyr, and every year there is an official victory celebration. Only when three further former members of Dubinski's commune are killed does the investigating detective realize that the murderer is looking for a photograph to prevent a long-held secret becoming public: contrary to official history, Dubinski had not been in Berlin on the day the students won the battle against the state in the "battle for the golden fleece." An avid fan, Dubinski had traveled to Hamburg to hear the Beatles play.

Writing about Dutschke, as all these examples show, means defining one's own attitudes to "1968." Journalists and politicians, depending on their political viewpoint, may portray him as the "chief ideologist" or "pied piper" of the movement. Former friends and comrades turn him into a saint or martyr, and writers add to the ever-changing image by focusing on the effect the attempted assassination had on his sympathizers. Only rarely do we encounter reflections on the risks of idolizing a "fallen hero." Gerard DeGroot has recently summed up this dilemma:

> The assassination attempt bequeathed the worldwide Student Movement a convenient martyr. Fallen heroes encourage speculation as to what might have been. The martyr is assigned an importance and nobility he never earned in life. So it went with Dutschke. The impracticalities of his utopian dream, and the violence it implied, were quickly forgotten. The myth subsumed the man. Dutschke became a symbol of the Sixties, a time when heroes had the guts to dream and were shot for doing so. Though the Student Movement had clearly failed, he escaped blame. Fallen heroes continue to block the path to understanding the decade.[38]

Joschka Fischer and Daniel Cohn-Bendit

Joschka Fischer became known internationally as Germany's vice-chancellor and foreign minister of the red–green coalition government from 1998 to 2005. He famously challenged the American Defense Secretary Donald Rumsfeld in the run-up to the second Iraq War in 2003.[39] He has been described as "the one who made it through," referring to Rudi Dutschke's "Long March through the institutions." At the height of his political career, one of his biographers described him as "the most exciting political expression of the 68ers, the personification of their successful march to the top of the institutions."[40] However, this description is a projection, the result of careful construction and political spin.

In fact, Fischer had never been a leading figure in the late 1960s and only came to some prominence as a member of the "Putztruppe" (clean-up gang) in the Frankfurt scene of squatters and sympathizers of the Red Army Faction in the 1970s.[41] He realized that the movement had been caught in a vicious circle of violence, and convinced many of his comrades to try a different tack to effect change, using the dual strategy of participating in the democratic process via the Green Party (the *Standbein* [support leg] in soccer terms) and in a broad oppositional green movement (the *Spielbein* [free leg]). As the first *Grüner* (member of the Green Party) to take a ministerial role in the state parliament of Hesse—famously appearing in jeans and sneakers for his swearing-in ceremony—he became the personification of a 68er who was trying to work with (and through) the system. He and his friend Daniel Cohn-Bendit, a French-German veteran and figurehead of the French May who initially entered local politics to influence policies on childcare and integration, became the living representatives of "1968" in Germany in the 1980s and 90s. Always available for interviews or a quote, they have been the go-to 68ers for the media for decades. The difference between them and the activists who did not survive or had turned their backs on the movement is that both Fischer and Cohn-Bendit are unrepentant supporters of their youthful ideals and, surprisingly, have won the grudging admiration of their former opponents. Furthermore, and this is important for our discussion of the constructedness of "1968" in Germany, both have influenced the debate through their publications.

In September 1998, just weeks before the red–green coalition was formed and took over after sixteen years of a conservative government, Joschka Fischer wrote a wide-ranging and highly significant article for a *Spiegel Special* looking back on "fünfzig deutsche Jahre" (fifty German years).[42] In it, he identified himself with the idealistic aims of the 68er movement and distanced himself from them at the same time, claiming that after three decades the world was a very different place and needed different strategies to solve its problems. He mocked those who claimed that the 68ers had caused a decline in moral values and the disintegration of society:

> A perfect family, an intact society, an ideal world working with highest productivity and maximum consumer orientation—yes, all these things would have been ours if this damn 1968 hadn't come along. The order of the German world—in spite of 16 years of Helmut Kohl and his "moral revival," appears to have been comprehensively destroyed since 1968. Since then, like the brave St George, an upright conservatism battles against the dragon named 1968, against its pestilential stench and the destruction of all the values of the occident.[43]

But, he wrote, the reality was different. Old enemies had become fleeting shadows, and the contradictions of Western societies at the eve of the new millennium could no longer be explained by the *Wertewandel* (change in values) from 1968. Fischer argued that, while playing a significant part in changing society, the 68ers had merely played a catalytic or accelerating role. And yet, 1968 was not just about events like the shots on Rudi Dutschke, the fight with the Springer press or the protests against the Vietnam War: The year 1968 has a greater significance. In addition to the real events of the time, it has remained a metaphor for a fundamental transformation of Western societies.

The fundamental changes in social and cultural values, as well as institutions, Fischer continued, had been a precondition for the transformation of capitalism, which had taken place around 1968. To this extent, it was appropriate to think of "1968" as a cultural revolution, and its impact had to be seen as historic. The shift had opened people's eyes to the fact that the West German elite still contained large numbers of Hitler's helpers and supporters, and caused the 68er generation to turn their backs on their parents. While Germany had seemed the same after the revolt, everyday culture and the rhythm of life had fundamentally changed, and even though much of this change had been set in motion throughout the 1960s, 1968 had been the year when the various elements came together and exploded. With victory at the general election in sight, Fischer concluded, the 68er generation now had to focus on a new phase of change and leave "1968" to the process of historicization. To help this process along, he offered his own assessment that would become a dominant narrative during the "red-green years":

> The fact that our political system and democratic culture are today much more permeable, adaptable and open when faced with new challenges [...] is one of permanent achievements of the magical year 1968.[44]

Fischer has continued to write his own script since he left office in 2005. In Pepe Danquart's film *Joschka und Herr Fischer: Eine Zeitreise durch 60 Jahre Deutschland* (Joschka and Herr Fischer: A Journey through 60 Years of Germany, 2011), for example, he provides a coherent, if selective, narrative of "1968" where the silence of the war generation and their unreconstructed way of thinking inexorably led to the revolt of the students and a new consciousness. But this interpretation no longer holds the same power as in 1998 or in 2003. When he presented the second volume of his autobiography in 2011, the normally pro-68 newspaper *taz*, in a neat reversal of roles, doubted his relevance and concluded: "Fischer ist Geschichte" (Fischer is history).[45]

This verdict is surprising. Ten years earlier, Wolfgang Kraushaar had characterized Fischer as the personification of a generational conflict, but also as prime example for the successful integration of the 68ers and the reconciliation between the state and its rebellious children.[46] As such, it would be equally valid to argue that Fischer, and by extension "1968," have become *geschichtsmächtig*, that is, that he and the movement have made history, perhaps even changed the course of history.

Next to Fischer, Daniel Cohn-Bendit has become one of the most recognizable 68er in Europe. As "Dany le Rouge" he had been one of the figureheads of the French May but has also become one of the key "voices" of the German student movement. Like Fischer, Cohn-Bendit claims that "1968" has had its day: "It has worked so well that it is over now."[47] Ironically, though, he has done more than most to keep the era alive. Starting with his book *Der große Basar* (The Great Bazaar) in 1975, and especially with his continent-spanning film-series and book *Nous l'avons tant aimée, la révolution* (We Loved It So Much, the Revolution, 1986; the German translation *Wir haben sie so geliebt, die Revolution* was published in 2001), he has played a major role in the construction of "1968." Characteristically hyperbolic, he describes the unique experience of being young in the late 1960s:

> In 1968 the world caught fire, as if in response to a global signal. [...] Supported by a rapid development of the media, we were the first generation that experienced the physical and daily totality of the world through a torrent of sounds and images. Our yearning for social and individual change freed incredible amounts of energy. These in turn made possible fundamental changes in our thinking as well as life in revolt.[48]

Cohn-Bendit is clearly aware of his role as keeper of the flame. I will return to his *1968: Die letzte Generation, die noch nichts von dem Ozonloch wusste* (1968: The Last Generation That Didn't Know about the Hole in the Ozone Layer, 1988) in the next chapter but for now simply cite from a volume he edited for the fortieth anniversary. *1968: Die Revolte* (1968: The Revolt, 2007), written to counter a "schlechte Realität" (bad reality),[49] is aimed for a younger readership, and promises to inform them of the key events and the context in which they occurred. In reality, though, it seeks to strengthen the narrative that asserts a vital historical role for the 68ers as modernizers and constructive citizens:

> Child rearing, education, sexuality, challenging established lines of authority, confronting the horrors of the German past, the relationship between the sexes and between generations, the relationship between citizen and state, political participation, co-determination in factories, insight into ecological interdependencies—all these things were on the agenda in those tumultuous years and were newly defined through action by the debates and activities of the 68ers. Society as it is today has grown out of these processes.[50]

In this list of achievements, Cohn-Bendit conveniently forgets to mention any of the "dark" aspects of "1968," including the experimentation with children in the name of "sexual liberation," which made him the center of a scandal in 2001 and again in 2014.[51] But, like Fischer, Cohn-Bendit is an experienced politician (he is an MEP and co-chair of the Greens in the European Parliament) and knows that the wider public is by-and-large sympathetic to the 68ers. Certainly the media continue to turn to him to interpret current events. Following the terror attack on the *Charlie Hebdo* cartoonists in Paris in January 2015, he declared that the democratic majority in France and Germany was waking up to the fact that it needed to defend the liberties won by the 68ers:

> When one defends "Charlie Hebdo," one defends the most radical form of anti-clericalism. [. . .] The magazine is radically atheistic, anti-militaristic and libertarian. It represents the spirit of the 68er-generation. It is their biting irony that we defend. The radical right to ironically challenge everything. And that is exciting at a time when part of the population in France and Germany demands that we lay to rest once and for all the pipedreams of the 68ers. Suddenly, everyone feels moved to defend this libertarian time with all its contradictions.[52]

In statements like this, Cohn-Bendit displays an acute awareness of the dialectic between the "conservative" mainstream and the "progressive" avant-garde, and the changing balance of power between the two over recent decades. At the same time, his suggestion that the democratic majority owes its freedoms to the protest of his generation demonstrates how much the construction of "1968" owes to hubris.

Ulrike Meinhof

The case of Ulrike Meinhof is an instructive one for an analysis of the way "1968" is constructed in Germany and particularly of the role the written word has played in a fundamental reevaluation of her thinking and actions. Her name does not immediately spring to mind as a "68er" since she was not a student any more, but her role as political commentator in the magazine *konkret* and her proximity to the events make her one of the key faces of "1968" in Germany. She had attended the first sit-in at the Freie Universität in May 1967, when the budding author Peter Schneider gave his speech "Wir haben Fehler gemacht" (Yes, We Made Mistakes, see chapter 4), and it was her open letter to Farah Diba, the wife of the visiting Shah of Persia, that was widely circulated before the fateful demonstrations on June 2, 1967. It was her analysis of the death of Benno Ohnesorg that contributed to the radicalization of many students, as did her reinterpretation of the arson attack committed by Andreas Baader and Gudrun Ensslin in Frankfurt in April 1968.[53] A week later, Meinhof was visiting the SDS center in West Berlin when Rudi Dutschke was shot, and her blistering article "Vom Protest zum Widerstand" (From Protest to Resistance, 1968) is widely seen as a clarion call for a further radicalization of at least part of the movement.[54]

Meinhof's "journey" from well-known left-wing journalist, who wrote influential opinion pieces, to ruthless terrorist, who wrote some of the key documents of the Red Army Faction, has been told many times. It has been the subject of several biographies,[55] dramas (e.g., *Ulrike Maria Stuart* by Elfriede Jelinek), and filmic representations (the actress Martina Gdeck memorably played her in *Der Baader Meinhof Komplex* [The Baader-Meinhof Complex, 2008]). Her portrayal in the media as a hysterical or atypical woman has been analyzed in several studies,[56] while her writings have been studied in depth[57] and recently translated into English.[58] Looking at the descriptions of her life, it is interesting to note the change in tone over the years, from distanced and neutral in Stephan Aust's *Der Baader-Meinhof-Komplex* (1985), to hagiographic in Jutta Dittfurth's *Rudi und Ulrike: Geschichte einer Freundschaft* (Rudi and Ulrike: The Story of a Friendship, 2008), or, on the other hand, bitter and sarcastic from the point of view of her daughter Bettina Röhl.[59] In her afterword to the English translation of her mother's writings, Röhl observes:

> Ulrike Meinhof's influence seems to be underestimated in historical and factual terms, while she is morally overestimated as an icon of the 1968 movement, a figure of German history.[60]

The most fascinating attempt to reinterpret Meinhof for a new audience, however, is Alois Prinz's biography *Lieber wütend als traurig* (Rather Angry Than Sad, 2003), which is specifically written for readers from the age of fourteen (it won the Deutscher Jugendliteraturpreis in 2004). One might wonder why a terrorist's life may be of particular pedagogical value, but Prinz is clear that Meinhof's moral absoluteness, her commitment to the oppressed, and her determination to fight for a better world are important character traits, while her romantic persona (brought up by a friend of her mother, jilted by her husband, fragile womanly features, tilting against windmills) engender sympathy and make her an ideal object of identification for teenagers.

Prinz, born in 1958, describes the moment when he and his fellow pupils first heard the news of Meinhof's suicide in prison:

> I remember how the news hit us [...] and caused embarrassment and confusion. The fact that somewhere out there there was a "gang" that had declared war on the state and our parents' generation was hard to believe and disturbing. Did they not want a better world, a more meaningful life and a fairer society? That much at least was known about their motives, and it was easy to link this with one's own dreams and desires. [...] On the other hand, they weren't just risking their own lives. Their path was littered with corpses. And these two sides were difficult for me to bring together. What remained was an unsettling question that I struggled to formulate

and that couldn't be appeased by phrases like "no end justifies every means" or "violence is never an option." On the one hand, there was this yearning for a life that was broader, better and wilder. And on the other, this cold-blooded killing and the implacable hatred.[61]

By putting his finger on the moral dilemma that many Germans felt about Ulrike Meinhof, Prinz invites the reader to appreciate the difficult decisions many 68ers themselves had to make. The book differs markedly from a representation that interprets "1968" from subsequent events. At the same time, an over-sympathetic approach risks to paper over fundamental differences between the German student movement and the Red Army Faction. Their first major pamphlet, *Das Konzept Stadtguerilla* (The Concept of City Guerrilla, 1971), was written mainly by Meinhof, and the claim made there that the RAF sees the history of the German student movement as its own history does not mean that the movement as a whole intended a 30-year killing spree. However, this is how many observers have chosen to interpret the connection (see chapter 3). Thus Butz Peters, in his study of the RAF, describes the ideological and strategic debates dominating "1968" as an "Ideensteinbruch" (quarry of ideas) to which the RAF freely helped herself:

> Moreover, the Student Movement is centrally important for the foundation of the RAF two years later: in their first written statement—mainly penned by Ulrike Meinhof—the group expressly describes the history of the Student Movement as part of its own history. Over a number of years ideas and demands of the Student Movement appear in the ideological pamphlets of the RAF. The RAF helps itself to this "quarry of ideas," and transforms itself into a kind of "illegitimate child" of the Student Movement.[62]

The fact that these ideas and new forms of communication also led to a myriad of other, nonviolent associations and activities ranging from the Jusos and K-groups to citizen's initiatives and the modern German women's movement tends to be forgotten in such narrow readings. As with Rudi Dutschke, then, we can see how "1968" can be constructed—by interested parties who aim to set the record straight and create a myth in the process. Because Dutschke and Meinhof polarized opinions, and because they died young, they became the perfect objects for the imagination. Romanticized, sanitized, idealized, vilified, they colonize the memory of "1968." Felix Ensslin, the son of Gudrun Ensslin and Bernward Vesper, is keenly aware of the way complex individuals can be turned into cyphers by those who write about them. In an afterword to a recently published correspondence between his parents, he describes the process of projecting desires and anxieties on the dead:

Consequently, they represent the possibility, beyond the opportunism of a grey world, beyond a threatening and deceptive veneer of liberalism, and beyond the silent approval of inequality and falsehood, to choose a different life or, rather, a different death. For this is the precondition for the projection of one's desires: that they are dead. The images can no longer be tainted by traces of new life.[63]

Or new information, one might add. The case of Gudrun Ensslin is certainly an instructive one for the construction of "1968." As one of the four arsonists who set fire to a department store in Frankfurt on April 2, 1968, partner of Bernward Vesper,[64] girlfriend of Andreas Baader, cofounder of the RAF, terrorist and inmate of the Stammheim high security prison who died during the Todesnacht (death night) on October 18, 1977, she has become the subject of numerous films and books.[65] But she is also associated with one of the most famous soundbites of "1968." After the shooting of Ohnesorg, she is supposed to have shouted, "This is the Auschwitz generation—and there is no arguing with them,"[66] a quote that has found its way into almost every account of the German student movement.[67] However, there is serious doubt that she ever spoke those words.[68]

Summary

The discussion has shown that "faces" like Benno Ohnesorg, Rudi Dutschke, Joschka Fischer, Daniel Cohn-Bendit, and Ulrike Meinhof serve as a convenient shorthand for the period. Of course, others could have been chosen, and I am well aware that my selection, in itself, will be seen by some as privileging one interpretation of "1968" over another. For example, we could have highlighted members of Kommune I like Dieter Kunzelmann, Rainer Langhans, or Fritz Teufel, all of whom led their life, through the incessant attention of the media and their own efforts,[69] in the public imagination of "1968." We could have looked at film student Holger Meins, who produced a short film on how to make a Molotov cocktail for the anti-Springer campaign and died in prison following a hunger strike in 1974,[70] or Horst Mahler, founder of the "Republican Club" in West Berlin, defense lawyer for Fritz Teufel, Rudi Dutschke, and other 68ers, and cofounder of the RAF. After all, they were part of a network of individuals with similar aims and objectives, even though their methods differed significantly.

As personifications of "1968" they have *all* become projection screens. The dead have been appropriated (by family, friends, and fellow travelers) and constructed as martyrs (by their comrades, the media, historians, and writers) for a grand, often melodramatic, narrative: Ohnesorg as *Everyman* struck down by evil forces, Dutschke as the *Idealist* and reluctant leader of an antiauthoritarian movement taking the bullets on behalf of the movement, and Meinhof as the tragic *Heroine* in a drama of her own making.[71] The living continue as the eternal activists who, though wiser and accepting of their mistakes, can be relied upon to continue the struggle against the establishment (in the case of Mahler, ironically now from the far right). They have accepted the role of heroes of and for their generation, striking impressive poses, coming to the rescue, and generally reassuring their audiences by their interventions that the movement lives on, even though they themselves are adamant that "1968" is well and truly over.

2: Chroniclers and Interpreters

THE YEAR 1968 IN GERMANY continues to offer a rich field for historians, political scientists, and sociologists. They share this field with a number of former activists who are engaged in writing their own history, and journalists who understand the continuing attraction of the era for the wider public. I explore the role of the media in the construction of "1968" in chapter 6, but for now will focus on those individuals who have been particularly active in writing narratives that aim to explain the events, put them into a wider historico-political context, and offer an interpretive framework. My contention is that these chroniclers and interpreters have tended to ignore the extent to which "1968" has become removed from the historical events and has developed its own momentum as a discourse on the identity and aspirations of Germans today. Ironically, their "expert" status has given them privileged access to interpret "1968" for a variety of audiences, but they rarely openly reflect on the reasons why they chose the topic. Similarly, few acknowledge that their interpretations may be determined by their own attitudes to the era or that their verdicts themselves influence the direction of future research. Moreover, while the two other memory contests over Germany's Nazi and Socialist past were essentially backward-looking and largely politically sponsored, the discourse on "1968"—in spite of and perhaps also because of the efforts of its historians—is forward-looking and fueled by a sense that the period represents "unfinished business." A good example for this is the American historian Jay Winter, who regards "1968" as a key moment in the twentieth century when "minor utopians" succeeded in putting the notion of liberation in the minds of millions of their contemporaries. While conceding that their immediate achievements were meager or nonexistent, he argues that their visions of an alternative reality precipitated "a series of moments of possibility, of openings, of hopes and dreams rarely realized, but rarely forgotten as well."[1] This chapter will demonstrate that the historicization of "1968" has not led to its deconstruction but added further layers to it.

It is worth noting that from early on, participants and observers were united in their view that "1968" was an important moment in West German history, and the first accounts of what had happened were published almost immediately. Indeed, one of the first books on the student protests came out in 1967. In their final chapter, the authors of *Was wollen die Studenten?* (What Do the Students Want?) already offered an interpretive framework that would form the basis of a narrative and, with minor variations, be endlessly recycled over the following decades:

> The student protests of the spring and summer of 1967 have discomfited and provoked the democratic affluent society, which has just placed its economic and political worries trustingly into the hands of a grand coalition, to such an extent that it allows us to draw conclusions about the lability, insecurity and lack of secure foundations in this society. Its responses, exemplified by its brutal measures to rid itself of the students, are proof in retrospect that they had good reason to criticize such a society.[2]

In 1969, the sociologist Jürgen Habermas published his political statements and analyses of the protest movement, especially regarding university reform. While broadly supportive of the protests, he lamented certain "irrational" impulses within the movement, which made it easier for the "other side" to maintain the status quo. To an extent, the students had demanded what he himself had proposed, an integration of the curriculum with the experiences and interests of the students, and a broader democratization of universities. In his view, the students' "grand refusal" was a direct consequence of the ineffectiveness of political opposition in Western democracies, which had led to the creation of "Gegenwelten" (countercultures). Crucially, in spite of his criticism of Rudi Dutschke's strategy as "left-wing fascism" and the revolt as a "Scheinrevolution" (a pretend revolution),[3] he credited the movement with a consciousness-changing power, an assessment that has also found entry into many of the histories of "1968": "The protest movement has decisively changed the consciousness of those studying at the universities of the Federal Republic."[4]

However, it wasn't until 1977, ten years after the death of Benno Ohnesorg, that activists realized that the movement was well and truly over. Against the sobering background of the German Autumn, Peter Mosler's *Was wir wollten, was wir wurden* (What We Desired, and What Became of Us) gave them a melancholy voice. Mosler did not aim to provide an objective account but rather eulogized the revolt as a moment "in which the dry chaff of our existence burned brightly." The result of dozens of interviews with former activists and participants, Mosler's book takes stock of what the movement meant to the protesters and what happened to them when it had run its course. He is acutely aware that he is collecting memories of his generation for the use of future generations:

> This book is not an "objective" treatise on the student revolt. The demon objectivity and the slimy kraken subjectivity, these two monsters are only peaceful when they go together. This is what they attempt in these chapters. I want to describe what was going on—for

the sympathizing citizens who were not allowed to find out in the Bild-Zeitung or on TV; for the young comrades, so that we recall some of the strengths that we gave up so thoughtlessly.[5]

Mosler offers a kaleidoscope of exemplary biographies to capture the "feeling" of the time. By mixing different personal experiences with accounts of the events and excerpts from some of the key theoretical texts read by the students at the time, he romanticizes the movement as a dream of heightened sensitivity and lost youth.

The volume *Studentenbewegung 1967–69: Protokolle und Materialien* (Student Movement 1967–69: Records and Materials), also published in 1977, painted a very different picture. The editors, Frank Wolff and Eberhard Windaus, provide a sobering insight into the bickering, positioning, and self-referential character of the movement. They observe that not only had the movement self-destructed, but its failure to achieve its objectives had caused many activists to give up and forget what they had once fought for:

> That the revolt is over is a convenient lie and a reality; disavowed she lives in ridiculous dungarees of totalitarian cut, in obscure miracle cures, in second-hand furniture, and in shabby pubs with stupefying music. A convenient lie: it makes us backward-looking, wanting to hold on the past. It destroys the continuing validity and acute necessity of the struggle for freedom which cannot exist without a worthy memory. It blinds us to the weaknesses and greatness of the worldwide rebellion that took place ten years ago.[6]

By confronting their former comrades with the (painful) truth of a movement that was arrogantly searching for strategies to turn its utopian ideas into reality and struggling with the quixotic task of challenging and replacing all the basic tenets of West Germany's political, social, and cultural life, Wolff and Windaus provided one possible blueprint for a future historicization and a "worthy memory" of "1968." Indeed, with the inclusion of the report on the student revolt by Minister of the Interior Erich Benda to the Bundestag on April 30, 1968, and excerpts from the ensuing debate, the volume has a distinct air of closure. But "1968" refused to go quietly.

"1968" as a Generational Narrative

The impetus to record and pass on what had happened was strong among 68ers for a number of reasons: they felt that their revolt had been an intense experience by bringing together thought, action, and emotion. They also believed that it had been misrepresented by the conservative press and politicians eager to maintain the status quo. While the revolt had been unsuccessful in actually changing the world, it had changed them in a fundamental way. And by changing themselves, they still held the potential to change the world in the future. Moreover, writing down what happened and pontificating what people should think about the past was, post-"1968," no longer the privilege of tenured professors (who were also civil servants and thus owed allegiance to the state) in ivory towers. After all, the students had experienced firsthand how the historical "truth" had been twisted by their parents' generation. While some historians rejected a "Politisierung der Wissenschaft" (politicizing of science) the majority of West German historians accepted that "Zeitgeschichte" had in fact become "öffentliche Streitgeschichte": history had arrived in the public sphere and was subject to public challenges.[7] Rudi Dutschke had declared that "Geschichte ist machbar" (we can make history), which can be understood in two ways: he believed that by their actions the students had the chance to change the course of history, but it also meant that learning from history and understanding one's role in a political moment was a dialectical process, feeding back into one's political praxis.

With the first "anniversary publications" in 1977, a sense of "generation" came into the mix. In two essays in the *Kursbuch*, the journalist and former activist Klaus Hartung was the first to reflect upon the "self-annihilation" of those of his former comrades who had chosen to join totalitarian or terrorist groups and the need for the continuing cohesion of the vast majority of former students who had been active in the movement and shared the same experiences.[8] But it wasn't until the twentieth anniversary of "1968" that the terms "68er" and "68er generation" became widely used by researchers and the media (also allowing for a line to be drawn between 1967 and 1977). From those who had been activists at the time, this construction from "outside" was noted with equal amounts of pride and irritation. Literary scholar Silvia Bovenschen, for example, observed wryly that her generation had become "marked":

> Given that we are members of a "historically marked" group, it seems as if certain sections of our memory can be turned into "the truth." That makes us self-opinionated, but also vulnerable to attack.[9]

Also in 1988, Daniel Cohn-Bendit defined his generation in contrast to the following generation: with the Greens in parliament and ecological issues at the top of the agenda (a year before the fall of the Wall changed the political coordinates completely), he wrote that the future no longer held a promise but had become a distinct threat. This had had a major influence on the mood of the next protest generation: instead of joyfully "making history," those who came after the 68ers were merely trying to prevent the worst consequences of global environmental pollution. Against this grim picture he evoked the idealistic hopes of his own generation:

> The excitement was massive, the mood euphoric [. . .]. A magical moment came to join the mixture of imagination and reality. The "principle of hope," at last, seemed on the verge of becoming reality, and the present was filled with an alternative reality. Our urge to do something was as intense as the feeling that we had left yesterday's humdrum reality behind.[10]

It wasn't until 1995, though, that the concept of a "68er generation" received serious scholarly attention. The sociologist Heinz Bude found that in spite of coming from very different backgrounds, those born between 1938 and 1948 were united by the apocalyptic childhood experience of the war and postwar period and a distinctly critical attitude toward the political system of the Federal Republic. He described the social construction of the 68er generation during the 1980s as a "retrospective propagation": "The more membership of a certain year group was declared to be the defining characteristic, the more members wanted to be part of it."[11] Given that the truly active core numbered 15–20, the committed activists (according to Rudi Dutschke) no more than 150–200, and those who could be mobilized no more than 10,000, it seems counterintuitive to speak of a generation. However, a "generational elite" may excite a "generational multitude," and, given the overlap between the political and the cultural revolution in the late 1960s, it seemed plausible to speak of a distinct generation. Bude added that the movement set free "enormous subjective forces" and that this outpouring of revolutionary fervor was experienced collectively: "If the term wasn't so suspicious-looking, one could speak of a collective ecstasy, which nevertheless did not mean rapture as it was definitely taking place in this world" (58).

By 2001, the position of "1968" as a generational marker seemed secure enough that the editors of the German equivalent of Pierre Nora's *Les Lieux de mémoire* (The Places of Memory, 1984–92) felt that they could include it as a distinct *Erinnerungsort*, a "place" where memories could come together. They asked Heinz Bude to write the entry, who explained the metamorphosis of the movement into the "68er generation" with the creation of a "foundational myth." Thus, when President Richard von Weizsäcker's acknowledged the historical achievement of the 68ers in his speech on German Unification on October 3, 1990, he set out to integrate the unruly 68er generation into the fold by offering them a stake in the broader national and intergenerational narrative. Bude writes:

> By reducing our historical knowledge in hindsight to a few catchy signs and symbols, the myth creates a tradition which represents a continuity bridge between generations, above all caesuras and beyond all controversies.[12]

In contrast to 1945 or 1989, Bude argues, "1968" offers itself as a "sicherer Erinnerungsort im Kollektivgedächtnis" (safe place in collective memory, 122), since the original political intentions of the protest generation have been stripped away and are now so far removed from the present that the former enemies of the state can be welcomed like prodigal sons and daughters. In this way, the "68er generation," in spite of its dark shadow in form of the RAF, no longer stands apart from the collective but is constructed as part of a "Familienroman":

> 1968 also stands for a specific chapter in West Germany's family novel, continuing on from National Socialism. It is a history of rebellion and reconciliation, where the intense conflict of separation of the younger intellectual generation is seen as a collective success story and proof of social civilization. (133)

While the term "68er generation" has thus been sanitized, there have been critical voices as well. The historian Axel Schildt challenges the term's validity and usefulness, pointing out that the assumption that one can "coral" a whole generation depends on listening to those elements who are most able to articulate their case. In the case of "1968," these are well educated, are male, and have produced literary texts or been subject of generational narratives themselves. He therefore sees the term "68er generation" as "overvalued and overused." As a consequence of their self-stylization and subsequent external construction, the originators must now live with the fact that they have become, for better or worse, the object of permanent attention and dependent on the fluctuating interest of the press.[13]

The question as to what extent generations can be constructed has been the focus of a number of research projects recently. According to Lutz Niethammer, the very fact that experiences are given generational form—contemporaneously or retrospectively—is increasingly understood as a means of mobilizing and lending legitimacy to a group identity. Talking about a generation is not a process that takes place in isolation from actual experience, however. There are limits to the power of (retrospective) narrative construction. In the case of the "68ers," a feeling of collective belonging based on the performance nature of the protests and the need to endow the events with meaning while they were happening stood at the beginning of a long-term process of generation building, nurtured further by the commemoration of common experiences over time. Niethammer concludes that there may always be an element of fiction involved in claiming membership of a generation, but rather than condemning such narrative strategies, studying the very act of construction has much to reveal about how activists—and those who observed them—made sense of "1968" and why the narratives of collective experience they fashioned often unfolded a powerful mobilizing potential.[14]

Obviously, the concept of a generation associated with "1968" is not unique to Germany. In the United States one speaks of the "baby boomers"[15] or the "Woodstock generation," and the year 1968 is widely seen as topping off the "sixties."[16] In Western Europe each country has its own term for an age cohort that is associated as much with its hippie lifestyle, music, and fashion as with its radical political agenda. Historian Anna von der Goltz has attempted to address the contradictions inherent in this generation building.[17] While a generational bond may strengthen the social ties between individuals, in the case of "1968" suggesting homogeneity where there was none may risk depoliticizing historic events and individual experiences. We also need to be clear, she reminds us, what we mean by the "68ers": Do we include all people of a particular age cohort (born during or at the end of World War II, all students of a particular age cohort, the core of 1960s activists, the wider circle of those who sympathized with the protesters, or all those who describe themselves as 68ers retrospectively, even if they had not participated at the time? Referring to Kristen Ross's study of the "afterlives" of May 1968 in France, von der Goltz points out that "generation" can be "a flawed construct, a somewhat sinister and calculated fabrication by a small group of former activists who sought to distance themselves from their radical pasts with the sole aim of political self-promotion in the present" (11). As "1968" was immensely political, the efforts to construct and define generations of "68ers" are equally political and have to be understood as such. And just as different political groups jostled for position in 1968, so today different groups lay claim to membership of the "68er generation." I will return to this in chapter 8, but it is worth mentioning briefly that in recent years former members of the conservative Ring Christlich-Demokratischer Studenten (RCDS), former policemen who were mobilized during student demonstrations, individuals who were living in the GDR and were prevented from political protest but felt sympathy for the student revolt, and even former journalists working for the Springer publishing group have declared themselves "68ers." I would therefore agree with von der Goltz when she cautions:

> While the left-wing West German 68ers have undoubtedly been the most vocal—and most self-conscious—group and have set the agenda for constructing a coherent generational narrative, their sense of themselves as a collective only emerged through complex and twisted processes of generation building. Although they represent the largest group of activists and could count on the West German media to nurture their fame, they are not the only yardstick of what constitutes a generation.[18]

Linda Shortt has recently defined generational belonging as an "identity anchor" that enables individuals to see themselves as part of an imagined community.[19] In a chapter dedicated to the way literary representations of the era differ if written by 68ers or "78ers," she explores the emotional pull the 68ers had on subsequent generations. She relies on a single text, Stephan Wackwitz's *Ein unsichtbares Land* (2003; An Invisible Country, 2005), a narrative that aims to dispose of the past in order to gain independence from a youthful identification with "1968," and enable the narrator to identify himself as a postrevolutionary. I will discuss the role of those critical of the student rebellion in chapter 3 and return to the phenomenon of the *Zaungast* (onlooker) in chapter 8, to show how "latecomers" contribute to the construction of "1968."

"1968" as a History of the SDS

The first scholars who made a sustained attempt to come to terms with the historicity of "1968" are the political scientist Tilmann Fichter and the sociologist Siegward Lönnendonker. Together, they have written a number of books detailing the history of the Socialist German Student League, especially in West Berlin. Lönnendonker has also built up the APO archiv, which has grown into one of the key repositories for documents, flyers, posters,[20] and gray literature emanating from the Extraparliamentary Opposition. As former members of the SDS and later employees of the Freie Universität, Fichter and Lönnendonker were ideally placed to undertake their decade-long project, even though by focusing on the SDS as the "most active" political student group in the late 1960s they relegate the other groups, ranging from the Sozialdemokratischer Hochschulbund (SHB) to the Ring Christlich-Demokratischer Studenten (RCDS), to the sidelines.

Their first book, *Kleine Geschichte des SDS* (A Short History of the SDS, 1997), is very open about why they had decided to write it—they felt that books like the one by Wolff and Windaus had lacked a political statement and simply used the history of the movement as a *Steinbruch* (quarry), picking only those bits that suited them. While the *Kleine Geschichte* is indeed much more factual of the events leading up to and during "1968" and attempts to adhere to academic standards, the authors are nevertheless partisan in their verdicts. A good example of their approach can be seen in their assessment of the Kommune I:

> The key claim of Kommune I, the removal of the separation of private sphere, civil existence and political praxis which was supposed to allow the individual to find his identity in the collective, was a complete failure. The parody of the Faustian dream of German philosophy, the creation of a new man, ended pathetically.[21]

It is understandable that former members of the SDS—which had been vilified in the Springer press and ignominiously dissolved when different factions began to establish communist cadre groups (K-Gruppen) — wanted to set the record straight. But Fichter and Lönnendonker had struck on a formula that could turn defeat into victory through the construction of a narrative that gave the movement a new meaning and a second life: they would continue the revolution by other means. In their essay "Berlin: Hauptstadt der Revolte" (Berlin: Capital of the Revolt, 1980), for example, they assign "1968" a number of achievements that had a significant impact on the political culture and everyday life in the Federal Republic. Moreover, they argue that the movement had begun to ask critical questions of the state that so far had been ignored:

> To be sure, the student revolt has had a greater impact on the political culture of the Federal Republic than any other event in the 60s. A new relationship with the Third World, antiauthoritarian child-rearing, grass-root movements, the situation of women in an advanced industrial society as well as a sensitivity for the destruction of the environment, not to mention a renaissance of Marxism at universities, are some of the most important results, all normal parts of our everyday life today. At the same time, other themes of the revolt became taboo, for example the political function of the judiciary, the right to resistance, the imperialistic character of the Federal Republic.[22]

Three years later, Fichter and Lönnendonker, together with political scientist Jochen Staadt, published the fifth volume of a history of the Freie Universität. Covering the years 1967 to 1969, the documentation focuses on the confrontation between university authorities, students, local media, and Berlin politicians following the shooting of Benno Ohnesorg, the subsequent debates about political responsibility, the wave of strikes, demonstrations, and responses, the Vietnam debate, all the way to the "battle at Tegeler Weg," and the debate about violence and planned new university laws. On the one hand, the volume is aiming to present a balanced picture. For example, it shows that the conservative student group RCDS (which bitterly fought the radical SDS within the student parliament) was critical of the US-American strategy in Vietnam and insisted on the right of students to debate political matters on campus.[23] It also contains a moving letter by one of Benno Ohnesorg's professors to the president of the Freie Universität (FU) urging him to challenge the grotesque character defamation in the Springer press.[24]

On the other hand, as in their earlier publications, the authors argued that the revolt had a number of deep, lasting, and positive effects. Extending their previous statement, they now claimed that "1968" was responsible for a broad liberalization of West German society, the invention of oppositional strategies, the formation of the social-liberal coalition under Willy Brandt and a *sozialpsychologischer Klimaumschwung* (sociopsychological change in climate) which enabled people to experiment with alternatives to the nuclear family in an atmosphere of tolerance. Given that this interpretation would become a widely shared take on "1968," it is worth quoting at length:

> Starting from the universities, the revolt has had a far-reaching impact on society. Even if many of the former participants consider it a failure, given that it achieved few of the aims and objectives they had set themselves, it has had a sustained impact on the cultural and political climate in the Federal Republic and West Berlin. For the first time, we saw fundamental opposition in action, something that opened the door for citizen's initiatives, self-help groups and political parties like the Greens or the Alternative Lists. The change in public opinion, caused by the Student Movement amongst the young generation and the intelligentsia, created important conditions for the social-liberal coalition to come to power. Willy Brandt's slogan "let's dare to have more democracy" promised the realization of a key aim of the protest movement. The change in the cultural and socio-psychological climate of the time weakened the claustrophobic conditions of private life in the 1950s and the restrictions of the nuclear family; in communal living, child centers, antiauthoritarian school projects and the first women's groups, productive centers of disruption developed that forced an extension of the tolerated space for minorities, nonconformism, fashions, etc.[25]

Two things should be noted here: against a general sense of failure among the former activists, the authors redefine "1968" as a successful failure. They suggest that while the original intentions of the movement may not have been fulfilled, its collateral and medium-term impact ought to be understood as leading to significant political and cultural change. Furthermore, we can see that such a reinterpretation was only possible once the paralysis of the German Autumn in 1977 had been overcome and the success of new social movements like the women's movement or the Green movement had become apparent.

Almost two decades later, Lönnendonker, Staadt, and the sociologist Bernd Rabehl, a close friend of Rudi Dutschke and a leading member of the SDS in the late 1960s, presented an updated version of the history of the SDS, this time focusing on the key years between its ousting from the Social Democratic Party in 1961 and the eruption of the "antiauthoritarian revolt." By this time, the authors were not just presenting new and detailed information about the SDS but took the opportunity to defend "1968" against its critics. This was certainly necessary from their point of view: in the context of 9/11 and the revelations about Joschka Fischer in 2001, the whole movement had been accused in the Bundestag of a dangerous dalliance with violence (an aspect notably absent in Lönnendonker and Fichter's interpretation cited above). Interestingly, they address the difficulties in writing about "1968," challenging both the view that "you can only write about 68 if you were there" and the opposing view that only outsiders who were born later could be objective about the revolt. Their aim now was to historicize and contextualize the German "1968" as part of a global phenomenon "in der das linke Denken mit Gewalt zum Handeln durchbrach" (when left-wing thinking violently turned into action).[26]

Clearly stung by the accusations that the SDS had opened the door for a culture of violence that had bred the RAF and was, certainly post-9/11, difficult to defend, Rabehl took great pains to explain how "einzelne Führer" (the odd leader, 512) had mistaken the spontaneous protests following the attempted assassination of Rudi Dutschke as a revolutionary situation and started to believe that it was their historic mission to bring this to fruition. Crucially, he also suggested that following the explosion of revolutionary exuberance a "Lebensgefühl" and a "Lebenshaltung" had developed that was unique not only to the activists but also an entire generation:

> Only at this point did a living sense of "sixty-eight" develop that put all doubts to one side. Innumerable milieus and groups formed which trusted their own strength and no longer circled round one single center. The revolt became normal, and spread to almost every family, school, village and small town. It became the normal attitude to life for the new generations. (511–12)

Lönnendonker and Fichter's most recent book, *Dutschkes Deutschland* (Dutschke's Germany, 2011),[27] continues their quest to retain control of their interpretation of "1968." This unusual volume, a *Streitschrift* (a polemic or intervention) once again aims to "set the record straight" as far as the history and political legacy of the SDS is concerned, but this time in the context of a new debate that had gained traction in recent years. The authors observe that the Left in (West) Germany was conspicuously quiet when the Wall came down. It was unprepared for German unification, the reality of a revolution that was not a Socialist one, and failed to respond to a historical moment. This *Sprachlosigkeit* (inability to speak) cemented the public view that "1968" had little to offer a modern German society. Not only did politicians on the Left fail to gauge the public mood between November 1989 and October 1990 (both Oscar Lafontaine's SPD and the West German Greens suffered bruising defeats in the first elections in unified Germany), but the contribution of left-leaning intellectuals to a modern German state was later called into question. While "1968," the

Extraparliamentary Opposition and the German student movement had previously been variously viewed as a "successful failure," a "fundamental liberalization," and a "political watershed" in the old Federal Republic, it was now seen as irrelevant by critics in a "Germany without 68."

Fichter and Lönnendonker aim to prove that far from being an irrelevance, the ideas and impulses from the Socialist German Student League were vital to keep the German question alive both in the context of the Cold War, the *Ostpolitik* pursued by the SPD under Willy Brandt, and the increasing acceptance of German division by the Left. In particular, the authors cite the example of Rudi Dutschke, who had left East Germany to study at the FU in West Berlin. The narrative generally accepted on the Left that the two martyrs of the German student movement were victims of an unreconstructed authoritarian police state was dealt a severe blow by the revelations in 2009 that Kurras had in fact been a Stasi agent, giving rise to a number of high profile calls from the right-wing press to reevaluate "1968" and the role of the New Left. These critics argued that Adenauer's West Germany and the grand coalition of 1966–69 were anything but protofascist and that the rebellion of the students played straight into the hands of a Stalinist strategy to weaken the young West German state. In their book, Fichter and Lönnendonker set out to defuse the accusation that the German student movement had been a puppet of the East German regime and the Stasi. They explore the role of the SDS in the postwar period, where the student league (founded, among others, by later Chancellor Helmut Schmidt) played a significant role, as the youth organization of the oppositional SPD, in discussing possible strategies to overcome German division, to resist West German rearmament, to implement democratic structures in West Germany's universities, to address the Nazi past, and to defend itself against attempts of infiltration by individuals who were beholden to East Germany.

The volume is obviously a polemic against revisionists. In the context of German memory contests, it aims to show that Rudi Dutschke had a much broader outlook on the German question than previously recognized. It also provides a number of key documents that prove that the SDS had consistently addressed and discussed the "German Question" in the fifties and sixties, that Rudi Dutschke in particular was a fervent supporter of German unification and that the young intellectuals in the SDS had challenged the SPD to come up with better ideas, remember their socialist ideals, and formulate strategies to shape an alternative Germany. In this I would agree with them: the fact that Willy Brandt came to power in 1969, announced an amnesty for minor law-breaking by activists, and attracted thousands of former SDS members into the party is an indication that the students had been able to make (a little) history after all.

"1968" between Theory, Praxis, and Myth

Wolfgang Kraushaar is the most prolific writer about "1968" in Germany. He studied political science in Frankfurt and describes himself as a "Tangential-68er."[28] His first contribution to the construction of "1968," "Notizen zu einer Chronologie der Studentenbewegung" (Notes for a Chronology of the Student Movement), appeared in Peter Mosler's *Was wir wollten, was wir wurden* in 1977. In his preface, Kraushaar cryptically suggests that it is necessary to supply a timeline "um etwas mehr Licht in das Dunkel der Fakten zu bringen" (to bring some light into the darkness of the facts, 249), but then he reflects on the dangers inherent in doing so:

> Furthermore, the assumption that chronologically pinning down dates will directly support the cause of the historiographical process is pure fiction. Only by consciously amplifying certain phenomena by means of rather latent layers of meaning, which are not normally classified in politological calendars, can we make connections more transparent. Of course, omissions and abbreviations can serve exactly the same purpose. (249)

Kraushaar highlights a problem here that would challenge historians for decades: how to make sense of the sheer volume of facts and influences, disparate events, groups, activities, attitudes, issues, and emotions. At the same time, he stresses that this first attempt at chronicling the student movement is just that—and indeed he would go on to grapple with this problem for most of his working life. Today, he is widely regarded as a *Stichwortgeber* (he is a key participant in public debates, regular speaker and interviewee) and undisputed, though often challenged, authority on the German student movement. His work has become essential reading for all researchers working on "1968." In 1987 he joined the Hamburg Institute of Social Research,[29] funded by the philanthropist Jan Philipp Reemtsma.

Clearly committed to understanding the complex relationship between the provocative actions of the students and the theories of their intellectual fathers in the Frankfurt School, Kraushaar announced his presence with a trenchant analysis of the "Organisationsreferat" (policy paper on the question of organising the protest) presented in September 1967 by Rudi Dutschke and his Frankfurt counterpart Hans-Jürgen Krahl,[30] but it was his three-volume "Frankfurter Schule und Studentenbewegung" (Frankfurt School and Student Movement, 1998) that established him as one of the key interpreters of the movement.[31] Cross-referencing a chronology of events from right after the war to the mid-1990s with an anthology of original documents and correspondence, the project successfully changed the focus of attention from West Berlin to Frankfurt and asserted the significance of philosophers like Max Horkheimer, Theodor Adorno, and Herbert Marcuse for the movement.

Also in 1998, Kraushaar published a volume focused entirely on the events of the year 1968.[32] In contrast to Tariq Ali and Susan Watson or Mark Kurlansky, who published similar chronologies,[33] he is acutely aware of the "dominance of the image worlds" and defends his choices, particularly a focus on "forms of action [. . .] which have broadened the repertoire of political action with new, imaginative and effective facets" (8). He is also aware that, thirty years on and in the middle of an election year that would bring red–green to power, "1968" had become "eine Münze im Kampf um das politische Selbstverständnis dieser Republik" (a key factor in the struggle for the political identity of this Republic, 313). The students had failed in their radical attempts to change society, he conceded, but they had been successful in their emancipation from their parents, in sensitizing society to the Nazi past, and in their demands for an expansion of education, for sexual self-determination, for women's emancipation, and for democratization of some institutions. While the movement had had negative side effects, it had demonstrated that a minority could make a significant difference. His conclusion summed up the very positive view that was to become, at least for a couple of years, the dominant narrative of "1968":

> The year 1968 has changed everything in the Federal Republic. The extra-parliamentary opposition had called for a veritable attack on the institutions—schools, universities, legal courts, local authorities, prisons, psychiatric wards, political parties and parliaments. Hardly any of these institutions has been spared awkward questions about its legitimacy. Once the obsolete and inappropriate revolutionary rhetoric had dissipated, the excess of utopian energies generated the strength for reforms that had been long overdue. Even though the extra-parliamentary opposition failed in almost all of its immediate political objectives, it still changed the attitudes and mentalities in a sustained way. It is only thanks to the APO that the thing that defines human beings in their subjectivity has been placed at the center of public interest. The traditional concept of politics has been expanded by a vital dimension. Political action is no longer determined by those in power, or limited to governments, parliaments and political parties. Initiative, maturity, civil courage, nonconformism and collective responsibility have gained an indispensable position. (323)

In marked contrast to most other researchers of his generation, Kraushaar has been upfront about the challenges facing anyone trying to write a history of "1968." While the tension between the "Erlebnishorizont" (experiential horizon) of the participant and the "Erklärungshorizont" (explanatory horizon) of the historian can be productive, there remains a "diagnostic uncertainty."[34] His next book, the influential *1968 als Mythos, Chiffre und Zäsur* (1968 as Myth, Cypher and Caesura, 2000), attempted to confront the issue head-on. In the introductory chapter "Wie über 1968 schreiben?" (How to Write about 1968?), he relates his own personal experience when, at a demonstration in Frankfurt on January 30, 1969, he came face to face with political power (he was pushed against exchancellor Ludwig Erhard's limousine) and found himself the subject of distorting reports in the press. How does one stay objective in such a case, he wondered:

> Writing history means, in spite of all the legitimate criticism of the predominantly narrative-oriented stance of the historian, to tell a story. Thus, the primary question is this: which position does the author adopt as narrator, and what quality do we attach to it in terms of the art of narration?[35]

While such questions are routine methodological considerations any historian has to address, this problem went directly to the heart of the *Wissenschaftskritik* advanced by the 68ers, since the traditional approach in the arts and social sciences they had encountered was not to divulge any sociopolitical position for fear that it might endanger objectivity. Kraushaar expanded on this in an essay the following year when the country was gripped by the revelations about "Joschkas wilde Jahre" (Joschka's wild years).[36] Characterizing *Geschichtspolitik* as *Machtpolitik* (politics of history as politics of power), he took a dim view of the chances of a successful historicization of "1968," given its politically controversial nature. Kraushaar did his level best to contribute to a "Versachlichung" (Objectivization) of the debate, first through his book *Fischer in Frankfurt* (2001), secondly through a comprehensive review of the antifascist, anticapitalist, and antiimperialist foundations "1968," a task that no historian had ever attempted,[37] and thirdly through an appraisal of Herbert Marcuse's role as "mentor" of the German student movement.[38] However, it was a short essay in a small book published in-house at the Hamburg Institute of Social Research that turned many former 68ers against him.[39]

Kraushaar had been able to show that the concept of an urban guerrilla had existed as a clear strategy in Rudi Dutschke's thinking as early as 1966. Correcting his view expressed three years earlier that the RAF was a "Zerfalls- und Entmischungsprodukt" (product of fragmentation and separation)[40] of the APO, he now conceded that there was a direct link between the 68er movement and the RAF, as evidenced by the unambiguous references to the student movement in *Das Konzept Stadtguerilla* penned by Ulrike Meinhof in 1971.[41] While this argument in itself is hardly convincing proof, given that it was in the interest of the RAF to claim continuity in order to elicit the support of potential sympathizers,

Kraushaar's research into Rudi Dutschke's correspondence and diaries revealed evidence that violence was certainly always an option in his thinking. To Dutschke, it was the capitalist system that created violence by perpetrating oppression and exploitation. In order to defend oneself against a form of the violence that was not immediately obvious in the Western world, direct action seemed the appropriate strategy to Dutschke, though he qualified this by stating that revolutionary violence was always counterviolence.[42] Despite toying with the idea of terror, he was at pains to stress the difference between violence against things and violence against people. Kraushaar concluded that Dutschke was the first student leader to talk about an urban guerrilla, even though he later argued that terrorism was "against socialist ethics."[43]

This reassessment of *the* iconic figure of the German student movement led to a highly charged debate in the countercultural newspaper *taz*, which lasted from March to May 2005. As this debate is a clear example of the difficulties involved in historicizing "1968," I will summarize the arguments that were put forward. Stefan Reinecke conceded that Kraushaar was right in locating "collective fantasies of violence"[44] in the student movement but argued that this did not automatically make Dutschke the founder of left-wing terrorism. Indeed, if Dutschke was guilty of lifting the taboo on violence, then so were the *Bild* with its outrageous headlines and the West Berlin police with its "civil war mentality."[45] Klaus Meschkat pointed to Oskar Negt's speech "Under the Sign of Violence" held at the Angela Davis Congress in 1972, which in his view had drawn a clear line between the APO and the RAF,[46] but maintained that both student movement and RAF had to be understood as responses to the "most murderous actions perpetrated by the most advanced democracy in the world."[47]

In response to a number of accusations in an increasingly animated and personal debate, Kraushaar stressed that he was only interested in historicization, even if that meant acknowledging uncomfortable truths and past mistakes. More importantly, he upped the stakes by describing Dutschke as an "Eskalationsstratege" (escalation strategist) who had fed the flames of latent violence, especially during the Vietnam Congress in February 1968 when his behavior "was largely responsible, in an already heated atmosphere of latent violence, for using the criticism of the Vietnam war as a vehicle to discuss tactical questions about the organized use of violence."[48]

Isolde Charim suggested that the debate showed a dangerous romantic and nostalgic identification with the past. In her view, the real issue was self-empowerment, and as this concept could pertain to both student movement and the RAF, it was obvious to her "that self-aggrandizement is the secret call to arms in a campaign designed to do away with the entire project of the Left."[49] Claus Leggewie argued in a similar vein, interpreting the feverish search for skeletons in the cupboards of the 68ers as an attempt to deny the protest movement any positive impact on the Federal Republic, and as such should be seen as part of a conservative strategy to hasten the demise of the red–green coalition.[50]

It is evident from this heated debate that "1968," at least in 2005, was still very far from historicization. In the context of Al Qaida terror attacks that had hit Madrid and London and were expected in Germany as well, a general soul-searching about how far one might go in tolerating violence was clearly the intention. Furthermore, the controversy demonstrated that the construction of "1968," in this case of one of its "faces," had done its work. It had become almost impossible to integrate new facts into a narrative that had been broadly accepted.

By the time of the fortieth anniversary, Wolfgang Kraushaar was ready to offer a compromise solution that would bridge the interpretive gulf between theory and praxis, peaceful protest and violent revolt, ideology and lifestyle. Subtitled "a balance sheet," his new book indicated, perhaps precipitously, that "1968" was well and truly over.[51] In recognition of the fact that by now historians favored to set the German student movement in a transnational context, he started the story with the Beat poets and the hippies in the United States. It was the countercultural attitudes that emanated from them, he argued, that influenced the mind-set of "1968": a disregard of the promise of material security in a bourgeois existence, a liberated sexuality beyond social conventions and norms, and the expansion of consciousness through experiments with drugs. In terms of an overall assessment of "1968" after four decades, however, he saw three domestic interpretations dominating the debate: as a dangerous aberration that needed to be exorcised, as an involuntary catalyst for a comprehensive modernization, and as a national revolution against the United States and the Soviet Union (43–44).

Kraushaar concluded his "Bilanz" with an extraordinary paragraph:

> In its volcanic core, "1968" was a foundational revolt. [...] At home and abroad, people searched for something pristine, something not yet deformed, manipulated or alienated. They searched for something authentic—in the individual, in the collective, in politics. [...] The uncovering of the original source—of fantasies, desires, wishes and dreams—was supposed to heal the wounds which society had inflicted under National Socialism. (253)

In this ecstatic description (volcanic core, foundational revolt), "1968" is turned into a force of nature, and its protagonists into seekers of truth. Not an "Ursprungsmythos" (origin myth) but an "Ursprungsrevolte" (origin revolt); the radical questioning of everything, not in a destructive but an almost childlike way, in the belief that by getting to the root causes of social, political and emotional problems one might overcome them; an attitude that would encourage later generations to make full use of their freedom. Much of this smacks of romanticism and even religion, and Kraushaar gives this due consideration (cf. chapter 9). However, compared to his list of the achievements of "1968" ten years earlier (1968 has changed everything), he is decidedly more circumspect about the successes. The challenge to prove that the German student movement actually had long-term effects is formidable, and requires a new set of evaluative criteria.

"1968" as a Revolution of Perception

The historian Ingrid Gilcher-Holtey has worked on this question for more than two decades. An expert on the French student movement, she has been one of the organizers of the DFG-funded collaborative research center *The Political as Communicative Space in History* at the University of Bielefeld and led a number of projects on "1968" as a communication event. Of particular interest for my analysis of the way "1968" has been constructed is her volume *1968: Vom Ereignis zum Gegenstand der Geschichtswissenschaft*. Not only was this the first time historians in Germany made an explicit statement that the era had become historic and therefore no longer belonged to the activists,[52] but Gilcher-Holtey also claimed to have developed the analytical criteria to approach the movement and its legacy objectively. She argued that the protests occurring in Western industrialized nations around 1968 should be understood as an expression of a social movement, following a definition of Neidhardt and Rucht as "a system of mobilizing networks of groups and organizations, intended for a certain duration and buttressed by a collective identity, which cause, hinder or reverse social change by means of public protests" (7–8).

In subsequent publications, Gilcher-Holtey focused on identifying the factors that made these social movements possible and united them across national borders and differences. Specifically, she analyzed their indebtedness to the New Left, their strategies for action, their processes of mobilization, and their disintegration and afterlives. She concluded that while "1968" had exhausted itself by the 1970s, it had, through the formulation of a concrete utopia that encompassed society as a whole, provided a blueprint for an alternative society that future movements lacked:

> None of the movements that came after (i.e., the women's, alternative and ecology movements) was capable of producing an overarching counter-concept to the existing social order that was comparable to the concrete utopia of the 68er-movement. The utopian energies inspired by the 68er-movement seemed spent and exhausted by

the 1970s. We can therefore say that the 68er-movement was the last social movement that had a counter-concept to the existing economic, social and hegemonial order.[53]

Describing the 68ers as an "Erinnerungsgemeinschaft" (community of shared memory, 124), Gilcher-Holtey observed that many former activists distanced themselves from the movement when its lofty aims were tainted by the radicalization of a minority, but that these aims had meanwhile found broader acceptance in subsequent generations and wider society. In *1968: Eine Zeitreise* (1968: A Journey in Time, 2008), she homed in on this puzzling aspect of "1968"—its continuing attraction. To her, this fascination existed in the unfulfilled promise of "1968," the collective feeling that a utopian moment had been within their grasp. This, she argued, had led to a "Wahrnehmungsrevolution" (revolution in perception):

> Rebelling for almost exclusively moral reasons, the students rediscovered a dimension of human existence which the 18th century had termed "public happiness"; a happiness that somehow belonged to "complete happiness" but was only attainable to those who acted publicly. (60)

What was left tantalizingly vague in 2008 was given a bit more substance recently. In *"1968"—Eine Wahrnehmungsrevolution?* ("1968"—A Revolution of Perception, 2013) and its English version *A Revolution of Perception? Consequences and Echoes of 1968* (2014—not a straight translation as it contains different chapters), Gilcher-Holtey once again asks how we can determine the impact of the movement for social change. She believes that cultural producers play a key role in changing if not the reality itself, then the symbolic representation of reality.[54] Taking her clue from a dictum by Herbert Marcuse[55] and the French sociologist Pierre Bourdieu, who had defined the political as the space where the perception of the empirical world is questioned, Gilcher-Holtey now viewed "1968" as a "cognitive subversion." Since changing history was a key impetus for the 68ers, "1968" was no longer about bygone events but the possibility of change in the future. Silja Behre, one of her PhD students, added that, consequently, remembering "1968" was in fact a political act:

> The history of remembering the 68er-movement is not summed up in its diachronous narrative structure, a tale of departure and disappointment, nor in the coming-of-age story of a generation. It is the history of a struggle for the end of the horizon. (110)

Gilcher-Holtey and Behre represent a crucial link in my analysis of the construction of "1968." Their argument is that, by broadening the "horizon of the political," the 68ers demonstrated the essentially formable nature of history, and, by theory and praxis, inspired subsequent protest-movements that have since become a "persistent challenge to top-down institutions."[56] With a copyright on challenging the political status quo, "1968" is thus constructed as the template for every modern social protest from the Arab Spring to Occupy. Indeed, it is in this thesis that Kraushaar and Gilcher-Holtey meet, where the narratives of "Ursprungsrevolte" and "Wahrnehmungsrevolution" colonize our understanding.[57] But there remains a nagging feeling that these interpretations are the product of an unreflected or unacknowledged *Übertragung*, a transmission of the observer's relationship to the object of his or her investigation. There is a risk that academics get too close to myth making. The question is whether a new generation of scholars without personal experience of the revolt can avoid such pitfalls.

"1968" as Countercultural Revolution

On the face of it, the intense political debates in the SDS about limited provocation and the seminar discussions in the Institute for Social Research in Frankfurt about the role of the authoritarian character on the one hand, and the colorful lifestyle, music and fashion of the hippie movement on the other, seem worlds apart but are linked by their synchronicity. The 68ers did not necessarily compartmentalize their lives into a private and a political section. Indeed, the whole point of the revolt, the creation of an authentic, autonomous, and antiauthoritarian identity, was to bring the two sides together, perhaps not in the extreme form of the Kommune I, but certainly more so than had been possible in the generation that came before. Focusing on the countercultural aspect of "1968," Sabine von Dirke argued in 1997 that the advent of the German student movement marked the beginning of the West German counterculture which had, over the years, metamorphosed into a significant political force in the shape of the ecology movement, but also a number of alternative milieus and subcultures with their own distinct aesthetic concepts and artistic practices.[58]

The historian Detlef Siegfried (Kopenhagen) developed this approach in a number of publications, focusing less on the specific year 1968 but the 1960s as a whole. He believes that the true meaning of "1968" lies "in melting together a political movement and a commercially expansive, youthful counter culture."[59] The advantage of locating "1968" in the "long 60s" is obvious. It allows the chroniclers and interpreters space to look beyond the political and ideological debates and incorporate slower social and cultural changes. In doing so, they inflate the already complex term with developments in consumer society, schools, army, and the media, and changes in values and mentalities. While acknowledging that this approach makes it even harder to disentangle causes and effects, Siegfried insists that this approach is necessary to ensure that the "Strahlkraft" (radiating force) of "1968" does not completely eclipse previous events and developments:

> The Student Movement represents just one of many groups responsible for the change, yet up to now it has caused the fiercest debates and garnered most of the attention. [. . .] As "1968" represented a patchwork of different groups, each fusing together counter culture and political opposition in their own way, it occasionally presents us with a confusing Janus face.[60]

In his major study *Time Is on My Side: Konsum und Politik in der westdeutschen Jugendkultur der 60er Jahre* (Time Is on My Side: Consumption and Politics in the West German Youth Culture in the Sixties, 2008), Siegfried focused on an area that had until then received only little serious academic attention: the convergence and divergence of political protest and commercial pop music within the hippie and counterculture. In the ironically titled chapter "Die wunderbaren Jahre" (The Wonderful Years) he analyzes the "Wertewandel" (change in values) that took place around 1968 and was characterized by an increasing preference for antiauthoritarian education, hedonistic lifestyles, an extension of participatory elements in decision making, and the growth of "alternative" social milieus.[61] He is aware that this "soft" research area is very difficult to bring into focus through the study of political organizations or social movements but argues that a culturally holistic approach is much better suited to capture the interdependence of political idealism, cultural experimentation, and commercial exploitation of "1968":

> The more private elements of youth-specific lifestyles and explicit political demands came together between 1967 and 1969 in a climate of departure which, symbolically compressed in the label "1968," has hardly lost any of its evocative power. The socio-cultural collectivization found here—at the time termed "underground" and "counterculture"—encompassed political as well as cultural elements. It contained, in a nutshell, the comprehensive claim to completely change the everyday experience of the individual as well as social conditions on a large scale. (750)

Sven Reichardt, a historian at the University of Konstanz, has recently followed the trajectory of countercultural impulses emanating from "1968" into the 1970s and early 1980s.[62] Like Siegfried, Reichardt argues that the alternative milieus that developed in West Germany in the late 1960s continued the utopian agenda of "1968." Characterized by a need for togetherness and warmth, the creation of an alternative press, a plethora of alternative projects, a variety of forms of cohabitation, a focus on antiauthoritarian education, new age spirituality, a willingness to experiment with drugs, and a marked emphasis on subjectivity, these milieus provided an alternative to the rigidly organized and ideologically driven communist groups that sprang up after the implosion of the SDS in 1969. Taking issue with Wolfgang Kraushaar's characterization of the left-leaning alternative milieu as "Zerfalls- und Entmischungsprodukt" of the student protest, Reichardt argues that the movement coalesced into a larger group that now defined itself through their countercultural lifestyle. Former members of the New Left, the Old Left, communist groups, environmentalists, and land communes attempted to live a concrete utopia on the edges of a society that they experienced as cold, alienating, materialistic, and exploitative.

The problem with an interpretation of "1968" as a predominantly countercultural movement is that it leaves out the political edge of its revolutionary fervor. It also leaves out the vital transnational impulses that inspired the movement in the first place. At the beginning of the new millennium, a new generation of scholars decided to develop research paradigms that reflected their experience of a globalized world with instant communication. Working in interdisciplinary networks, they began to construct "1968" as a transnational phenomenon.

"1968" as a Transnational Phenomenon

While the German "1968" has from the outset been understood as part of a global movement (cf. the International Vietnam Congress in February 1968 or the BBC TV feature "Students in Revolt" on June 13, 1968), historians and political scientists took some time before they seriously accepted this aspect. In addition to Arthur Marwick's landmark publication,[63] two PhD dissertations in the late 1990s hinted at the potential of a broader approach. While Ingo Juchler explored the impact of revolutionary liberation movements in the "Third World" on the student movements in the United States and West Germany,[64] Michael Kimmel focused on the similarities and differences between student movements in West Germany, France and the United States.[65] The latter study is of particular interest, as it established not only commonalities in terms of ideology, forms of protest, and key issues but also specific national characteristics that differentiated them. Thus, in contrast to broad-brush statements that the "global 1968" was a generational revolt against postwar materialism and authoritarianism, Kimmel identified national characteristics that determined the protest culture in West Germany, specifically the primacy of theoretical debate and the desire to develop a new form of consciousness (238).

However, it was the publication of *1968: The World Transformed* in the same year that set the research agenda for the next decade. The eminent Heidelberg historian Detlef Junker and his coeditors argued that academics had hardly begun to treat "1968" as a global phenomenon, while it had been so blindingly obvious to the students and intellectuals at the time that their revolt against capitalism, imperialism, and colonialism was shared by like-minded groups across many countries. The editors thus felt encouraged to formulate an ambitious research agenda:

> By interpreting 1968 as a global or transnational phenomenon, we propose to explain the simultaneity of the crises that erupted throughout the world. By stressing the international dimension, we hope to stimulate further comparative research on the global history of 1968.[66]

Building on the work of sociologists Immanuel Wallerstein and George Katsiaficas[67] historian Martin Klimke, linguist Joachim Scharloth, and media scholar Kathrin Fahlenbrach founded the International Centre for Protest Research in 2006,[68] which has since led to a number of conferences and publications focusing on "1968" in a global or European context. There are a number of advantages in conceiving of "1968" in such a way: it suggests that it was bigger, modern, international, and fashionable. It deflects attention from specifically German issues (e.g., the emergency laws, the grand coalition, or the Nazi past), and it suggests continuity as it allows for a "long 1960s" frame. The disadvantage in subsuming the German "1968" under a transnational paradigm, from a German point of view, is that it makes it appear less special and perhaps even parochial. There is also a risk that with a broader perspective individual actors, issues, and conditions can lose their specificity. In the following, I will analyze some of the key studies of this new generation of researchers in terms of their impact on the construction of "1968" in Germany.

In their introduction to *1968 in Europe: A History of Protest and Activism, 1956–1977*, Klimke and Scharloth argue that "what happened in one part of Europe had an almost immediate impact elsewhere"[69] and imbue the events, such as the International Vietnam Congress held in West Berlin in February 1968, with a global significance. As a forum to discuss tactics and platform for expressions of international solidarity between student movements, it certainly gave activists the opportunity to experience the interconnectedness of their struggle and "to prepare a global revolutionary strategy that would result in a revolutionary transformation of the Cold War system" (4).[70]

By 2009, Klimke and his colleague Philipp Gassert had declared not only that "1968" had become a legitimate object of the historical sciences, but that as a key research paradigm, the transnational, global, and international nature of "1968" required empirical studies,[71] which Klimke duly delivered in the form of his monograph *The Other Alliance* (2010).[72] The book explores the numerous personal, organizational, and ideological links between the students in Berkeley and West Berlin, but also the close attention authorities and university administrations paid to these countercultural exchanges.

It should be noted at this point that Gassert and Klimke show considerable awareness of their own role in the construction of "1968":

> At first glance, this simultaneous politicization and historicization of "1968" may strike observers as a paradox: Does writing the 1960s into history not mean that they lose their contemporary usefulness? This perspective, however, overlooks historiography's perpetual (and not disinterested) role in the process of translating events into bits and pieces of cultural memory. [. . .] memories of specific historical events often gain in their potential to generate controversy before being absorbed into a new consensus. Historical master narratives are generated by preceding controversy. "Historicization" and "mythologization" are not necessarily opposed to each other. Rather, they may be two sides of the same coin. (8)

Clearly, these historians see themselves in competition with other "sources of influence," such as media outlets, politicians, or contemporary eyewitnesses, but unfortunately they do not expand on their comment about their "not disinterested" role. Neither did they make clear their own *Erkenntnisinteressen* (cognitive interest), or simply the reasons why they believe "1968" is worthy of their sustained professional attention. In *The Other Alliance*, Klimke edged a bit closer to an answer. Acknowledging that historians and academics were not innocent bystanders in the discourse on "1968," he argued that it was his generation that had brought new perspectives. In the final paragraph, he hints at his own fascination with the period's "richness":

> Regardless of whether we judge the decade's legacies as positive or negative, a thorough investigation will keep alive its philosophical, artistic, cultural, and political richness as a significant, if at times contradictory, site of memory, and not allow the sixties to be turned into a site of partisan bickering or oblivion. (244)

Returning to the transnational paradigm, Timothy Scott Brown's recent study *West Germany and the Global Sixties* (2013) expands it considerably by exploring "the intersection of global vectors across one local terrain" and combining radical-political, generational, countercultural, and transnational narratives. According to Brown, who gives reductionist and activist representations of "1968" short shrift as "historiographical psychotherapy," a consensus interpretation has emerged among historians that regards the German "1968" as firmly embedded in a global "1968":

> From the travels of radicals to the transplantation of books, movies, music, and other cultural goods; from solidarity with Third World

liberation struggles to attempts to import the goods and ideas of the international counterculture; key West German events were constructed out of non-German materials and in relationship to extra- and trans-German patterns of emotional and ideological affiliation.[73]

Brown points out that the global—encompassing transnational exchanges and virtual ones stemming from the globalizing imagery—has to be viewed in conjunction with local conditions and actions.[74] In the case of Germany, he argues that the transnational was an "especially active affair," with key individuals choosing to import, translate, and re-create the raw material of the global revolt from the writings of the Beat poets and the experiences of the Civil Rights and Free Speech Movements to the manifestos of the Prague Spring and the liberation movements in South America.

"1968" and the Politics of History

Edgar Wolfrum is one of Germany's leading experts on its contemporary history. He is a member of the "public history" cluster at the University of Heidelberg and advises publishers on the reconceptualizing of history books used in German schools. Over the last two decades, he has not only located "1968" in the political history of the old Federal Republic of Germany but also used it as a case study to describe the politics of remembrance in contemporary Germany. Fundamental to the development of his ideas was his seminal essay on "1968" and the politics of history published in 2001.[75] Like Kraushaar, Wolfrum understands "1968" as a myth that connects a significant number of Germans who have accepted it into their collective memory. Analogous to the revolutionary year 1848, he argues, "1968" marks a significant caesura in (West) German history, neatly bisecting the forty years between 1949 and 1989 into a conservative-led postwar period and a period characterized by increased democratic participation and more liberal lifestyles. With the fall of the wall and a general decline in support for left-wing world views, "1968" has become the site of a "Kulturkampf" (cultural contest)[76] and the object of a third *Vergangenheitsbewältigung*, a public battle over hegemony and the right to interpret the past which legitimized present and future political action. Wolfrum stresses that historians do not have a monopoly on the interpretation of "1968"; the task of constructing and reconstructing the past is shared with other actors who have a vested interest.

He admits that "1968" is contested between historians (not only) from the left and right but also within each group. While some read it as an emancipative act, others focus on surreal behavior or diagnose a dangerous romantic relapse. Recent research has variously interpreted "1968" and its legacy as a political protest movement, a generational conflict, a cultural revolution, a renaissance of Marxist thinking, a confrontation with National Socialism, a sexual revolution, the birth of a new women's movement, and a legitimization of violence up to and including terrorism. These readings were combined with trends like contingency theories or the transnational or global character of "1968," and a determined attempt to regard it as an expression of a social movement, not merely the result of the activities of individuals (29).

Wolfrum is fairly relaxed about the marriage of myth and scientific endeavor but believes that historians and social scientists have an obligation to reconstruct the past truthfully and critically. In this context, they have a special responsibility with regard to their role as producers of "history" that is intended for the general public. The aim of their debates and disagreements, he reminds his colleagues, is to foreground certain interpretations of history and defend them in public:

> Discourses about the politics of history [. . .] have one key function: Not only do they mediate between everyday stories and a fundamental narrative, but they also represent the authority in which the competing interpretations of history are institutionalized. In other words: what is at stake in public conflicts about the politics of history is the legitimate view of the past. Here the political actors attempt to shape a baseline narrative by formulating key messages which are potential elements of other, modified narratives. The question which messages will be included in the fundamental narrative is decided in these conflicts and in confrontation with alternative views. (30)

Taking his cue from Friedrich Nietzsche's essay "Vom Nutzen und Nachteil der Historie für das Leben" (On the Use and Abuse of History for Life) (in *Unzeitgemäße Betrachtungen* [Untimely Meditations, 1874]), Wolfrum differentiates an antiquarian, a monumentalist, and a critical approach to "1968." The antiquarian view focuses on the time before 1968 when, according to conservatives, the Federal Republic was set on a pro-Western, democratic, and moral trajectory from which it was diverted by the revolt. The Social Democrats would counter that after the election of Willy Brandt as chancellor in 1969 they had introduced much of the students' antiauthoritarian agenda. Part of this antiquarian approach is the debate over who was responsible for the peaceful revolution in the GDR and German unification: Willy Brandt's *Ostpolitik* or the Helmut Kohl's firm stance against an ideological arrangement between the two German states. History thus becomes a "Themenpark" (theme park, 33), arranged around memory icons which can always be added to with further elements. Their emotional charge creates an "Identitätsdruck" (identity pressure, 33), either positive or negative.

The monumentalist approach promises that what was great once can become great again. By comparing "1968" to "1848," the year becomes equated with emancipation, liberty, and hope. 68ers consequently saw themselves as freedom fighters in solidarity with the Third World, on a mission to transform the Federal Republic into a truly democratic and modern society. This approach creates a "foundation myth," the interpretation that Germany wasn't really founded until the students and the extra-parliamentary opposition forced the older generation to face up to their Nazi past and break with their authoritarian tradition. Such an interpretation goes hand in hand with the narrative that Willy Brandt had represented: the "other Germany" which had valiantly fought the Nazis, along with a nostalgia for the old Federal Republic and its achievement of a pacifist civil society. The obvious problem lies in the dark shadow of "1968," the terror of the Red Army Faction, which has to be isolated as an "inversion" to maintain the monumentalist interpretation.

A critical approach to "1968," Wolfrum argues, would cut through the illusions and mythicization. In contrast to the collective and communicative memory of the Third Reich, which is passing into cultural memory, the *Zeitzeugen* however are still dominant, both as apologists and vociferous critics of the era.

In *Die geglückte Demokratie* (The Successful Democracy, 2006), his critically acclaimed history of the Federal Republic, Wolfrum has since integrated the 68ers into a grand narrative of a successful state,[77] however only at the cost of a rather vague bird's-eye view (68ers might call it a "history from above"):

> What may be regarded as "the 68ers" was in fact a rather heterogeneous movement. There was no such thing as "the" ideas of "1968," at best perhaps a conglomerate of very different thought-fragments from Marxism, as the critique of capitalism, theories of class and imperialism, and especially from undogmatic and at the time completely forgotten authors from the fields of psychoanalysis and analytical social psychology. The "children of Karl Marx and Coca-Cola" were full of idealism but also unworldly dogmatism; new insights and alternative social plans combined with absurd notions and a surprising number of blind spots. (264)

Surprisingly, his final judgment on "1968" is mainly positive, along the lines of President Richard von Weizsäcker's pronouncement twenty years earlier:

> The politicization of the young generation increased the vitality of democracy in the Federal Republic; most importantly, they were successfully integrated into the democratic system which had shown its ability to reform. (271)

As to the question at what time historians would be able to wrest control over the story from the 68ers, the anniversary year 2008 provided new ammunition for Wolfrum's thesis that the time had not yet come.[78] While it was ironic that the state was now actively celebrating a movement that had tried to sweep it away, the uneasy truce simply reflected the political reality of another grand coalition between conservatives and Social Democrats in the Bundestag, which meant that the continuing skirmishes between supporters and critics of "1968" were relegated, pro tem, to academics and former activists. It was noteworthy, he added, that even the conservative party and its leader Angela Merkel were resigned to the reality of "1968" as legitimate part of a shared German history. In 2005, four years after attacking Joschka Fischer for his militant past and utopian ideas, the woman who would soon be chancellor of the Federal Republic of Germany observed:

> Much of the social change that in 1968 and after worried the old Federal Republic and also the CDU is shared heritage today. We cannot, and will not return to the image of families and women of the 1950s. We cannot, and will not return to the socio-political framework of that time. We have all moved on since then.[79]

I would agree with Wolfrum that the politics of history play an important role in the construction of "1968." However, it is one thing for a politician to pay lip service to the achievements of former political opponents (especially on the campaign trail), but quite another to actually engage with the movement's utopian agenda.

"1968" as a Utopian Conundrum

In her 2002 study *May '68 and Its Afterlives*, Kristin Ross asserts that, as far as the French "1968" is concerned, the management of its memory is "at the center of the historical problem of 1968 itself."[80] Overtaken as they have been by subsequent representations and struggling against social amnesia and instrumentalization, she believes that the events "cannot now be considered separately from the social memory and forgetting that surround them." Apart from the obvious question whether her own intervention isn't in itself a contribution to the afterlives of the French "1968," one should note that there is a major difference between the situation she describes for France and the one in Germany. Ross asserts that an "enormous amount of narrative labour" has been expended to forget (she uses the terms "liquidate," "erase," and "render obscure") the events in France:

> The official story [...] is one of a family or generational drama, stripped of any violence, asperity, or overt political dimensions—a

benign transformation of customs and lifestyles that necessarily accompanied France's modernisation from an authoritarian bourgeois state to a new, liberal, modern financier bourgeoisie. (5–6)

One might almost claim the opposite for Germany. While "1968" has been the object of severe criticism from former enemies and renegades (see the following chapter), it has been constructed (and survived) as a utopian time and space by a surprisingly wide range of interpreters, very much in line with the interpretation Ross strains to keep alive herself: "a time when people once envisioned a world different in essential ways from the one in which we now live" (20). In the following, I will explore a selection of such efforts.

Oskar Negt, professor of sociology in Hannover and former "mentor" of the German student movement at the Frankfurt Institute for Social Research, has long warned that the debates about "1968" ignore its utopian aspirations:

> The year 68 opens up history for a few moments; it is a year that is rebellious and offensive [anstößig] in every way, a year that gives us beginnings and hopes. Even the defeats and disappointed hopes become part of our collective memory, which, the further away the original events are, is cut to size to make it fit with the prevailing reality.[81]

Railing against organized forgetting, he argues that the students' "Entwurfsphantasien" (imaginative fantasies, 9), their theoretical and practical advances in the areas of self-realization, internationalism, the politicization of the private sphere, and new organizational forms of direct democracy are significant intellectual and emotional achievements that have had a lasting effect on German society. More recently, he has described "1968" as an irritant that keeps reminding Germans that there is an alternative to the status quo:

> Like a thorn in the flesh, Sixty-Eight irritates a society that is increasingly looking for structure and dependable order. If we didn't have this excess, this realistic day-dream of a better world, [. . .] the movement would have been forgotten long ago.[82]

In his study of the philosophical foundations of the German student movement, Gerhard Fels admitted that there was no coherent ideological or theoretical understanding that united the protesters. At the same time, many were attracted by the idea that history was moving inexorably toward a socialist society, which gave them a long-term mission: if something could be imagined, then it could be turned into reality. Searching for a "third way" between capitalism and Stalinism, the students imagined a "new man," a moral ideal that could be maintained indefinitely:

Following the geo-political reversal, the utopias of the 68ers have retreated into a timeless realm of ideas. From thence, they can flow back into the here and now. This is more than likely if the world were to return to a form of unbridled capitalism and overlook the social consequences of global industrialization.[83]

Social geographer Michael Watts believes that the long-term effects of 1968 are not yet visible and suggests that it has created "spaces of hope" that are both radical and relevant to the present. Like Negt, who described the continuing efforts of 68ers as "Maulwurfsarbeit" (mole-like tunneling), he sees the Long March happening just out of sight:

> We now take this complex mix of civic, popular-participatory and extra-parliamentary politics for granted but perhaps we should not. The sixties were central to this way of doing politics and as such they did not so much stop in defeat in 1968 as "disappear" underground, working on and through institutions, networks and new organisation, building in their polyp-like activity a veritable reef of oppositional practice.[84]

The (West) German historian Norbert Frei argues that the 68ers' belief in their mission and the amelioration of mankind, "the faith in the utopia and the New Man" has kept them going while movements in other countries have either given up hope or have been assimilated.[85] The (East) German historian Stefan Bollinger maintains that following the collapse of communism the politically motivated neutering of the movement can only be resisted by a determined counternarrative that focuses on the utopian potential of "1968":

> In times when TINA, that is *There is no alternative*, renders taboo any radical criticism (even any socialist questioning of the best of all systems, modern capitalism), looking back to the year '68 reminds us that things could be different. [...] For the West, which has once again become one world, the capitalist world, the critical confrontation with a society characterized by exploitation and with the democratically disguised rule of capital remains a permanent memory. This society had to be challenged; exploitation, alienation and manipulation were seen as and attacked as the core elements of capitalist society.[86]

In his study *Utopia or Auschwitz: Germany's 1968 Generation and the Holocaust*, Hans Kundnani analyzes the impact of the German student movement on the foreign policy of the red–green government between 1998 and 2005, in particular its decision to engage in Kosovo and Afghanistan. By exploring the relationship of leading German 68ers with the country's Nazi Past, he discovers a "psychodrama"[87] that put the generation of "1968" into a double bind: with traumatic memories of the war and postwar period, 68ers grew up with the knowledge that their parents had been responsible for the most horrific crimes of the twentieth century. It was a strange mixture of guilt and moral superiority, Kundnani adds: "Many of them would spend their lives struggling to break free from Nazism while at the time fearing that Nazism was, in fact, 'in' them" (10). As children of the perpetrator generation, the 68ers felt they had an existential obligation to make amends for the sins of their fathers:

> The students coming of age in 1968 did not merely dream of a better world as some of their counterparts in other countries did; they felt compelled to act to save Germany from itself. It was an all-or-nothing choice: Utopia or Auschwitz. (12)

The Germanist Richard Langston has recently argued that multichronicity should be regarded as the defining hallmark of "1968." Challenging the "structural straightjacket that the date implies," he brings us full circle back to Oskar Negt:

> To argue that '68, the unfulfilled revolutionary spirit of the year 1968, is still with us today is [...] only valid if and when we acknowledge that '68 never resided wholly in its own time and that this uncompleted past has also never been entirely fulfilled in our own. Herein resides the utopian conundrum [...] that the often overlooked German thinkers Oskar Negt and Alexander Kluge ensconced as the motor of their political philosophy after 1968.[88]

This "utopian conundrum," then, can help explain the continuing uncertainty among historians and critics how to write about "1968." But it is not enough.

Why Is It So Difficult to Write a History of "1968"?

There is no doubt that "1968" provides a unique challenge to historians. Apart from dealing with the methodological question of how to "frame" the succession of events (from "June 2, 1967" to "1968" to the "long 60s"), their protagonists (individuals, students vs young people, political groups and organizations, social groups or movement, intellectual fathers, the 68ers) and their locations (local, regional, national, transnational, global), they have to contend with conflicting narratives from participants (depending on their political allegiance, position, and world view) and changing cultural and geopolitical constellations that in turn have an influence on the selection of their research paradigms. The oft stated optimism with which historians looked forward to the opening of archives and the transition of "1968" from memorialization to historicization was certainly premature.

None of this is surprising. For a start, memories are fallible. Introducing one of the first oral memory projects on "1968," Ronald Fraser observed:

> Memory, as is well known, is always conditioned by the events that have succeeded what is remembered. It is thus always "fallible" if we expect it to reproduce exactly "the thing as it was." But what people felt (or, more accurately, what today they remember having felt), what they hoped to achieve as much as what they in fact achieved, what should have happened and what would have been better if it had not happened, constitute historical facts as much as the events themselves.[89]

Secondly, memories are prone to wishful thinking. Günter Amendt, a former activist and social scientist who reached a broad audience with his "revolutionary" studies on sexual behavior among young people, observed pointedly:

> The 1960s are so infused with legends that it would be illusory to believe that one might be able, with the help of contemporary witnesses, to get to the truth about this time. The opposite is the case: every witness continues to build the legend, by using, consciously or unconsciously, the opportunity for self-promotion and self-stylization. The consequences of these reflections are, in the words of Sloterdijk, historical falsifications. [...] There simply is no truth about the 60s. There is only the truth of every individual who was there at the time. The greater the temporal distance to the event, the harder it is to tell apart legend and truth in the self-representations of the protagonists.[90]

Thirdly, conflicting memories may lead to "memory wars," as the editors of *The Sixties: A Journal of History, Politics and Culture* admitted in their inaugural issue in 2008.[91] Fueled by nostalgia and the ready availability of iconic images, some memories may dominate debates while other struggle to be heard. Power operates through representations of the past, the editors suggest, but immediately admit that such an instrumentalized view risks ignoring the more elusive aspects of "1968":

> One may already feel so inundated with all things Sixties that it is tempting to pit history against memory and try to rescue the Sixties *as a period*, accessed through careful research, from "the Sixties" as a *popular mythology*, spun largely by mass entertainments, middlebrow commentary, commercial bromides, and pedagogic clichés. Though we certainly champion rigorous inquiry, this is a temptation worth at

least partially resisting. Above all, it is neither easy nor even advisable to separate history categorically from myth, let alone the past from its representation. Far more fruitful is to explore their dialectic—the means by which history converts to myth, as well as how the past itself may resist certain forms of mythmaking. (4)

Norbert Frei agrees that "1968" has transcended the boundaries of the actual events:

> "68" is more than the byword for a real event. "68" is an associative space filled with social attributions and all-knowing self-analysis: a flourishing meeting place where the statements of activists and the responses of their critics, the perceptions of contemporaries and the observations of those born later collide. "68" is the sum total of interpretation and imagination in the global "appearance of simultaneity." And this is precisely where historians run into difficulties.[92]

Does that mean that one should give up the attempt to write a history of "1968"? The opposite seems to be the case. In *1968: Eine Kommunikationsgeschichte* (1968: A History of Communication, 2011), Joachim Scharloth suggests that it is exactly *in* the contradictions between the narratives of "1968" that a new discursive space has opened up for innovative research. By critically engaging with the popular myth of "1968," exploring individual phenomena and then searching for commonalities, scholars have the opportunity to write about "1968" "beyond the cypher."[93]

Summary

The analysis of some of the key research paradigms of "1968" has shown that historians have to battle with others who want to control the story. Putting their faith in the tools of their trade, historians have so far failed to dispose of "1968"—like nuclear waste, the political and emotional radiation levels are still too high to put it into the long-term storage of history books. This shouldn't come as a surprise. Contemporary history researchers always have to contend with accusations of indulging in a "Jubiläumswissenschaft" (anniversary science),[94] and with the irritation that *Zeitzeugen* claim to know better than professional analysts. Wolfgang Kraushaar has met this challenge head-on, with some considerable success in the case of the debate about Rudi Dutschke and violence. But there are still many historians who are practicing "historiographical psychotherapy,"[95] or simply act as "Erinnerungsunternehmer" (memory entrepreneurs).[96] They claim to write history while writing their own history or a history they would like to see. This is legitimate in fiction but highly problematic in academia. Tom Hayden, veteran of the US-American student movement and coauthor of the Port Huron Statement, believes that those involved in the cultural discourse over the meaning of "1968" inevitably have to align themselves to one of three broad views: those who want to restore and revitalize the heritage of "1968" to propel future social movements; those who want to bury "1968" to make the world safe for their various supremacist ideologies; and those who want to manage the stories of "1968" to prove that the institutions always reform themselves and prevail.[97]

While this may be overstating the issue, the question is a valid one: Do historians have the integrity to admit that their *Erkenntnisinteresse* is leaning toward one of these categories, or do they continue to assert that theirs is a disinterested science and that they are only interested in what happened? There are only a few historians who acknowledge that their historiographical perspective is not only subjective but also influenced by ever-changing national and international paradigms. It is a courageous act of taboo-breaking when they do so, but it is also, one might argue, a direct consequence of an exposure to the ideas of "1968." Detlef Siegfried is one of these and makes a welcome difference by putting himself in the picture:

> Though this study lays claim to academic rigour, I cannot state categorically that I have treated the object of this study as a distanced observer. Amongst those who—like myself—grew up in the 1960s, there is a keen, occasionally romantically coloured, awareness that we were marked by the upheavals of that time. This awareness is not just the product of subsequent construction, but also the consequence of an everyday, and often collective, appropriation of the world in the early and mid 1970s.[98]

Philipp Gassert, in a very useful survey of the literature and research trends on "1968," has recently suggested that historians should focus not only on the events of 1968 but also on the "making of 1968," including their own role in the creation of cultural memory.[99] While this may sound plausible and laudable, the reluctance of so many of his colleagues to declare their *Erkenntnisinteresse* in this field makes one wonder whether they should be given even more power in the politics of memory. Gassert's privileging of "archivalische Knochenarbeit" (hard graft in the archives),[100] the historian's belief that the truth can only be found in the sources, ignores the fact that the German student movement was an organic, dynamic, and emotional phenomenon where individuals did not, as a rule, put pen to paper until after the event. While visits to the APO Archiv in Berlin or the Protestarchiv at the Hamburg Institute for Social Research help researchers to get a feel for the era, I would argue that they cannot replace an imaginative and (self-)critical engagement with the hopes and dreams of the revolt.

The examples given in this chapter have shown that writing and interpreting the history of "1968" is a tricky balancing act. In the next chapter, I will look at individuals who have no problem in declaring their interest, though their efforts in deconstructing the myth, paradoxically, end up adding to the construction of "1968" as well.

3: Critics and Renegades

THERE IS VERY LITTLE RESEARCH on the effect renegades and critics of the movement have had on the continuing debate about the legacy of "1968" in Germany. While their headline-grabbing theses are duly reported in the press (see chapter 6), their vociferous attacks on the politics, behavior, ideology, sexual proclivities, and utopian dreams of the protesters have contributed to the longevity of "1968" in Germany. Some of the criticism is rational and rooted in a different political worldview, mainly formulated by those who opposed the radical students at the time. But there is also a different form of criticism, one that burns with such a fierce hatred that, almost 50 years on when even former enemies have found an accommodation, requires an explanation. Such venomous attacks on the 68ers and their legacy, in nonfiction and fiction, are often made by individuals who were born well after 1968. A special case exists when former activists change their minds and attack the very ideals they once held so dear. In some instances, this may amount to autobiographical psychotherapy; in others, to an honest reflection of, and confrontation with, their former beliefs. This chapter presents some of these critical voices and demonstrates how they have contributed to the construction of "1968" in Germany.

Before we look at Germany, though, it is useful to acknowledge that a critical attitude toward "1968" can be found in many countries. I have already mentioned Kristin Ross's account of the afterlives of the French May, and there is certainly no shortage of "68er bashing" in the United Kingdom.[1] As far as the United States are concerned, the gently ironic tone of cultural critic Joe Queenan aptly sums up the situation: "Baby Boomers, like bubonic plague, will continue to be a scourge on the planet for many years to come."[2] Queenan criticizes a generation that promised not to "sell out" and then did, their "incessant invocation of sixties mythology" (30), and the "premature nostalgia" (31) that surrounds the era. This raises the question, why write a book about them and give them all this attention?

Gerard DeGroot, an American historian working in the United Kingdom, has attempted to "unplug" the sixties and view its historical significance without the amplification of the myth. He argues that real events have been replaced by imagined constructs:

> The Sixties is [...] a collection of beliefs zealously guarded by those keen to protect something sacred. Idea has been turned into ideology, with the effect that the Sixties has come to be defined not by time but by faith. Believers object violently to any attempt to redefine the decade, dismissing rebel analysis as reactionary, revisionist, or neoconservative. For forty years, a battle has raged over ownership of the decade, with those who dare to question hallowed truths bombarded with a fusillade of consecrated dogma. In no other period of history has canon been allowed so freely to permeate analysis.[3]

DeGroot is distinctly cagey about his motives for writing his book. On the one hand, he reveals that, though only born in 1955, "he was there." On the other hand, he claims that he has formed his opinions on the basis of recent research rather than on "golden memories of a life once lived" (2). While admitting to his own list of sixties heroes, for example, Cesar Chavez, Bob Dylan, or Robert Kennedy, he maintains that his analysis is not driven by a political agenda. To him, the past is what happened, while history is the way we view it. Consequently, the coherence of the sixties in terms of meaning and structure that have been assigned to it by historians and analysts is largely constructed. DeGroot's central thesis is that most of what happened in the 1960s lacked coherent logic, that the era was more chaotic than commonly described, and that omissions have produced a misleading and reductive image. Thus the "summer of love" becomes the "summer of rape" (301ff.), and Rudi Dutschke one of the "shiniest myths" of 1968 (340). For DeGroot, the memorialization of the sixties now smells of incense:

> After the decade died, it rose again as religion. For quite a few people, the Sixties is neither memory nor myth, but faith. [...] They imagine into existence a world where everybody is rendered peaceful by the power of love and where greed, ambition, and duplicity are banished. Reality itself is suspended. (449)

Of course, the observation that much of the student idealism was unrealistic is not a new one, certainly not in West Germany. In 1968 Jürgen Habermas publically criticized the agitators, mentors, and "poets of the fake revolution" for encouraging the students in their "lächerlichen Potenzphantasien" (ridiculous fantasies of power).[4] Two years later, Richard Löwenthal, professor of political science at the Freie Universität Berlin with first-hand experience of the brutality of totalitarian regimes, formulated his critique of the German student movement as a "romantic relapse" into Marxism.[5] While initially sympathetic to the students and their utopian inspired rebellion, he believed that by imagining themselves as part of the struggle of third world revolutionaries they were acting in romantic despair and ignoring the realities of modern industrial societies. Since the New Left had lost the hope and conviction that social justice would be achieved when capitalism had finally been defeated, the "believers" had no alternative but to storm the barricades of heaven to force the issue. Löwenthal described this as a "Rückfall in eine primitivere Art von Diesseits-Religion" (a relapse into a more primitive form of religion in this world, 68) and concluded that the antiauthoritarian movement was in fact suffering from a lack of role models:

> What appears to us today as a revolt against every authority is often a bitter frustration with a lack of authority—not in the sense of a lack of strictness, but in the sense of the presence of conviction which provides convincing role models for life. (81)

Political Opponents

While former activists use the anniversary years to remind readers about the achievements of their movement, their erstwhile opponents use them to point out its failures. One of the first was Franz Schneider, a professor of political science in Munich, who, 25 years on, described the revolt as a "Fehlgeburt" (miscarriage).[6] Schneider was particularly enraged that, in his view, the "spirit of 1968" had permeated many, if not all aspects of life in Germany. A key characteristic of this spirit was a "reservatio mentalis," an internalized rejection of the state and its institutions:

> This mental reservation means that the "system" is accepted as impregnable for the time being, but rejected internally (without a viable alternative). The permanently available readiness for aggression is unleashed on specific occasions when it becomes symbolic, signifying that one is against the whole "system." (17)

Gerd Langguth was a member of the RCDS in the late 1960s and its president from 1970 to 1974. As a "68er on the other side," he had a long career as member of the German Bundestag for the CDU, director of the Bundeszentrale für politische Bildung (Federal Agency for Civic Education), head of the European Commission's representation in Germany and professor of political science in Bonn. He is best known for his biographies of Angela Merkel and former president Horst Köhler. In contrast to many other critics of the student movement from the conservative side, Langguth actually engaged with its ideas. Indeed, he wrote his PhD thesis about the protest movement and the New Left[7] and returned to the topic in 2001, following the debate about Foreign Minister Joschka Fischer's militant past.[8] He argued that the former activists had been less interested in analysis than in "Verschönung" (positive spin, 9) and "Verklärung" (glorification, 9), which enabled them to monopolize the interpretation of "1968." Against this, Langguth proposed a "saubere wissenschaftliche Analyse" (10), which would judge the movement by their aims, and not by their alleged impact.

According to Langguth, the SDS was a "Kampfverband" (militant association) with a questionable attitude toward violence, one that had planned to turn West Germany into an "Erziehungsdiktatur" (educational dictatorship, 11). At the same time, he is not oblivious to the fascination that emanated from the "elitist, romanticizing, utopian and irrational theories" (15) and attracted many young intellectuals. However, his own "clean academic analysis" (10) breaks down when he turns to Rudi Dutschke. For example, he claims that Dutschke's "Gewaltphilosophie" (philosophy of violence) had prepared the "geistigen Nährboden" (mental breeding ground, 58) that eventually led to the terrorism of the RAF. These are semantically loaded terms, particularly in the context of the heated debates about Fischer's past in 2001 (and four years before Wolfgang Kraushaar published his research about Dutschke's flirtation with violence). On the one hand, we can interpret these accusations as belated revenge for the ritual humiliation of RCDS members by the SDS in the late 1960s; on the other hand, his words echo those spoken by Angela Merkel when she demanded that 68ers publicly renounce their former ideals.[9]

Langguth argued that it was hard for conservatives to wrest control of the interpretation of "1968" from former activists and a media that uncritically perpetuated the myth and cemented public perception through the use of images that served as symbolic *pars pro toto* (197). The role of the media in the construction of "1968" will be explored in chapter 6, but it is instructive in this context to hear two voices who did not feel such a handicap.

In 2005, *Focus* journalist Michael Klonovsky described the 68ers as "Demokraten wider Willen" (democrats against their will) who were still manifesting the "reservatio mentalis" that Franz Schneider had diagnosed back in 1993:

> To be a 68er does not mean to be a member of a generation, but rather the exponent of a world view, one that claims to be critical, anti-authoritarian and emancipated. Those who adhere to this world view, while ever ready to adapt if it suits their careers, have never let go of the idea that capitalism is the wrong economic system, that the Federal Republic is the wrong state and that the Germans living in it are the wrong people.[10]

More impactful, however, was a book published in 2007 by the editor of Germany's best-selling tabloid, *Bild-Zeitung*.[11] The title of the book *Der große Selbstbetrug* (The Grand Delusion) does not mention 68ers, but they are the main target of this polemic. Kai Diekmann claims that 68ers are seldom criticized or ridiculed, though they deserve to be. As self-styled "Gutmenschen" (do-gooders, 12), they are responsible for the "madness" of political correctness that shows greater empathy for perpetrators than victims and that torpedoes every attempt at excellence in the name of equality. In Diekmann's eyes, modern Germany is characterized by lack of common sense, anti-Americanism, intolerance, lack of individual responsibility, and corruptible politicians. Following a broad secularization, marriage and children are out of fashion while excessive feminism dominates political culture. People lack manners and show tolerance for fundamentalists (in spite of the obvious failure of the integration of migrants). Germans are eco-mad. The country risks its own future by kowtowing to political correctness. And it is all the fault of the 68ers.

Diekmann argues that following the "march through the institutions" the student rebels had gained influential positions in schools, local authorities, and criminal courts, as well as in politics and the media. Here, their world view of indiscriminate tolerance now determines grades, decisions on asylum requests and social benefits, laws and the reporting of news. He concludes with a sarcastic "Lob der Achtundsechziger" (praise of the 68ers, 251), in which he ridicules them for their political and aesthetic failures, their lack of hygiene, and, most importantly, their lack of joy. With their tendency to refuse to see the world as it is, there is little reason to remember "1968":

> The achievements of Sixty-Eight are therefore found on the other side of reality, reflecting a deeply romantic view of the world. A few beautiful poems were written, a few great song lyrics. Apart from that, all that can be remembered about Sixty-Eight is negative: a bet on the wrong horse whether it's multi-culturalism or the contempt for state, nation, family, property, hard work, diligence or patriotism. (254)

It is not surprising to see the key values espoused by the German conservative parties mentioned here. Together with "Ordnung, Sauberkeit, Pünktlichkeit" (order, cleanliness and punctuality)[12] they form the Prussian catalogue of virtues that were responsible for Germany's ascent to a world power before World War I and ensured the reconstruction and *Wirtschaftswunder* (economic miracle) following 1945, for which the CDU claims credit. The 68ers challenged these virtues, arguing that they had been responsible for the creation of the German "authoritarian character," the country's descent into barbarism, and the Holocaust. It is obvious, then, that Diekmann's polemic aims to undo the "damage" he believes "1968" has caused in the medium and long-term and convince his readers that a return to the status quo ante would be a good idea. At the same time, in order for his polemic to work he needs to acknowledge that the 68ers *did* have an important impact on German society, which accords them an (albeit negative) significance that they might not have had without this high-profile intervention. Diekmann thus inadvertently contributes to the construction of "1968."

In 2008, the former prime minister of Rhineland-Palatinate Bernhard Vogel and the then chairman of the conservative student association RCDS presented a *Streitschrift* that attempted to both criticize the 68ers and assert that the conservatives belonged to "1968" as well, no matter which side one had been on at the time.[13] In the preface, Vogel claimed that while some of the critique of the 68ers had been justified, the resilience of the West German constitution and democratic system in the face of their challenge ought to be seen as part of its "Erfolgsbilanz" (successful track record, 8).

In the various chapters, conservative politicians and journalists, some of them contemporaries of left-wing protesters, aim to "set the record straight" and wrest the interpretative hegemony of "1968" from former SDS activists. Wulf Schönbohm, for example, argues that the disquiet about the stuffiness, authoritarianism, pettiness, and intellectual narrowness in the families and wider society was shared by most students at the time (17) but that it was the SDS who, as "useful idiots" (21) allowed themselves to be used by East Germany to discredit the West as a whole. Similarly, Ruprecht Polenz observes that former radicals still maintain that they were right and that it was their protest that led to a belated democratization of the Federal Republic, while in reality that had never been their objective:

> The apologists behave as if the society as we have it today had been the objective of the 68ers. The opposite is true. Nothing was further from the minds of the left-wing radical Student Movement than to reform our society, to improve it incrementally. The 68ers denounced the rule of law, parliamentary democracy, market economy, a pluralistic and open society as the "system" that had to be overthrown. They were radical, fanatical, and militant. (112)

Not all political opponents of the dominant narrative of "1968" come from the right. For some, the 68ers were not radical enough: the journalist and publisher Wolf Wetzel argues that former activists and their opponents are now collectively engaged in the historicization and "decontamination" of a time when citizens dared to challenge "the system" not only with slogans but also with direct action.[14] Wetzel believes that it wasn't the 68ers that changed the state, but the other way around. As "ZivilgesellschaftlerInnen" (proponents of a civil society, 20), both 68ers and their former enemies are now engaged in the obliteration of the experience and realization that in order to radically change the existing order, radical means were, and continue to be, both justified and necessary.

Another form of political critique of "1968" comes from Uwe Wesel, who came to the FU Berlin in 1969 as professor of law and served as its vice-president for a number of years.[15] Wesel's ambiguous view is already present in the title of his book: "Die *verspielte* Revolution" can both be understood as a homage to the playful, creative, and imaginative nature of the student protest but also as a comment that the revolution had in fact been within reach and had been gambled away. Wesel stops short of the latter interpretation but argues that the activists have gambled away years of their lives while the determined response of their opponents and their wholesale condemnation of "1968" has led to a loss of "Diskussionskultur (debate culture, 321)."

Generational Opponents

Former political enemies of the rebelling students today find themselves in the paradoxical position of feeling vindicated in their erstwhile opposition but also acknowledging the historical necessity of the protest. Subsequent generations do not have this nostalgic generational bond. When the red–green coalition came to power in 1998, young members of parliament criticized the dominance of the 68er generation in (tenured) positions of power and influence. These "Besserverdiener and Besserwisser" (those who earn more and know it all)[16] were, according to these young parliamentarians, occupying posts due to a well-organized system of networks and mutual patronage. In fact, the 68ers had become the "establishment" and needed to be removed. This minor parliamentary revolt quickly fizzled out as ministerial posts were allocated, but the generational critique did not.

An interesting constellation emerges when the children of the 68ers begin to critically engage with their parent generation. In 2004, Sophie Dannenberg's novel *Das bleiche Herz der Revolution* (The Pale Heart of the Revolution) caused a stir with her searing indictment of the "crimes" of the 68ers and the psychological damage they allegedly had inflicted on their children and their parents. In one of the most vitriolic attacks on the peace-loving and reformist image of the German student movement, Dannenberg (born 1971) "reconstructs" the events at the Frankfurt Institute of Social Research where Aaron Wisent (Theodor W. Adorno) is pressured by Bodo Streicher (Horst Mahler) to write a defense of the notorious Kommune I flyer "Burn Warehouse, Burn" which is reproduced in full in the text. When Wisent refuses to publicly exhibit "academic and armed resistance" by condoning this incitement to violence, militant members of the SDS turn against him:

> We are sick of the dialectic yackety-yak. What should be done? is our question. We don't want to talk, we want to fight. We want a

strategy debate. We want weapons. We want to know how we can blow up this shitty university, all universities, America houses, America, capitalism. We want class struggle, we want war, we want the victory of the working class. We want the final victory. Here and now.[17]

In this passage Dannenberg echoes a scene from Uwe Timm's *Heißer Sommer*. But while the SDS member there is allowed to explain the ideology of the "great refusal," here the reader is supposed to learn the darker motives of the SDS. By giving it the voice of thugs and the words of terrorists and fascists, Dannenberg "exposes" the consequences of the "nihilistic" teachings of critical theory—they have become just another vehicle for power struggles and corruption.

The militant minority, described by Dannenberg as lazy, drugged-up, fanatical bullies, not only interrupt Wisent's lectures but organize a full-blown pogrom. Shouting anti-Semitic slogans ("Pentagon-Jude!" [Pentagon Jew!]), they throw a Molotov cocktail and Wisent dies in agony (106). His brilliant assistant Hieronymus Arber, who had tried to save Wisent's life, is later outmaneuvered by a corrupt coalition of another assistant, the scheming Heinz Müller-Skripski (Jürgen Habermas), and the thugs, who quickly manage to gain influential posts in government, media and universities. In an intrigue reminiscent of Dietrich Schwanitz's *Der Campus* (The Campus, 1995), Arber's academic career is successfully torpedoed, and he is lucky to find a post at a polytechnic in the provinces.

In a second strand, Dannenberg introduces the reader to Kitty Caspari, one of the "antiautoritär verwahrlosten Kinder" (antiauthoritarian derelict children, 134) of the 68ers. Kitty's father, Borsalino von Baguette (Klaus Croissant) lays down his mandate as defense lawyer for terrorist Susanne Albrecht when he is coerced by Streicher to smuggle weapons into prison. He relocates his family to the "Freie Republic Wendland" and makes a living defending the antinuclear protesters. From an early age Kitty is subjected to what her grandfather describes as permanent brainwashing, learning about the corruption of the capitalist world and the need for permanent revolution. Her home life is stifling: her mother is completely focused on herself; she is subjected to harrowing sexual experiments by her father and brother, and sent to a quack therapist when she refuses to accept their worldview. It takes years for Kitty to undo the damage caused by this upbringing. She meets Arber, who encourages her to write about her experiences, but even in the present he is thwarted by his nemesis Müller-Skripski, who ensures that Kitty's story does not get published.

The third strand deals with the relation between the 68ers and their parents, the "Nazi-generation." The 68ers have broken all lines of communication with them, refused their traditions, but not, Dannenberg suggests, out of moral revulsion, but because they lack the curiosity, the empathy, and the willingness to accept their parents' failure. Significantly, it is not the war, but that they lost it that caused the 68ers to turn against their parents:

> The fact that we lost the war, [...] that we weren't the mighty avengers we ought to have been but cripples and Germans who had their backbone broken. They hate the fact that we mourn and yearn for our lost homeland, that we remember. They live in the here and now, in happy despair. (303)

In an interview with *Der Spiegel*,[18] Dannenberg suggested that her generation's hatred of the 68ers was as strong as that of the 68ers toward their parents. She professed to be disgusted by the "false anti-fascism" of the 68ers, their "specific sweaty stench," their "destruction of traditional values" such as decency, reliability and homeliness, and the "Pornographisierung der Kindheit." More importantly, she argued that the generation that invented "progressive aesthetics" and tried to present the RAF terrorists as victims was, at least in part, responsible for modern day terrorism: "There is a direct line from Che Guevara to Al Qaida."

Predictably, her polemical attack on the 68ers attracted a lot of attention. Initially reviewers focused on side issues such as the question about her motivation for this debunking of the myth of 68 (she claimed to know young people who had experienced fates like Kitty), her identity (Dannenberg is a pseudonym, her real name is Annegret Kunkel) and the identity of "Alexander Oronzov" (credited in the book for penning the authentic-sounding passages in the jargon of critical theory). Eventually, though, the debate homed in on the question of violence. As Ursula März observed, the 68er's predilection for mixing idealism and violence continues to pose a problem for German society:

> 68 is still relevant as a historical conflict. It symbolizes the susceptibility of idealist thinking to forms of destruction, cruelty and violence. Society can deal with the consequences of 68. But to come to terms with 68, with terrorism or the anti-Semitic impulses and learn to see them as consequences of history is obviously something that will take a lot longer.[19]

Dannenberg's attempt to deconstruct the 68ers and show their repressive, militant, and hypocritical character seemed to have run into the buffers of what was, in 2004, unacceptable to say. However, in spite of almost blanket panning of the novel (the book was almost uniformly rejected as clichéd, even "blasphemous"[20]), her critical voice seems to have hit a nerve. As the critic Robin Detje grudgingly admitted, the book "versprüht auf grandiose Weise Hass, mit grellem Mut und der Ästhetik der Verzweiflung" (in a grandiose way, it spreads hatred, with fierce courage and the aesthetics of despair).[21] The words "greller Mut" are, I would argue, indicative of the pressure that is building against the monopolization of history by the 68ers and against their tendency to put a positive spin on their own past.

Dannenberg's fundamental critique of the 68ers is partly autobiographical and reflects a deep understanding of (though not agreement with) the main ideas of "1968." Similarly, the "young" academics Harthmut Becker, Stefan Winkler, and Felix Dirsch (born either 1966 or 1967) delineate the "intellectual resistance" of conservative publicists against the 68ers from a position of political integrity.[22] However, there is a small but vocal group of neonationalists who believe that "1968" is responsible for a weakening of the national fiber, a fatal *Wertewandel* that has led to a cultural, economic, and political downfall, the loss of meaning and orientation. Typically, they place their books with fringe publishers and there is very little information about the authors. However, their polemics reach a broad audience through the Internet and are modelled on the "straight talking" of populists like Thilo Sarrazin. One of these authors is Torsten Mann, who believes that the 68ers were witless victims of a global conspiracy to subjugate the German people:

> The 68ers are the children of the "Frankfurt School," or they have come through Marxist-Leninist organizations. They have successfully completed their "march through the institutions." The spiritual fathers of the "Frankfurt School" prepared the re-education of the German people during the Second World War while living in the United States. Their aims were to destroy the spiritual tradition and values of the Germans, to annihilate any sense of patriotism. All authorities were supposed to be overthrown and families dissolved. Typical German virtues like diligence, duty, faithfulness and willingness to sacrifice oneself for the greater good were supposed to be replaced by a fun-seeking society characterized by its obsession with obtaining maximum pleasure. Today, the children of the "Frankfurt School" occupy key political, legal and social positions and turn their ideology into action—with fatal consequences for Germany and the German people.[23]

Rolf Kosiek argues in a similar vein, suggesting that the 68ers completed the work of the Frankfurt School, namely the "Zerstörung der deutschen geistigen Tradition" (destruction of the German intellectual tradition):

> Returning to Frankfurt after 1945, their objectives were the obliteration of the German intellectual tradition, the annihilation of a sense of belonging to the collective and to the Fatherland, the demolition of authorities, and the dissolution of family and state.

Prussian virtues that were once held in high esteem: a sense of duty, altruism, a willingness to serve and sacrifice oneself, they all were replaced by the pursuit of pleasure. The sorry consequences of this development, aided by the occupying powers, can be found everywhere today. One cannot understand the dominant conditions in Germany unless one knows about the Frankfurt School and its continuing corrosive effects.[24]

Kosiek is coming dangerously close to the language of the Nazis in this passage: the juxtaposition of a group of Jews plotting against the German people from abroad, the phrase "Vernichtung des Volksbewußtseins" (the annihilation of a sense of belonging to the collective), and especially the term "zersetzen" (corroding), suggesting an undermining or corroding influence, emit the stench of Goebbels' propaganda machine. But this, ironically, is the argument of these authors: it is they, the "proper" Germans, who are now the persecuted minority, victims of a pervasive political correctness and a dominant culture that has jettisoned key German values.

One could go on. Holger Pinter speaks of a "68er Verschwörung" (68er conspiracy), where the 68ers have become the totalitarian rulers they once attacked:

> What the Dutschke-generation has achieved is not the opposite of Nazi-ideology but twisted Nazi-ideology, similar to the way that devil-worship is twisted Christianity. That's why devil worshippers are really closet Christians and 68ers closet Nazis.[25]

Perhaps the most outspoken example of these views is the activist Markus Willinger, an Austrian exponent of the far-right "Generation Identity" who believes that the 68ers have jettisoned Germany's cultural identity.[26] In his "declaration of war against the 68ers," Willinger intones a litany of complaints about the parent generation:

> You have promised yourself a utopia, a peaceful, multi-cultural society of affluence and tolerance. We are the inheritors of this utopia, and our reality looks very different. Your peace is bought by more and more debt. Your affluence is disappearing across Europe. For us, your multi-cultural society means hatred and violence. In the name of tolerance you persecute all those who criticize you, and then you call those you persecute intolerant. We are sick of all that![27]

What comes across in this cri de coeur, allegedly of a lost generation, is the disappointment of an idealist with a utopian dream that came to nothing, but also an awareness that, if the 68ers were able to change their reality, so can their children. As such, these fierce critics of the 68ers need the narrative of "1968" to achieve their own goals and, ironically, engage in its construction.

Renegades: A Family Affair

If one defines a renegade as a person who rejects a religion, cause, allegiance, or group for another, Klaus Rainer Röhl could serve as a blueprint. Born in 1928, he isn't part of the 68er generation, but as founder, owner, publisher, and editor in chief of the magazine *konkret* he was instrumental in the amplification and multiplication of the ideology and aspirations of the New Left in West Germany. Together with his wife Ulrike Meinhof, he provided the Extraparliamentary Opposition and the German student movement with a platform but also influenced the strategy debates with a Marxist slant. Following Meinhof's radicalization and decision to set up the Red Army Faction with Baader and Ensslin, Röhl became disillusioned with the movement and increasingly clashed with his reporters over the political direction of the magazine.

Röhl's first public statement as a renegade, the polemic *Fünf Finger sind keine Faust: Eine Abrechnung* (Five Fingers Are Not a Fist: A Reckoning, 1974) laid the foundation for a narrative that has plagued "1968" to the present day. Casting himself as an errant husband who did have affairs but did not mean to drive his wife into terrorism, Röhl reflects:

> So, was it just a tale of love and adultery? It was indeed, but one with serious consequences. Step on a butterfly, and a thousand years later you get a famine. If one could undo everything, create a time paradox, change this one thing—would the history of the Left have taken a different direction? Of course not. What we can be sure is that Baader would not have been freed by Ulrike Meinhof. Perhaps he wouldn't be in prison now, having served his time for his arson attack. And, of course, the group would have not been called "Meinhof-group." Perhaps there would have been no "Red Army" either, none of the others would have been capable enough. But the question is moot, there is no paradox, no return, and no correction.[28]

Constructing the entire history of the APO and the student movement as a background to and consequence of a failed personal relationship that led to one of the most traumatic periods in West German history reveals a supersized ego and a dangerous level of delusion, but this version of events has had a significant impact on the popular imagination of "1968" to the present day: for example, in Uli Edel's film *Der Baader Meinhof Komplex*, Röhl's infidelity is foregrounded and offered as a plausible motive for Meinhof to become a terrorist.

Röhl describes himself as a petit bourgeois, a socialist with a working-class background who is fascinated with the children of the bourgeoisie (Gaston Salvatore, Bahran Nirumand, Christian Semler) playing revolution. Even in his angriest moments, though, he is able to describe the attraction of the movement, for example in his depiction of the "flood" of forty thousand protesters at a demonstration against the Vietnam War pushing through the streets of West Berlin:

> Of course, what swept them along was the empty Kudamm, what moved them was the pure air of a Berlin spring. And yet, everyone shared the feeling that it was possible to sweep away capitalism, so loud, so joyous, so breath-taking was the running procession, so tightly knit was the community of linked arms, so convincing was the *Ho-Ho-Ho Tschi Minh* that drowned out every doubt. It was an intoxication, beautiful and pure, and let no one scold the man who took part in it and could not help but be moved by it. (236)

Röhl's complete break with the ideas of "1968" occurred in 1974, when he realized that the articles that he had published in *konkret*, for example Peter Schneider's article "Gewalt in den Metropolen" (Violence in the Metropoles, 1968; see chapter 4), had unforeseen consequences. Röhl describes Schneider's essayistic flirt with violence as "Beautifully written, Seductively beautiful. But it was wrong. It had devastating consequences" (245). Following this realization, Röhl shows remorse and contrition:

> It was I who published these first open discussions about violence. I did not take them seriously enough. Did not know that words could become 9mm projectiles, that the beauty of utopia could become an impatience that would stop at nothing. (245)

Over the years, this contrition has turned into a vitriolic attack on the values and ideals Röhl had once espoused. In 1995, for example, he set out to reveal the "Lebenslügen" (grand delusions) told by the 68ers, in particular the widely held view that the student movement had been staunchly antifascist. This, he asserted, was simply a ruse by the GDR and the Soviet Union to hoodwink naive Westerners. Similarly, Röhl challenges the view that the movement was essentially nonviolent. Indeed, from his point of view, "1968" is the product of a very successful "campaign of disinformation" while in reality it had only three consequences: drug abuse, terrorism and "excessive feminism."[29]

I have already mentioned Klaus Rainer Röhl's and Ulrike Meinhof's daughter Bettina in my discussion of the faces of 1968. Following her high-profile attack on then Foreign Minister Joschka Fischer for his militant past, Bettina Röhl published a book that recasts "1968" as a family drama.[30] Much like her father, she challenges the dominant narrative of the 68ers as a positive force in German history. In her interpretation, the liberal middle classes were too naive to realize that they had been taken in by apolitical, self-deluded, and stoned madmen:

> The middle classes did not realize that they were being taken for a ride by apolitical children of affluence on their revolutionary trip.

> Like madmen, the middle classes wanted to have serious debates with madmen, but the latter took LSD or put on a Rolling Stones record, laughed themselves silly and told their elders to stuff their "middle-class shit." (539)

Returning to the tragic story of her mother, Bettina Röhl describes in unsparing detail how Ulrike Meinhof had lost her moral compass when she redefined the sordid acts of mass murderer Jürgen Bartsch as the fault of an uncaring society or when she applauded the killing of Israeli athletes by Black September terrorists at the Olympic Games in Munich in 1972. One cannot help but sympathize with Bettina Röhl's quest to find someone to blame: for her traumatic childhood, for the abduction of herself and her twin sister by "friends" of her mother, for the memory of seeing her mother in jail and learning about her suicide. Seeing the mindset that destroyed her family (with the active help of her father) becoming redefined as the best thing that could have happened to the Federal Republic, the private has become political indeed.

Renegades: 68ers Turned Critics

Two high-profile critics of the 68ers come from their own ranks: Gerd Koenen and Götz Aly. Koenen, who had joined the SDS following the death of Benno Ohnesorg, became a member of the Maoist Kommunistischer Bund Westdeutschland (KBW, Communist League of West Germany) in 1973, while Aly was the founder of the radical paper *Hochschulkampf* (University Struggle) in West Berlin and active in the Rote Hilfe (Red Aid), an organization that provided support for the imprisoned members of the RAF. Both have made their name as independent historians—in Koenen's case with a focus on the history of communism and Germany's relationship with Russia, in Aly's case the history of National Socialism and the Holocaust.

Koenen's book *Das rote Jahrzehnt: Unsere kleine deutsche Kulturrevolution 1967–1977* (The Red Decade: Our Little German Cultural Revolution 1967–1977) was rushed to publication in the wake of the national debate about Joschka Fischer's militant past in 2001. It provided ample ammunition for "68er-bashing" but, more importantly, suggested a new way of looking at the history of the German student movement. Koenen argued that there was a continuum that linked the birth of the student movement in June 1967, when Benno Ohnesorg was shot, with the *Deutscher Herbst* of 1977 when the Red Army Faction held West Germany to ransom with the abduction of the president of the employer's association and the hijacking of a Lufthansa airplane. The student protesters of the late 1960s were thus lumped together with the actions of a violent terrorist group in the 1970s, and therefore, especially in the politically sensitive times after September 11, seen as progenitors of modern terrorism. The term "red decade" was picked up quickly,[31] helping to shift the dominant narrative of "1968" from a watershed that turned authoritarian West Germany into a liberal society, to one that declared the whole decade from 1967 to 1977 one of aberration and collective delusion.

Koenen had a point: by criticizing the students' belief in a "erfüllte Zeit" (historic moment), the "eigentümlicher Wahn" (peculiar delusion), and "Halluzination"[32] that many of the activists suffered, he put a finger on the irrational aspects of "1968" that had been missing in the narrative. On the other hand, he can be accused of mistaking his own experience in a tiny Maoist group that had strict behavioral codes and a very blinkered worldview with the experience of a much larger cohort. After the demise of the student movement, many activists joined the SPD or went on the Long March as teachers, professors, journalists, and doctors, while others continued their protest in countercultural milieus that included *Kinderläden* (literally: children shops, i.e., antiauthoritarian crèches), land communes, bookshops, local newspapers, *Wohngemeinschaften* (apartment-sharing community), self-help groups, and youth centers.

Koenen was acutely aware of the challenges inherent in becoming a historian of his own biography. Still, he suggested, it was time to uncover the sociopsychological connections that had led many of his comrades to the fringes of society:

> We cannot hide forever in the shadow of the "old Nazis" who were supposedly everywhere. We have to talk about ourselves—about our subconscious feelings and obsessions, our delusions and narcissistic imagined victories. (10)

By talking openly about *his* generation and their mistakes, as reflected in the title of his book, Koenen felt he could come closer to an explanation as to why so many young people had broken with mainstream politics and culture. He claimed that only with the demise of the APO and the SDS in 1969 did the antiauthoritarian youth movement become a generational mass movement with a shared "jargon of a pseudo-revolutionary authenticity" (19). Significantly, he believed that academic discussion of "1968," which had just begun in 2001, was but a belated manifestation of this "Zeitstimmung" (mood at the time):

> Entire mines of documents await their discovery, fruitful research projects their grant applications, and broad paradigms their unfolding. Here, where text and images have acquired a rich patina, it is possible to delight in romantic-utopian dreams, if only in the sober jargon of science. (22–23)

Koenen challenged Oskar Negt's view that drew a line between the events in the late 1960s and the groups that developed as a consequence of the events. He argued that once we include the extremist, sectarian, and terrorist offshoots of the student movement in the narrative of "1968," it is no longer possible to claim that it led to a liberalization, democratization, and Westernization of the Federal Republic. What we would get instead is an idea of the "almost autistic" character of the 68ers:

> The desire to cast a still indistinct attitude to life in metaphors and formulas, and to create an alternative sphere of theory, history and literature—in today's terms: a *virtual reality*, which transcended and broadly replaced the empirical present. (46, italics in original)

Koenen followed up his reinterpretation of "1968" with a book on the lives of three individuals who were minor figures in the student movement but came to greater prominence in the context of the RAF.[33] In the postscript to this book, Koenen explains that the story of Bernward Vesper's autobiographical book *Die Reise* (The Trip, published posthumously in 1977) was initially intended to sit at the start of *Das rote Jahrzehnt*, "since all the important themes and motifs of 'our little cultural revolution' were contained within it" (341). While this may be the case, it also conveniently serves Koenen's purposes to draw a direct line between Bernward Vesper's Nazi father Will Vesper, and the terrorists Gudrun Ensslin and Andreas Baader, thus constructing a "linksradikale Familienszene" (224) that redefines the fringe as the epicenter of "1968." In this context, Wolfgang Kraushaar has observed that by denying the qualitative difference between an oppositional movement that acted publicly and a clandestinely operating terrorist sect, Koenen was in fact displaying the ideological blinkers that he accused the 68ers of.[34]

In his introductory essay to a collection of images depicting "1968" published in 2008, Koenen seems to have had a change of heart, though. Romanticizing what he used to parody, he now described "1968" as a "revolution of rising expectations," an "eruption of erotic life-energies and hallucinatory emotions," and a highly subjective historical moment that was shared by many in such intensity that its experience formed a political generation, a generational lifestyle, and a way of thinking that influenced the rest of society.[35] Admitting that they were "far removed from the leaden time" of 1977, he remembers a "dreamlike situation of delimitation, a magic moment of coming out of one's shell" (20) that contained the potential for a different reality. Significantly, Koenen contradicts his thesis of the "red decade" when he declares:

> Thus the women's movement, as well as many other developments of the 1970s, from citizen's initiatives to ecology, was part of the

broad stream of energy and movement that emanated from 1968, but it doesn't really belong in the context of this year. (26)

I would argue that you cannot have it both ways—if the modern German women's movement, born in 1968 (see chapter 5), does not belong to the context of "1968," then neither does the RAF, which was set up in 1970. Moreover, the romanticizing of a collective magic moment of experiencing countless possibilities does not sit well with a description of his generation as ideologically blinkered. In this case, Koenen's projection of his own disappointment over his wasted years onto the canvas of "1968" undermines his argument.

If Gerd Koenen's thesis of a "red decade" challenged the cozy narrative of "1968" as essentially beneficial for Germany's political culture, Götz Aly's *Unser Kampf 1968: Ein irritierter Blick zurück* (Our Struggle 1968: An Irritated Look Back, 2008) provoked an outright scandal. Here was a 68er who suggested that his generation had more in common with their Nazi-parents than they would like to admit. By focusing on the experiences of intellectuals who found themselves in the firing line of the activists, he claimed to have found compelling evidence for his uncomfortable diagnosis:

> Very few share the realization that the German Sixty-Eighters were driven to a large extent by the pathologies of the 20th century, and that they pathetically resembled their parents, the generation of Thirty-Three. Both saw themselves as a "movement" that wanted to sweep the "system" of the Republic from the historical stage. They despised [...] pluralism and adored [...] fight and action. They combined megalomania with cold ruthlessness.[36]

Aly argued that the 68ers were more interested in writing stories to maintain control over their history instead of actually writing history. Just like their parents, they were joined together by the "Schicksalsgemeinschaft des Kampfes" (fated community of the struggle, 22) and still engaged in a "Manipulation der öffentlichen Meinung" (manipulation of public opinion, 102) while denying how wrong they had been when they had celebrated the brutal oppression in the Chinese Cultural Revolution as an example to be followed. They were thus "Kinder der Nazis" (children of the Nazis, 115) who had uncritically repeated the mistakes of their parents.

Unsurprisingly, Aly's book met with an angry response. The title *Unser Kampf*, referencing Hitler's autobiography, was a provocation in itself but also suggested that Aly was speaking for all 68ers. Equally unsurprisingly, Wolfgang Kraushaar took him to task for methodological errors and the holes in his argument.[37] Kraushaar pointed out that, similar to Gerd Koenen, Aly was merely projecting his personal feelings of guilt about belonging to an extremist organisation and coming close to criminal acts onto an entire generation. Furthermore, Aly's experience of "1968" began when the focus of the student movement had moved from West Berlin to West Germany: "Aly's role was thus that of a belated arrival on the radical leftist scene" (89). For good measure, Kraushaar added that, in spite of claims to have scoured the archives for new material, Aly's main resource was his personal experience. Kraushaar conceded that Aly has a point when suggesting that the student movement was "a very German, belated offshoot of totalitarianism" (Aly, 8):

> Both groups disregarded the institutions of a state governed by the rule of law, idealized their own members as a "movement," developed a form of activism that was more radical than the usual forms of political praxis, adhered to an unchecked version of utopianism, and were inclined to anti-bourgeois attitudes and to unrelenting anti-liberalism. (93)

Knowing that his rebuttal would have little impact given the high profile Aly's book had in the media, especially the conservative press, Kraushaar concluded:

> Aly has [...] done the job of the most adamant and unrelenting opponents of the 1968 movement. Yet he has also played into the hands of the most undeviating supporters and glorifiers of the history of the 1968 movement in Germany, among whom there is now a rare consensus about the need to challenge Aly's assessments. (95)

Self-Criticism and Repentance

There is no shortage of former activists who have publically repented the errors of their ways. I will return to the journalist Thomas Schmid, onetime member of the SDS in Frankfurt and, together with Joschka Fischer and Daniel Cohn-Bendit, founder of the radical group Revolutionärer Kampf (Revolutionary Struggle), who was chief editor of the *Welt* newspapers in the Springer publishing empire from 2008 to 2014 (see chapter 6). Others with a lower profile were assembled in a volume that bade farewell to "1968" on occasion of the thirtieth anniversary. The journalist Werner Olles for example regards his time in the movement as a "failed marriage."[38]

Peter Schütt, member of the SDS in Hamburg and one of the founders of the *Deutsche Kommunistische Partei* (DKP, German Communist Party) was ousted from his party in 1988 and has since become a *Wertkonservativer* (someone who believes in conservative values) and converted to Islam. For him, the "march through the institutions" was mainly taken by those who had watched the action from the sidelines. The "uprising of a generation" was, he observed, a fabrication:

> The greater the distance to the events of that short summer of anarchy, the greater the glorification of that magical year. In reality, committed activists only came from left-wing elitist circles—I would estimate that until 1968 there were at most five hundred activists and protagonists of the revolt in the entire Federal Republic, including West Berlin.[39]

But it was Klaus Hartung, the journalist and writer who had helped to develop the concept of a 68er generation in the *Kursbuch* in the late 1970s (see chapter 2), who produced one of the most complex self-critical introspections for the fortieth anniversary in 2008. In this wide-ranging essay, Hartung not only thematizes the errors of his fellow activists but also queries the motives of those who are expecting the 68ers to reflect on their past actions and show remorse.[40] He suggests that the continuing "Mythenproduktion" is not due to his former comrades, which raises the questions who is actually interested in the perpetuation of the myth, who is asking the 68ers to repent, and what exactly it is that they are supposed to repent for. Perhaps, he muses, it is the acceptance of "das Unerledigte," the things that have been left unsaid and undone, that keeps "1968" alive in Germany:

> The 68ers have dispersed into all walks of life of the nation, and they have taken with them the motivations, intentions and experiences of their revolt. However, I believe that this sense of unfinished business has always created a kind of unconscious and unresolved community. I think that the "68ers" must accept that they have been too passive when it comes to the ever-changing public image of "68."

Hartung points out that those who expect the 68ers to eradicate their own history have nothing on the 68ers themselves who, starting with the fragmentation of the movement into dogmatic communist splinter groups, began a process of "Selbstliquidation" and "Selbstopfer" (self-sacrifice) in the name of party discipline. Meanwhile, the ripples of "1968" reached the provinces and changed everyday life and culture:

> The impulse of the anti-authoritarian movement changed our understanding of work, it dissolved the authoritarian state. On the other hand, its life-reforming tendency and its institutions, the communes, antiauthoritarian crèches and local groups flourished. The more the Left became a creative part of society, the more it seemed to see itself as an alternative that was now dreaming the dream of a "different Republic" instead of the revolution. [. . .] And when the old Federal Republic ended, the West German Left realized that it had

been their secretly desired Republic all along, now glinting in the evening sun.

Hartung accepts that the 68ers cannot distance themselves from the consequences of their rebellion. He does not deny that their antiauthoritarian euphoria became dogmatic rigidity, their intellectual desire for enlightenment a barbaric infatuation with violence:

> It is always difficult to discern limits and illusions within positive experiences. It is even harder to accept that it is the best intentions which can become the most perverted, that good can create evil. Self-criticism must be able to see both: the immense experience and its disturbing metamorphoses.

In order to come to terms with "1968," Hartung argues, one has to enjoy a good paradox. None of the primary objectives of the rebelling students were achieved, yet they are credited with heralding in a more liberal society and a more representative political system. The state, seen with suspicion and avoided whenever possible, has become a giant bureaucracy that relieves the individual of every responsibility. Whether all this is the responsibility of the 68ers, though, is open to question. The problem with "1968," according to Hartung, is that it has often been declared dead but never been concluded politically. Instead of engaging in reform of the existing state and its institutions, the 68ers continued to live in a "Gegengesellschaft" (countersociety) with "Gegenkultur" (counterculture) and "Gegenöffentlichkeit" (counterpublic):

> The problem, as I see it, lies in the fact that the "68ers," the "New Left," the "alternative scene" and the Greens were always strong enough to dream of a "different Republic," but never strong enough to actually build it.

The essay concludes that the politics of memory, as far as "1968" is concerned, sit on a tightly packed foundation of self-made taboos. While the solidarity among those on the Left has disappeared, 68ers continue to oppose unorthodox thought:

> Now the pendulum of the Zeitgeist has swung the other way. It is our veil that is torn. We lack the values, a sense of common purpose, the willingness to get stuck in. We are silent, it is no longer possible to say that all this is conservative demagogy. We can sense that our values are turning into their opposite. [...] We can sense that the social coldness that we feel does not emanate from the neo-liberals, but from the heart of what we thought was social. More often than not, our multi-cultural tolerance was simply ignorance and indifference. Now we bemoan the disintegration of family bonds, the loss of civic culture and responsibility.

Hartung's essay demonstrates that the 68ers are well aware of the two-edged nature of their legacy. With their halcyon days long gone, they have to live with the long-term consequences of their youthful idealism and ideological fervor. Secretly, they may even agree with some of their critics, though to openly admit it would negate the core of their beliefs, which still define them, for better or worse.

Summary

In contrast to the historians discussed in the previous chapter, the critics of "1968" are not shy about their agenda. For some, it remains "eine Münze im Kampf um das politische Selbstverständnis dieser Republik" (a token in the contest about the self-conception of this Republic),[41] while for others it holds a more personal significance. It offers a convenient screen for the projection of resentments old and new, real or imagined. The vehemence of some of the criticism has tarnished the positive image of the student rebellion, while the public statements of self-criticism, ranging from defiance to apostasy, have weakened the perception of the 68ers maintaining a united front. Paradoxically, writing against "1968" has kept the debate over its legacy alive and cemented its status as a major moment in German history.

4: Tale Spinners and Poets

From Literary Representation to Imaginative (Re-)Construction

ACKNOWLEDGING THAT THERE ARE elements that the chroniclers and interpreters of "1968" have failed to capture, Wolfgang Kraushaar has suggested that there exists a role for writers and artists in preserving the creative energy of the movement:

> It may be that only a writer or an artist possesses the necessary freedom to protect his memories—where the imagination seems to have survived—from the increasingly impertinent grasp of historicization.[1]

In spite of this (guarded) admission, the significant body of fictional texts set in, or against the backdrop of, the German student movement that has developed (and continues to grow) since the early 1970s has hardly featured in the debates about the historicization of "1968" discussed in the previous chapters. This is a serious oversight by historians, sociologists, and political scientists as it is in these novels that we find preserved the *emotional memory* that simply cannot be recovered in the archives. There are reasons for this oversight: historians, as a rule, are reluctant to accept fiction as evidence since it is subjective and almost impossible to corroborate. Moreover, some of the key literary texts about "1968" were written years or even decades before the historicization of "1968" was attempted in earnest. And yet, to ignore the evidence of these texts means to forego an insight into the psychological makeup of the 68ers, a ground-level perspective on what the abstract ideological debates meant to them, and a deeper understanding of the motives behind their protests and the impact of their experiences on their lives.

In this chapter, I discuss the specific contribution that literary authors have made to our understanding of "1968" and summarize the debate on the social function of literature. While there are many German-speaking authors who have engaged with "1968,"[2] six well-known writers have returned to the subject again and again over the past five decades. I will explore to what extent texts by Hans Magnus Enzensberger, Peter Schneider, Uwe Timm, Friedrich Christian Delius, Erasmus Schöfer, and Jochen Schimmang, authors who have made their name by writing about "1968," represent a continuation of the revolt by other means. Far from being a self-indulgent and melancholy response to the demise of the German student movement, their texts have played, and continue to play, a significant part in the construction of "1968" in Germany as a utopian moment.[3]

It should be noted that the desire to represent the experience of "1968" in literary form is not unique to Germany. The sheer exuberance of events caused the British poet Stephen Spender to travel to the epicenters of the protest and report back on his impressions,[4] while the Dutch novelist Cees Noteboom waxed lyrical about the liberating effect of the "longest conversation ever" in the French May.[5] There exist a considerable number of novels set in, or against the backdrop of, the global "1968." In France these include Michel Houellebecq's *Les particules élémentaires* (The Elementary Particles, 1998), Roger Bichelberger's *Le mai, le joli mai* (The May, the Pretty May, 2001), and Olivier Rolin's *Tigre en papier* (Paper Tiger, 2002), in Italy Andrea De Carlo's *Due di due* (Two Rows of Two, 1989), in the United Kingdom John le Carré's *Absolute Friends* (2003), Hari Kunzru's *My Revolutions* (2007), and Derek Johns's *Wakening* (2009), in Iran Azar Nafisi's *Reading Lolita in Tehran* (2003), in Mexico Paco Ignacio Taibo's *'68* (1991), and in the United States Tom Wolfe's classic *The Electric Kool-Aid Acid Test* (1968), Thomas Pynchon's *Vineland* (1990), Jennifer Egan's *The Invisible Circus* (1995), Richard Powers's *The Time of our Singing* (2003), T. C. Boyle's *Drop City* (2003), Douglas Kennedy's *State of the Union* (2005), and Terry Bisson's *Any Day Now* (2013). However, compared to the ongoing production in Germany, they are few in number. Indeed, the family of texts that has grown around the German student movement now covers five decades, with more than fifty novels, as well as autobiographies, novellas, short stories, plays, poems, and song lyrics.

Even though the German student movement only lasted for two years, it holds a lifetime of "magic moments" for the individuals who were part of it. Seeking to get to the "essence" of "1968," writers imbue it with a unique hope and a common political message: what might be possible if a whole generation were to refuse to replicate their parents' values, and confront social conventions and dominant behavior patterns. Holding individual and collective experiences together are a set of "nexus points" that represent formative moments for the 68ers but are equally relevant for later generations: the tension between the private and the political; the realization that democracy and freedom can never be taken for granted; the complex issues of sexual awakening and personal relationships; the confrontation with Germany's troubled past; the elusive unity of thought, action, and feeling; the desire to show solidarity with people living in abject poverty; the liberating effect of nonmainstream music and hallucinogenic drugs; the energy released by political activism; the challenge of a monolithic press; and the search for "socialism with a human face"; as well as attempts at self-organization and mobilization for a cause.

The breadth and diversity of the movement is reflected in the social background of the writers and their protagonists: there are accounts from the perspective of the nobility, the working class, army conscripts, university professors, feminists, poets, pupils, professional writers, students, gays and lesbians, psychoanalysts, journalists, and the legal profession. Various "regional settings" create verisimilitude and connect the centers of protest with the periphery—we see events unfolding and individuals caught up in them in Berlin, Hamburg, Munich, and Frankfurt, but also in smaller places like Bremen, Münster, Tübingen, or Heidelberg. In terms of stylistic variety, we find the whole range of modern literature: from simple stories via diaries and letters to multiple points of view and stream of consciousness; from documentary realism to magical realism and surrealism; from sober party-political correctness to irreverent fun; from gently ironic satire to farce and cabaret. We have texts written during LSD trips and texts set in an alternative future; we have the "traditional" bildungsroman, a travelogue, a road movie script, and even a tragedy-cum-thriller. We have elegies and any number of love stories. And there is no shortage of sex.

German critics have, as a rule, had little time for the literary representation of the German student movement. It is a complex terrain, particularly when political and literary imperatives collide or the expectations of a revolutionary aesthetic in a literature emanating from the spirit of "1968" is projected onto a literature about "1968." Of course, Germanists and critics have not completely ignored the literary representations. Keith Bullivant includes the early literary representations of "1968" in his study on the "Death of Literature" debate.[6] Martin Lüdke published a number of perceptive essays on the "Literatur im Umbruch" (literature in a period of change).[7] while Andrew Plowman discussed five books as autobiographical writing,[8] and Ingeborg Gerlach another five as an expression of "New Subjectivity" in a "requiem for a revolt."[9] Ralf Schnell has analyzed an even wider range of texts. In his *Geschichte der deutschen Literatur nach 1945* (History of German Literature After 1945, 1993) he was the first to argue that these were "thematically linked texts."[10] His interpretation was largely psychological, suggesting that most of the literary representations of "1968" were acts of imaginary wish fulfillment in the face of an unsatisfactory reality. This sort of interpretation, under the label of "romantic relapse," has unfortunately plagued the discussion for a long time. It is reflected in the labels critics have come up with for these texts: *Erfahrungsliteratur* (literature of experience), *Erinnerungsliteratur* (literature that remembers), *Besinnungsliteratur* (literature that reflects), *Veteranenprosa* (the prose of veterans), *Verständigungstexte* (communicative texts), *literarische Verarbeitung der Studentenbewegung* (literary processing of the student movement), *literarisierte Revolte* (revolt turned into literature), *Literatur des Abschieds von der Revolte* (literature that bids farewell to the revolt), *epische Aufhebung der Studentenbewegung* (epic conclusion of the student movement), and, most condescending, *Literatur zum Wohlfühlen* (feel-good literature).

One reason for the unwillingness by many critics to seriously engage with or look at the whole range of the literary representations of the German student movement is that they span so many styles and issues. Furthermore, with texts ranging from the subversive to the melancholy, from "traditional" to experimental, there is little chance of finding the (lowest) common denominator. In *Abschied von der Revolte* (Farewell to the Revolt, 1994), Ingeborg Gerlach suggested that we should distinguish two strands: the "Literatur des Abschieds von der Studentenbewegung" and "Politisierungsliteratur" (literature intended to politicize the reader).[11] Focusing on the former, and using mainly texts from the 1970s, she interpreted the "farewell" as a reluctant return to "normality" which often leads to disillusionment and apathy:

> The return of the protagonist who failed when pitted against the immovable world ends with a broken individual robbed of his objective. (26)

Ignoring for a moment the fact that in spite of the "Abschied" the novels kept coming, Gerlach's argument raises the question of what to make of the other strand, which offered a more optimistic outlook and retained the utopian vision. Specifically the books published in the AutorenEdition, a writers' cooperative founded in 1972, asserted that the movement had led to a lasting politicization of many of the 68er generation. Characteristically, the protagonists in these books overcome their sense of loss and continue on the Long March, often join the communist party, finding new hope in political cooperation between intellectuals and workers. Critics have been particularly scathing and dismissive of these texts, arguing that they "improve" history and memory to such an extent that the result has lost touch with reality.

In their book on representation in literature and history, Mary Fulbrook and Martin Swales point out that representation as a concept was itself changed by the student unrest in the sixties, with the postwar, "modern" approach of New Criticism yielding to a dialectic approach.[12] Thus our perception of the texts discussed in this chapter is twice refracted, and the traditional process of copying the extraliterary world, and making an aesthetic artefact from it, no longer suffices. The question whether a historical account is "false" or not may indeed have become irrelevant. Fulbrook and Swales argue that even without historical "truth," the texts can still create meaning:

Communication can lead to significant changes in perception, new insights and understandings. It may not, in principle, be possible to "know the past as it really was," in all its lost entirety; but it is entirely possible to engage in genuinely meaningful, intersubjective communication about "what is really significant in the past" in the present—and to do this without abandoning some notion of at least good faith or commitment to honesty, if not, perhaps, a more elusive, indefinable and absolute notion of historical truth.

I have argued elsewhere[13] that what is thus created is not only a representation but also a reinvention: a reconstruction of the past in order to make it understandable, meaningful for the present, and useful for the future. In doing so, the literary representation of the German student movement shows many similarities with the approach of the romantics who looked back not to the classics but to the "countercultural" middle ages, which represented a different kind of social order. Much like the romantic movement, the German student movement had distinct phases, and it can be argued that the literature representing it can be divided into phases as well: revolutionary enthusiasm; exploration of new freedoms; resignation; historicization; mythologization; reorganization in new movements; and finally reflection.

According to Cornelia Klinger (*Flucht, Trost, Revolte: Die Moderne und ihre ästhetischen Gegenwelten* [Escape, Consolation, Revolt: Modernity and Its Aesthetic Counterparts, 1995]), the impulse to hold on to the elation of a revolutionary experience by romanticizing it need not be regarded as escapism. In romanticizing the movement, these texts aim to create intimacy in a world perceived to have ignored its original message. The issue for the critic is to determine whether the union of literary form and political content as an aesthetic whole actually works and what it can achieve. Forty years ago Hermann Peter Piwitt, himself an active participant within the wider Extraparliamentary Opposition of the late 1960s, asked:

> What do the novelists of the Student Movement actually achieve when they confine themselves to dressing up for the veterans their shared experience, that is, a reality that has already been decided upon?[14]

The question is still valid today: What is the motivation behind these novels; what do they hope to achieve? What can these texts offer that we haven't already heard, that we aren't already agreed on? What is the point of writing ever more accounts? I would argue that the increasing distance to the German student movement inspires writers to reconstruct a sense of collectively experienced past, a sense of shared identity that has been under attack from the very start. The fact that the impact and historical achievement of the German student movement is still hotly debated in Germany indicates that there is by no means a *vorentschiedene Realität* (a reality that has been decided on in advance) for everyone, that reality is created backward and forward by historians and writers to allow readers to recognize themselves and their desires.

However, almost five decades after the events, the question whether the literary representation has sufficient quality to allow the reader to enter that world becomes more relevant. It is here that the more recent books have the advantage over the older accounts—they can build on a wider experience and create a sense of honesty and intimacy, which was lacking in earlier attempts. Hand in hand with an evaluation of the literary merits of the texts has to go an evaluation of the "collage" that emerges from a synoptic reading of this body of texts. Does the picture we see match the historical evidence? Does it explain why the movement failed and why the protagonists took so long to overcome their sense of loss to convey what they had learned to the rest of society? There are several answers to these questions. The emotional shock of the immovability of the establishment (and its heavy-handed response via the "decree concerning radicals" in 1972) meant that many activists retreated into subcultural milieus. The vocal exponents of the 68ers, on the other hand, quickly got on people's nerves. They were, and still are, portrayed as *ewige Rechthaber* (constantly self-opinionated). This impression is reinforced in the early fictional accounts of "1968": they are characterized by their *Gefühl, recht zu haben* (convinced they are right); they are *die mit den festen Meinungen* (those with firm opinions). They claimed, and still claim, the *Deutungshoheit* (cultural hegemony) and insist that they have something that needs to be said and understood. However, the memory of dreams unfulfilled, of hope denied, now pervade the narratives of the 68ers: *Das kann doch nicht alles sein!* (that cannot have been all!). What matters to them now, and this is borne out by the recent publications, is to be honest with themselves, to preserve their identity in a vast memory project, and to ensure that their legacy is not forgotten.

The Social Function of Literature

One of the reasons why the literary representations of "1968" did initially receive short shrift from critics can be found in the different expectations associated with a "literature emanating from 1968" and a "literature about 1968." The Germanist Klaus Briegleb indignantly observed that in the wake of the German student movement writers should have focused on the political function of literature and eschewed the more traditional ("affirmative") techniques of narration, instead of jumping on the bandwagon of the "Neue Innerlichkeit" (new subjectivity).[15] This reflected a tendency by many activists to regard literature as just another tool in the hands of the establishment to provide an emotional escape vehicle for people who would otherwise become aware of the reality of their situation. Calling for a politicization of aesthetics, student protesters ridiculed the writers of the Gruppe 47 as "Papiertiger" (paper tigers) in October 1967[16] and staged a go-in at the Frankfurt Book Fair a few weeks later.[17] In Hamburg, a working group of the local student union defined literature in the spirit of Benjamin Franklin, with a twist:

> A specific form of constructive mirroring of a segment of reality, with the aim of making visible certain social interactions. The artistic text as a consciousness-raising means of communication is thus directed towards an emancipatory praxis, insofar as it uncovers, through a "biased" depiction of society, its institutionalized forms of repression. It therefore creates the knowledge-based preconditions for socially-oriented action.[18]

But "literature about 1968" did not automatically have to adopt postmodern aesthetics or cajole the reader to engage in revolutionary action. One might also argue that the focus on subjectivity in the 1970s could not have held such a fascination for German writers if they had not experienced the revolt first. That is not to say that the literary representations of "1968" did not attempt stylistic experimentation (some did), but to many writers it was more important to represent (and reflect on) the experience of the revolt, while the question of the revolutionary content and message initially took a back seat or could be conveyed by more conventional means. Obviously, the revolutionary bluster and conviction did not last indefinitely, and the literary representations of "1968" have become increasingly preoccupied with the processes of memory and forgetting.[19]

The dilemma for German writers post-1968, having to chart a course between their aesthetics and the social relevance of their texts, has been a major theme for scholars of German literature for many years. The writers themselves saw the choices clearly. In 1975, Nicolas Born likened the challenge of writing the revolution and attempting to change the consciousness of their readers to a "erschütternden Zusammenprall" between the imagination and the factual:

> At such a point literature must lose its key function—that for good reasons remains unspoken—namely to show the destructive and constructive, but always bone-shaking, collision of the imagination with the factual, or to be this collision itself.[20]

The title of Peter Weiss's magnum opus *Die Ästhetik des Widerstands* (1975–1981) reflects this dilemma in a nutshell. As Frederick Jameson observed in his foreword to the English translation, the *Aesthetics of Resistance* marked "a powerful intervention in German historiography, or more precisely into the sense of history and the construction of the past."[21] However, to understand the complex discussions about literature's potential for social change and the way tale spinners and poets responded, we need to turn to the German writer Hans Magnus Enzensberger, who played and continues to play a pivotal role in the literary construction of "1968."

Enzensberger had come to the attention of an anglophone audience with an essay in the *Times Literary Supplement* in 1967, in which he roundly declared the political system in the Federal Republic as "quite beyond repair."[22] The choices the German people had, he argued, were to accept that state of affairs, or do away with their political system and build a new one, by means of a revolution. With a rhetorical flourish, he declared: "Tertium non dabitur."[23] This oft cited opening salvo in Enzensberger's public critique of the way West Germany had opted for restoration instead of reform or revolution after the war needs to be read in context: the essay, and its place of publication, indicate that this is not an intervention into party-political politics but into the politics of literature. Frustrated with the ineffectiveness of his fellow writers in opposing the grand coalition and its support for the US-American war in Vietnam, he declared that writers needed to confront the fact that they were powerless to effect social change and ask themselves whether it made any sense to continue their tacit complicity in keeping the masses quiet. The piece was widely picked up in the West German media, particularly in *Der Spiegel*, which gave a broad selection of German writers the opportunity to comment on the question whether a revolution was indeed, as Enzensberger had suggested, inevitable.[24]

Enzensberger developed his critique further in the *Kursbuch*, a cultural magazine that he had edited since 1965.[25] In his contribution "Commonplaces, Regarding the Latest Literature,"[26] he built on Herbert Marcuse's essay on affirmative culture (written in the 1930s but not published in German until 1965) and argued that if writers had any function at all, it would be for them to join the "march through the institutions" advocated by Rudi Dutschke only a few months earlier. In the footsteps of radical writers like Ludwig Börne (1786–1837) or Rosa Luxemburg (1871–1919), they should cut themselves free of the shackles of the "Bewußtseins-Industrie" (awareness industry) and educate the public through their writings. Enzensberger went on to ascribe the writer a key role in bringing political awareness to the masses:

> Teaching Germany the rudiments of politics is a gigantic project. Like any such undertaking, it would ideally start with teaching the teachers. Even this is a long and difficult process. [. . .] The writer who embarks on this project suddenly experiences a critical interaction, a feedback-loop between reader and writer, something he

would not have dreamed of as a conventional writer. [...] Perhaps the teacher will one day achieve what he was denied as long as he aimed to produce art: that the practical value of his work surpasses its market value.[27]

Enzensberger had expressed similar views a year before at a meeting of the Gruppe 47 in Princeton.[28] He had become increasingly skeptical as to the subversive and critical power that writers and intellectuals could wield as a counterbalance to the political and economic elites. As far as he was concerned, and in the context of what he perceived as a prerevolutionary situation at the height of the German student movement, there was an urgent need to ask about the social relevance of literature. Provided that writers entered into a critical dialogue with their readers, he felt that there still existed the potential to shake the audiences out of their consumerist apathy. The passage above certainly shows no lack of confidence in the power of writers to make a difference, even if their "Kunst" (art) might suffer in the process.

While some student slogans, such as "Schlagt die Germanistik tot, macht die blaue Blume rot" (Kill German Studies Dead, Turn the Blue Flower Red; during the occupation of the German Department at the Freie Universität Berlin, implying that academic study had lost all connection to reality), suggested that he had thrown out the baby with the bathwater, and Jürgen Habermas felt that Enzensberger had become a "harlequin at the court of the movement"[29] who could never be pinned down in a logical argument, the ensuing debate produced a determination among many writers to support the Extraparliamentary Opposition. This newfound confidence would manifest itself in a whole spectrum of social activism ranging from Heinrich Böll's public speeches against the introduction of the emergency laws, via Uwe Timm's association with the AutorenEdition, to Erasmus Schöfer's involvement in the Werkkreis Literatur der Arbeitswelt (Cooperative Literature of the World of Work).

There are good reasons to suspect that Enzensberger's call for a "politische Alphabetisierung Deutschlands" (political alphabetization of Germany) is the ground zero for the literary construction of "1968," but the assumption is difficult to verify. German writers responded in a variety of ways to the political and intellectual challenges of the protest movement. Peter Handke insisted on plowing his own furrow but, in doing so, only brought the reach of its antiauthoritarian message into focus. Günter Wallraff began his career as investigative journalist, and Peter Weiss dedicated his *Viet Nam Diskurs* (Viet Nam Discourse, 1968) to the proletarian revolution. The budding author Peter Schneider, who had impressed students with his poetic-polemical speech "Wir haben Fehler gemacht," put his writing skills at the disposal of the movement during the short-lived anti-Springer campaign. F. C. Delius also attests to the impact Enzensberger's essay had on his generation.³⁰

Enzensberger's own path as "writer of the revolution" is certainly "vexing."³¹ He abruptly ended a fellowship at Wesleyan University in Connecticut and spent a year in Cuba. Disillusioned with the reality of socialism there, he embarked on a "documentary novel" about the life of the Spanish anarchist Buenaventura Durruti. In the preface, he reflects on the process of writing history in which history becomes a "collective fiction," with several stories converging to create a single story:

> In the end, what the Long March means to us is what is narrated about the Long March. History is an invention, with reality supplying the materials. But it is not an arbitrary invention. The curiosity it creates is based on the interest of those who tell the story, and it allows the listeners to recognize and to be clearer about their own interests and those of their enemies.³²

Ten years after 1968, Enzensberger published *Der Untergang der Titanic* (The Sinking of the Titanic), a "comedy in verse," which deals with humanity's inability to learn from mistakes. In the third "Gesang" (Song), the poet remembers the "sonderbar leichten Tage der Euphorie" (the strangely light days of euphoria) in Berlin, where the feeling was "als stünde etwas bevor, // Etwas von uns zu Erfindenes" (as if something was about to happen, // Something that we had yet to invent).³³

Enzensberger's idea that enlightenment and a new consciousness could be achieved through a gradual change in perception obviously wasn't new. Bertolt Brecht had developed a similar theory for the theater, but, in the context of the Cold War and the hardly revolutionary "socialist realism" practiced by East German writers, a new form of literary and intellectual debate was needed. Henning Marmulla has recently shown how Enzensberger's *Kursbuch* became a manual for the "politische Alphabetisierung der Deutschen" (political alphabetization of the Germans), by creating a politically engaged counterpublic.³⁴ Published by the Suhrkamp Verlag, the *Kursbuch* gave the movement a forum to try out new ideas. In 1968, the *Kursbuch* contained, inter alia, an essay by Peter Weiss (on Che Guevara), a documentation on the events surrounding June 2, an essay by Oskar Negt (refuting Jürgen Habermas's idea that the strategy of the SDS was akin to "Linksfaschismus" [left-wing fascism]³⁵), an issue discussing what the future might look like (including a conversation with SDS thinkers Rudi Dutschke, Bernd Rabehl, and Christian Semler), and the famous issue on the "death of literature." With the exception of issue 12 on the situation in the universities, Enzensberger regularly used the platform to offer his own thoughts on the possibility of a radical transformation of society in his column "Berliner Gemeinplätze" (Berlin Commonplaces).

Reading the *Kursbuch* today, one cannot help but feel that the magazine must have played an important part in influencing its readers' perceptions, perhaps not immediately (that would have been the case only for those who were already active in the movement), but certainly for those who wanted to hear what left-wing intellectual and literary voices had to say in response to the challenge of the movement.[36] It is also obvious that, contrary to some accounts, the magazine actually celebrates poetry and prose, demonstrating that literature was far from dead. In fact, the debates on the pages of the *Kursbuch*, for example between Peter Schneider, who argued that literature could only play a minor role in articulating desires and pointing the way to political action (issue 16), and Hans-Christoph Buch, who argued that one should keep faith in the consciousness-transforming character of art (issue 20), demonstrated the continuing hope that, by writing the revolution, authors could bring it a little closer to realization. Marmulla is therefore right when he observes:

> With the Kursbuch Enzensberger focused the themes of the international 68er movements and created a communicative space where themes were politicized and the perceptions of different actors synchronized. A student like Peter Schneider came to the literary field via the Kursbuch, literature was politicized here. This space that newly negotiated the political and the literary, that provided a link to the international 68er movements due to Enzensberger's de-nationalized and de-nationalizing habitus, thus represented an influential and publically effective forum for interventions in the political field of the Federal Republic. (260)

Between Scylla and Charybdis

Peter Schneider, a student of German literature and aspiring author in 1968, personifies like no other the challenges faced by a writer determined to radically change society. In his rhetorically polished speech "Wir haben Fehler gemacht" at the Freie Universität Berlin on May 5, 1967,[37] he told his fellow students that their protest had been ineffective up to that point because they had been playing by the rules of a system that was impervious to arguments, and that it was time for a refusal to play by these rules any longer. While in this case the suggested sit-in was intended to challenge the university authorities, the wider target of Schneider's speech was the students' naive expectation that a "sachliche Diskussion" (a discussion based on facts) would change the minds of the establishment. Wolfgang Kraushaar believes that this speech, and its call for direct action, planted a dangerous seed. While accepting that Schneider's "Pathos der Empörung" (pathos of indignation) correctly identified why a protest adhering to the rules laid down by the authorities (the police and the judiciary) was bound to fail, he also observes that within a short period of time the rhetoric changed from breaking the rules to outright violence.[38] Schneider himself quickly became an important figure in the German student movement. He was asked by Rudi Dutschke to organize the campaign against media tycoon Axel Springer[39] and was part of an "anonymes Autorenkollektiv" that openly propagated the use of "counterviolence" in the struggle:

> In principle the question of violence ends with the question whether we are determined to achieve our objectives. Once and for all we want to prevent people being beaten and crippled in spirit and body after which they can only work, shop and hate. We will not wait until another generation is irreparably damaged, we will defend ourselves now. We will only get socialism if we let our enemies know that we will use all necessary means to make it happen.[40]

As to the role of the writer in this struggle, Schneider was equally radical. In *Kursbuch* 16, he had two opportunities to develop his arguments, first in the essay "Die Phantasie im Spätkapitalismus und die Kulturrevolution" (The Imagination in the Era of Late Capitalism and the Cultural Revolution),[41] which was originally supposed to appear in the previous issue on the "Death of Literature," and in a "Kursbogen," a folded poster inside *Kursbuch* 16 confidently entitled "Rede an die deutschen Leser und ihre Schriftsteller" (Speech for the German Readers and Their Writers). In the former, Schneider asked how individual and collective *Wünsche* (a term steeped in German romantic tradition denoting a dream and desire of an alternative reality to the harsh conditions created by those in power) could ever prevail against the combined strength of the police, the press, the legal system, and the vested interest of the employers. He argued that to end the alienation experienced by the individual, a cultural revolution was needed, and that it was the role of the revolutionary writers (by means of agitation and propaganda) to create a consciousness of the alienating conditions via a "great lament" and show in their work examples of a successful "conquering of reality through imagination." By "mobilizing" the wishes and desires against reality, writers would soon find out which of their works were useful in the struggle:

> Let us chase all the painted desires out of the museums and into the streets. Let us pull down the written dreams from the groaning bookshelves in the libraries and put a stone into their hands. Their ability to defend themselves will determine which of them will be useful in the new society, and which will gather dust. (37)[42]

By the time the essay was published, however, the movement had imploded. Schneider was en route to spend six months working for the revolution in Italy, from where he was expelled back to Germany. These experiences were the basis for his novella *Lenz* (1973), published in the newly formed Rotbuch cooperative.

Condensed in these ninety pages are the author's experiences of elation and frustration in the movement, the joy of political solidarity and the complications in human relationships due to class and upbringing. Schneider's protagonist, much like his namesake Lenz in Georg Büchner's novella from 1836, suffers from the unresolved contradictions between idea and reality, in this case his Marxist and Maoist politics and the reality he experiences with workers in a factory in Berlin and his elusive girlfriend. In Italy, after a disappointing stay with champagne socialists in Rome, he befriends revolutionary workers in Trento and for the first time feels that it might be possible to reconcile "Anspruch und Wirklichkeit" (pretension and reality). When he is forced to return to Germany, he resolves to embark on the Long March.

Lenz signals a conscious decision on Schneider's part to continue to write the revolution, but from a subjective point of view. The reader shares the protagonist's dreams, insecurities, doubts, and frustrations. His acute sense of alienation is real, but not just because of the oppressive authorities and conservative press in West Berlin but also his dogmatic comrades and their empty phrases. In Italy, he slowly finds his own self again, rediscovers who he is and what he wants to do. The light, the sounds and smell, the sea, and an actress friend combine to relax Lenz, who, as Peter Schneider himself, is emotionally scarred by the war and the separation of his parents. At a party he observes the gulf between fashionable political attitude and reality. "Why are they constantly saying things they don't mean?" he asks. As an outsider, he realizes how hermetically sealed are the political groups that he moves in, how pathetic the need to appear a guerrilla because everyday political work does not lead anywhere. The workers certainly have good reasons to keep their distance:

> How long will you stay and stick with this? Your excited commitment for our cause, where does it come from? You do not have the same problems we have, because you do not have to do the same work that we do.[43]

Lenz realizes that for him to deal with his personal problems and his political disorientation, he must talk and write about them, that he must slow down and tackle them patiently.

The initial reception of the book was mixed due to the author's apparent political and literary U-turn, but it soon became a bestseller. Oliver Sill described the book as a "literary event" that summed up the experiences of the movement and signaled the renunciation of the earlier revolutionary voluntarism and the end of hopes for an early, fundamental social revolution as well as a reappraisal of, and return to, the possibilities inherent in literature.[44]

More recently, Thomas Krüger has read *Lenz* as a product of the transitional period between the protest movement and the "Neue Innerlichkeit" of the seventies. For him, the novella is a nostalgic look back to a lost opportunity, though he is careful to leave the door open for a more positive interpretation:

> Nostalgia is not simply a negative, resigned category, but instead a sometimes painful return to a narratively reconstructed past. In effect, nostalgia has a strong utopian dimension.[45]

Peter Schneider continued to wrestle with the question whether it was possible to be a revolutionary and a writer at the same time.[46] He returned to the student movement as a topic in the postunification novel *Eduards Heimkehr* (Eduard's Return, 1999) and has defended its legacy in numerous essays and an autobiographical confrontation with his former self.[47] But it was his novel *Skylla* (2005), an essay on Napoleon Bonaparte's observation: What is history but a fable agreed upon? that provided a genuinely new perspective on "1968." The protagonist is Leo Brenner, a former activist in the German student movement, now a successful Berlin solicitor specializing in divorce cases. Fleeing rainy Tuscany one holiday, he buys a plot of land on a hill in Latium and builds a house with a view for his family. He and his young wife Lucynna, an archeologist, unearth a mosaic below their terrace, and explore the myth of the monster Skylla as they become involved in a race to reconstruct a sculpture that was the original source for the mosaic. Among the daily frustrations of housebuilding and a second narrative strand that explores the time of emperor Tiberius, in whose cave in Sperlonga the sculpture was originally set, we come to what appears to be a minor narrative detour, but which proves to be the center of the novel. Brenner encounters a former comrade from his student days, Paul Stirlitz. This down-on-his-luck drifter, who scrapes a living helping affluent 68ers to build their second homes in Italy, confronts Brenner with his past as agitator and student leader.

Brenner initially has no recollection of Stirlitz (an indication of the passage of time and his "successful" integration into bourgeois society) but is forcefully reminded that not all 68ers managed to leave their past behind. Skillfully reflecting the debate of the time, Schneider lets his characters take opposite sides on how to remember the German student movement, either as a time of "brutale[n] Parolen und Welterlösungsformeln" (brutal slogans and formulas for saving the world), or as a "wunderbare und notwendige Revolution" (wonderful and necessary revolution).⁴⁸ It soon becomes clear that Brenner and Stirlitz are not only fighting about the historicization of their own past but also its legitimization. For Stirlitz, the accepted history of "1968" is one big lie:

> Memory is a tricky thing. [. . .] In retrospect, perpetrators are always innocent, and they love to play the role of the victim. This was the case with our fathers, and it's no different with us, the self-styled anti-fascists and revolutionaries. Most innocent of all are always those who plan a deed in their mind, but leave the dirty work of execution to others. Murderous slogans, shouted at a teach-in, are much easier to forget than murder, don't you think?⁴⁹

Stirlitz reminds his former comrade of the time when Rudi Dutschke was shot, willing Brenner to admit that as a leading figure in the movement he had been instrumental in enticing many young people to violence with the slogan "Sprengt Springer!" (Blow Up Springer!). Faced with this "self-appointed judge (208)," Brenner adamantly refuses any admission of guilt that Stirlitz so eagerly expects from him. The reason for this becomes obvious when Stirlitz confesses that he had interpreted the slogan as a call to action. He had prepared a bomb that was intended to damage the Springer headquarter in Berlin but instead had killed two innocent people. Brenner feebly protests that his slogan had had no militant meaning, that it had simply been a case of following "der Logik des Stabreims" (the logic of alliteration, 209), but Stirlitz, eaten up by his feelings of guilt, demands that Brenner accepts his part of the responsibility for the consequences of his actions.

Initially, the solicitor defends himself vigorously: "I never planned a bomb attack, let alone participated in one. The only thing you can accuse me of is having been too lax in my choice of words," but he begins to have doubts when Stirlitz steals the mosaic, an act that causes the disappearance of Lucynna and Brenner's "Läuterung" (purification):

> And should I not accept a share of the blame, a moral complicity? Did my slogan not contribute to a climate in which someone like Paul Stirlitz could imagine himself a hero by doing what—truth be told—everyone wanted to do? (231)

At this point, Schneider widens the scope of his archeological dig. Brenner meets with one of the archeologists who are trying to recreate the Skylla sculpture, who explains to him:

> People want to know where they come from, and through this hope to find out who they are and where they are going. Historiography is a battle over memory, one that never ends—no matter whether we are talking about the history of an individual or the history of entire nations. Out of the testimonies of their forefathers, each generation

creates a new history for itself, a history that it wants to inscribe into mankind's collective memory. The important thing is not what happened, but which elements of what happened are formulated and preserved. A history that has never been written down will get lost—in the end, it never even happened. (248–49)

Asked whether this means that there is no difference between original and reconstruction, the archeologist responds:

I wouldn't go that far. But if no original has been preserved, not even a copy of the original, then the reconstruction will prevail. And at some point, it replaces the original. (252)

In an interview shortly after the publication of the novel, Peter Schneider explained why he had tackled the problem of reconstruction:

Even the 68ers [. . .] displace and repress their past. In remembering, everyone produces their own version of their own past, a version that suits them. In the end, the reconstruction of history replaces the original—in my novel, this happens when the Scylla-sculpture is reconstructed. Perhaps we cannot help but lie about our past, but at least we should be aware of that.[50]

Schneider has chosen to illustrate the dual process of historicization and legitimization of the German student movement with the mythological image of Scylla and Charybdis. This may be helpful in that it signals how easily we may be pulled toward one or the other, but there is also a sense of arrogance, of affording the 68ers a mythical significance by aligning their past ("Eigenmythologie") with powerful imagery traditionally associated with more significant historical moments. But that is exactly Schneider's point: he demonstrates that it is in our nature to want to legitimize our past actions and that our own actions, as long as we can convince the next generation, may one day be as "mythical" as those of the past.

With *Skylla*, Schneider appears to exorcise a ghost. Both the protagonist and the author were actively involved in the student revolt. Both avoided violent conflict but share a certain responsibility for the actions of others whom they might have inadvertently incited to violence. Indeed, Peter Schneider was more involved in the movement than is commonly remembered today. He was part of the group that prepared the "Springer tribunal" in 1967 and one of the signatories of a pamphlet against Springer's press monopoly in West Berlin. He was also, as he revealed himself, one of the originators of the "Wanted" Poster during the visit of the Shah of Persia in West Berlin that led to the demonstrations where Benno Ohnesorg was killed, and the subsequent escalation of the conflict between students and the state.

The author seems to say that "1968," like the myths of the monster Scylla or the shy emperor Tiberius, has undergone numerous retellings, has in fact become a myth itself, unrecognizable beneath countless opposing interpretations, and that it may be impossible to reconstruct "the truth." Like Tiberius, who attempted to legitimize his hold on power by creating a mythical bloodline to Odysseus, the 68ers are busy justifying themselves; their legend "is pushed into collective memory by all available means" (*Skylla*, 131).

Peter Schneider is aware of how much he himself has contributed to the "mythical" power of "1968." His *Lenz* had attempted to put some distance between himself and the "unpoetic" dogmatism and futile violence that had destroyed what had been intended, and yet become one of the "iconic" texts on the German student movement. *Skylla* can be interpreted as a further aesthetic and creative allegory of the movement: once a beautiful maiden, corrupted through no fault of her own, she kills those who come too near. Innocence and violence are the two halves of her being, and Odysseus thought she was the lesser of two evils.

An Archeology of Desires

Next to Peter Schneider's *Lenz* sits Uwe Timm's *Heißer Sommer*, the other iconic literary representation of the German student movement. Timm, born in 1940 like Schneider, was a student on an exchange year in Paris when he heard the news of the death of his friend Benno Ohnesorg and returned to Munich where he joined the movement, engaging in agit-prop and street theater. He also spent several months in Hamburg, and his experiences are reflected in the novel. While *Lenz* explores the feeling of disorientation at the end of the movement, *Heißer Sommer* attempts to reconstruct the essence of "1968" by following an average student through the main phases of the revolt from the summer of 1967 to the autumn of 1968. The protagonist, Ullrich Krause, studies German literature in Munich when the death of Benno Ohnesorg shakes him out of his apathy. He decides to move to Hamburg and stops at his parents' house on the way. The confrontation with his father, a former Nazi and strict authoritarian, illustrates the emotional and ideological distance between the generations. In Hamburg, he experiences his first "go-in" when members of the local SDS disrupt a lecture. Ullrich becomes involved in the movement, begins to read Marcuse, distributes flyers, participates in the toppling of the statue of a colonial officer on campus, and joins the demonstrations against the Springer newspapers following the attempted assassination of Rudi Dutschke. When the protest dissipates, Ullrich experiments with drugs, joins a street theater group, works in a factory to get closer to the working class, and finally decides to return to Munich to become a teacher and embark on the Long March through the institutions.

Despite its simple, almost clichéd storyline and its laconic style, *Heißer Sommer* is meticulously composed and offers several layers of meaning. Its leitmotifs (the weather, already signaled in the title; the fear of authority; the cheeky slogans by graffiti artist Peter-Ernst Eiffe; the suppressed anger and hope for liberation) are reinforced by regular quotes from German literature.[51] By channeling the plethora of events, sounds, ideas, images, and emotions through the sensorium of this "average" young man, Timm enables the reader to see deep into the consciousness of the 68ers. We experience Ullrich's narrow-minded parents, his sexual inexperience and inability to openly talk about his feelings and desires, his fear of anyone in authority, and his need to belong. It is this last characteristic that makes Ullrich the ideal observer of events, but also provides a clue to the paradox that while the number of activists in the German student movement was small, it attracted such widespread support at critical junctures.

Timm combines a variety of sources into his text, including quotes from critical theory, newspaper clips, and radio announcements, but it is his technique to cut between a description of an event (through Ullrich's eyes) and a focus on Ullrich's reactions through the voice of the narrator that enables him to construct a differentiated picture of, and allows the reader a variety of access points to, "1968." This can be best demonstrated with the scene where Ullrich first experiences the "sprengen" (breaking up, literally: exploding)[52] of a lecture by members of the SDS. In the Audimax, the University of Hamburg's main lecture hall that had been the scene of the unfurling of the banner "Unter den Talaren, der Muff von tausend Jahren" (Beneath the Academic Gowns, the Stench of a Thousand Years; referring to the Nazi past of some of the professors and, more broadly, their authoritarian attitude) on November 9, 1967,[53] students gather as if expecting an entertainment or a gladiatorial fight. A small group of activists from the SDS take the microphone from the professor and the group's leader delivers a speech that covers the grievances of the students, an analysis of what is wrong with West Germany's political and economic system, an analysis of the authoritarian character, and a call for action (*HS*, 121–23).

The speech, delivered by an energetic young activist called Connie (a combination of Dutschke, Cohn-Bendit, and Schneider), allows Timm to introduce the reader to the ideology and underlying message of the student movement. It mirrors the vocabulary that Herbert Marcuse had used in his speeches to West German students in 1966 (*Vietnam: Analyse eines Exempels* [Vietnam: Analysis of an Example]) and 1967 (*Das Ende der Utopie* [The End of Utopia]), but blends it with a critique of the authoritarian structures at the university. Crucially, Timm interrupts the speech to show how Ullrich and the audience react, thus giving the reader a sense of "being there" and an opportunity to empathize with the listeners:

> Let us show, above all, how democratic control ends exactly at the point where it could interfere with the interests of the ruling classes. Let us force the professors, who until now were allowed to give their opinions without opposition, to talk about these opinions. Let us force them to come clean about in whose interests they defend these opinions. Let us challenge their unquestioned authority. (There was applause and shouts of "Bravo" in the lecture hall.) Lets us challenge repressive institutions, like this lecture hall. All the seats in this hall are oriented towards this one point, where normally the professors stand and are allowed to talk without being challenged. (Ullrich applauded. I never noticed that before, he said.—What? asked Christa.—This thing about the lecture rooms.) (122)

Timm enables us to interpret this passage in various ways. We might observe the demagogical and dogmatic character of the oratory. We may focus on Ullrich's naivety in believing the undigested mélange of critical theory and Maoist agitation, or his inability to actually understand what is going on (when Ullrich attends a SDS meeting, the narrator drily comments: "Ullrich couldn't quite keep up"). We can enjoy the uncomfortable moment when gleeful naughtiness turns into taboo-breaking (a heavily pregnant woman uses her body to push the professor away from the lectern). We may perhaps even remember that one of the professors present at the "Unter den Talaren" protest had called out: "You all belong in the concentration camp!"[54]

For Timm, this central passage represents just one element in a three-pronged strategy to construct "1968" as a magic moment when students experienced the unity of thinking, feeling, and action. The pursuit of happiness, in Ullrich's case a diffuse awareness of his isolation, is of equal importance to the political emancipation for the students. The potential of happiness free from alienation, the alternative to traditional bourgeois or petty-bourgeois behavior and thought, becomes a concrete utopia for Ullrich. In the company of new friends and comrades in Hamburg, he finds himself slowly shaking off his emotional numbness and begins to understand that it is up to him to overcome his sense of alienation:

> He had linked arms with them, he could laugh and talk with them, as if he had known them for ages. What he feels is joy, a feeling that is bigger than himself, something that gives him a sense of space and strength. A joy determined by hatred, but a hatred that changes things. (217)

Turning his alienation into action, Ullrich participates in the toppling of the Wissmann statue, a symbol of German imperialism and racism that had been erected in front of the university's main building in 1922[55] and begins to explore viable options. It is during this period that he encounters the radical thoughts of Herbert Marcuse:

> Fighting for freedom, in the interest of the whole against the specific interests of oppression, terror can become a necessity and obligation. In this context, violence, revolutionary violence, manifests not only as a political means but as a moral duty. (152–53)[56]

Yet he ultimately realizes that blind "Aktionismus" (actionism), for example by setting fire to a police car, does not change anything. For Ullrich, the solution lies in solidarity with the working class, while Connie, the speaker at the go-in, chooses the armed struggle. There is no doubt, though, that Timm sides with his protagonist. Ullrich puts his faith in Marcuse's promise: "There is a happiness that can be realized for all: a pacified world, a world without exploitation and oppression" (339).

What appears to be a traditional bildungsroman reveals itself to be an attempt to use it as a vehicle to make readers think, and act, on the information given to them. As such, the text is biased in favor of those individuals and groups who aim to change society. One of Ullrich's housemates (we only learn his surname, Petersen—a character who will return in Timm's novel *Rot*) speaks of "die tendenziell bewußtseinsbildende Funktion von Literatur" (consciousness-raising role of literature, 234), while Timm himself was very clear about his politics at the time. As a member of the German Communist Party (DKP), he was committed to fighting the economic and political "Aberglauben" (superstition) that he felt was dominating the Federal Republic:

> The superstition that this country is the land of freedom, the superstition of the democratic order which in reality ends in front of the factory door, the superstition that employers give you work when in reality they take your labor, etc. Behind this superstition hides the capitalist reality.[57]

Against this "superstition" Timm cofounded the AutorenEdition, a publishing collective with writers who were committed to a "Versuch einer neuen realistischen Prosa" (the experiment to write new, realistic prose)[58] that was targeting a broad audience with texts that had a broader appeal and would deal with problems of the readers, not those of the writers. He also followed up on his interest in Germany's colonial past with a solid piece of research culminating in his description of the genocide perpetrated by German soldiers in German South-West Africa in his novel *Morenga* (1978) and his volume of photographs from German colonial times, *Deutsche Kolonien* (German Colonies, 1981).

Morenga not only reflects the break by the 68ers with the traditions of their fathers but also the escalation of the confrontation that had occurred after the demise of the student movement. While the majority of students had "moved on," many, like Timm himself, had joined communist groups, and a small minority had turned to guerrilla warfare against the state. Thus we find both the "ideas of '68" and the new vocabulary of the "armed struggle" of the Red Army Faction reflected in the narrative of the veterinarian Gottschalk, who is intrigued and fascinated by the culture of the Herero but realizes that with his colonial mindset it will be impossible for him ever to identify fully with them.

Timm summed up his own conclusions from his *Morenga* project in the preface to *Deutsche Kolonien* in 1981. He notes that the Africans had tended to live in classless societies, and this had been a constant challenge to their colonial masters, who realized that, unless there was greater competition for resources among the Africans, very little profit would be made. Timm comments,

> This [. . .] is typical of the ideology of the colonizers. It stems from economic thinking and is determined by an unquestioning sense of superiority, which in turn is based on a belief in technological progress. In this way, any life form that is different becomes the Other in the eyes of the colonizer; it becomes something alien, primitive, without his ever reaching a position where he would be able to see this other culture as rich and complex in its own right.[59]

There is a clear link between the moral outrage of the students against the Wissmann statue and the outrage Timm himself feels against the treatment of the colonized as children who need to learn the German virtues of punctuality, order, and diligence. In fact, it was against these "German virtues" that the generation of 1968 rebelled.

Timm returned to the topic of the student movement repeatedly, for example in *Kerbels Flucht* (Kerbel's Escape, 1980), where the euphoric sense of a new beginning has disappeared, reflecting the author's own disillusion with the communist ideals. Christian Kerbel, a former activist working as a taxi driver, now regards the theories that once gave him a sense of purpose as nothing but "abstract rubbish."[60] He views his own activism as "activism without results" and "wasted time" (20). The "Veteranen der 68er Jahre" (veterans of the 68s) drink their beer in a pub suitably named "Alter Ofen" (Old Oven, 22). Kerbel realizes that there was a mismatch between what they thought and what they felt: "Our insights and understanding are still far ahead of our feelings" (100).

In his novel *Rot*, Timm revisited some of his characters from *Heißer Sommer*. The protagonist Thomas Linde is a former student rebel now working as a "Beerdigungsredner" (funeral orator) and jazz critic. In his midfifties, he has found love again with Iris, a young "Lichtdesigner" (light designer). But his precariously balanced existence, conforming to and yet subverting the rules of the "system," is shaken when he is asked to research a speech for a former comrade, Gustav Aschenberger, who has died before he could carry out his plan to blow up the Victory Column in the heart of Berlin as a signal of defiance against this "system." Linde is drawn back into the world of his former ideals, trying to rediscover what he once stood for. He is reluctant to follow in Aschenberger's footsteps, but as his relationship with Iris deepens, he finds his way back to the moral imperative of his youth and, via flashbacks of other wakes and meetings with former comrades, seems to be on the verge of setting off the bomb himself when he is killed crossing a street at a red light. As the accident happens at the beginning of the book, we relive his life up to the moment of his death.

Two themes are central to an understanding of Thomas Linde. The first is the color red—the title of the novel and the subject of his private research. He has been compiling the associations and connotations of the color for years, from the obvious political ones to the metaphorical, mythical, romantic, theological, and psychological, as well as the ephemeral and anecdotal. The question of whether the color red represents a unifying worldview or a fragmented experience exercises Linde. Like Goethe in his *Farbenlehre* (Theory of Colors, 1810), Linde is a seeker of meaning beyond the boundaries of consensus reality. The second theme is the passage of time and the loss of ideals and convictions. Linde begins to feel that few actions actually make a difference. "Das kann doch nicht alles sein!" (This cannot have been all there was!)[61] is a recurrent sentiment, fueled by his regular (professional) exposure to the experiences of death, of unfulfilled dreams, of continuity broken. In marked contrast to those "von der Konkurrenz" (those from the competition, i.e., organized religion, 157), Linde cannot offer any reassurance of continuity beyond death to his clients, and while this lack of transcendental assurance has not bothered him before, "der Sinn des Seyns" (the point of existence, 151) now becomes an urgent question.

Linde sets out to find out what drove Aschenberger to contemplate such an extreme act. He remembers them marching together at demonstrations, holding up banners against the Vietnam war, and selling communist newspapers at factory gates, but he fails to understand what could have driven him to such despair that he would resort to such a violent form of protest. If anything, their utopian dream was built on the notion that society had to be replaced by another, more peaceful, enlightened, and empathetic one. Linde discovers that, while he himself has been able to extricate himself from the communist party and to accept reality and change, Aschenberger has remained "true" to the cause. Alone, in his own hermetically sealed world of revolutionary literature and a milieu that stubbornly refuses to acknowledge that the socialist alternative has reached a dead end, his despair must have festered for years.

Linde is at pains to explain to his young girlfriend how anyone could ever have taken a set of beliefs like communism seriously. The Großer Stern, with the Victory Column as its focal point, for Aschenberger and Linde the intersection of German history with its dictatorships and dreams of world domination, is simply the place of the Love Parade for Iris. The meaning of life, which Linde once believed to lie in the creation of a just and equal society, has degenerated to "shoppen und ficken" (151) in modern Germany.

Aschenberger's death moves Linde deeply: he sees it as a black hole, "eine Implosion des Sinns" (an implosion of meaning, 167), as if his political comrade should have had more of an impact. Perhaps this expectation is not unreasonable: a whole generation had set out to march through the institutions to change society, but instead society, the institutions, and the passage of time have changed them. *Rot* is full of such cases: Linde's former comrade Edmond has lost his revolutionary zeal and become a wine dealer. Another former comrade, Ulrich Krause (the protagonist of *Heißer Sommer*, here spelled with one l), works as a teacher in the new East and maintains an APO archive. Linde learns that Aschenberger had visited Krause shortly before his death to look for a manual on guerrilla resistance fighting to learn how to make his bomb.

Timm spends considerable time exploring this fascination with violence as a last resort when idealism cannot convince others of the right path. One is reminded of the young Holger Meins who showed his short film on how to make a Molotov cocktail at the "Springer tribunal," and also of the bizarre episode in Rudi Dutschke's life when he carted explosives around Berlin in the pram of his infant son.

What Linde reminds us of in his final speech on Aschenberger, as his consciousness drifts away after his fatal accident, is that we must accept that, for some, the eternal contradiction between freedom and equality can lead to the conclusion that "ein Signal setzen" (to send a signal, 395) is more important than daily compromises. If this is now an old fashioned or unacceptable viewpoint, then so be it.

Initial reviews of *Rot* were enthusiastic. *Di Zeit* critic Ulrich Greiner argued that Timm had produced his best novel so far, perhaps because it enabled readers to feel that Linde's story was very much their own. Dealing with the passage of time, in this case with reference to the student movement, does not create a sense of closure, though, because there are many unfulfilled hopes, and because the dead are not dead yet. Linde's occupation as "Beerdigungsredner" is fitting: there is cause for mourning, but there is consolation, too:

> Why is there cause for mourning? Because ideals that could not stand up to reality are buried. [. . .] Timm reminds us of the history of a generation that had wanted all, achieved a lot, but also lost a lot. But there is one thing they can say about themselves: they were serious about happiness for all and social justice.[62]

Ursula März is less sanguine in terms of any positive epitaphs for the 68ers. She understands Aschenberger as the metaphor for a "Haufen

Asche" (a heap of ash), which is all that is left of the revolutionary spirit of the movement.⁶³ Both interpretations are valid. However, März may be taking Timm's choice of names too literally: Looking around Aschenberger's vast collection of revolutionary literature, Linde comes across a copy of Marcuse's *Versuch über die Befreiung* (An Essay on Liberation, 1969). A dedication in English signed by Herbert Marcuse himself reads: "The ash is not only the rest, it's also new fertility" (*Rot*, 72).

Timm continues to work on his own reconstruction of "1968." I have already mentioned his autobiographical text *Der Freund und der Fremde*, in which he reflects on Benno Ohnesorg as a former friend and as a media construct. Following on from his previous memory project, the celebrated *Am Beispiel meines Bruders*, Timm finally found a suitable form that allowed him not only to compose a requiem for his friend but to rediscover and confront his own former self which was profoundly affected by his friend's death. Inevitably, like Peter Schneider's *Skylla*, the book turns into an essay on the significance and power of myths: of the ancient Orpheus myth or the modern myth of the 68ers, of which Timm's friend has become a significant part. For the death of Benno Ohnesorg has become a "moment" in time: one that is invested with a special significance. For a minority it provided the excuse to form terrorist groups (e.g., Bewegung 2. Juni, or the Red Army Faction). For many it has become a key date to be commemorated. It is endlessly revisited by historians and novelists, and used by the media as shorthand for a generational narrative and experience. And yet, while Timm accords himself the role of Orpheus who can bring back the dead, he does not only add to the myth but also deconstructs it, reminding his readers that Benno Ohnesorg was a real person who became the unlikely hero in a struggle for a better world with better beings in it.

The Geography of Memory

Friedrich Christian Delius has written both about the German student movement and the RAF. In his Deutscher Herbst Trilogy, *Ein Held der Inneren Sicherheit* (A Hero of Home Security, 1981), *Mogadischu Fensterplatz* (Mogadischu Window Seat, 1987), and *Himmelfahrt eines Staatsfeindes* (Apotheosis of an Enemy of the State, 1992), he explored the collateral damage and discontinuities in individual biographies caused by terrorist violence, while in *Amerikahaus und der Tanz um die Frauen* (America House and the Dance around the Women, 1997) he reconstructed the atmosphere of the student movement before 1968. *Amerikahaus* consciously avoids revisiting the iconic moments of the movement and instead focuses on its beginnings in West Berlin. The protagonist Martin, a student of German literature nicknamed "Buster" for his shy and reticent nature, experiences the first demonstrations against the Vietnam War. A virgin, he struggles with his petit-bourgeois background, forbidden sexual desires, and borrowed utopian dreams, only managing to be himself in the pages of his diary. Longing for company and acknowledgment, he halfheartedly joins a demonstration but remains an observer:

> No matter whether the passers-by reacted disapprovingly or approvingly, for the demonstrators everything seemed like a reward: they were noticed. Martin did not assume that people would be impressed by their posters and demands, and perhaps change their views. That wasn't the point. The protest march had a different meaning. The spectators needed the demonstrators, and the demonstrators needed the spectators. It was the gazes from outside that melted the motley crew of protesters into something they were not: a uniform group.[64]

In passages like these, Delius offers the reader an insight into the dynamics of the movement: the mutual interdependence of protesters and onlookers, the threshold of fear that had to be overcome by well-brought-up young Germans to join a protest march, the need for recognition of their minority view that simply did not register in the press, the radio, or television unless the demonstrations turned to provocation.

When the first eggs are thrown against the white walls of the Amerika Haus (the United States maintained cultural centers in all larger West German cities), Martin is once again a spectator:

> The eggs had flown through the air with such lightness and freedom that Martin viewed the scene with a rare rush of serenity. He forgot whether he should be outraged or amused. The four eggs, of which three had hit their target, may have been a parody of the four thousand bombs that were dropped on Vietnam every day. But it meant more. The eggs worked like a liberating theatre-effect: what was happening became removed from the spectators, slipped away from reality and disappeared onto a stage. (95)

The police respond by beating the protesters with batons, while Martin manages to slip away. He struggles to come to terms with what he has seen. Was this a performance or a protest? He is aware that something unheard-of has happened:

> A small rebellion, a great embarrassment, a democratic happening, an act of violence, Martin was unable to interpret it. A premiere which he didn't dare to criticize. (99–100)

Delius tries hard to shield his narrative from the knowledge of what would happen to the movement in the months to come. The advantage of this approach is that the reader is introduced to "1968" in *statu nascendi*, where the lines of confrontation are just beginning to be drawn, where students are caught between the conflicting motives of their libido (and need to impress others), their moral outrage over their government's support of the Vietnam War, their instinctive rebellion against their authoritarian upbringing, and the euphoric experience of collective action. He also reminds the reader of the claustrophobic atmosphere in West Berlin that had such an important role in creating the conditions for the rebellion to reach critical mass.

In *Mein Jahr als Mörder* (My Year as Murderer, 2004), Delius returns to the student movement and examines one of the root causes for the escalation of violence, drawing on historical events around which he constructs his narrative. On December 6, 1968, a student in West Berlin decides to kill a former Nazi judge who has just been acquitted. Hans-Joachim Rehse, one of the judges in Roland Freisler's Volksgerichtshof (People's Court), had not only sentenced to death his best friend's father, the physician Georg Groscurth, but also caused untold misery to Groscurth's widow Anneliese, who was persecuted as "communist witch" in the fifties and sixties and dragged through the courts while her tormentor got off scot-free. An inner voice tells the student: "Someone will set an example and kill this murderer, and this someone will be you."[65]

The first-person narrator feels enraged by what he considers is a corrupt system. He decides upon a "double strategy": gathering material for a book about this gross miscarriage of justice and at the same time planning the murder. In contrast to the endless debates that lead nowhere, he feels an obligation to carry out his plan, experiencing the exultation of actually doing something concrete: "Word and deed were the same, finally" (45):

> When Berlin judges [. . .] acquit the murderer and sentence his victims, someone has to point out the difference, and in a spectacular way. Then the finger must point to the real perpetrator, even if this finger is a pistol. (259)

He is careful not to let on what he is up to, but Delius allows us an insight into the student's thoughts. When an American acquaintance suggests that "all violence is bullshit," we learn:

> I would love to have answered: you are right, I used to think like you when I was in London. But you come from California and not from the most infamous place on the map of Europe, from a country inextricably tied up in its own past, a country that drags you into its abyss, into the Nazi swamps that no-one can drain or circumvent, that makes us flee into work and even makes me a murderer! (135)

A second motive is a very personal one. He learns that his mother, who lived in the same village as the Groscurth family, had done nothing to protect them when the Nazis came to arrest Georg, and feels the moral imperative to atone for her lack of courage: "She had stood by, and I had to atone for her traitorous act, atone for the shame, I just couldn't stand by and do nothing" (224).

Slowly, though, he begins to have doubts about the wisdom of his plan when he experiences the escalation of violence all around him. In the bars frequented by the student activists, journalists and tourists gather to catch a glimpse of "bad boys" like Andreas Baader, thrill seekers "looking to become part of the wild world of the revolution" (32). Following the Schlacht am Tegeler Weg (Battle of Tegeler Weg), where militant students and politicized apprentices for the first time beat the police in a protracted street fight, he realizes that the word violence had acquired "a pathetic aura" (34) and becomes acutely aware that the student movement has come to an end. The fanatics are now calling the shots. At this point he is swayed by Hellmut Gollwitzer's admonition following the fighting: "For fascists violence isn't a problem, but a socialist must always be accountable for the use of violence; any violence against a person is inhuman" (269). The student realizes that he has deluded himself, that his action would be counterproductive and misconstrued, and therefore abandons his plan.

Mein Jahr als Mörder is a case study that shows how manifest injustice can lead a peaceful, intelligent young man to contemplate becoming a perpetrator of violence.[66] It is also a searing indictment of the role of the West German legal system. Delius was well aware of its power, having fought an extended battle against accusations of libel following the publication of his polemic satire *Unsere Siemens-Welt* (Our Siemens World, 1972). By adding to our understanding of the student movement with the complicated personal (as opposed to collective) motives of the activists, he provides us with a much needed corrective to the dominant narrative of "1968" and its often one-dimensional protagonists.

The Labors of Sisyphus

As a founding member of the writing cooperative Werkkreis Literatur der Arbeitswelt and vocal proponent of the unity between workers and intellectuals, Erasmus Schöfer has lived his politics and paid the price of limited public acceptance. *Ein Frühling irrer Hoffnung*, Schöfer's first novel in a tetralogy entitled *Die Kinder des Sisyfos* (The Children of Sisyphus), takes us back to the spring of 1968. The book covers the milestones of the movement and how they influence the lives of Viktor Bliss, a leftwing intellectual, and his wife Lena, a dressmaker at the *Kammerspiele* theater. The focus is on the siege and brief occupation of the Springer printing press in Munich following the attempted assassination of Rudi Dutschke. Viktor is arrested as one of the "Rädelsführer" (ringleaders),[67] and his friend Martin Anklam, a shop steward at the Ford motor plant in Cologne, is seriously injured. The resulting radicalization of Viktor and Lena, their desire to change society and their struggle to stay true to themselves, make up a large part of the book.

One particular aspect that is seldom covered in accounts of the movement is the political stance that certain theater companies took: during one performance the director and the cast go on "strike" for a few moments and read a solidarity address to the Vietnam people from the stage. This event, and the resulting furor, has serious consequences for Lena, whose contract is terminated. She blames Viktor for his role in instigating the strike, and the frustration of their defeat is ultimately also the cause of their separation.

Schöfer successfully combines a portrait of the era with a portrayal of its impact on the participants and their relationship to each other. The dream of being honest with one another and following one's desires, as described in the fashionable theoretical texts of the time (e.g., Herbert Marcuse's *Eros and Civilization* [1955, in German as *Triebstruktur und Gesellschaft*, 1965]), and the problem of protecting their private lives from what is happening in the world, proves too much for them. In a description of Viktor's consciousness that is both realistic and poetic, Schöfer articulates the dilemma that ensues when the barriers between the private and the public are intentionally dissolved:

> "The bottomless truth about one human being is unbearable for another; most likely everyone is an abyss but not everyone is self-aware enough for that."[68]

Here we can see Schöfer's conviction that, unless the conditions that determine everyday life and alienate people from each other are changed, no amount of self-awareness raising and communal living can counter them. This, of course, is one of the main thematic threads that run through the movement: the whole point of all the demonstrations and idealistic attempts by the protesters to make history, to change the world, and to emancipate themselves. By exploring the gap between ideal and reality with considerable sensitivity, Schöfer offers one explanation for the ultimate failure of the students' quest to create a "neuer Mensch" (new Man).[69] Indeed, one could argue that the author's ability to get inside his protagonists thoughts and feelings, as well as juxtaposing different viewpoints on the same page, gives the fictional mode of representation a distinct advantage over the plethora of documentaries and theoretical texts that have tried to capture this vital aspect of the student movement.

The second relationship explored in the novel is that between Viktor the intellectual and Martin Anklam the worker. Each is representative of his class and profession; they serve Schöfer as examples of a successful bridging of the gulf that, had it happened on a larger scale, might have changed history. Their experience of physically fighting the overwhelming power of the police and water cannons with their own bodies, another one of the central experiences of the movement, is described in a mixture of literary and political statement:

> In this moment, all his doubts about where and to whom he belongs are gone, the barriers between barely recognizable fronts, between the rulers and the ruled are sprayed away, the burden of understanding both sides of the argument, the painful decision for or against alternatives that have nothing to do with the living world: with water the police decided that he belonged with the powerless, and for that he was unconsciously grateful. (167)

The experience of emancipation, Schöfer concludes, is bought at the price of all that a man has. In Viktor's case, this means the loss of his child (alienated and taken away from him), of his wife (unable to live with the consequences of their political activism), of his health (there is an unspecified accident later in his life that leaves him disfigured and leads to his living the life of a recluse),[70] and, most importantly, of his ideals. Their dream has failed because socialists have become dishonest, he will tell his granddaughter one month after the fall of the wall; all his hopes and aspirations have come to nothing, he is a "widerlegter Utopist" (utopian proved wrong, 12). And yet there was a time, during the intense struggle to avert the passing of the emergency laws in May 1968, when the country seemed on the verge of a revolution, when he believed it possible that the unions would join the protest. It is this belief in the "Machbarkeit der Geschichte" (feasibility of creating history) that Schöfer is keen to pass on.

Predictably, the fact that Schöfer wears his politics on his sleeve did not go down well with reviewers. Harald Jähner conceded that Schöfer tries to update the jargon of the New Left by means of a more "relaxed" language and multiperspectival "tricks," but, he complains, there is nothing beyond the "political litany" that shows the world of 1968 other than in stereotype.[71] Schöfer's publisher and some reviewers point out that his significant contribution is that he describes the era through the eyes (and with the consciousness) of the time, instead of reflecting back on it with the benefit of hindsight. This may be true to a certain extent, but it is also true that the events are narrated as they are because of his ideological position. He wants them to be this way because he believes, then and now, that the formation of a communist party and solidarity between workers and intellectuals is the only way to change society.

The second part of Erasmus Schöfer's *Die Kinder des Sisyfos* project continues with the reconstruction of the history of the New Left from an orthodox communist perspective. In *Zwielicht* (Twilight, 2004), he describes the aftermath of the student movement, the processes of emancipation in factories, villages, and workers' writing circles, all reflecting the political climate of the 1970s when citizen initiatives offered some hope for those who felt that the Long March had been stopped before it had begun. One of the case studies is the budding resistance against the building of a nuclear power plant in Whyl, where politicians and energy companies collude to break the "peaceful resistance" of local farmers and their supporters. Through the eyes of Armin Kolenda, a young communist journalist, the reader is given insight into the difficulties citizens' initiatives encountered when militant groups used the confrontation for their own ends:

> The hatred came with the others, they brought it in the 2CVs and VWs with split rear windows, in backpacks and sleeping bags hitchhiking from Berlin, Bremen and Hamburg, coming from their battles with the system in the big cities where they had learnt from batons and bullets and killing words that the rulers will bite back if the status quo is threatened. [. . .] But they used the great words of the revolution like pennies, chucked them against closed windows and heads, and used the pavement not just for walking.[72]

In *Ein Frühling irrer Hoffnung*, Schöfer had demonstrated that in 1968 the movement was a continuum, with debates about the proper strategy an integral part, and solidarity among its members a given. In *Zwielicht*, Schöfer draws a line between communists and militant action. There is a palpable sympathy for grass roots resistance and people who realize where their true interests lie (a process in which the various communist protagonists are only too happy to assist), and Armin Kolenda is convinced that the peaceful protest of the citizens' initiatives is a direct consequence of the 68er movement. But he quickly realizes that the communist dream of a popular front will once again come to nothing if the violence of the RAF is allowed to give those in power an excuse to denounce all resistance as illegal and dangerous. Thus, the militants are described as "Kaoten" (chaotic types), who have little understanding of the daily struggle of "real" people when they fight their private war as "the most difficult kids of the victorious affluence" (248).

Against the background of the public hysteria during the Schleyer kidnapping, Kolenda and his friends struggle to maintain the party line. He feels that the terrorists are acting rationally, even though they lack a basis in the working class. Desperate and alone, they are doomed to fail:

> Kohl says they are a rabid band of murderers. They do everything to declare them mad. But they are their own children. Challenging their corrupt fathers. Probably out of despair or something. Revolution in no-mans-land. (361)

For the academic Viktor Bliss, a pupil of the eminent German political scientist Wolfgang Abendroth, the terrorists are enemies of the working class. He argues that, from a communist party standpoint, "a handful of crazy students" (442) have even helped to secure the state and those in power. Ironically, it is the worker Martin Anklam who shows understanding for the RAF:

> Lost their mind! Please, Vik, don't say that. Ulrike Meinhof wasn't mad. She was as sane as Fidel and Che and Ho Chi Minh. They couldn't bear it, the injustice, the lies, the exploitation. [. . .] What drove them I would call political despair Vik, no, that is wrong, it is moral despair, of seeing any sense in political action since politics are corrupt and full of lies, and if someone tries to act honestly in politics he falls into the swamp like the others. (442–44)

From Anklam's idealistic reflections Schöfer takes the reader to the arena of publishing. Kolenda, sent by his newspaper to cover the 1977 Frankfurt Book Fair, attends a press conference by the Association of German Writers. Bernt Engelmann's speech is quoted at length (468–69), not just because he shares the orthodox party view of the "violent acts of a handful of pseudo-revolutionary desperados" (469) but because it allows Schöfer to use authentic material to reconstruct the outrage felt by intellectuals at the time at being systematically hounded as sympathizers of the RAF by conservative politicians and journalists who in their past had themselves been willing members of the Nazi regime. Engelmann makes clear that the witch hunts against supposed RAF sympathizers are reminiscent of the Nazi era and that antifascists are not only supporting the constitution but are in fact the real defenders of the Federal Republic. *Zwielicht* concludes with Kolenda's resigned observation: "It's become horribly cold and dark in this country" (593). The hopes and aspirations of "1968" have been replaced by the gloom and despair of "1977." The RAF, whatever its intentions, has produced a climate that tarnishes all legitimate protest with suspicion.

Volker Dittrich believes that Schöfer's tetralogy, which in its totality provides a history of the (New) Left from 1968 to the fall of the wall, represents a counterbalance to the "official" history of the Federal Republic. Written as a "history from below," his protagonists think, act, and speak as protesters would have at the time, without the nagging awareness of the ultimate failure of their struggle. This certainly sets this representation apart, in that the reader is confronted with "real" people, with all their hopes intact and all their wrong choices still ahead of them. The point of this approach, he argues, is to preserve the experience of a radical departure so that future generations can learn from it.[73]

As such, and especially if seen together with Schöfer's involvement in the Werkkreis Literatur der Arbeitswelt, which he founded in 1970, we can interpret his project as one author's contribution to Enzensberger's *politische Alphabetisierung der Deutschen*. At the same time, the emphasis moves away from the student movement to the broader struggle of the working class, which the majority of students never really understood but which they nevertheless revitalized by their example. The Sisyphus motif signals an almost hopeless endeavor but one that has to be undertaken again and again. After all, the endeavor is not completely hopeless. In a poem accompanying the text, Schöfer concludes: "Bleibt der Brocken wieder nicht oben // schleifen wir diesmal den Berg" (If the rock won't stay up // then it's time to level the mountain).[74]

Other Representations

What makes Jochen Schimmang's *Der schöne Vogel Phönix* so irresistible to the reader is his insistence that he has had the time of his life:

> Then this May 1968, this brief moment when everything seemed possible and perhaps everything was possible, this short moment that after all lasted for two years.[75]

For Schimmang's protagonist, the real achievement of the movement is the development of a collective identity that allowed the individual to endure the contradiction between romantic utopian vision and unyielding reality:

> The fact that they were able to deal with the contradiction between their own actions, its intentions and the reactions of the public was mainly due to the intact political identity of the Student Movement. It included the acting individuals in its politics and tactics, had the courage to admit to its above average political and moral sensitivity and the resultant isolation from the wider population without trying to deny it opportunistically. (243)

While this passage mirrors the experience of Schneider's Lenz, Timm's Ullrich Krause, Delius's Martin, and Schöfer's Viktor Bliss in that they felt isolated from the majority of the population and therefore needed to form an even closer bond with their comrades, the reader also gets a sense of the arrogance with which the activists viewed them. Schimmang's narrator characterizes the students as courageous, with an "überdurchschnittliche politische und moralische Sensibilität." Once again the affinity to the romantics is palpable, and by painting the activists in this light, the author equips them with a nobility of purpose and a tragic fate. Unsurprisingly, life after the movement is "Leidensgeschichte" (tale of suffering), the bitter realization of failure, a struggle for survival. The only comfort lies in comradeship and the faint hope that the mythical bird Phoenix will one day rise out of the ashes again:

> It is not certain that there will be a new flood. Of course, we all hope there will be, and quite a few see the beginning of a new movement when they see a glimmer somewhere. [...] But in truth we are all trying to survive the winter, and this winter can last forever. (281)

It is in short paragraphs like this that the literary construction of "1968" is at its most potent: having built up the movement as a "magic moment," everything that came after must necessarily pale in comparison. The experience of collective emancipation and liberalization, the overcoming of fear and doubt, and the glimpse of an alternative to the status quo are described in such romantic terms that they acquire infinite desirability. Their loss, in the face of sobering political and cultural reality, recalls the biblical fall from grace, the Arthurian legend, Promethean rebellion, or any other myth constructed by humans to give failure a silver lining. In this case, it is the myth of the Phoenix that will rise out of its own ashes (the device also used by Marcuse and revisited in Uwe Timm's *Rot*) that sustains the hope of disappointed activists that one day there may come another "flood" that will sweep away the unyielding "system." Yet Schimmang's narrator is realistic enough to know that the chances of this are small—not only because the "system" has absorbed the students' challenge and adapted but also because the students' rebellion was of such intensity that he cannot imagine any other group ever topping it. Having turned it into an infinitely desirable, yet at the same time near unattainable, unique moment, the writer's task is complete: he has constructed an unassailable fortress where the spirit of revolution, like Wagner's Brünhild, must wait for a hero to free her and start the cycle again. I will return to this paradigm in chapter 10—in the meantime it should have become clear that literature has the edge compared to history when it comes to harnessing myth, emotions, and imagery in order to construct "1968" at a subconscious level.

A good example of the use of imagery is Bernd Cailloux's *Das Geschäftsjahr 1968/69* (The Business Year 1968/69, 2005). The novel demonstrates that the era does not have to be portrayed exclusively in terms of its directly political significance. Instead, Cailloux resurrects the year as the time when the concrete utopia of living an "alternative" life seemed within reach of quite ordinary young people. Three friends—the unnamed first-person narrator and Andreas Büdinger, both disillusioned local reporters, and the inventor Achim Bekurz—set up a small business in a garden shed in Düsseldorf. This is a cottage industry with a difference: inspired by the young art professor Josef Beuys and his circle, they wait for an idea that will enable them to become artists themselves, ideally without too much effort. Before long they form the Muße-Gesellschaft (Leisure Society), hoping to create a kind of subversive counterculture while making a living outside the rules of the capitalist market. Bekurz is to be responsible for the technical side, while the others take care of logistics and marketing. They agree to take decisions together and to divide profits equally while supporting an increasing number of drug-hazed hangers-on.

Their first product is the "revolutionary" strobe light, which they plan to manufacture for discos and live events. It is an invention that perfectly fits the mood of the time and the alternative scene of young people eager for new kicks and experiences. The friends get their breakthrough in Hamburg's Golem disco, where the proprietor plans to cash in on the unique mix of politics, art, and lifestyle of the late sixties. The psychedelic lightshow installed by the Muße-Gesellschaft creates a euphoric effect that proves a success once Büdinger demonstrates to them the new possibilities:

> He ran through the ring in all his jerking height, as if hit by electric shocks, and twisted his gangly body, his long arms and legs, into rhythmically exact, endlessly flashing strobe-images.[76]

The dancers love the new effects; it is, the narrator comments, as if "a mental jerk had gone through everyone, dividing time into a Before and an After."[77] The owner of the strip club next door is impressed as well, but the Muße-Gesellschaft, riding high on the success of their first sale, refuses to deal with a representative of the "system" they despise.

Even at this early stage, the three friends realize that by selling their product they are selling a part of themselves. They have tripped over the stumbling block at the heart of the 68er philosophy: the realization that it is impossible to live an "authentic" life within the falsehoods of the present-day reality. They begin to understand that their dream of a countercultural enterprise in a capitalist reality is full of contradictions, for example, when the owner of the Golem tries to haggle over the agreed price. It is Büdinger, the most entrepreneurial-minded of the three, who papers over the cracks that are beginning to appear in their philosophy. He refuses to take the dream of a nonprofit organization too seriously and pragmatically sets up the Muße-Gesellschaft as a limited company. He tells the others that the flash of the strobe light stands for the start of the counterculture: "We bring a new light into the world, and with it we will change the habits of a whole generation—what more do you want?" (48). Yet the first-person narrator is not persuaded. He is aware that the hyperbole in Büdinger's statement runs counter to his own ideals, but is unable to convince his partners that he is right.

A few months after their debut, they get the opportunity to show off their product to a wider audience when they are hired to provide a massive strobe light and the swirling psychedelic images on the screens behind the performing bands at the Internationale Essener Songtage (the German equivalent of the Woodstock festival, headlining Frank Zappa and his Mothers of Invention). For all those present, the night of September 28, 1968, proves to be the pivotal moment of their lives:

> An event that would stay forever in the memory of those who were there—a fundamental experience and yet only a stolen second in the history of the world, just like the whole windy year of which it was part. Only afterwards, when we tried to give form to this era, did it become clearer that this night marked a turning point, when an avant-garde of future cultural practice broke with old norms and escaped—into lifestyles and behavior patterns that would ultimately define them and others. (66)

In passages like this, Cailloux, like Schimmang, romanticizes the moment, investing it with significance beyond the individual and the singular. He uses the strobe light as a metaphor for the consciousness-changing import of the liberation of young people who feel for an instant that their lives could be so very different, that the rules of the consumerist society need not be obeyed. But the magic moment cannot last. The Muße-Gesellschaft is in demand: theaters, artists, manufacturers, and advertising agencies beat a path to their door, bringing about the inevitable descent into commercialism. As the narrator begins his own plunge into drug addiction, he realizes that his company is doing exactly the same as his dealer: by supplying them with accessories to reach a desired state of mind, they feed and exploit the need of young people to escape reality.

Eventually, Büdinger becomes the company director, while the narrator anaesthetizes his scruples with ever-increasing amounts of drugs. To meet the costs of expansion, the company sells its strobes to the strip clubs they once abhorred, moves into "respectable" premises, and employs new people, while the narrator is edged out. Unsurprisingly, given his drug addiction, the narrator is unable to oppose Büdinger. Instead, he attempts to justify to himself his continued participation in the company during long car journeys from customer to customer. He still believes that they achieved something without, he says, the aid of "irgendwelcher studentischer Heißmacher" (some overzealous student agitators, 111). What the students were discussing in theory, he muses, the Muße-Gesellschaft had already put into practice and had thereby changed reality.

And yet the thrill has gone. The narrator is sent to open a branch in Hamburg, where he slowly recovers from his addiction and finds love with a woman who correctly sizes him up as a "hippy-businessman" (177). Encouraged by his new independence, he plans to outwit his former business partners, only to be thwarted when he contracts life-threatening hepatitis, a weakness that Büdinger exploits in order to persuade him sign over his share in the company. Years later, they meet again and laugh off their Muße-Gesellschaft as a "youthful error," sarcastically commenting that '68 had been "a grandiose, almost ingenious PR campaign, and one that cost almost nothing" (236). Yet the narrator has not given up on his ideals. He still believes that they had a unique opportunity to do "the right thing" and, even though they failed miserably, has no regrets: "After all, we came up with something useful"—the little flashing light (254).

Bernd Cailloux's novel was very positively reviewed and nominated for the German Book Prize. He was praised for conveying to the reader "the essence of '68" while refraining from jumping on the bandwagon of "68er bashing." Certainly, the author stays clear of the endless political debates without, however, entirely ignoring their significance. The student protests are always in the background, but they do not dominate the plot. Rather, Cailloux focuses on the way the era must have felt to the many people who were probably less interested in reading Karl Marx than simply having fun and freeing themselves of the austere and authoritarian norms of the postwar generation. His depiction of milieu, mood, and jargon communicates a sense of authenticity, while his imaginative use of the strobe light as a metaphor for the "spirit of '68" marks him out as a poetic and thoughtful witness to the period.

Cailloux's main achievement consists of his novel's representation of '68 as simply another financial year, with the student protests and countercultural ideals a minor irritation for business. Indeed, the manner in which everybody lines up to do deals with the subversive Muße-Gesellschaft, adapting and integrating their "revolutionary" invention into the mainstream, symbolizes what became of the cultural revolution of '68 more broadly: it was domesticated, packaged, and later sold as pop culture. The title *Geschäftsjahr* holds another meaning, however: a balance sheet on which those involved can enter the achievements of '68. For the narrator, a modern Parzival who has invested his whole identity in his ideals, there may be a small personal plus, even though he lost his health. For Büdinger, there may have been financial success, but for him as a person, the entry is empty.

"1968" under Local Anesthetics

Not all German writers have produced literary representations of "1968," and it is noticeable that those at the peak of their celebrity kept a wary distance to the revolt. A case in point is Günter Grass, who attended many debates in Berlin and shared the students' objection to the grand coalition, a chancellor with a Nazi past, and the emergency laws, as well as their revulsion over the shooting of Benno Ohnesorg and their portrayal in the Springer press, but utterly disagreed with the SDS-led radical tactics and strategy of escalation. He had been asked to remove the Kommune I when they had taken up residence in Uwe Johnson's apartment during his absence, and, together with his fellow Gruppe 47 writers, experienced the group's ignominious dismissal as "Dichter" (poets) and "Papiertiger" at their meeting in the Pulvermühle guest house and at the Frankfurt Book Fair in the autumn of 1967. As a *gebranntes Kind* (a child who had been burnt before) who had seen the Nazis' promise of a "national revolution" hoodwink the previous generation, he was naturally skeptical of the students' revolutionary fervor. Moreover, as a committed supporter of the Social Democrats and especially Willy Brandt, he believed that the radical students were endangering the fragile new parliamentary democracy in West Germany and a chance of evolutionary change at the national elections in 1969.

In a speech to members of the Sozialdemokratische Hochschulbund (SHB, the student organization of the SPD set up after the ousting of the SDS), Grass criticized the "Neoidealismus des deutschen Studentenprotestes" (neo-idealism of the German student protest) and the "Gratisproklamation der Revolution" (cost-free proclamation of the revolution) in a country that had no revolutionary base, no revolutionary tradition, and where the majority of voters leaned toward the conservatives.[78] He lambasted the students' elitist attitude and their arrogance toward the workers and prophesied that they would revert to their privileged middle-class mind-set when they left university. The student protest, he argued, was based on an irrational ideology and a rehash of German romanticism. Sarcastically, he added:

> The dead revolutionary "Che" Guevara cannot defend himself if he has to satisfy romantic yearnings as a pin-up in Germany today. (301)

In spite of this searing criticism of the German student movement, one senses that this tirade was more of a smoke screen in an effort to make the SPD, for which Grass had been writing speeches since 1961, more electable. Grass's conflicted views are evident in his novel *örtlich betäubt* (1969; *Local Anaesthetic*, 1970),[79] which received mixed reviews in Germany but was feted in the United States. Here, the protagonist Eberhard Starusch, a high-school teacher of German and history in West Berlin, discusses Germany's political past and present with his dentist during a series of complex treatments. Two of Starusch's brightest pupils, the seventeen-year-old Philipp Scherbaum and his girlfriend Vero Lewand, represent the voice of the disenchanted youth who are fed up with the country's materialistic and pragmatic direction. They side with the radical students and want to do their bit: Vero cuts the stars off the hoods of Mercedes cars, while Philipp plans to douse his dachshund Max with petrol and burn him alive in front of the Hotel Kempinski to protest against the German government's support of the Vietnam War.

Starusch is torn between his instinctive refusal of their protest, which he describes as "jugendlicher Anarchismus" (youthful anachism, 14), "Vandalismus" (vandalism, 33)" and "Sprechblasen" (speech bubbles,

45), and his secret admiration of these young people, which wants to urge them on: "Go on, do it. If nobody does anything, nothing will change" (138). In the end, though, he agrees with his dentist that the student revolution is not going to change anything. He takes Philipp to the place where he plans to set his dog alight to make him understand that he will have to live with the consequences of his actions for the rest of his life. In a passage that could be construed, with the benefit of hindsight, as an admission of Grass's own "radical" past (his SS membership at the end of World War II only came to light with the publication of his autobiographical *Beim Häuten der Zwiebel* [2006; *Peeling the Onion*, 2007]), he tells Philipp:

> Now it's your turn. But it won't make a difference. It will become a memory for you, a giant memory. You won't get over it, ever. You will always have to say: when I was seventeen, I was a perpetrator. (183)

German critics were unimpressed by the novel. Horst Krüger, writing for *Die Zeit*, argued that Grass had reduced one of the key political challenges of the day to a simple conflict between adolescents and grown-ups.[80] Marcel Reich-Ranicki, in a wide-ranging review that criticized Grass for having lost his literary bearings, added that infantilizing the Extraparliamentary Opposition was a dangerous strategy:

> Without exception, the attempts in the novel to deal with the phenomenon that is called the protest movement of young people, the New Left, or the Extra-Parliamentary Opposition, are not just silly but dangerous. The fact that Grass chooses to make two youngsters the target of his well-meaning, condescending and simplistic critique, one of them a seventeen-year-old grammar school pupil who fights against the Vietnam War and for a smokers' area at his school, is both revealing and disastrous. Grass consistently infantilizes the protest movement, and as a consequence he diminishes and trivializes it. Consequently, a very serious political phenomenon of our time becomes a somewhat comical revolt which has its roots in the pains of puberty. Grass can be sure of the applause of squares and reactionaries, even if that was not his intention.[81]

When Ralf Manheim's English translation, *Local Anesthetic*, appeared in the United States, reviewers were surprisingly enthusiastic. Anatole Broyard, writing for the *New York Times*, praised its form as being "as efficient and economical as a Volkswagen."[82] *Time* magazine went as far as putting a picture of Grass dressed as a dentist, with a dachshund reflected in his head mirror, on its title page.[83] The cover pronounced the author to be "a novelist between the generations, a man who can speak to the young." In the article itself, the anonymous reviewer argued that the author's concern about "the generation gap, the morality of revolutionary protest, the apparently helpless and surely tragic bankruptcy of liberalism" seemed "as American, and as unsettling, as the latest home-made-bomb scare."[84]

Günter Grass repeatedly returned to the German student movement, though only in passing. In *Aus dem Tagebuch einer Schnecke* (From the Diary of a Snail, 1972), he reiterates his view that humanity can only progress at a snail's pace, and in *Kopfgeburten, oder Die Deutschen sterben aus* (Headbirths, or The Germans are Dying Out, 1980), he briefly satirizes a couple of German 68ers who are deeply shaken by Rudi Dutschke's death in December 1979 but are ignoring everyday injustice while still holding on to their "all-encompassing design" for a better world.[85] In *Mein Jahrhundert* (My Century, 1999), Grass includes "1968" in a series of vignettes. His anchor for the years 1966–68 is a failed revolutionary-turned-academic who fled the action in the city to study in provincial Freiburg. The implication is that the majority of 68ers may not have been the ardent revolutionaries we are supposed to take them for. The verdict at the end is devastating when a young student tells her professor: "Von Ihnen kommt sowieso nichts mehr" (There is nothing you can offer us anymore).[86]

Surprisingly, Grass seems to have moved away from this outright condemnation of the German student movement soon after. In a dialogue with the French sociologist Pierre Bourdieu in 2002, Grass summed up his position on "1968" as follows:

> I was in the middle of all these events. The student protests were justified and necessary, and have achieved more than the spokespeople of the pseudo-revolution of 1968 would have liked to admit. The revolution did not take place, there was no basis for it, but society did change.[87]

It is interesting to note that while Grass's almost allergic antipathy to the "spokespeople of the pseudo-revolution" (i.e., Rudi Dutschke and Daniel Cohn-Bendit, as well as his fellow writers Peter Schneider and Uwe Timm) continues, he now believes that the movement had a beneficial effect on German society in the long term, specifically in challenging authoritarian behavior and unquestioning obedience, Grass's own life-long targets.

Critical Assessments

As far as the American Germanist Monika Shafi is concerned, there is a disconnect between the intensity of memorial work on the German "1968" by historians and journalists, and what she regards as a "relative dearth" of literary representations:

Within the realm of scholarly political and historical discourse, 1968 may cause both vituperation and admiration, but as a literary topic it has, with the exception of the two classics *Lenz* (1973) by Peter Schneider and *Heißer Sommer* (1974) by Uwe Timm, not been able to generate the same level of intense discussion and long lasting attention.[88]

Shafi suggests that the texts dealing with "1968" are "but a minor phenomenon" in postwar German literature, and puts this down to the movement's "ultimately narrow membership and outlook" (205) that privileges the point of view of white, male, and middle-class former activists and ignores the experiences of women and non-Germans. As such, it "undercuts the 1968ers claim to privileged access to cultural memory." Moreover, the focus on retrospection "yields a memory discourse that locks the characters into their past, a narrow social and national realm that seems to avert productive or self-empowering insights" (216).

While I would agree that the literary representations have been largely absent in public debates, that does not mean that they do not play a crucial role in the construction of "1968." I will address Shafi's point about the apparent lack of literary representations by female writers in the next chapter but want to challenge her claim that by looking backward the authors of "1968" novels and their protagonists somehow miss out on "self-empowering insights." In literary representations of the German student movement of the last fifteen years, authors have juxtaposed revolutionary characters with their older (but not necessarily wiser [see chapter 9]) selves precisely because they are interested in conveying their insights, which they believe to be as relevant today as in 1968, to a new audience. As to Shafi's assessment that these texts are only a "minor phenomenon," I would argue that cultural memory does not coalesce overnight, and that literature has a much longer half-life than scholarly and newspapers articles. In addition, she ignores the existence of a substantial body of German literature that focuses on "1968." For their *Lesebuch* (reader) accompanying the exhibition *Kurzer Sommer—lange Wirkung* at the Historisches Museum Frankfurt in 2008, the editors have selected excerpts from fifty-six texts by 50 authors (9 of them women). Given that the anthology offers only a cross section of the overall production (missing out important authors such as Jochen Schimmang, Erasmus Schöfer, or Peter Paul Zahl), one can confidently state that these texts represent more than a sideshow. In the words of the editors:

> It is the specific ability of literature to track the long-term effects and intense power of this belated "intellectual re-founding of the Federal Republic." It succeeds, beyond the biographies of individuals or generation, to trace the ambivalences of the time and follow its impulses to the periphery.[89]

Susanne Rinner, another American Germanist, has recently explored the role literary representations of "1968" play in the (re-)construction of memory. Choosing as her examples texts from the 1990s with an emphasis on noncanonic representations reflecting East German, Turkish-German, and Transatlantic experiences, she sets out to demonstrate that the literary imagination makes a unique contribution to the construction of "1968":

> My analysis of 1968 memory novels reveals a hybrid genre that represents processes of remembering and forgetting as well as the heterogeneous nature of the cultural memory of 1968. This hybrid genre makes use of additional layers of distancing and reflection.[90]

Rinner argues that fiction shapes the memories of "1968" and provides postmemories for those who did not experience the era themselves. While this is true for any fiction that is linked to historical events, she believes that the literary representations of "1968" form a unique genre due to the way they transcend space and time:

> I argue that "disrupted time" and "fragmented spaces" reveal themselves in the processes of remembering and forgetting and that these processes constitute the genre of 1968 memory novels. (13)

Rinner concludes:

> The distinction between the literary text as a simple representation of historical events and the political sphere where power and action are located is obsolete. The interpretation of the 1968 memory novels in this study supports the notion that literary texts actively engage in the recuperation as well as the recherché of the past for the aesthetic and educational benefit of the present. (147)

In marked contrast to most of the secondary literature on the German "1968" examined so far, Rinner is refreshingly upfront about her sympathies for the era:

> While I am not a 68er I am sympathetic to the goals and motivations of the 1960s Student Movement. At the heart of this study lies the conviction that utopian thinking and attempts to improve one's own living conditions and to support others in the struggle for freedom, equality, and justice are as important as ever and will never be outdated. (7)

That does not mean, though, that she is uncritical of her subject. In fact, Rinner, much like Shafi, obliquely criticizes the literary representation of "1968" for excluding a female, hybrid, or transnational perspective, and sets out to correct this apparent gap by choosing examples that do. However, the problem with aligning oneself so closely to the research agendas that have filed "writing about 1968" under the paradigms of cultural memory, gender discourse, and modes of transnational or hybrid experiences is that one is unlikely to be surprised by one's findings. Moreover, by identifying the cultural memory discourse as the main raison d'être for the literary representation of "1968," we risk losing sight of the other key aspects of these novels: their utopian aspiration, and their subversive intent.

What Is the Point of a Literary Representation of "1968"?

Almost five decades' worth of sustained literary engagement with the events and ideas, the hopes and dreams, as well as the experiences and failures of the student rebellion has produced a body of texts that defies simple categorization. These texts play a central role in the construction of "1968" as they aim to reveal the "inner monologue" of the movement, to show what was going on inside people's heads. In doing so, authors contribute to preserving its memory but are also engaged in forming public opinion about it. Insofar as they were active participants in the movement, their task becomes even more challenging, as the literary representation may be interpreted either as a continuation of the revolt by other means, or a melancholic and protracted letting-go of an important period in their lives. The sheer variety of literary approaches, interpretations, and perspectives mirror the diversity of lived experiences. The question is whether we see this collage as a random assembly of found fragments or whether we are prepared to see these texts as attempting something more than preserving the past. If we subscribe to the former, we will be able to do justice to the individual work, its unique message, form, and aesthetics. If we tend to the latter, we are bound to discern a collective endeavor with thematic, ideological, formal, and semantic affinities that represents an implied *Bedeutungszusammenhang* (nexus of meanings) that all these authors are working toward.

The early efforts to capture the essence of "1968" in literary form were attempts to continue the struggle that had been lost in the streets. They aimed to record vital experiences and keep alive an individual and collective "moment," to remember, to mourn, and to convey to the next generation what had been achieved in terms of raised consciousness (practicing what Ullrich's comrade Petersen in Uwe Timm's *Heißer Sommer* calls the "tendenziell bewußtseinsbildende Funktion der Literatur" [tendentially awareness-forming function of literature]). Just as in the autobiographical and historical accounts of "1968," though, an increasing distance to the events inserts layers of other experiences and memories, not to mention the ever-changing sociopolitical context that inevitably colors the representation. In the case of "1968," an enormous amount of effort, especially by interested politicians and journalists, has been spent on either neutralizing or appropriating the utopian and subversive elements of the movement.

By preserving the emotional memory of the movement, literary representations both complement and resist its historicization, retaining its rebellious spirit. They can also give us an insight into the psychological makeup of a generation, the seesaw of emotions between fear, exultation, and despair that is rarely conveyed in the historical accounts of the era. Of course, there is a risk that these emotions are falsified or misrepresented. Sophie Dannenberg's *Das bleiche Herz der Revolution* is a case in point here, with her depiction of 68ers as self-centered and intolerant thugs without an ounce of compassion for the feelings of others. The initial outcry following the publication of the novel wasn't so much because she criticized the 68ers but because many observers felt that by turning up the intensity of her satire to such an extent that the protagonists became obvious caricatures, she had overplayed her hand and lost the trust of her audience.

Compared to historians who can claim veracity by quoting from their sources (though, as Götz Aly has shown in *Unser Kampf*, the selection and interpretation of sources is as subjective as a fictional account), writers face an uphill battle to convince their readers of their trustworthiness. But there are some simple methods for both to create a bond. Does the milieu and tone have a sense of authenticity? Are the related emotions and experiences embedded in historical events? Do they sound contrived? There is a noticeable difference in the depiction of the Ohnesorg shooting in Uwe Timm's *Heißer Sommer* and Leander Scholz's *Rosenfest*, with the latter quickly showing up as fabricated. We face a similar dilemma when it comes to the portrayal of violence and the connection between "1968" and the RAF. On the one hand, the protagonists in 1968 cannot know how their words or actions may influence others in ten years' time. On the other hand, it is very difficult for authors to refrain from imparting a bit of hindsight (though Friedrich Christian Delius in *Amerikahaus* and Erasmus Schöfer in *Ein Frühling irrer Hoffnung* have shown that it is perfectly possible). We could of course depend on the law of averages and decide that we are likely to get to the truth if we read all the representations. However, reading fifty or a hundred novels in the hope of finding "the truth" is impractical, and the reader will normally have to rely on his or her emotional intelligence vis-à-vis a single work. But then this would be the same case with the average reader interested in the era consulting just one historical account.

The continuing production of texts that revisit "1968" can be interpreted as a stubborn reaction on the part of activists-turned-writers to come to terms with their own aging (see chapter 9) or a response to the demise of a socialist alternative to capitalism. It can also be seen as an outright challenge to the countless accounts of the era that reduce it to "sex and drugs and rock and roll" or a heap of moldy books and files in a damp cellar (one of the abiding images in Uwe Timm's *Rot*). They are like "Flaschenposten" (messages in bottles) that have been cast into the sea in the hope that someone, somewhere, might find them and respond.[91] As to the continuing attraction that "1968" holds for authors, I would draw a comparison to the literary representation of the Red Army Faction. As Julian Preece has shown in his recent study, when the original historical event provides such a rich source of myths, it offers authors "a semi-blank screen on which they project ideas, scenarios, and fantasies."[92]

On another level, the literary representations reflect a continuing and powerful need to canonize the movement as a vital part of modern German heritage. By persistently returning to the period of student unrest in the late 1960s, writers engage with a central debate about Germany's past and its meaning for the present. The act of remembering and its significance for the survival of utopian ideals that were formulated in the late 1960s is crucial for the literary representations of the German student movement. We need to remember, though, that the memory of "1968" is, for the moment, a *kommunikatives Gedächtnis* (communicative memory), in that it is still being created, debated, manipulated and challenged, and not yet a cultural memory that can be filed away. The tale spinners have learned that you can, literally, change history.

I would argue that the many literary representations of the German student movement have made an important contribution to this process: they have attempted to provide balance and reflection to the interpretations given in politics and the media. However, such literary representations of the German student movement must not be mistaken for repositories of "culture" in a traditional sense: rather, they are a repository of counterculture and therefore not an element of the affirmative, easy consensus that characterizes other memory contests. In the late 1970s, Martin Lüdke hinted at this aspect when he described the function of these texts as holding important lessons in cryostasis against a hostile environment. For German readers who have grown up in the old Federal Republic, one of the attractions of reading a novel about the German student movement is that they can recognize some part of themselves, or their parents, in it and know more about their own place in history. This may be stating the obvious, but there are specific effects to be anticipated when reading a representation of events that unite a generation in memory. As time passes, we are beginning to realize what we have lost. In recovering it, we cannot help but change its context. What we are really looking for in the literary representations of "1968" is reassurance, a promise and a moral touchstone for the present as we make the choices that determine our future.

Summary

There is no doubt that Hans Magnus Enzensberger kickstarted a process of self-examination that involved most West German writers in one form or another. His program of the *politische Alphabetisierung der Deutschen* is comparable in its vagueness and attractiveness to Rudi Dutschke's *langer Marsch durch die Institutionen* (long march through the institutions), with equally diverse reactions and impacts that are difficult to pin down. For authors like Schneider, Timm, Delius, Schöfer, Schimmang, and Cailloux, the German student movement has become "eine Art Lebensthema" (a lifelong obsession).[93] Writing about its spirit, mythicizing the "magic moment" that had been experienced and then lost, they have constructed "1968" as a precious memory, but also a utopian promise. Their message is that a different life is possible, exemplified in the lives of their protagonists. By revisiting the era again and again, they discover new layers of meaning and ensure its continuing social relevance.

A collage of texts emerges that recreates and explores a breakthrough of consciousness, a feeling of awareness of others, both in moments of joy and great sadness. Following a romantic tradition, this literature preserves moments of intense *Welterfahrung* (experience of the world), not just *Selbsterfahrung* (experience of the Self) against sobering reality. Some of these "moments" have been painted so exquisitely that they attain infinite desirability. And herein lies the subversive potential of these texts: the historical "event" is romanticized so that the reader may wish for a similar experience. The unity of thought, feeling, and action becomes reality for a moment, and as Schimmang's image of the phoenix implies, may become reality again. The literary representation of the German student movement seeks to distill the intensive experience of youth, to hold on to collective advances in consciousness, and to convey what is hardest to convey: the experience of a *konkrete Utopie* (concrete utopia).

Faced on the one hand with Hermann Peter Piwitt's dictum "Es ist Aufgabe des Schriftstellers, die Realität, nicht die Fiktion zu erfinden" (It is the writer's job to invent reality, not fiction)[94] and Che Guevara's reminder "Die Pflicht jedes Revolutionärs ist es, die Revolution zu machen" (It is each revolutionary's duty to foment revolution),[95] and on the other a writer's natural urge to spin a tale, the writers studied in this chapter have managed to do both. With their references to Greek mythology: the phoenix bird that rises out of its own ashes (Jochen Schimmang's *Der schöne Vogel Phönix*), the sad story of Skylla (Peter Schneider's *Skylla*), the labors of Sisyphus (Erasmus Schöfer's *Ein Frühling irrer Hoffnung*), the optimism of Orpheus, who attempted to free his beloved from the clutches of the underworld (Uwe Timm's *Der Freund und der Fremde*), and to Germany's national epic, the *Nibelungenlied* (Uwe Timm's *Rot*), writers have not only contributed to the construction of "1968" but have elevated it to a mythical status, thus ensuring a longer shelf life, if not immortality, for their young heroes. I will return to these writers in chapter 9 to see whether increasing age and a very different political reality have changed their stance, but for now switch focus to explore the role women played and continue to play in the construction of "1968."

5: Women of the Revolution

ONE OF THE BEST EXAMPLES of the manipulative and corrective power held by those who are constructing "1968" in Germany can be found in the way female activists were excluded and later (partly) reintroduced into the dominant narrative. While today there is general agreement that the modern German women's movement was born in 1968 (via the Aktionsrat zur Befreiung der Frau [Action Council for the Liberation of Women] and the famous Tomatenwurf [tomato-throw], see below), the 68er women who were an integral part of the movement had been progressively written out of its history, or relegated to a "schmückende Nebenrolle" (decorative minor role).[1] Over the first three decades, their role had been reduced to a collage of media images and clichés. In *1968: Ein Zeitalter wird besichtigt* (1968: An Era Revisited, 1997), for instance, the photographer Michael Ruetz includes a series of images of female activists: they are shown sitting around a table, looking glamourous, smoking, and apparently waiting for their male comrades to return from their revolution.[2] The title Ruetz gives these photographs is "Bräute der Revolte," literally *brides of the revolt*, but, in a more accurate translation of the colloquialism, *tarts of the revolt*. Only in recent years have we seen attempts to correct this blatant manipulation of the history of "1968."

Again, such phenomena are not specific to Germany (though they are more keenly felt due to continuing debates about "1968" here). In her autobiography *Promise of a Dream* (2000), Sheila Rowbotham, a noted socialist feminist theorist, talks about the way women were written out of the history of the sixties in the United Kingdom:

> Many obvious questions about the left in the sixties have simply never been asked and many areas of political and social experience have been curiously ignored. For example, amidst all the words expended on the sixties, women make very limited entrances, usually as legs in miniskirts. Radical young women suddenly arrive in the record during the seventies as the Women's Liberation movement emerges. But what of us in the sixties? Where did all those ideas about reinventing ourselves come from after all?[3]

In the following pages, I provide a counterpoint to the male-dominated and -constructed narrative of "1968," with the same categories of "faces," historicization, and literary representation I used in chapters 1, 2. and 4.

Female Faces of "1968"

We may start with the woman who was present when Benno Ohnesorg was shot on June 2, 1967. Immortalized in the ubiquitous photograph by Jürgen Henschel, hardly anyone knows her name. To Uwe Timm, she was the angel who eased his friend's parting, but in most accounts of this pivotal moment of the student movement, she is identified as an "unknown opera-goer." In fact, her name is Friederike Hausmann (née Dollinger). She was a student at the Freie Universität Berlin and had put on a black dress and smart coat to have a better chance to get close to the demonstration against the visit of the Shah of Persia.[4] The death of Ohnesorg, and his blood on her hands, radicalized her like so many others: she joined the SDS, then a Maoist splinter group, and for a number of years proselytized among factory workers in Stuttgart. Unable to become a teacher due to the Radikalenerlass (decree concerning radicals), she left Germany for Italy and started to write history books, including a monograph about Giuseppe Garibaldi.

Another female "face" of the German student movement was Ursula Seppel, an SDS member in Hamburg. Charged for protesting loudly against the *Klassenjustiz* (class justice) when a comrade appeared in a different court case, she appealed against the verdict and organized an unusual protest at the Hamburg District Court in December 1968. On a signal she and eight female comrades removed their tops and sang, bare-breasted, the "ballad of the asexual judges."[5] The action was widely reported. *Der Spiegel* described it as a "solidarity striptease," while *Die Zeit* talked about "weibliche Wunderwaffen" (female wonder weapons) and expressed itself surprised at the dominance of women in the local SDS chapter.[6]

Other female 68ers made their mark in a variety of ways. Sigrid Fronius was the first woman president of the ASTA (student union) at the Freie Universität Berlin in 1968 and went on to fight for social justice in Chile, Argentina, and Bolivia.[7] Silvia Bovenschen was a member of the SDS in Frankfurt and one of the authors of the notorious "Befreit die sozialistischen Eminenzen von ihren bürgerlichen Schwänzen" (Free the Socialist Leaders of Their Bourgeois Dicks) flyer.[8] She wrote about the jealously guarded legacy of the 68ers (see chapter 2), published one of the key studies in German language on the cultural and literary representation of the female (*Die imaginierte Weiblichkeit* [The Imagined Femininity, 1979]), and addressed the challenges of aging in her recent novel *Nur Mut* (Be Brave, 2013).[9] Irmgard Möller, the girlfriend of communard Fritz Teufel, was involved in the discussions about the use of violence at the International Vietnam Congress and went on to participate in the Knastcamp (jail camp) in Ebrach in July 1969. She was the only surviving RAF-member following the Todesnacht in Stammheim in 1977.[10] Helga

Reidemeister was an SDS member from 1966 and lived in the *Wohngemeinschaft* that Rudi Dutschke used when he was in West Berlin in the 1970s. She became a noted scriptwriter and film director. In 1988, she produced the film essay *Rudi Dutschke: Spuren*, which includes her photographs of Dutschke and Ernst Bloch in Aarhus and an interview with Bloch's widow, Karola Bloch.[11]

Beate Klarsfeld, a secretary working for the Deutsch-Französische Jugendwerk (German-French Youth Foundation) who had married a French Jew whose parents had perished in Auschwitz, publically slapped Chancellor Kurt Georg Kiesinger in the face at the CDU party congress on November 7, 1968, to signal her protest against a former Nazi as the leader of West Germany. She was arrested and sentenced to a year in prison but did not have to serve the term. In 2012, she was the presidential candidate for Die Linke, and in 2015 she and her husband Serge were awarded the Bundesverdienstkreuz (Order of Merit of the Federal Republic of Germany) for their work hunting Nazi war criminals.[12]

An ever-present "face" of the German "1968" is Gretchen Dutschke-Klotz, the American-born widow of Rudi Dutschke. Cast in the Yoko Ono role as the one who stood between her husband and the revolution, historians and journalists tend to see her as an "irritant" who diverted Dutschke's attention and energy. Their marriage was regarded as an anachronism when the original plan was to participate in Kommune I, and her own activism was belittled. But it was she who had to make decisions when he was shot, oversee his recovery, look after their children, and find a new home when one country after another refused to grant them asylum. Following her husband's death, she coedited a number of books about Dutschke and published a substantial biography (1996)[13] and his diaries (2003). In 2009 she appeared in the semidocumentary biopic *Dutschke* (dir. Stefan Krohmer).

Alice Schwarzer is universally known in Germany as one of the most outspoken feminists and editor of the magazine *Emma* (since 1977). What few Germans were aware of, until her recent autobiography,[14] is that Schwarzer started her career as a journalist in 1968. She worked for the satirical magazine *pardon* and was sent to write a feature about the emancipation of women in the SDS. Unable to locate organized women a few months after the Tomatenwurf, she set out to raise awareness of the discrimination of women in her articles, with far-reaching consequences.[15]

Perhaps the most famous female face of "1968," though, is Uschi Obermaier. A model from Bavaria, she moved to Berlin in 1968, became the girlfriend of communard Rainer Langhans, and helped turn Kommune I into a media circus. In contrast to the politics of communard Dieter Kunzelmann, she was more interested in the countercultural aspects of the movement, went out with Jimi Hendrix, Mick Jagger, and Keith Richards, briefly fronted the band Amon Düül, and escaped to Munich with Langhans when Kommune I imploded. Here, they set up the Haifisch-Kommune

(Shark Commune) which was notorious for its parties and drugs.[16] In 2007 the movie *Das wilde Leben* (The Wild Life; in English as *Eight Miles High*, 2008) depicted Obermaier's unconventional lifestyle. The voice-over goes: "She loved her life and lived her love. She lived the dream of an entire generation." At the same time, the *Bild-Zeitung* serialized her autobiography, with a number of nude images of her. Describing her variably as "68er-Ikone" (68er icon) and "Sex-Ikone" (sex icon), *Bild* used the opportunity to sensationalize the life of a party girl-turned-revolutionary: "For breakfast, I had apple juice, heroin and sex."[17]

Unsurprisingly, Obermaier's media presence and commercial nous did not find favor with former activists or the sisterhood. Sabine Reichel, herself a model and communard in the late 1960s, argued that Obermaier had been chosen by the media to represent the 68ers but was in fact the very opposite of what "1968" was about:

> The problem is that Uschi Obermaier does not represent the "68ers," nor anyone else but herself. A mixture of Bavarian original, a bit of Playboy Bunny, a dash of Domina, instinctive and anti-intellectual—why exactly should she represent a generation when she wanted to be the very opposite?[18]

Reichel wryly comments that Obermaier is the only female 68er who became famous without being on the most wanted lists for terrorist acts. In her view, the reason for Obermaier's "success" (apart from her willingness to undress for the camera) is that she can be paraded as a warning example of what might happen if people are given (or help themselves to) too much freedom:

> In addition to female terrorists and groupies, and leaving aside female artists, film makers and politicians for the moment, there were countless interesting and engaged women who actually changed or influenced things in their daily lives. Unfortunately, there are no references to her fellow sisters in Uschi's egocentric universe, even though it is thanks to them that she lived in a time when she could act with such abandon. One reason for the fuss about Uschi is likely to be that many people are uneasy about the late 60s and early 70s, and Uschi functions as a less threatening medium that allows them a voyeuristic glimpse into a forbidden world.

The Historicization of "1968" from a Female Perspective

The main reason why women have been underrepresented in the historical accounts of "1968" (apart from the male-dominated internal discussions, public demonstrations, and media debates) is the fact that at the very moment when they became visible as a distinct group, they actively split from the SDS. At the delegate conference of the left-wing student association in January 1968, about 100 active members founded the Aktionsrat zur Befreiung der Frau. They had realized that combining study, political activism—especially a few weeks before the International Vietnam Congress—and childcare presented real challenges and that their male comrades proved less than helpful when it came to sharing the burden. Out of this grew the very first antiauthoritarian *Kinderladen* which in turn would have a significant impact on the theory and practice of childcare and childrearing in Germany. On September 13, 1968, at an SDS meeting in Frankfurt, Helke Sander gave her famous *Frauenrede* (women's speech), in which she outlined their position:

> We want to try and realize models of a utopian society within the existing one. However, within this counter-society there must finally be a space for our own needs.[19]

Arguing that the revolutionary men were contradicting themselves when they preached emancipation while behaving like machos in their home lives, Sander presented the SDS leaders with an ultimatum: listen to our case or we will leave. When the men ignored her and laughed, another female activist, Sigrid Rüger, flung a tomato at Hans-Jürgen Krahl. The altercation was widely reported, and Ulrike Meinhof wasted no time in showing her solidarity in one of her opinion pieces in *konkret* (which by this time had its own contradictions when its editor Klaus Rainer Röhl introduced cover images of seminaked women to increase circulation).[20] In recognition of the new direction of the debate, the *Kursbuch* dedicated issue 17 to the topic "Frau, Familie, Gesellschaft" (woman, family, society). Karin Schrader-Klebert's essay "Die kulturelle Revolution der Frau," which introduced the *Kursbuch* readers to the idea that "women are the Negroes of all peoples," is widely regarded as a seminal text of the modern German women's movement.[21]

The underlying tension in strategy and culture—the male activists, especially in the SDS, regarded the *Frauenfrage* (the female question) as a *Nebenwiderspruch* (secondary contradiction) that would solve itself once the main battle between labor and capital had been won—created a split in the movement from which it would never recover. Thus, (male) historians of the German "1968" tend to describe the women activists and their emerging new movement in a separate chapter, as "Abgrenzungsbewegung" (movement of delineation), "Revolte in der Revolte" (revolt within the revolt), or "Entmischungsprodukt" (product of separation).[22] However, it wasn't until 2002 that a book appeared that depicted the life stories of female 68ers.

Ute Kätzel's book *Die 68erinnen* (The Female 68ers, 2002)[23] makes an important contribution to the construction of "1968." In this oral history project, the author interviewed fourteen women who describe how they joined the movement and what their personal involvement was. They then reflect upon the impact their activism had upon themselves and wider society. Kätzel observes that even those who see "1968" as a cultural revolution hardly mention its main consequence: that the role of women changed fundamentally during and in the aftermath of "1968." What becomes clear, though, is that women began to have a separate agenda to the men: while they wanted to change the world like their male comrades, they also wanted to change their own position in it, a difficult task as a new and positive female identity was yet to be established.

Kätzel claims that the visual evidence of the involvement of women in the German student movement has been removed from the press archives, though she does not give any details to support this assertion:

> Over the years [. . .] many pictures of women, which had been published around 1968 in newspapers and magazines, were separated out in the picture archives and especially the press archives. (12)

She argues that it is mainly men who control the discourse on "1968," even though women played an important part in the SDS and the wider movement by making the Federal Republic less authoritarian and patriarchal:

> They had to fight many battles and gained from them personal strength. But they also had to deal with numerous injuries which were the consequence of being champions in many ways. The female 68ers conquered new lifestyles and areas of politics that ran counter to the established gender roles of the 50s and 60s. They broke taboos, revolutionized the private sphere, and because of this had a much greater impact on changing the world than many highly theoretical speeches. (18)

Kätzel reminds us that women were at the front line of the protest, getting beaten up at demonstrations just like their male comrades, and actively involved in the intense political debates in universities and political student groups. But she also makes clear that women were less interested in blowing their own trumpet and that the revolution was not the be all and end all of their activism. The men may have started the revolution, but it was the women who went through a process of emancipation.

In her review of the book, Erica Fischer, the author of *Aimée & Jaguar* (1994) and herself a prominent feminist in Austria, argues that the achievement of the female 68ers is especially noteworthy since they lacked "positive Frauenvorbilder":

> The fierce determination with which the young women broke with their traditional roles as women and mothers is even more impressive

if one considers that most of them had been born in the Nazi-period and lacked any positive female role models.[24]

In the last fifteen years, research into the role women played in the movement has begun to redress the balance. Kristina Schulz, professor of history at the University of Bern, has published a number of essays and books on the intersection of "1968" and modern German women's movement, culminating in her thesis: "Ohne Frauen keine Revolution" (No revolution without women).[25] Belinda Davis, historian at Rutgers University, has worked on the way gender has influenced historiography in Germany,[26] while the academic journal *L'Homme: Europäische Zeitschrift für Feministische Geschichtswissenschaft* ran a special issue in 2009 "to counter the historiographical dominance of the male perspective on 68."[27] In her essay "Gespaltenes Gedächtnis?" (Split Memory?), Susanne Maurer, professor of education and gender studies at Marburg University, makes a point that is particularly pertinent to our discussion of the constructedness of "1968." She suggests that the "drifting apart" of the student movement and the women's movement had a direct impact on the way they are remembered and historicized: "Ein Auseinanderdriften von Bewegungen wirkt sich auch auf das Erinnerungs- und Überlieferungsgeschehen aus."[28] In the following section, I demonstrate that this "drifting apart" is especially visible in the literary accounts of "1968" written by women.

Writing the Revolution, from a Female Perspective

Elisabeth Plessen's novel *Mitteilung an den Adel* (Notes for the Nobility, 1976) focuses on the tense relationship between Augusta and her father, C.A., a rich landowner and member of the German nobility, who lives in Einhaus, a large estate in Schleswig Holstein. On her way to his funeral, Augusta reflects on their difficult relationship, caused by his being an ex-Nazi who smoothly morphed into a member of the conservative party after the war, as well as his staunch nationalist views and his authoritarian behavior. When she was a student in West Berlin and involved in protests, her activism was studiously ignored at home:

> When Augusta came home to visit, C.A. never asked how things were going in Berlin, and he was silent when others did. He did not want to know what a *teach-in* was, or a *lecture boycott*. He did not want to hear about demonstrations, after all, he knew all about them after reading DIE WELT, and he knew that version of things. Berlin irritated him, and he did not want to be irritated. He did not want to learn about what was going on, and when he was told, the

information was not information for him but a point of view. That saved him effort, and the topic Berlin became a taboo.[29]

The more radical his daughter becomes, the greater the confrontations at home. Plessen is an acute observer of the emotionally charged atmosphere in Einhaus, the constant sparring between father and daughter. When C.A. reads in his newspaper that his daughter has signed a resolution, he accuses her of besmirching their good family name. Trying to get through to his daughter, the father lets her read his war diary, and his daughter in turn makes an honest attempt to understand him and his actions. She even lets him visit her in her commune in West Berlin. However, the generational, political, and cultural differences have become unsurmountable, and father and daughter become estranged.

In his review, Christian Schulz-Gerstein argued that, even though the novel had been written by a real *Gräfin* (countess), Plessen's elegiac description of a dying world was in fact representative of many generational confrontations in "1968":

> How else could it be explained that, for someone who is neither a descendent of a count nor grew up in a castle nor was educated by private tutors, the consternated and indignant atmosphere of mourning is still so familiar? How else could we explain that we recognize as our own this fearful and terrifying still-life atmosphere, where parents ignore their children's questions about Hitler and the Jews, pretending not to have heard them until the children are finally muzzled and the parents complain about their sullenness, how could we take this childhood, one that denies any objection, to be our own, if this book were mainly about "notes for the nobility"?[30]

Relatively few women penned autobiographical accounts focusing on "1968," but they did have some limited exposure. Inga Buhmann's *Ich habe mir eine Geschichte geschrieben* (I Have Written My Own History, 1977) was marketed as an "autobiographisches Schlüsselbuch von großer Bedeutung" (a key autobiography of great significance) and provided a counterpart to Bernward Vesper's *Die Reise*.[31] Judith Offenbach's *Sonja: Eine Melancholie für Fortgeschrittene* (Sonja: A Melancholia for Advanced Readers, 1980) chronicled the lesbian relationship between Judith, the first person narrator, and her lover Sonja, both students at the University of Hamburg.[32] Sabine Reichel, who was so critical of Uschi Obermaier, published her autobiography *What Did You Do in the War, Daddy?* (1989) in English (she left Germany in 1975 to effect a "mental dislocation"). Like Plessen, she focused on the psychological impact of the Third Reich on the 68er generation:

A German girl in a worthless land, heir to an inescapable, unwanted legacy for which I was never prepared [. . .]. Who are you when you have no faith in your fatherland, no love for your countrymen, when your roots are chopped down to a stump without hope of regeneration because the soil is poisoned?[33]

It wasn't until the end of the last century, though, that books that focused on "1968," and were written by women, reached the attention of a broader audience and won critical and international acclaim. Significantly, it was a Turkish writer, Emine Sevgi Özdamar, whose novel *Die Brücke vom goldenen Horn*[34] (1998, *The Bridge of the Golden Horn*, 2007) was embraced by both the critics and the reading public. Combining a female and transnational perspective on "1968" in West Berlin and Istanbul, Özdamar added the spice of hybridity and showed that the ideas of the German student movement reached far beyond the campus but that the self-centered debates within the SDS ignored the reality of the working class.

The most powerful book written about "1968" written by a woman, though, is Ulrike Heider's *Keine Ruhe nach dem Sturm* (No Calm after the Storm, 2001).[35] Her female perspective allows deep insights into the spirit of the movement, where the private truly becomes political. Autobiographical but always relevant beyond the individual, Heider explains where the 68ers came from, their idealistic sense of solidarity, the experimental approach to sex borne out of repression (revisited in her book *Vögeln ist schön* [Fucking Is Beautiful, 2014]), and the complex reasons why the brightest children of the middle class in West Germany turned their backs on the values of a society that expected them to conform. Most importantly, her insider perspective comes across as honest and authentic, and her younger self as much more self-aware than many swaggering male protagonists in the literary representations of "1968."

Heider observes the meetings of the SDS in Frankfurt in the communal kitchen at the Kolbheim student residence, her initial bafflement by the sociological jargon replaced by her growing fascination with a more democratic, tolerant, and idealistic way of living. She quickly becomes aware of the different shades of political radicalism (she went on to write the study *Anarchism: Left, Right and Green* [1994]), but it is the challenge of turning theory into practice that is the real focus of the book. Often she sees her solidarity abused, but that does not weaken her determination. *Keine Ruhe nach dem Sturm* shows "1968" with all its contradictions and shortcomings, an antidote to inflated accounts yet sympathetic of those who grew up in its center. True to the title, the book continues after the demise of the student movement and encompasses the experience of Frankfurt squats where political antiauthoritarianism morphed into the alternative movement. What emerges is the portrait of an alternative "red decade" that links the individual with the collective experience. Heider is absolutely clear that the student rebellion was as much about lifestyle and attitude as it was politics:

> Their affront was not just directed at the old Nazis, the cold-war mongering of those in power in politics and business and at the imperialist war of the Americans in Vietnam, but also at the culture of the German philistine and his likes around the world: his pettiness and prudishness, his instinct to obey superiors, his performance fetish, his hatred of the weak, his willingness to report on other people, his meanness, his lies and cowardice. (58)

Laudably, her account does not leave out the darker sides and excesses of "1968"—the disintegration of the movement and the transformation of antiauthoritarians into authoritarian dogmatists, or the damage that drugs and violence would wreak on individuals. But even here the fundamental change in attitudes and the hard-won sense of solidarity make a difference:

> Even the most personal issues were interpreted politically, so that the individual neurotic no longer felt so alone and exposed to his symptoms. At last, we knew that others felt the same, and we began to understand why that was the case and the reasons behind it all. At last, we could show emotions, cry, shout or even rant and rage. (121)

Keine Ruhe nach dem Sturm received positive reviews at the time,[36] though neither from the larger papers nor, crucially, from literary scholars or historians. Given the almost hysterical levels of the debate in 2001 and the other key texts published in 2001 (Uwe Timm's *Rot*, Gerd Koenen's *Das rote Jahrzehnt*, Wolfgang Kraushaar's *Fischer in Frankfurt*), Heider's account provides a powerful counterpoint.

Summary

The construction of "1968" in Germany has seen significant changes over the last four decades, in tune with the political, social, and cultural upheavals of women's emancipation, German unification, and globalization. Female historians have corrected the male-dominated gendered discourse of "1968" to a certain extent, but there is more work to do, especially when it comes to the representation of female 68ers in the media. While some male writers like Peter Schneider or Uwe Timm continue to weave their tale of the great revolt, female writers have tended to portray the heady days of protest and emancipation as an episode in a longer struggle. Perhaps there is less reason to be nostalgic for women:

with the birth of the women's movement in 1968, which has its own historiography, literature, and media presence, women now have a separate (and more positive) legacy to identify with.[37] Even in the most elegiac accounts of "1968" written by women, there is a sense that they have moved on.

6: "1968" and the Media

APART FROM FORMER ACTIVISTS, historians, and writers, the media have the most vested interest in keeping "1968" at the forefront of public awareness in Germany. There are three main reasons for this: Firstly, the baby boom generation represents a large and educated audience with disposable income, and therefore a lucrative market for publishers and their advertisers. Secondly, many former 68ers on their march through the institutions found an influential job in the media and were therefore more likely to run stories about "1968" (Stefan Aust was editor in chief of *Der Spiegel* from 1994 to 2008; Thomas Schmid was editor in chief of *Die Welt* from 2008 to 2014; Christian Semler wrote for the *taz* until his death in 2013).[1] Last but not least, "1968" is still a reliable trigger to mobilize public opinion on issues as diverse as military engagements, education, terrorism, equality, sexuality, town planning, multiculturalism, and academic freedom. German tabloids still feed the hunger of their readers for drama and sensation with scandalous tales of free love, anarchy, and subversion, while the liberal press continues to employ "1968" to criticize its conservative competition. Both happily engaged in "68er-bashing" in recent years, but, as long as the 68ers maintain their sociocultural capital, the media grudgingly acknowledge their historic contribution and rely on them for soundbites.

In this chapter, I look at the fourth estate's continuing fascination with "1968" and then focus on the press as the most reliable indicator of how the era, its activists, and its ideas have been, and continue to be, depicted in print. I analyze the ongoing discourse on "1968" in the Springer press, the news magazine *Der Spiegel*, (and the rivalry between them) but also the publications of the Bundeszentrale für politische Bildung, a German federal government agency responsible for promoting civic education. Recognizing that the media encompasses radio, television, and the Internet, and that much of the material available in these formats is scripted, I include samples from public broadcasting channels Zweites Deutsches Fernsehen, Deutsche Welle, and Deutschlandradio. The discussion will show that the media plays a significant and often contradictory role in the construction of "1968."

The Symbiosis of the Media and "1968"

The German student movement of the late 1960s attracted enormous media attention and coincided with the proliferation of television and a concentration of the press in fewer hands. Even for those who lived through that era, their memories of "1968" are necessarily prosthetic,[2] and most often provided by the media, be it the images of the Vietnam War, the assassinations of Martin Luther King, the "Summer of Love" and Woodstock, the barricades in Paris, the Soviet tanks in Prague, the death of Benno Ohnesorg, or the shots on Rudi Dutschke. Content and message are merged in the footage of these events, but they remain ciphers until filled with a given value and meaning so that we have not only a notion but also an opinion of "1968." This is what journalists and media writers do, constantly reinterpreting the movement in the context of changing political, economic, and cultural priorities, thus creating a palimpsest with recycled images, words, sounds, tropes, biographies, and clichés.

As Wolfgang Kraushaar has demonstrated with his *Protest-Chronik* (Chronicle of Protest, 1996) of the 1950s,[3] it wasn't the case that there were no public demonstrations in Germany until the German student movement came along. The Kampf dem Atomtod (Fight against Nuclear Death) campaign and the protests against rearmament mobilized more people than the APO, but the public media, especially radio and television, hadn't developed to the point when they would regard the protests in the street as a "media event." Moreover, while the earlier protest movements were engaging people from different generations, the student movement was initiated by the young educated elite that was supposed to lead the fledgling West German democracy in the future. As such, and in the increasingly hostile political climate of the Cold War following the building of the Berlin Wall and the Cuba missile crisis, the vocal protest of a small minority against the country's political and economic order, its tainted leaders, and its traditional values became "big news." It didn't hurt that companies and manufacturers had identified the baby boom generation as a distinct and profitable target group with distinct product preferences and habits of consumption (the 68ers have, ironically, morphed into the Silver Generation—see chapter 9) or that the APO provided a *Gegenöffentlichkeit* (counterpublic) against the policy of consensus under the grand coalition, thus providing the headlines that would normally be generated by the political opposition.

The students were well aware of the paradoxical relationship they had with the press. They needed the *Massenmedien* (mass media), which they viewed as part of the manipulative system they aimed to overthrow, to gain visibility beyond the campus, while the media, which generally regarded the radical students with deep suspicion, needed the students to fill their pages and position themselves in the market. In terms of reaching a broader audience, the students were outgunned: Ulrike Meinhof's weekly column in *konkret* was no match for an editorial by Rudolf

Augstein in *Der Spiegel*, and laboriously produced flyers no match to the omnipresence of the *Bild-Zeitung*. The students also knew that access to the media meant risking the manipulation, simplification, or grotesque distortion of their message, a lesson that they had learnt the hard way in the aftermath of the shooting of Benno Ohnesorg.

The sheer number of articles, editorials, opinion pieces and dossiers, special editions, commemorative issues, and "news" items about the German "1968" printed over five decades is enormous and has at times (especially in 2001 following the revelations about Foreign Minister Joschka Fischer's militant past and in 2008 for the fortieth anniversary) reached hysterical levels.[4] The Springer group titillated its readership with the potential return of a fifth column with revolutionary intent when red–green came to power in 1998,[5] while smaller countercultural papers and publishing houses (e.g., Pflasterstrand, taz, Wagenbach, Nautilus) managed to establish a communicative network for the 68ers and their supporters (see chapter 8).

It would be no exaggeration to say that "1968" is the goose that keeps on laying golden eggs for the German media. The readers of *Der Spiegel, taz, Die Welt, Bild,* and *Die Zeit* are eager consumers of the latest revelation or update of the "where are they now?" kind, and even more excited by the antics of former 68ers who confirm their opinions of them. However, there is more to motivate the media than simple profit. Every time "1968" appears in one newspaper, rivals follow suit with their version, depending on political allegiance and editorial direction. Yet even this political jousting does not fully explain the fascination "1968" holds for the media. Right from the start, there was a strong symbiosis, a mutual dependency of movement and media. Bernd Rabehl, a former activist and close friend of Rudi Dutschke, has argued that the media ignored the serious questions the students were asking but engaged with the spectacle element of the movement, thus creating a "zweite Realität":

> The student revolt had become a media revolt, and this second reality often triumphed over actual reality and has shaped memories to the present day. In it, the situational dominates: demonstrations suggest rebellion, unrest, revolution. The media interpreted, distorted and falsified, they created a new reality which either upheld the values of the Cold War or aestheticized and personified the movement, reduced it to its symbols and events and hijacked it for the marketing of youth cultures. Education and critical assessment were the exception. Even the media of the opposition could rarely extricate themselves from these alternatives; often they were mirror images of the confrontation or the cult of youth.[6]

Monika Shafi, on the other hand, maintains that the essential message the students wanted to convey did get through:

> Despite media manipulation, the images disseminated into German society were potent primarily because of the intensity of the message that fueled them, and not because of how these images were presented by the German media.[7]

Obviously, we would be able to find plenty of evidence for both views. The media, afforded a special and privileged status by the German constitution following the disaster of the *Gleichschaltung* (enforced conformity) during the Third Reich, constantly evolves and struggles with often conflicting imperatives to inform and entertain, to warn but also to reassure, to question and to synthesize. The power of the media and its ability to manipulate are perhaps better understood today because of "1968," but the risks remain real. Media coverage has become the key criterion for judging the success of protest movements. In the case of "1968," the media also acts as an agent of memory work, though many journalists would deny that this is what they are doing.[8] Increasingly, though, 68ers and their chroniclers profess to be fed up with the endless recycling of 68er stories in the media. Hans Magnus Enzensberger famously talked about the "Misthaufen der Medien" (dung heap of the media)[9] under which the experiences of "1968" lie buried. Klaus Hartung described the "erinnerungsgeilen Medien" (media randy for memory) as "nervötend und widerwärtig" (tedious and disgusting),[10] and Quinn Slobodian recently wrote that "the grooves of the [68er] narrative in Germany are worn smooth through repetition in print journalism, memoirs of former activists, television documentaries, and feature films."[11] Ironically, that does not stop historians, writers, and journalists from revisiting the era, often with the active encouragement of the media.

"1968" as a *Medieninszenierung*

Kathrin Fahlenbrach, professor of media studies at the University of Hamburg, has charted the complex relationship between "1968" and the media in several publications. In her first monograph on the subject, she interprets the student protests as theatrical productions with a dynamic visual language.[12] She argues that the media then dramatized these "Inszenierungen" (stage productions)[13] further, which in turn convinced the activists to adapt their protests to the requirements of the media in order to bring their objectives to a broader audience. The students saw their actions justified and amplified in the media reflection, at the price of ceding control over their message. A good example of this process would be the focus of the media on "opinion leaders" and their insatiable appetite for celebrities, which contradicted the intentions of the "antiauthoritarian" movement. Fahlenbrach points out that the students initially accepted this drawback and strategically used the mass media to reach their own supporters but also the broader public (176). For example, the SDS arranged for Rudi Dutschke to speak to the press (e.g., *Der Spiegel* interview "Wir fordern die Enteignung Axel Springers") and on television (e.g., the interview with Günter Gaus on December 3, 1967). The Kommune I believed it could satirize the media (e.g., by exposing the tabloids' hysterical bias against students with its "pudding assassination" of US Vice-President Hubert Humphrey in early April 1967) but soon found that the media, especially the Springer press but also *Stern* magazine, could turn public opinion against them. Fahlenbrach concludes that the media "normalized" limited acts of lawbreaking through repetition and "standardized" the image of "1968" (222).

Elsewhere, Fahlenbrach argued that the German student movement encountered a "medienhistorische Schwellensituation" (media-historical threshold situation)[14] with the transition from print to television. Both media were forced to adapt their modes of reporting in favor of visual and emotional criteria, which in turn influenced the way the student movement organized and choreographed its protests. An "expressiver Proteststil" (expressive style of protest) was created, which indicated social demarcation lines, helped to polarize and mobilize protesters, and afforded them the illusion of a "Kollektivkörper" (collective body).[15] On occasion of the fortieth anniversary of "1968," Fahlenbrach described the German student movement as a key media event in German history but observed that its celebration itself had become a ritual, reflecting the continuing interest in the year due to its emotional charge, but also the media's attempt to own and define the event.[16]

In her most recent publication,[17] Fahlenbrach and her colleagues have broadened their scope to research the interrelation between mass media and protest movements more generally. Since the late 1960s, activists and the media are well aware that protest actions attract the attention of readers and viewers because of their dramatic character. By covering the protest events, the media act as a "social center" but also acknowledge an alignment of purpose: they both need public attention. While the protesters initially focus on their message and form of protest, the media have the power to frame this protest: the photographer can select which part of the actions to record, the journalist can choose how to contextualize and interpret the actions, and the editor decides which elements of the story to cover and how to present them. In this way, social phenomena are constructed by the media, and readers, listeners, or viewers are influenced in their interpretation of the events. While moderate movements will have no problem aligning themselves to liberal media, radical movements have a much harder task in getting their message across. Fahlenbrach therefore sees "1968" as primarily a media construct:

While the "mythological" value of 1968 and its effects, especially in terms of cultural change, are, in the collective memory of most western societies, intrinsically tied to the mass media, the Student Movement was, at the same time, the first movement that at some given moment lost control of its public image. In the end, and even today, the media dominated the public understanding of their goals, their motives, and even their collective identities. Thus, 1968 first demonstrated the non-intended and paradoxical effects that social movements in Western societies encountered in their communication with the mass media. (8–9)

In order to test this hypothesis, I will now look at the way the Springer press and *Der Spiegel* have engaged, and continue to engage, with the activists, ideas, and events of the German student movement over the last five decades.

"1968" and the Springer Group

The Springer newspapers and the rebelling students were bound to clash. Axel Springer had built up a considerable market position in West Germany before he expanded into West Berlin by taking over the Ullstein Verlag in 1959 and with it the *Berliner Morgenpost* and the *Berliner Zeitung* (BZ). Together with his tabloid *Bild* and the daily newspaper *Die Welt*, he had a market share of 65–68 percent in West Berlin in 1967. With a strict anticommunist and pro-American stance, the Springer newspapers were highly critical of the students' protests against the Vietnam War, particularly in West Berlin, which, due to its unique geopolitical position, was dependent on the US presence to survive. Following the shooting of Benno Ohnesorg, Springer newspapers accused the students of being responsible for the death of one of their own. Even when it was clear that a policeman had shot an innocent student in the back of the head, the *Berliner Zeitung* commented: "Wer Terror produziert, muß Härte in Kauf nehmen" (If you produce terror, you can expect a firm response).[18] The students fought back: In an interview with *Der Spiegel*, Rudi Dutschke demanded the expropriation of Axel Springer, citing the West Berlin constitution, which made provision for expropriation if private ownership was used to the detriment of the people.[19] The conflict escalated; students were regularly portrayed as long-haired, lazy, dangerous, and controlled by the GDR, and the cartoons depicting them in the Springer papers confirmed this image. The *Berliner Extra Dienst*, a small left-wing newspaper designed to counter the might of the Springer papers and financially supported by *Der Spiegel* editor Rudolf Augstein, wrote sarcastically:

The Springer-congregation—several incidents in West Berlin in recent months have demonstrated this—does not stand idly by when the students produce "terror": if they cause terror, "they have to expect a firm response." But these radical rowdies are tough: rough muscle types, armed with clubs, hairy like apes and covered in bandages. They resemble intellectual gorillas, and the student union of the Freie Universität could cast a number of gangster-film series with them. At least that is the image created by West Berlin's busiest Springer-cartoonist when he "portrays" these terrorists with their sub-human faces. Hans-Joachim Stenzel, who prefers his three-letter moniker, knows how to unmask the Dahlem-Mafia with his quick pen.[20]

But it wasn't the fact that they had become the target of the Springer papers that made students target the Springer press in response. In their view, Springer was symptomatic of the way the Federal Republic was controlled by unelected elites that had enormous power over public opinion, much like the media tycoon Alfred Hugenberg in the Weimar Republic who had helped Hitler to come to power. With his near monopoly in West Berlin and his staunch support of the American war in Vietnam, to the radical students of the SDS Springer represented all that was wrong with the West German system, and they set about to topple him. Peter Schneider was tasked to organize the anti-Springer campaign, which would culminate in a tribunal that was intended, like the unofficial War Crimes Tribunal on Vietnam organized by Bertrand Russell, which was taking place that same year, to publicly shame the publisher and educate the public about the manipulative practices of his newspapers. While the tribunal was more of a damp squib when a number of high profile supporters from the liberal press withdrew,[21] Schneider summed up the students' criticism of Springer in a polemical article in *konkret*. Demonstrating the rhetorical skills he had honed on campus, he argued that Springer was hoodwinking the masses by telling them that the interests of those in power were the same as theirs:

> When we talk about the manipulative instrument that is the Springer Press, we talk about the press for the masses. And when we talk about fraud, then we talk about those who have been defrauded of their interests. [...] And when we fight against Springer's press for the masses, then we do not fight it because of its biased reporting or because it evokes emotions, but because its reporting is biased towards the interests of those in power, instead of the interests of the masses.[22]

Following the attempted assassination of Rudi Dutschke on April 11, 1968, the rage of the students was immediately channeled against the

Springer papers, even though the assassin Josef Bachmann had got the idea from the vitriolic headlines of the far-right *Deutsche National-Zeitung* ("Stop Dutschke Now! Otherwise There Will Be Civil War").[23] Over the Easter weekend following the assassination attempt, the Springer headquarter in West Berlin and branches in Hamburg, Munich, and even abroad were attacked, with protesters setting fire to delivery vans and papers.

For 68ers, it was and remains an article of faith that Axel Springer and his papers were responsible for the attack on their figurehead. To them, Springer represented the past, an unyielding, staunchly anticommunist cold-war thinking, the fake hypocritical moralizing tone of the parent generation, and the capitalist "system" of control. The East German songwriter Wolf Biermann summed up their feelings in his song "Drei Kugeln auf Rudi Dutschke":

> Die Kugel Nummer Eins kam
> aus Springers Zeitungswald
> Ihr habt dem Mann die Groschen
> Auch noch dafür bezahlt
> Ach Deutschland, deine Mörder![24]
>
> [Bullet number one came
> out of the Springer stable
> and you even paid the man
> the dime for the deed
> O Germany, your murderers!]

The animosity between the 68ers and the Springer group has continued until the present day. A tiny minority chose violent means (a "Kommando 2. Juni" (Command June 2) of the RAF planted five bombs at the Springer branch in Hamburg on May 19, 1972, and in 1975 Axel Springer's chalet in Gstaad, Switzerland, was set on fire),[25] but the battle was enthusiastically kept alive in the press by both sides. From the left, *Bild's* practices of distorting the truth and inciting prejudices were lambasted by German writers Heinrich Böll and Günter Wallraff,[26] while the Springer papers missed no opportunity to tarnish the 68ers and their legacy. In 1997, for example, the conservative political scientist Hans-Peter Schwarz wrote an op-ed piece for *Die Welt* that sounded as if it had been written three decades earlier. Schwarz argued that "1968" had resembled an "Erweckungsbewegung" (revivalist movement), dominated by "unoriginelle Maulwerksburschen" (unoriginal foul-mouthed guys) and "wortgewaltige Radikalinskis" (word-strong radical rowdies) who had only belatedly returned to the "Inseln des gesunden Menschenverstandes" (islands of common sense).[27]

Behind the scenes, though, change was in the air. Mathias Döpfner, CEO of the Axel Springer media group since 2002, was keen to return the company to the middle ground and greater profitability. This included freeing the name Springer from toxic associations. In June 2006, *Der Spiegel* documented a debate between Döpfner and Nobel laureate Günter Grass.[28] Grass had not given any interviews to a Springer paper for almost forty years following a smear campaign against his friend Heinrich Böll and himself. The wide-ranging discussion covered Islamic fundamentalism and Germany's relationship with the United States, but the surprising element was their frank exchange about the role the Springer papers had played during the German student movement, and the failures and achievements of "1968." Grass criticized the continuing power of the *Bild-Zeitung*, which in his view appealed to the lowest human instincts, but conceded that the "Hassgesänge" (songs of hatred, 43) in 1967 and 1968 had come from the students as well as from the Springer papers. Döpfner accepted that there had been a "Bunker- and Barrikadenmentalität" (the mentality of the bunker and the barricade, 46) in his house at the time and promised a "selbstkritische Revision." When asked what would remain of "1968," Döpfner responded:

> In hindsight, Axel Springer was right on most counts. [. . .] However, the other side had the more successful campaign. After all, it had a stronger impact on the perception of reality than anything that the papers from the Springer publishing house were propagating at the time. (47)

It is worth analyzing this statement in some detail. Döpfner claims that Springer's strong stance against the student revolt was the right one at the time, but that the anti-Springer campaign had been more effective in the long run by inculcating in the population a "perception of reality," in other words: anything but the truth. This suggests that the public belief that Springer had crossed the line in attacking the students had led to a lasting and deep-seated trauma among the journalists of the Springer group (or the realization that the confrontation had damaged its reputation and balance sheet) but also a mindset that doesn't really acknowledge that they had done anything wrong. This is confirmed by Döpfner's remark that while he was willing to conduct a "selbstkritische Revision" of his company's conduct, he had not seen any willingness on the part of the 68ers and their supporters for an equally self-critical debate about "die inhaltlichen Verirrungen der 68er-Bewegung" (the ideological confusions of the 68er movement, 50).

Döpfner's next move was to establish a former 68er as editor in chief of *Die Welt* in November 2006. Thomas Schmid joined the SDS in 1968 and was a member of the radical group Revolutionärer Kampf with Daniel Cohn-Bendit and Joschka Fischer but had gradually moved away from his radical positions. He had worked under Döpfner at various papers in the 1990s and relished the opportunity to reestablish *Die Welt* as a paper that mattered. *Die Welt* readers didn't have to wait long to notice a difference in their paper's position on "1968." In December 2007, Schmid wrote a thoughtful essay that signaled the new approach.[29]

In an attempt to appease the paper's traditional readers while reaching out to a new audience, which might view it with some reservation due to its toxic reputation when it comes to "1968," Schmid offered what looked like a compromise: the Federal Republic had been "revolutionary" right from the start, in that it was the German's first serious bid to overcome its "Traditionen der autoritär-romantischen, quasireligiösen Staatlichkeit" (traditions of authoritarian-romantic, quasi-religious statehood).[30] But since this revolutionary break had happened silently, without much fuss, it had not been properly appreciated by the next generation, which rebelled against "das Unausgesprochene" (what remained unsaid),[31] the lack of overt enthusiasm for the radical newness the young republic represented. Schmid pointedly identified himself as a 68er and admitted to a Faustian sense of dual identity:

> Out of high spirits grew hatred, out of critical attitudes arrogance, and out of a republican and constructive world view a destructive one, in the guise of socialism. We young people who didn't really know much about anything seriously believed that this first successful German society in human memory was rotten to the core and doomed to fail. In a gesture of limitless (though groundless) self-assurance, we believed that the non-seller socialism—which had long proven its criminal character—was the remedy for the putative restorative society that could no longer be reformed from within.[32]

He explained this "rhetoric of negation" with an unconscious and unacknowledged continuity between the 68ers and their parents, thus solving the dilemma how to reconcile the generations. As far as the myth of "1968" as a second founding of the Federal Republic was concerned, Schmid rejected it completely. While his generation may have had a small part in the further democratization of the country, the real story should be the fact that West Germany's young democracy had absorbed and overcome the challenge:

> In reality, the Republic continued on its course unperturbed: more democracy, less authoritarianism, more West, more representative democracy, more complexity, more internationality, more empathy. And the few good ideas that "1968" has contributed: well, they have quietly entered state and society.

Obviously, a single editorial was not likely to change perceptions overnight, and rival newspapers continued to be wary of the conciliatory messages from Springer papers.[33]

The Struggle Continues

The fortieth anniversary of "1968" would have offered a good opportunity to bury the hatchet, but it was not to be. Instead, former and present Springer writers went on the offensive with a number of publications designed to challenge what they perceived to be the dominant narrative of the German student movement. In *Berlin 1968: Eine andere Perspektive* (Berlin 1968: Another Perspective, 2008), retired journalist Michael Müller, a former correspondent for higher education at the *Berliner Morgenpost* in West Berlin, recounts the events surrounding June 2, 1967, as he witnessed them.[34] He does not ask why the students were so angry with Springer, but just states that they wanted to create a "Gegenöffentlichkeit" to counter misleading and inaccurate reports in the media (from which Müller distances himself). The resultant confrontation, he argues, drove the majority of peaceful students into the arms of a radical minority, while "sugar daddies" like Rudolf Augstein (editor of *Der Spiegel*) and Gerd Bucerius (editor of *Die Zeit*) supported the anti-Springer line to harm their competitor. He feels that he and his fellow Springer colleagues were simply saying what the majority felt, and that Springer had been identified as a convenient target by the SDS to give their supporters a concrete enemy:

> Why do I recount all this? Because I am convinced that the campaign that was unleashed against the publisher Axel Springer in 1967 and 1968 was not just a reaction to the—hardly uniform—position of his papers on the rebellious students and their utopian objectives. The protest movement needed the publisher as an enemy, to rail against and to offer its followers a target. If Springer hadn't existed as a target, then the initiators of the rebellion would have had to invent him. Obviously, not every Springer-journalist had the necessary sensitivity in those days. But I never met anyone who had jumped into the trenches and demonized their critics to such an extent as they did with Springer. (164)

Müller casts himself in the role of the "honest reporter" who writes as he sees. Yet what he sees is filtered through his ideological lens. Unsparingly, for him it was the GDR who had infiltrated the SDS and started the anti-Springer campaign, and the students' view of Axel Springer was therefore based entirely on GDR propaganda. His portrait of Rudi Dutschke, whom he witnessed at the International Vietnam Congress, is equally determined by this point of view:

> He had got himself into a dream world, to such an extent that everyday reality was an irritation. [. . .] For him, the congress had global significance, and he saw himself as the prophet of a global revolution. (195)

The journalist Sven Felix Kellerhoff has been writing for the Springer press since 1993 and has worked as senior editor for the *Berliner Morgenpost* and *Die Welt* since 2003. His essay "1968 und die Medien" (1968 and the Media, 2008) explores the way the German student movement has been inscribed in the German collective memory by former activists and the "liberal" press.[35] Kellerhoff starts from the premise that "1968" is "ein widerlegter Mythos," a myth that has been shown to be false, and yet is still believed by many people. Like Schwarz and Müller, he argues that those who believe in the myth are blanking out reality in order to glorify the era. History is highly flexible in this regard, he believes, as it is mediated through mass media:

> The past is the reality of former times, history on the other hand the idea that a society has of its own past—generally mediated by the media. (105)

Kellerhoff sets out to demonstrate how the media constructed the myth of "1968." To a certain extent, he explains, it is the images of the revolt, for example the student holding a wooden cross who is hit by a water cannon, that have fed the myth. But there is also the broader imaginary of the movement, the widespread interpretation of "1968" as an "Umgründung der Republik" (refounding of the Republic, 87), a movement fought by Springer's "Medienhetze" (incitement, 87). According to Kellerhoff, these myths have been comprehensively disproved, but they linger in the public consciousness and can still cause harm. He suggests that historians generally lack the necessary media skills to see through the manipulation of the liberal press and offers as remedy his interpretation of the way "1968" has been mythologized. His first point is that there would not have been a revolt without resonance. By responding to the antics of the Kommune I, the media had given undue attention to the antics of half a dozen troublemakers while playing down their criminal intent (the "Pudding-Attentat" (Pudding Attack) and the flyer "Burn warehouse burn") and the damage they inflicted on the reputation of the city. Kellerhoff denies that the Springer papers overreacted: their articles about potential terrorist acts by the commune were "typische Verdachtsberichterstattung" (typical reporting on suspicions, 94). His second point is that one cannot have a battle without an enemy. Focusing on the anti-Springer campaign, he argues that while the Springer group had a large market share in West Berlin, consumers were entirely free to choose alternative papers or get their news from the public service broadcasters. In a revealing sentence, Kellerhoff repeats the old accusation that the campaign had been orchestrated by the GDR: "Bisher konnte nicht nachgewiesen werden, dass die West-Berliner Kampagne 'Enteignet Springer' ab 1967 direkt aus Ost-Berlin gesteuert wurde" (So far, it could not be proven that the West Berlin campaign "expropriate Springer" was controlled by East Berlin, 100). He admits that Springer journalists may have crossed the line themselves but argues that this was understandable given the provocation by the students:

> Obviously, within the various Springer papers there were attacks on the protesting students that came close to crossing the line of journalistic seriousness. There were gaffes, for example cartoons that showed demonstrators as long-haired apes, and aggressive headlines like "Stop the Terror of these Red Youngsters now." In response to the slogan "Expropriate Springer!" the papers responded in kind. But, given the overall amount of reporting, the articles about the protest movement represent only a small, and at times marginal, amount. (101–2)

Kellerhoff characterizes the student rebellion as a protest of a small minority, which should not be regarded as speaking for the young generation in general. While twelve thousand students marched at the end of the Vietnam Congress, ninety thousand West Berliners came to the counterdemonstration (city employees were given the afternoon off to attend this collective show of disgust with the policies and behavior of the students, a feeling that the Springer papers shared wholeheartedly). Moreover, Kellerhoff points out approvingly, the Berliner Zeitung had commented that a placard with the slogan "Dutschke Volksfeind Nummer 1" (Dutschke Public Enemy No. 1) had been "ein Schönheitsfleck" (a blot on an otherwise clean slate, 103).

His third point is that the movement could only have been "transfigured" into a positive and important historical moment by hiding or ignoring significant inconvenient and unsavory truths. Just as the public image of the Third Reich had seen paradigmatic changes (where an initial silence had been replaced by a focus on the perpetrators and victims, and then a focus on the suffering of the Germans), readers should expect similar seismic changes in the perception of "1968." While publications like Götz Aly's *Unser Kampf* and the articles by Thomas Schmid, new editor in chief of *Die Welt*, had created the odd "Riss im glattpolierten Geschichtsbild" (crack in the polished historical image, 105), they had not yet destroyed the myth of "1968," which would remain the task of future media historians.

Also in 2008, Hans-Peter Schwarz presented his biography of Axel Springer, in which the confrontation between students and the media tycoon plays a central role.[36] Compared to his op-ed piece in *Die Welt* in 1997, Schwarz tones down his rhetoric considerably. In the chapter "Im Roten Jahrzehnt" (In the Red Decade), Schwarz explores the reasons why the students attacked Springer (accepting former Nazis in positions of power; supporting the US actions in Vietnam; supporting the exploitation of the Third World; legitimizing the brutal police actions against student protesters), but also the psychological impact of the anti-Springer campaign on the publisher, which turned him, seemingly overnight, from a "Götterliebling" (favorite of the gods, 479) into a public menace. The attempted assassination of Rudi Dutschke had been a disaster for the Springer empire, and the tycoon himself never really recovered from the public condemnations and accusations, making him conclude that Germany had become a madhouse (470).

On July 2, 2009, Reinhard Mohr announced in *Der Spiegel* that Springer CEO Döpfner and *Welt* editor in chief Schmid were planning a "rematch" of the "Springer tribunal," and had invited, inter alia, Daniel Cohn-Bendit, Christian Semler, and Peter Schneider.[37] The intention, according to Döpfner, was to better understand the past. The Springer group had admitted that it had made mistakes in those days; now it was the turn of the 68ers. On August 22, 2009, however, *Der Spiegel* reported that the event was not going to take place after all. According to the report, Döpfner had expressed himself disappointed that the former student activists had rejected the opportunity to reflect on their past.[38] In the aftermath of this nonevent, Thomas Schmid and Peter Schneider engaged in an acrimonious exchange. Schmid accused Schneider and his former comrades of refusing to admit that they may have been wrong and only engaging in a debate when it was clear from the outset that only the Springer papers were to blame for the poisoning of the atmosphere in 1968:

> The collective of nay-sayers that is formed here is pathetic. And self-righteous. They have refused to talk! That is truly authoritarian. It is a poor show when former anti-Springer activists, four decades after 1968, still hold on to the old confrontational way of thinking. It's a really sad story.[39]

Predictably, the accused hit back with a collective statement that questioned Döpfner's and Schmid's motives.[40] A week later, Schneider published an article in the *Frankfurter Rundschau* arguing that their media critique had been essentially correct in 1967 and that Springer papers were continuing to manipulate public opinion, though now in a more sophisticated way. He did concede, though, that the concentration process of the media had developed differently to what he and his comrades had expected at the time:

> The manipulative power of the consciousness-industry [Bewusstseinsindustrie] has developed in such a way that its manifestations are hardly registered any more. The biggest danger for independent thought and public opinion formation now emanates from the increasing process of concentration of the media. This however does not develop as straight-forwardly as imagined by the 68ers.[41]

Opening the Archive

Döpfner's next move in the quest for the rehabilitation of his media empire was the announcement in January 2010 that the Springer group was making available online almost six thousand articles, editorials, and readers' letters published in *Berliner Morgenpost*, *Bild* Berlin, *B.Z.*, *Die Welt* Berlin, *Hamburger Abendblatt*, *Welt am Sonntag*, and *Bild am Sonntag* between 1966 and 1968 that referred to the German student movement. In his editorial, Döpfner wrote that knowing what really happened had always been the driving force of journalism and the humanities, and that the *Medienarchiv68* was intended to encourage a new and unbiased look at the way the Springer papers had reported on the 68er movement.[42] Citing the 2009 revelation that the policeman who shot Benno Ohnesorg had been working for the Stasi, he stressed that it was important that "independent academics" (as opposed to former 68ers) revisit the positioning of the Springer papers at the time. As far as he was concerned, he felt that the *Medienarchiv68* would lead to a more differentiated view:

> The thesis that the Axel Springer publishing house was a centrally controlled opinion-forming machine intent on stopping the student movement does, however, not stand up.

An unbiased observer, Döpfner continued, would realize that the same papers who had run headlines like "Stoppt den Terror der Jung-Roten jetzt" (Stop the Terror of the Youngs Reds Now, *Bild* Berlin, Februar 7, 1968) or "Wer Terror produziert, muss Härte in Kauf nehmen" (Those Who Terrorize Others Shouldn't Be Surprised by a Firm Response, *B.Z.*, June 3, 1967) had also printed "Es ist ein Unding, einen Dutschke zum 'Volksfeind Nr. 1' stempeln zu wollen" (It Is Nonsense to Declare Dutschke Public Enemy No. 1, *B.Z.*, February 22, 1968) and "Millionen bangen mit" (Millions Wait Anxiously, *Bild* Berlin, April 13, 1968, following the shots on Rudi Dutschke).[43] The long established negative views of the Springer papers were thus nothing more than the result of East German propaganda and Stasi disinformation. Reiterating that Springer was very interested in a debate in which the results were not predetermined, he invited a new generation of readers to see for themselves.

Unsurprisingly, the move created a lot of attention.[44] Georg Altrogge, chief editor of the media portal *Meedia*, observed that it was understandable that the Springer group wanted to set the record straight but equally that the 68ers were reluctant to revisit the past in order to exculpate Springer.[45] Sven Felix Kellerhoff wrote in *Die Welt* that the *Medienarchiv68* finally allowed anyone to test the truth of the widely held "Vorurteile" (prejudices) that Springer papers had hounded the students and were responsible for the escalation of violence in 1967/68.[46] Kellerhoff acknowledged that some headlines had crossed the line, and pointed out that Döpfner had apologized for these. These included "eine mittlere dreistellige Zahl von Texten, die [...] gegen publizistische Maßstäbe verstießen" (a three-figure number of texts that [...] breached publishing standards), and especially a cartoon by Hans-Joachim Stenzel that had compared the student protesters to the Nazis.[47] Steffen Grimberg of the *taz* ironically compared the opening of the archive with a sortie from a wagon circle in a desperate attempt to win the "Kulturkampf" between Springer and the 68ers.[48] Jan-Philipp Hein, writing in the *Kölner Stadt-Anzeiger*, noted that only the Springer group was interested in a "Korrektur des Geschichtsbildes" (a correction of the historic image), and that it was doubtful whether anyone outside the media industry would take much notice.[49]

The *Medienarchiv68* was also the topic of two lengthy radio features by Deutschlandradio, Germany's newly formed national radio channel that incorporates the old broadcasting houses Deutschlandfunk (Cologne), the former RIAS Berlin, and the East German Deutschlandradio Kultur (Berlin). In the first program, written by Michael Meyer and broadcast on January 18, 2010,[50] representatives of both "sides," including Tilmann Fichter, Gerd Langguth, Thomas Schmid, and Peter Schneider, gave their assessment of the initiative. Given the entrenched positions, it was left to Manfred Bissinger, a journalist who had worked for the magazine *Stern* in 1967/1968 and acted as go-between for *Der Spiegel*, *Die Zeit*, as well as the organizers of the anti-Springer campaign, to provide some perspective:

> They waged war against each other, and in this war or struggle, whatever you want to call it, things happened, transgressions, which one would rather not know about today. As such, it is right if they work through and come to terms with their past, and finally draw a line under it.

The second program, written by Wolf-Sören Treusch and broadcast on April 8, 2010,[51] explored whether Döpfner's initiative had in fact changed the image of the Springer-Verlag. Thomas Schmid was optimistic, arguing that by returning to the archives, it had been possible, for example, to determine that the slogan "Rudi Dutschke Staatsfeind Nr.1" (Public Enemy No. 1) had not been a Springer headline (the paper had printed a photograph of demonstrators holding up a banner with these words but argued in the text that demonizing Dutschke was not the way forward). Peter Schneider, on the other hand, maintained that the invitation for a second "Springer tribunal" was a ruse, with the intention to rewrite history. Jochen Staadt, coauthor of *Feind-Bild Springer: Ein Verlag und seine Gegner* (Springer the Bogeyman: A Publishing House and Its Opponents, 2009)[52] interpreted the continuing disagreements between Schmid and Schneider as a sustained "Familienkrach":

> This is really what you call a family argument. Once you were close within a family, then everyone goes their own way, and now we all come back for a family celebration and tell each other what we always wanted to say. That's probably a friendship and enmity for life, and it will never end.

Treusch concluded that Döpfner and Schmid's initiative was part of the continuing "Kampf um die Deutungshoheit," the contest over who controlled the interpretation of "1968" that had begun with the debate over its impact on (West) Germany's democratic culture, then focused on the 68ers' flirtation with violence, and had now turned to the role of the Springer papers during the revolt. I would add that the *Medienarchiv68*, in spite of its obvious agenda to reconstruct history and improve public opinion of the Springer group, was a significant step toward creating a "public sphere," where differences can be openly debated.

"1968" and *Der Spiegel*—A Never-Ending Story

The German weekly news magazine *Der Spiegel* has a proud history of investigative journalism (e.g., the "Spiegel-Affäre" of 1962 which briefly landed publisher Rudolf Augstein and *Spiegel* journalist Conrad Ahlers in prison under suspicion of treason and led to the resignation of Defense Minister Franz Josef Strauss).[53] Augstein had long challenged the growing market share of the Springer papers, especially in West Berlin. In a two-page editorial in 1966, he criticized the tycoon for presiding over a media empire that had been allowed to grow unchecked and was systematically manipulating the news as well as undermining West Germany's fragile democracy:

> No single citizen, be he the richest or most powerful, can flourish to the detriment of the common good, without the general public defending itself. A man whose existence is incompatible with the democratic order either challenges the democratic government, or he unmasks the democratic government as non-existent.[54]

A year later, Axel Springer's photograph was on the title page of the magazine (with the title "Gefahr für Deutschlands Zeitungen" [Danger for Germany's Newspapers]), and Augstein reflected in another editorial whether it would not be better to expropriate the media tycoon.[55] While he claimed to rule out a support for the student demand to dismantle Springer's newspaper empire, Augstein nevertheless showed sympathy for the way they had been treated by the Springer press. This sympathy turned into a modest financial support for the anti-Springer campaign but also, crucially, an increased interest of *Der Spiegel* in the students' agenda. The covers of the magazine, which feature a single topic every week, are a fairly accurate barometer of the key issues in (West) German political debate, and in 1967 students and their issues featured five times: "Die aufsässigen Studenten von Berlin" (Berlin's Rebellious Students, 24/1967), "Was denken die Studenten?" (What Do the Students Think?, 26/1967), "Gefahr für Deutschlands Zeitungen" (40/1967), "Die übertriebene Generation" (The Excessive Generation, 41/1967), and "Revolutionär Dutschke" (Dutschke the Revolutionary, 51/1967).[56] In 1968, the student movement and its issues featured six times on the title page: "Axel Springer" (1/1968), "Götter oder Fachidioten?" (Gods or Boffins?, 8/1968), "Studenten auf den Barrikaden" (Students on the Barricades, 17/1968), "Karl Marx" (18/1968), "Französische Revolution" (French Revolution, 22/1968), and "SDS Revolution in Deutschland?" (SDS Revolution in Germany?, 26/1968).[57]

While it is understandable that Germany's leading news magazine should take a keen interest in the student protest (after all, students were among its most avid readers and were likely to remain so), it is truly astonishing how often over the following five decades *Der Spiegel* has returned to "1968," sometimes to mark significant anniversaries, but occasionally without any discernible reason. Moreover, "Die wilden 68er" were the topic of the very first issue of a new venture for the *Spiegel* publishing group. In 1988 *Spiegel Special* no. 1 reprinted individual articles by Wilhelm Bittorf, Harald Wieser, Rolf Rietzler, Hans-Joachim Noack, Peter Brügge, and Jürgen Leinemann, all part of the *Spiegel* series "Träume im Kopf, Sturm auf den Straßen" (Dreams in Their Heads, Trouble in the Streets), and presented them in a single edition.[58] The aim of the series, according to the introduction, was to do justice to the complexity of the movement and explain it to the reader as "history" and "continuing present."

In 1996 *Der Spiegel* ran a series of articles on "Rudi Dutschke und die wilden Jahre der Studentenrevolution" to coincide with the publication of Gretchen Dutsche-Klotz's biography of her dead husband,[59] and, only a few months later in 1997, a series "Vollstrecker des Weltgewissens" (executors of the global conscience).[60] The first article, written by Cordt Schnibben, is particularly interesting because of the inclusion of photographs that had by then become part of the canonic images of "1968," inter alia a picture of Rudi Dutschke and his comrade Gaston Salvatore trying to break through a police barrier, one of communards Rainer Langhans and a bare-breasted Uschi Obermaier, Friederike Hausmann ministering to the dying Benno Ohnesorg, images of Andreas Baader and Ulrike Meinhof, and one of Günter Zint's famous photographs of protesters holding up a wooden cross in helpless defense against the water cannons (see chapter 7). The final image shows revelers at the Berlin Love Parade, thus drawing a connection between "1968" and the more relaxed and allegedly hedonistic lifestyle of young people in the 1990s. While the general level of discourse in the series is surprisingly elevated, the magazine is not above employing the sensational and racy headlines Rudolf Augstein had disapproved of in the Springer press. Thus, in part 5 of the series, entitled "Die Tage der Kommune," the introduction reads:

> They drank jasmine tea, had endless discussions and regarded sex first and foremost as a problem. The members of Kommune I became the pop stars of the student revolt and changed everyday life in Germany.[61]

In 2000, *Der Spiegel* returned to "1968" with a title story on the "Generation Ich" (Generation "Me"), which focused on 68ers as members of the red–green government and unlikely establishment figures.[62] By now, the magazine suggested, the 68ers had lost their relevance, certainly in the eyes of the next generation that rejected their antimaterialistic values. However, it offered the 68ers a right to reply, and Peter Schneider once again employed his rhetorical skills to defend his generation:

> How on earth could a half-way intelligent young man in those days have managed to stay clear of this movement, not become infected and carried along? And this in a Federal Republic where the activists of the Nazi-generation were in their prime and confronted us after their miraculous metamorphosis as upright democrats and friends of the constitution. This republic's teachers, judges, professors, doctors, police commissioners, politicians and business leaders had all started their careers in the Third Reich and were generally able to continue after the war without any trouble. A republic where, for young people, there was an inexplicable, resounding silence, a silence that not only asphyxiated the question about the past, but also other, much more harmless ones. For example, why stepping on the grass, crossing an empty road on a red light, singing in the yard and on the stairs was immediately seen as an attack against public order.[63]

"1968" on Television

Public broadcasting in Germany plays a significant though intermittent role in the construction of "1968." I have already highlighted programs broadcast by the Deutschlandradio that engaged with the *Medienarchiv68*, and it is no surprise that in particular the two main German television channels, that is, the Arbeitsgemeinschaft der Rundfunkanstalten Deutschlands (ARD) and the Zweites Deutsches Fernsehen (ZDF), have repeatedly commissioned programs on the German student movement. Meike Vogel, a member of the DFG-sponsored research project *"1968": Ein Kommunikationsereignis?* ("1968": A Communicative Event?) at the University of Bielefeld, has suggested that the image of "1968" in Germany at the time was largely defined by television, as it gave the movement an enormous reach and carried the iconic images of protagonists and events into every sitting room. Moreover, she argues that the intense reporting at the time was in itself part of the "politisches Kommunikationsereignis (a political communication event)."[64] I would agree with her that some television programs provided real insights into the mind of the protesters, for example the interview with Rudi Dutschke broadcast on December 3, 1967,[65] or the debate broadcast by the Austrian channel ORF on June 13, 1978. In this programme, Rudi Dutschke, Daniel Cohn-Bendit, the journalist Matthias Walden, and the political scientist Kurt Sontheimer debated for more than three hours (!) with only minimal interference from the host Günter Nenning.[66]

In 2003, a four-part series *Was war links?*, commissioned by Südwestdeutscher Rundfunk (SWR) and Sender Freies Berlin (SFB) and produced by noted documentary filmmaker Andreas Christoph Schmidt, was broadcast on the satellite channel 3sat (a public, advertising-free television network, comprising Germany's ARD and ZDF, Austria's ORF, and Switzerland's SRG/SSR, that specializes in cultural programs).[67] The programs, though ostensibly exploring the vanishing phenomenon of a left-wing worldview, which seemed endangered after the fall of Communism and the German unification, mainly focus on the 68er generation, their ideological and cultural influences, and their memories of their heyday. Part 1, "Protest und Theorie" (Protest and Theory) sets the scene with an interview with the "Alt-Linker" (veteran leftist) Klaus Theweleit, who proclaims that what drove the 68ers was a "generationelles Lebensgefühl" (generational feeling) and thus as much lifestyle choice and cultural desire as an exclusively political agenda. The following parts, "Dutschke und Konsorten," "Lärm und Gewalt" and "Kunst und Klassenkampf" (Dutschke and his Ilk; Noise and Violence; Art and Class Struggle), explore the key moments of the German student movement, the escalation of violence, and, interestingly, the challenges writers, playwrights, and filmmakers were faced with when it was fashionable to produce "socially relevant" art (see chapter 7).

In spite of this example, which attempts to capture the idealism, hedonism, intellectualism, and fascination, but also the contradictions and self-delusions of a generation, there is no evidence that "1968" has remained a serious topic of investigation, debate, or revision on television as it has in the pages of Springer newspapers or *Der Spiegel*. Images require context, and on television this is normally triggered by anniversaries, which inspire broadcasters to program chat shows, roundtable discussions, interviews, or commemorative films, often using repeats or reassembled material that is updated according to a given political, socioeconomic, and cultural situation and editorial preference. A good example of such programming is the "Thementag 68er," broadcast by 3sat on April 6, 2008. Starting off at six o'clock in the morning, the twenty-four-hour television marathon included a program on rock and pop music that was played in 1968, a concert by the British rock band Cream, a debate about what constituted left wing politics in 1968, Roman Brodman's documentary film *Der Polizeistaatsbesuch* (The Policestate Visit, 1967), the premiere of a documentary film by Kurt Rosenthal on the blockade of Springer printing presses, documentaries on the invasion of Czechoslovakia by Warsaw Pact troops and the Vietnam War, the movie *Hair* (1979; based on the 1968 musical), a documentary on "1968" in the Swiss province of Graubünden, the movie *Zur Sache, Schätzchen* (Let's Get It On, Darling, 1967), a film exploring the impact of "1968" on theaters, a film exploring how different 68ers had fared on their Long March (including a portrait of Tom Koenigs, who became a prominent politician of the Green Party and special UN envoy in Kosovo and Afghanistan), a studio debate on the myth of "1968," the movie *Rote Sonne* (Red Sun, 1969, featuring Uschi Obermaier), a biopic of Rudi Dutschke, the 1978 debate between Dutschke, Cohn-Bendit, Walden, and Sontheimer, the documentary *Die schwarzen Panther* (The Black Panthers, 1998), and a film about the American folksinger Arlo Guthrie.[68]

Obviously, the impression that this themed 68-marathon was a major media event is misleading: the 3sat program directors were able to assemble individual programs, movies, documentaries. and studio debates from their archives, in this case productions from four national public-service broadcasters over four decades. The single new program was *Kulturzeit extra: Mythos 1968; Die Revolte und ihre Archäologen* (The Revolt and Its Archaeologists, 2008), moderated by Cècile Schortmann.[69] Guests included the journalist Franziska Augstein, the historian Götz Aly, the philosopher Axel Honneth, the writer Klaus Theweleit, and the film director Andres Veiel. The overall impression left by the "Thementag 68" was one of exhaustion and confusion. What may have been intended as a noble attempt to capture the multifacetted reality of "1968" became a bewildering collage of unrelated and often jarring elements that more often than not simply confirmed clichéd views of "1968" as a period of sex, drugs, and rock and roll.

"1968" Online

With the advent of the Internet, proponents and opponents of the German student movement have gained another medium through which to inscribe "1968" in public memory. The era features prominently in resources such as *LEMO* (Lebendiges Museum Online, hosted by the German Historical Museum)[70] and the national oral history project *Gedächtnis der Nation* (Memory of the Nation).[71] The latter is particularly interesting as it contains interviews with former activists, such as K. D. Wolf and Gerd Koenen, but it lacks any kind of contextualization or critical challenge. For the anniversary year 2008, most newspapers established online dossiers, though in many cases they simply reused articles that had been published previously.

The Bundeszentrale für politische Bildung (bpb), financed by the Federal Ministry of the Interior, plays a special role for the construction of an "official" memory of "1968" as it supplies teachers and "Multiplikatoren" (educators, journalists, etc.) with resources for their work in schools, universities, and adult education.[72] It has published two special editions of its journal *Aus Politik und Zeitgeschichte* that focus specifically on "1968": *Die 68er-Generation* (2001)[73] and *1968* (2008).[74] Both contain original articles by established academics that engage with, and present the latest research on, complex issues, such as the ideological foundations of the student protesters, the role "1968" played in the GDR, the historicization of "1968," or its transnational aspects, but are written in an accessible style so as to be suitable for a broad audience. In addition, the Bundeszentrale subsidizes reprints of selected publications on the topic. In the past, these included books by Gerd Langguth and Götz Aly, while at the time of writing Norbert Frei's *Jugendrevolte und globaler Protest 1968* (BPB vol. 699) and Stefan Wolle's *Der Traum von der Revolte* (BPB vol. 728) were available for one euro.

For 2008, the Bundeszentrale also created a web portal on "1968" with material in a variety of media.[75] It includes videos of interviews with "Zeitzeugen," a historical survey "Jahre der Revolution" (Years of the Revolution) as well as contextual material on the "Hintergrund und Vorläufer der Bewegung" (background and precursors of the movement), a picture gallery on different "Protestformen" (forms of protest) a section on "1968" as an international phenomenon, and a section on "68 heute" (68 today). A particular feature of the site is a "virtual discussion" where former activists Silvia Bovenschen, Daniel Cohn-Bendit, Martin Dannecker, Gretchen Dutschke-Klotz, Beate Klarsfeld, Barbara Köster, Bahman Nirumand, and K. D. Wolff discuss "1968" under a variety of headings.[76] While some of the texts in the dossier had been reused from previous publications (including essays by Axel Schildt, Wolfgang Kraushaar, Stefan Wolle, Kristina Schulz, Kathrin Fahlenbrach, and Detlef Siegfried), a significant number of the resources were commissioned especially for this site by the producers.

Similar to the BBC's *Radio 4* website and participatory oral history project in 2008,[77] the bpb had to negotiate the challenges of impartiality and different levels of previous knowledge on the topic among its online audience. Thus, its introduction to the section on the "Jahre der Rebellion" is both generic and broad-brush:

> They were years of departure and rebellion: emergency laws, the lack of a strong opposition in the Bundestag, and an ossified society—but also the still patchy confrontation with the Nazi-past—were key causes for the formation of the extra-parliamentary opposition. After the radical changes that affected the Federal Republic at this time came processes of political, social and economic modernization.[78]

Other interesting features of the site include a link to a discussion between former activist Peter Schneider and former RCDS leader Eberhard Diepgen (who later became major of West Berlin), held at the Amerika Haus Berlin in January 2008,[79] and the transcript of a live chat with journalist Reinhard Mohr and the political scientist Gerd Langguth on June 3, 2008.[80] The most impressive set of resources, however, must be the video statements by fourteen German artists, film directors, dramatists, and writers (inter alia Günter Grass, Christa Wolf, Edgar Reitz, Jürgen Flimm, and Volker Ludwig) who give their verdict on "1968."[81]

There are a number of issues with this kind of construction of "1968." Firstly, while the Bundeszentrale für politische Bildung is expected to present material impartially, it is also an agency of, and an institution within, the very "system" that the students were challenging. By presenting "1968" in the same way as other historical moments of the twentieth century, it necessarily downplays any continuing relevance of the movement. More pragmatically, we may ask what the half-life of a website is. Certain resources will become out of date, but in contrast to history books in schools, which become tatty and are replaced, a website remains "frozen" but can also be subtly altered without anyone noticing, and it can slowly disintegrate when links no longer work. A good example for this is the site's link page to the dossiers on "1968" by German newspapers, many of which have been taken down in recent years.[82]

Summary: The Construction of "1968" in the German Media

The analysis has shown that the German media have a vested interest in keeping "1968" in the public consciousness. It serves as a convenient marker of political positions and values, and continues to generate healthy sales and salacious headlines. It also provides a touchstone for the evaluation of other social movements and political developments ranging from environmental issues and anticapitalist movements to terrorist attacks. While the newspapers of the Springer group and *Der Spiegel* are at the forefront of the media construction of "1968," other print media like *Die Zeit, taz, Frankfurter Rundschau, Frankfurter Allgemeine Zeitung, Süddeutsche Zeitung, Stern,* and *Focus* regularly feature articles by, and publish interviews with, former activists. German television tends to paint a nostalgic picture of "1968," though recent productions like the semidocumentary biopic *Dutschke* (ZDF, 2009—see chapter 7) have attempted to counter this perception. The Bundeszentrale für politische Bildung holds a unique position as quasi-official interpreter of events, though we must remember that its editors report to, and serve, the government. There is no shortage of websites depicting various aspects of "1968," and YouTube has a significant number of videos that enable interested users to track down material that used to lie hidden in the archives of broadcasting houses.

Returning to Kathrin Fahlenbrach's thesis that "the media dominated the public understanding of their goals, their motives, and even their collective identities," I would argue that while this may be true, there is little evidence to assign a specific understanding of "1968" as a consequence of editorial and journalistic endeavor over the last five decades, unless one presupposes a reader who will only consume one particular newspaper. At most, a kaleidoscopic image emerges that continues to allow a wide range of interpretations, even if they cannot compete with the psychological empathy and intensity of literature or the historical detail and critical analysis of academic studies. Moreover, with many 68ers entering the media, schools, and universities on their "march through the institutions," these very institutions have themselves become more critical of autocratic behavior by elected leaders, or, where this has not been the case, at least the audiences are better equipped to recognize when they are being manipulated.

7: "1968" and the Arts

THE TENET OF THIS BOOK is that the construction of "1968" in Germany is effected primarily through the written word, in historico-political discourse, in literature, and in the media. However, the discussion of the representations of the German student movement in the pages of newspapers and magazines, on television, and on the Internet has shown that they feed on intermediality and intertextuality, creating an overall contextual framework where images and sounds serve as shorthand for complex arguments, memories, and emotions. In this chapter, I explore artistic representations of "1968" in a variety of art forms, including museum exhibitions, plays, paintings, popular music, photography, and film. Given that at least some of these are scripted, or conveyed and interpreted via the written word, I argue that they make a significant contribution to the collective idea of what constitutes the German "1968."

It is widely accepted that "1968" caused a major reevaluation of the function of artistic production. The debate that Hans Magnus Enzensberger had initiated in the realm of literature was replicated in theaters, art galleries, cinemas, museums, concert halls, and broadcasting houses. The focus of all these discussions was not artistic expression in itself, but rather the question of in whose name and for what purpose artists, painters, musicians, designers, playwrights, and film directors created their works. Basing their analysis of "Kunst als Ware der Bewußtseinsindustrie" (art as commodity within the consciousness-industry) on a mélange of the writings of Karl Marx, Mao Zedong, and Theodor W. Adorno, members of the Berlin SDS had published a radical critique of the way art had become a tool for the economic and political elites to maintain their position:

> The art industry thus becomes [. . .] a means to rule over the masses, a concept widely accepted in public consciousness. This control—intellectual domination—offers the essential prerequisite for control in all areas.[1]

According to the students, this "geistige Beherrschung" had become particularly oppressive in popular culture, where "products," such as *Heimatfilme* (films set in a conflict-free world), *Schlager* (hit songs sung in German), and romantic novellas, created a false sense of harmony and told their audiences that all was well and that there was therefore no need for a challenge to the status quo. To combat the instrumentalization and commodification of art, the students recommended a campaign of awareness-raising measures, an evaluation of existing methods of cultural production, and a critical confrontation with bourgeois aesthetics:

> If art is seen as a means for the creation of consciousness, then a number of tasks emerge for the emancipatory movement within the cultural superstructure: first we will have to examine the conditions of production in the art industry, recognizing that we need to lay the foundations for our work. At the same time, it would be necessary to confront bourgeois aesthetics in the form of critical analysis (actions, discussions) and through our own productions. In doing so, we cannot pretend that a socialist society already exists. For the time being, progressive art can only be understood as reaction to the poor existing one, as critique.

As we have seen in the case of the literary representations of "1968," the artists representing the student rebellion in the wake of "1968" needed to make a choice: if art was an essential element of all political action, they would need to "take sides," to engage with the ideas and utopian dreams of the students and assign their work an appellative function. On the other hand, with increasing temporal distance from the events, they could attempt to remain "objective" or choose a position that acknowledged that "1968" had since been refracted and reconstructed, thus enabling the audience to approach the work of art with critical distance.

"1968" in Museums

This second option has recently been favored by curators in the United States and Germany. For example, the traveling *1968 exhibit*,[2] produced by the Minnesota Historical Society in partnership with the Atlanta History Center, the Chicago History Museum, and the Oakland Museum of California, links in with national and state educational standards in history and social studies. It aims "to introduce or expand students' knowledge of the events of 1968, to develop a more nuanced understanding of the complexities of the 1960s, to uncover multiple perspectives on the issues of Vietnam, race, politics and the popular culture of 1968, to analyze the importance of image in shaping opinion, and to discover and construct narrative history."[3]

In Germany, the Deutsches Historisches Museum in Berlin and the Haus der Geschichte in Bonn currently have no major exhibitions on "1968" but subsume the era into their permanent offerings. Local museums hold their own artefacts connected to the German student movement (for example Rudi Dutschke's knitted sweater in Luckenwalde).[4] The fortieth anniversary of "1968" saw a number of exhibitions in the centers of the revolt in Berlin (*'68: Brennpunkt Berlin*, Amerika Haus Berlin; *berlin 68: sichten einer revolte*, Stiftung Stadtmuseum Berlin) and Frankfurt. The exhibition *Die 68er: Kurzer Sommer, lange Wirkung* (May 1–November 2, 2008) at the Historisches Museum Frankfurt[5] was arguably the most significant in terms of ambition and media impact. The catalogue accompanying the exhibition combined an overview of the main topics and exhibits with a series of articles.[6] In his introductory essay "Die 68er: Ins Museum?," Jan Gerchow, the director of the museum, reflected on the conceptual and political challenges of putting "1968" into a museum. He argued that a museum—especially one that in 1968 had embraced a broader mission than preserving "high culture" and supporting the social reproduction of the elites—was exactly the right place to reflect on the historical meaning of the era. In contrast to the fast-moving mass media of radio, television, and the press, and with the institutional support from the city and the state, the museum was ideally placed to mediate between competing constructions and bring together former activists and subsequent generations.

Reactions were predictably mixed. While the curators claimed that they had intentionally refrained from presenting an "abschließende Mastererzählung" (concluding master narrative, 19), the historian Claus Kröger pointed out that the exhibition's title already contained the postulate that "1968" had had a significant and long-term social impact.[7] The journalist Arno Widmann described the exhibition as "pathetically helpless," "disturbingly small," "parochial," and, most scathingly, "stupid":

> The exhibition is stupid. Not because it doesn't offer any answers. It is stupid because it doesn't pose any questions. Neither about the origins of '68, nor what became of it. Instead we see found objects in glass cabinets, and photographs and posters on the walls. It has become exactly what the curators allegedly wanted to avoid: a nostalgic event for veterans.[8]

There is no doubt that the curators of these exhibitions are well aware of the tensions inherent in such projects. They not only have to cater for visitors with widely differing knowledge about the period but also have to accept the responsibility of selecting, prioritizing and artistically interpreting elements of an era that is still hotly contested. At the same time, due to their high visibility, educational mission, and "official" support, the exhibitions are likely to reach a wide audience and will therefore play an increasingly important part in the construction of "1968."

"1968" on Stage

The Grips-Theater in Berlin, founded by Volker Ludwig in 1972, was initially an emancipatory theater for children that grew out of the

APO-*Kinderläden*. It is best known for its musical revue *Linie 1* (Line 1, 1986), and remains one of the most important theaters for young audiences. In 1980, Grips premiered its first play for adults, *Eine linke Geschichte* (A Weird History / A History of the Left). Cowritten by Ludwig and Detlef Michel, a former member of Kommune I, *Eine linke Geschichte* follows the lives of three students who first meet in 1966 in West Berlin at a demonstration against the Vietnam War. Karen, Johannes, and Lutz represent student types: the shy young woman eagerly soaking up the opportunities for self-realization and emancipation, the serious intellectual with moral certitude, and the hedonistic libertine. The audience sees them caught up in the excitement of the utopian moment, but, and this is the genius of the play, their story does not end with the demise of the student movement. In subsequent scenes, we see them exploring various options on their Long March—Karen leaves her boyfriend Johannes and marries Lutz, who ditches his radical views and works in the media. Johannes eventually ends up supporting the Social Democrats. They grow older, quarrel, and separate but are always drawn back to each other. The unique element of the play over twenty years was that, following the penultimate scene set in 1978, Ludwig would always write a final scene that brought the story right up to the respective present. Thus, the protagonists would find themselves discussing their experience with members of subsequent generations and movements, reflecting on their past, and always hoping that their utopian dream would one day come true. Eventually, these "updates" were no longer credible, and from 2007 the play reverted to the original ending, as Ludwig explained:

> The story of three students who meet in 1966 at a demonstration against the Vietnam War, whose lives we then follow to the present day, is also part of the story of its authors and the GRIPS Theatre itself. And since the audience always wants to know what happened next (something we also wanted to know), the last scene was always set in the present day. However, the distance between the penultimate scene, set in 1978, and the last became longer and more difficult to portray convincingly. Over 25 years, Detlef Michel and I had to think of a dozen new concluding scenes. The audience came back each year, to see what happened to their and our flower-power dreams, and to see how we managed to make the link to the final sentence, the "unheimlich starken Anfang" (really cool beginning) of a new LINKE GESCHICHTE. Today, we go back to the historic conclusion from 1980.[9]

Ludwig is right in observing that *Eine linke Geschichte* reflects first and foremost his and Detlef Michel's personal history and that their audience consisted mainly of former 68ers and their sympathizers. What he omits to say is that the play was taken off the program in 1999 and not revived until 2007. As Barbara Burckhardt commented sarcastically, with red–green in power, there was no point in chronicling a project that had become reality, though not in the form the authors had hoped for:

> Maybe it wasn't much of a surprise that the last performance took place in March 1999; the project of the Left was no longer a project, and a swan-song about the anti-utopian power of the factual could not really be expected from the determined optimists of the Grips Theatre.[10]

If Volker Ludwig's *Eine linke Geschichte* was a play that looked back to "1968" with sympathy and interest, Christoph Schlingensief's play *Rocky Dutschke, '68*, which premiered at the Volksbühne Berlin in 1996[11] and was also broadcast as a radio play in 1997, pulled no punches. Schlingensief, at the time the enfant terrible of the German theater world, mercilessly ridiculed the 68ers, who in his view had long sold out and become the sated, lazy, and opportunistic burghers they had once opposed. The *Berliner Zeitung*, predictably, was amused and called the spectacle a "fröhliche Leichenschändung" (cheerful desecration of the dead).[12]

"1968" on Screen

Given the plethora of cinematic representations of the Red Army Faction, there are surprisingly few feature films that take "1968" as their topic. The standout production is Hans Weingartner's *Die fetten Jahre sind vorbei* (The Years of Plenty are Over, 2004, in English as *The Educators*, 2005) which transposes the students' critique of capitalist society to the next generation. When the young anarchists inadvertently kidnap the fat cat Hardenberg, it turns out that he is actually a former 68er, who gleefully exploits their naive idealism.[13] Achim Bornhack chronicles Uschi Obermaier's eventful life in *Das wilde Leben*, though her time at Kommune I is but a brief episode. Similarly, "1968" serves merely as background to the main story in Uli Edel's *Der Baader Meinhof Komplex*. In spite of the producers' obvious commitment to verisimilitude in recreating crucial events of "1968," for example the demonstrations against the visit of the Shah of Persia or the International Vietnam Congress, the focus is very much on the future members of the RAF, and Edel follows Stefan Aust's book too closely to escape the simplistic message that Ulrike Meinhof's bad marriage and Klaus Rainer Röhl's infidelities were the ground zero for West Germany's descent into terrorism.[14] What is interesting, though, and relevant for the construction of "1968," is the way the film's representation of the German student movement skewers the audience's imagination so that the movement is much more firmly associated with the one of many "Entmischungsprodukte" (Kraushaar) that happened to be the most cinematic in its dramatic potential. Consequently, the film favors Gerd Koenen's problematic interpretation of the "red decade" and an uncritical equating of discussions about resistance/provocation with an agenda of targeted bombing/murder.[15]

Other recent films that claimed to be faithful to the "historical truth" include Stephan Krohmer's docudrama *Dutschke* (ZDF, 2009), which combined original footage with recreated scenes and interviews, and Andres Veiel's *Wer, wenn nicht wir?* (Who If Not We Ourselves?, 2011). Veiel's film closely follows Gerd Koenen's book on Bernward Vesper, Gudrun Ensslin, and Andreas Baader and, like Krohmer's *Dutschke*, mixes newsreel footage and acted scenes. In contrast to *Der Baader Meinhof Komplex*, these two films make a serious attempt to engage with the complex politics of the era and with the difficult relationships between the protagonists. However, all of the films mentioned here cannot escape the fact that they are commodities in the market place. The trailer for *Wer, wenn nicht wir?* entices potential viewers with the promise of scenes of a sexual nature and unruly behavior: "They are the new generation. They dream of a better world. And they are willing to act."[16] To this extent, the SDS students writing in *Die Zeit* in 1968 had a point, though Veiel, to his credit, refuses to give in to commercial pressures. He shows the audience the real challenges Vesper and Ensslin faced when confronting the Nazi generation (which were not an abstract but in Vesper's case a complex relationship with his father), and has no doubt angered many RAF sympathizers with his sympathetic portrayal of Ensslin's jailor.

"1968" on Canvas

"1968" has featured prominently in the works of a number of German artists, sometimes very obviously, as in Wolf Vostell's *Nur Die 1* (1968), which juxtaposes modern consumerism and the image of the brutal killing of a suspected Vietcong by Saigon's police chief, sometimes in more abstract form, as in the works of Josef Beuys or Anselm Kiefer.[17] An excellent example of the constructed nature of "1968," and the role of art in this process, can be seen in the works of Gerhard Richter and Hagen Bonifer. Richter's *Zyklus zum 18. Oktober 1977* consists of 15 paintings, which in turn are based on photographs of dead RAF terrorists and their funerals.[18] Given their highly controversial nature (planned suicide or state-sanctioned murder?) and global reception (the cycle toured widely and was acquired by the Museum of Modern Arts in New York in 2005), the connotations and associations of these paintings evoke an interpretation of "1968" through the lens of the events of 1977.[19]

In 2009, German artist Hagen Bonifer presented his own cycle *Vom Nutzen zu zweifeln: 2. Juni 1967* (The Benefits of Doubt: June 2, 1967) of fifteen oil paintings based on photographs taken on or around June

2, 1967.[20] These paintings are a conscious mirroring of Richter's cycle, using the same formats, technique, and colors (though slightly brighter tones of gray) so that the cycles enter into a conversation. Bonifer believes that Richter's cycle has sidelined the idealistic, joyful, and positive elements of "1968," including the necessity for emancipation and critique.[21] Each of the paintings responds to one of Richter's, including one of a young Gudrun Ensslin, one of communard Fritz Teufel, and one of students engaged in a street fight with the police (reproduced on the cover of this book). In an interview, Bonifer explained that he did not want Richter's interpretation of the past to remain uncontested. As far as he was concerned, the "historic moment" of June 2, 1967 was a "Zeitenwende" (historical turning point), its "fühlbare Sinnlichkeit" (palpable sensuality) in danger of being forgotten or overwritten by later emotions of hate and despair.[22]

"1968" in Popular Music

The German student movement coincided with the explosion of a global countercultural or "underground" music scene, which fed on and at the same time satirized the commercial rock and pop music of the time. This movement was led by American acts, such as The Grateful Dead and Frank Zappa and the Mothers of Invention,[23] but increasingly also by German "Krautrock" bands, such as Amon Düül, The City Preachers, Floh de Cologne, Guru Guru, and Tangerine Dream. Characteristic for them was a mixture of experimental music and a political message that aligned itself with the objectives of the protest movement. Both sides met at the Internationale Essener Songtage in September 1968,[24] including the *Liedermacher* (singer-songwriters) Hannes Waader and Franz Josef Degenhardt, who, in the tradition of protest singers like Woody Guthrie and Bob Dylan, added a German voice to proceedings. While Wolf Biermann was not allowed to leave East Berlin to perform his "Drei Kugeln auf Rudi Dutschke," Degenhardt sang his "2. Juni 1967" and the sardonic "Vatis Argumente" (Daddy's Points),[25] a *Rollengedicht* (a poem read through the voice of a specific character) intended to expose the conformist nature of the Nazi generation.[26]

While musicologists and fans will be able to untangle the myriad of influences and metamorphoses of this "underground" music, I am interested in the contribution popular music and politically engaged songwriters make to the construction of "1968." An excellent example for this is the song "1968," written and performed by German multitalent Rainald Grebe.[27] Grebe poses as a narrator who tells an audience of children the "catastrophic" story of the year 1968 and the rebellion of the students. He declares, in wide-eyed incomprehension, that the people then lived in the best possible world of full employment and generally accepted moral values, and yet that the students destroyed this paradise with their revolt: "Ich verstehs nicht. // Ich werds auch nie verstehen. // So gut wie damals // wirds uns nie wieder gehen." (I don't get it. // I will never get it. // We will never have it as good as we did then.) The singer/narrator concedes that the older generation had been ardent Nazis, but at least they had been "normal." He concludes that "die 68er sind an allem schuld" (the 68ers are responsible for everything) and suggests those who still believe in the revolution should "nach drüben gehen" (bugger off to the GDR)—a piece of malicious advice many 68ers heard during their protests, but which of course after Unification is no longer an option. The song mirrors Degenhardt's *Rollengedicht*, but Grebe changes the tone in the last stanza, when the utopian dream seems to take over, the present intrudes, and he reaffirms that protest was and is necessary: "Lass deine Haare flattern // für eine bessere Welt" (Let your hair fly // for a better world).

In an interview with the *taz*, Grebe explained that he felt it was appropriate to remind his audience that the 68ers had opened doors and developed a comprehensive critique of the capitalist system that was still valid. Moreover, he felt that history had increasingly become "historytainment," where a few images suffice to construct a simplistic and often misleading portrait of the past:

> Everything is simplified these days. Five minutes represent a whole year, and the images are always the same: Well, dear children, here we have a few naked men and women standing against a wall, next to them a child, that's 1968. That's all you need to know.[28]

"1968" and Photography

Photography does indeed play an important role in the construction of "1968."[29] As historical documents and artistic expressions, they help us visualize an increasingly distant reality, and the provocative pose of naked communards up against a white wall and presenting their backsides is not the worst image to summarize the playful as well as radical message of the movement.[30] The responsibility for the selection of "representative" images that travel the world and underpin the global collective memory of the era lay and continues to lie with editors and publishers but ultimately depends on gifted photographers to record the "moment." The global "1968" would not have burnt itself so deep into the public consciousness without the key images of the Vietnam War, the French May, the "Summer of Love" and the Woodstock Festival,[31] or, in the case of West Germany, the images of Benno Ohnesorg or Rudi Dutschke.

One of the key purveyors of images of the German "1968" is the photographer Michael Ruetz,[32] who was a well-known face to the rebellious students in West Berlin and with his camera recorded hundreds of "moments" between 1966 and 1969. Two-hundred fifty-six of his photographs can be seen on the website of the Deutsche Fotothek,[33] including the one that was chosen by Hagen Bonifer for his cycle *Vom Nutzen zu Zweifeln*.[34] Ruetz's photographs of the German student movement have been widely exhibited (including at the Deutsche Historische Museum in Berlin) and published in three large-format volumes, all sold via the "alternative" bookshop Zweitausendeins. In *"Ihr müßt diesen Typen nur ins Gesicht sehen": Die APO Berlin 1966–69* ("You Just Have to Look These Guys in the Eye": The APO in Berlin 1966–69, 1980), the photographer explained that he considered his work a contribution to the history of the Extraparliamentary Opposition. His main motivation for developing thousands of film rolls, apart from a strong sympathy for the cause, was the fact that the reporting of the APO, especially in Berlin, was "mangelhaft" (inadequate) and often highly manipulative.[35] In *Sichtbare Zeit* (Visible Time, 1995), Ruetz reflected further on his role as "eyewitness to the Zeitgeist" and the significance of what he was recording:

> The APO was a means of getting rid of your negative identity and replacing it with positive identification patterns; you were given the opportunity to barter off your collective guilt for a clean conscience. I think this was the APO's most genuine achievement.[36]

Two years later, though, on the thirtieth anniversary of 1967, Ruetz was no longer sure whether "1968" would have a lasting impact. Nevertheless, *1968: Ein Zeitalter wird besichtigt*, is an impressive publication, not only in the sheer variety and intensity of key "moments" but also in the sense of "normality" when the heroes or villains of "1968" appear in more private or unexpected contexts. Ruetz is also self-aware in his role as selector and interpreter of his images, something that becomes particularly obvious in the ironic or playful titles he gives to individual photographs or chapters. A particularly evocative image of Rudi Dutschke carries the title "Aura,"[37] while a group of shots of female students is entitled "Die Bräute der Revolte" (202–6). Similarly, the photographs collected in the Deutsche Fotothek include one of Rudi Dutschke and Gaston Salvatore ("Pflichtbewußt" [Dutiful]), one of Herbert Marcuse giving a lecture to thousands of students ("Die Einsamkeit in der Menge" [Loneliness in the Crowd]), and one of Gudrun Ensslin at a demonstration ("Die heilige Johanna von Tempelhof" [St. Joan of Tempelhof, i.e., West Berlin's airport]). Most poignantly, the image of students throwing stones at the Tegeler Weg is entitled "Ende der Unschuld" (The End of Innocence).

It is no surprise that photographers felt they had to choose sides in "1968." Günter Zint, who took the emotive image of demonstrators holding up a wooden cross while being drenched by police water cannons[38] (in 2008, the Haus der Geschichte [House of History] in Bonn ran an small exhibition *Wilde Zeiten* with his photographs[39] and the Bundeszentrale für politische Bildung included several in its exhibition *'68: Brennpunkt Berlin*[40] at the former Amerika Haus Berlin) has been very vocal about the social responsibility of the "eyewitness."[41] Of course, their products are as much commodities in the market place as songs or movies, and occasionally one gets the impression that these large-format books have been produced to meet an artificial demand during an anniversary year and may end up as coffee-table adornments. It is indeed doubtful whether we learn anything new from the photographs in *Baader Meinhof: Pictures on the Run 67–77* (1998)[42] or *K1: Das Bilderbuch der Kommune* (K1: The Picture Book of the Commune, 2008).[43]

In his editorial note to *1968: Bildspur eines Jahres* (1968: Tracking the Images of a Year, 2008), Andres Veiel describes how he and his coeditor Gerd Koenen trawled through tens of thousands of pictures in the archives to develop a "picture-trail" of the events:

> Sometimes we found hundreds of photographs of one of the key events, but only one photographer had selected the optimal section, had achieved the ideal relation between the foreground and the background, had waited for the one, correct expression in the faces of those who were photographed.[44]

This, I would argue, is a perfect example of the constructedness of "1968": editors and publishers make decisions about the "optimal" detail, the "ideal" relationship between foreground and background, the "correct" expression in a face. This presupposes that they have already made up their minds and are engaged in selecting those facets that they want the public to see. Depending on the type of audience, they may well wish to have their chosen worldview reaffirmed, but readers of these books may also look for an unbiased account. The very fact that the publishers of these *Bilderbücher* (coffee-table books with large images) see a market for them could simply reflect that former 68ers are aging and nostalgic for the days of their youth (see chapter 9). On the other hand, with control over the visual record of "1968," the media, editors, and publishers have a powerful role in shaping the cultural memory of the era.

"1968" and the Printing Press

One of the reasons why "1968" remains so contested in Germany is the fact that right from the start, the students managed to set up their own channels for the distribution of information. It is no accident that one of the exhibits at the Historische Museum in Frankfurt was a spirit duplicator (known as "ditto machine" in the United States, "Banda machine" in the United Kingdom), which was used for the production of flyers. The printer Peter-Paul Zahl, whose reprint of Georg Büchner's *Hessischer Landbote* (Hessian Courier, 1834) with the motto "Friede den Hütten! Krieg den Palästen!" (Peace to the shacks! War on the palaces!) inspired many protesters, was instrumental in professionalizing the APO's modes of communication, for example with the anarchist paper *Agit 883* (from February 1969). Within the pages of the underground press and magazines like *konkret*, the protesters could also indulge in the lighter side of the revolution, lampooning the inept behavior of the police (a specialty of cartoonist Gerhard Seyfried) or poking fun at their own leaders (for example in a spoof image of Leonardo da Vinci's *Last Supper* that replaced the disciples with prominent activists). The students and their ideas also had a significant impact on established publishers, from small establishments like the Wagenbach Verlag in West Berlin, where Friedrich Christian Delius worked as Lektor,[45] to the influential Suhrkamp Verlag, led by Siegfried Unseld. Indeed, as the *Chronik 1970* (Chronicle of 1970, 2010) makes clear, "1968" had a major impact on the artistic, as well as the commercial direction of the publishing house.[46]

Summary

In spite of the students' critical attitude toward the "Bewußtseinsindustrie," the arts responded creatively to their protest and have, over the past five decades, contributed to the construction of "1968" in Germany. While initially mainly a conduit for the students' radical message, in recent years art has become a mediator between new audiences and an increasingly distant past. In imaginative reinterpretations like Hans Weingartner's *Die fetten Jahre sind vorbei* or Hagen Bonifer's *Vom Nutzen zu zweifeln*, "1968" is neither repackaged as a commodity nor crudely regurgitated to fight a battle that was lost long ago. Instead, in these examples, it is reimagined for a present that risks forgetting what was truly inspiring.

8: *Zaungäste*

No account of the construction of "1968" in Germany would be complete without a look at the curious phenomenon of the *Zaungäste* (those looking in from the outside—literally over the fence). Initially, this was the term used by journalist Reinhard Mohr in 1992 for his own generation, the "78ers," who were too young to have participated in 1967/68 but had nevertheless inherited their forebears' antiauthoritarian values and often wished that they had been part of the action.[1] Given that the SDS had actively targeted schools (initiating the so-called *Schülerbewegung* [movement of high school students])[2] to politicize the next generation, it should come as no surprise that many high-school students were eager to follow in the footsteps of their heroes—only to discover that many activists had moved on by the time they themselves left home and started university or jobs. At the same time, we need to remember that the demise of the movement was not a given in 1969 or 1970, that the 68ers had younger siblings, and that each new cohort of eighteeen-year-olds leaving home could, as one of their life choices, become part of the countercultural milieus that had developed in the wake of the revolt.[3]

This chapter, though, will focus on specific *Zaungäste*: individuals who were not part of the German student movement and yet are actively engaged in the construction of "1968" by asserting that either their peer group or they themselves were part of it. These are writers, academics, and journalists who have made it their business, in some cases their life's work, to keep the era in the public eye. Much like modern romantics who wish they were living in the fictional worlds of Jane Austen or James Cameron's *Avatar*, these *Zaungäste* compensate for their lateness or exclusion by an even stronger identification with the era than shown by the former activists themselves.

Writing the Revolution, Secondhand

"One would have to invent Reinhard Mohr if he didn't already exist—as chronicler of a time that he yearns for, even though he never knew it." These are the words of Daniel Cohn-Bendit, describing his coauthor on the cover of their book *1968: Die letzte Revolution, die noch nichts vom Ozonloch wußte*. Mohr himself explained that he was politicized in 1972, before he became a part of the left-wing Frankfurt "scene" that also included Cohn-Bendit and Joschka Fischer. They all felt it essential to demonstrate solidarity with the imprisoned RAF terrorists, and, in the face of an uncompromising state and a mainstream society that appeared to them as cold and vengeful, affectionately remember the "Wärmestrom" (current of warmth) of the countercultural milieu.

Mohr has written for a range of magazines and newspapers, including *Pflasterstrand, taz, Stern,* and the *Frankfurter Allgemeine Zeitung,* but it was as editor for the culture section of *Der Spiegel* and contributor for *Spiegel Online* throughout the 2000s where he really engaged in shaping the discourse on "1968." A good example is a rousing article in January 2001 when the "scandal" about Joschka Fischer's militant past broke. In "Zorn auf die roten Jahre" (Angry with the Red Years, 2001), Mohr argued that the polemic attacks against Fischer were in fact an organized campaign to exorcise "1968" from German history. To counter these attacks, Mohr defended the 68ers, describing their actions and values as "fully justified" in an era of political repression, historical amnesia, and sexual inhibition, while denouncing the conservative politicians leading the charge as ill-informed and hypocritical backbenchers who were jealous of the exciting past of their rebellious contemporaries. He conceded that the 68ers had become the object of caricature to subsequent generations, and their revolutionary fervor inexplicable even to themselves, but imbued the era with a romantic aura: it was a "lost age," full of "craziness" and with a "strange attraction" that had allowed young people the freedom to create their own "Lebenswirklichkeit" (reality):

> Life in the collective, whether in a commune, an alternative project or a Sponti discussion, had become the new normal in the mid-1970s for thousands of male and female "comrades." It was the attempt, in the spirit of Adorno, to live an authentic life within a false one, to establish a sub-cultural, hedonistic and life-affirming counter-culture in opposition to the destructive capitalism which, together with its state, was our declared enemy—no matter who happened to be chancellor at the time.[4]

In February 2008, as part of the magazine's series to mark the fortieth anniversary of "1968," *Der Spiegel* published three excerpts from Mohr's book *Der diskrete Charme der Rebellion* (The Discrete Charm of the Rebellion, 2008).[5] In it, he ironically confronted the paradox that "1968," in the view of many conservatives, was responsible for the demise of traditional German values, the decline of educational standards and the disappearance of the nuclear family while at the same time just a historic "blip," completely negligible in its social impact. His response was equally dialectic:

> The revolt of this distant "Planet 68" has failed politically if we look at its original utopian aims of socialism and global revolution. And

yet, its deeper, contradictory and strangely iridescent impacts continue to the present day—as much as the debate about them. Its glowing core that we can still feel today was the idea of a free and happy society, the utopia of the "liberated" individual free from oppression and loneliness within an alienated, hollow existence. The secret of 68 lies in the sudden radical, intense and absolute spirit in which this promise of happiness, and perhaps even redemption, was received, pursued and "lived."[6]

It is worth pausing for a moment to analyze the imagery employed in this passage. In the tradition of German romanticism, the reality of the movement's failure to change the political system is quickly dispatched, before Mohr focuses on the more elusive impacts of the movement that he characterizes as "deep," "contradictory," and "strangely iridescent." The "glowing core" of the revolt, on the other hand, seems to be unperturbed, an ageless, unaltered, and eternal idea of a free and happy society, a utopia of collectively "liberated" individuals who are free of oppression and loneliness. The following sentence raises the stakes even further, elevating "1968" to a quasi-religious promise of happiness and deliverance, which, Mohr suggests, was experienced and "lived" by its disciples. All this is a "secret," only visible to the initiate, and therefore obviously not to thick-skinned pragmatists who have forgotten how to dream (I will return to the question of romantic influences on "1968" in chapter 10).

In another highly revealing passage, Mohr observes:

The academic verve of theoretical analysis and the rhetoric of explaining the world had their own erotic attraction. The almost naive faith in the written word, in the power of an argument, in abstractions and concepts which were supposed to shine a light on, and explain the irritating world of phenomena—the desire to "put things in a nutshell"—all this contained a fascinating promise, a Faustian moment of true cognitive breakthrough. Within it lay the wonders of ideological-critical unmasking, if you will: an intrawordly revelation. (50)

Again, while conceding that the 68er's faith in the written word was "almost naïve," Mohr accords the works of the Frankfurt School an "erotic" quality which contained not only a "fascinating promise" but "a Faustian moment of true cognitive breakthrough." Returning to religious imagery, he then describes this faith as encompassing the "wonder of critical unmasking," which in turn would lead to an "intrawordly revelation" (Mohr knew his Heidegger). What should be noted here, though, is that in these passages a *Zaungast*, not the 68ers themselves, is assembling considerable intellectual artillery to defend "1968." Moreover, the 68ers were avid readers of Adorno, Habermas, Marcuse, and Bloch, but they were engaged in fighting for a utopian, radically different, future. In *Der diskrete Charme der Rebellion*, Mohr asserts that "1968" was in fact already the realization of that dream.

A year later, though, reality encroached on Mohr's carefully constructed interpretation. As chief apologist for the 68ers, he not only had to defend the 68ers from accusations of cowardice when they refused the invitation to participate in a Springer Tribunal 2.0 (see chapter 6), but also the revelation that Karl-Heinz Kurras, the policeman who had shot Benno Ohnesorg, was a Stasi officer[7] and that Rudi Dutschke's assassin, Josef Bachmann, had close ties to German neo-Nazis.[8] Wondering whether the history of "1968" had to be rewritten from scratch, he mused what would have happened if these facts had been known at the time. Would the students' rage have found other targets than the Springer-Verlag? Would they have been more radical and militant? Unsurprisingly, his conclusion once again asserted the necessity of "1968":

> The recent Spiegel-discovery illustrates, once again, that the Federal Republic in 1966/67 was very different to Germany in 2009— that there were, beyond all ideology and conspiracy theories, good, very good reasons for an antiauthoritarian protest movement: reasons that ranged from world politics to the private sphere and the biographical.

"1968" and the GDR

Since German unification in 1990, historians like Heinrich August Winkler have observed that the former GDR did not experience a "1968" and that this lack of a common frame of reference points to an obvious fault line in the German collective experience.[9] Mary Fulbrook speaks of a "revolution that did not take place,"[10] while Timothy S. Brown comments that "it is scarcely possible to speak of a Western-style "protest movement" in the GDR."[11] Brown points out, though, that the events and ideas of 1968 had a long term impact on East Germany:

> The year 1968 in the GDR did, however, play an important role in the politicization of figures who would later be active in the peace and citizen's movements in the GDR, and in this sense the year may be seen as an important marker on the way to the revolution in 1989. (194)

In an interview in 2008, the East German writer Christa Wolf, who had struggled to get her novel *Nachdenken über Christa T.* past the state censors in 1967/68, confirmed that many of the critical intellectuals perceived the student rebellion in the West as an important moment, but that their attention was focused on developments in Czechoslovakia, where Alexander Dubček's reform programme and the work of dissidents like Vaclav Havel illustrated that it might be possible to change the socialist system from within:

> We on the Left in the GDR viewed the 68ers in the West with great sympathy, but the events in Czechoslovakia were much more important to us. That was an existential question: "Socialism with a human face."[12]

To what extent is it then possible to speak of an East German "1968"? There are two possible answers. Some argue that, as part of a global revolt, individuals in different countries participated as much as they could (some, especially in totalitarian regimes, perhaps more in spirit than action) and applied the ideas of imaginative resistance to their local situation. Others say that "1968" was a purely Western phenomenon and that claims that East Germany was part of it are simply attempts to rewrite history. What is of interest for this book is how an East German "1968" is retrospectively imagined as an equivalent to the West German "1968" and as the forerunner of the 1989 revolution that led to German Unification.

As in West Germany, East German "68ers" were a relatively small minority, and without doubt subject to much greater repression by the institutions and organs of their state. This is confirmed by the findings of the parliamentary commission of inquiry "Aufarbeitung von Geschichte und Folgen der SED Diktatur in Deutschland."[13] Ulrich Bock, who studied theology at the University of Jena in 1968, describes the few who rebelled as "mosaic pieces which pull the GDR out of its sad gray and give it some color."[14] Similarly, the film director Barbara Metselaar Berthold speaks movingly of a small group of individuals inspired by the student protests in the West who dreamed of participating in them:

> We would have loved to have been heroes. There are generations where the age-typical sense of life corresponds with the general social mood. Things were not so with us. Born into the GDR at the end of the 40s or beginning of the 50s, we experienced the youthful energy of a new beginning when all over the world change was in the air, revolts broke out, and with it the hope that old restrictions and rules would be swept away. With the exception of the Prague Spring in 1968, all this happened in countries that were inaccessible to us, but, because of this, its glow had an even greater impact on us. This euphoric time full of zest and moments of happiness did not last long. The state authorities did their best to strangle those who did not follow the rules. The country fell into paralysis. The hippie-era was over.[15]

Metselaar characterizes the situation of her group of friends with a mixture of fatalism and nostalgia: their idealized image of the revolt in the West and the German student movement was more projection and wishful thinking than reality. Crucially, though, it wasn't just the lifestyle and fashions that excited them but the antiauthoritarian message, the idea that rebellion against any form of oppression was justified. Living their alternative lifestyles behind closed doors, under constant surveillance and pressure by the Stasi and the conformist majority, they soon felt paralyzed. They would have loved to have been heroes, but they could not.

Dieter Althaus, the former conservative first minister of Thuringia, was only ten years old in 1968 but has contributed to the debate with an essay in the *Streitschrift* published by the Konrad Adenauer Stiftung (see chapter 3). He points out that memories, even conversations about "1968," had been taboo in the GDR until 1989. These memories were not dominated by Benno Ohnesorg or Rudi Dutschke, though, but by the Prague Spring and its brutal squashing by Warsaw Pact troops:

> The people between Rügen and the Erzgebirge look back to their own "68": they perceived "1968" as an important and very political year that formed them no less than their West German compatriots. It was the year of the Prague Spring. For the first time since the bloody crackdown on the rebellion of 17 June 1953, people dared to hope for more democracy, that the door to freedom would open a little bit. And then Soviet tanks flattened all these hopes of freedom—and with it the reform movement, which came to a standstill in the GDR for two decades.[16]

And while the lifestyle revolution did not stop at the German–German border, Althaus claims that East Germans were shaking their heads at the antics of Kommune I and the students' anti-Springer campaign:

> Many citizens of the GDR had no sympathy for the protests against the Springer publishing house—in fact, they would have been glad to have had the chance to read the *Bild-Zeitung*." (216)

It is obvious that "1968" can be instrumentalized for political point-scoring, in this case between two different narratives of German history: on the one hand, the conservative version, where Adenauer's politics of Western integration and commitment to the capitalist system had guaranteed West Germans the freedoms that their East German cousins would eventually demand for themselves, and on the other hand, the social democratic version, where Willy Brandt's *Ostpolitik* enabled the two Germanys to coexist peacefully and where dialogue and cultural exchange eventually broke down the determined resistance of the East German regime. Neither side is particularly enamored with the 68ers, but given that "1968" is too important to omit from unified

Germany's grand narrative, it has become the object of overtures and attempts of appropriation from both sides.

The historian Stefan Wolle has researched the response of the GDR regime to the West German student movement.[17] While the regime initially perceived a "natural unity" between those who wanted democratic socialism (as defined by the party) and those who wanted an anticapitalist revolt, it was also deeply averse to what was termed "angelsächsische Überfremdung" (anglo-saxon cultural takeover).[18] While Ulbricht and Honecker viewed the SDS as a potential ally, they were concerned about the association's influence on East German critical intellectuals and young people eager to be "wo das Leben tobt" (where life is happening, 96). The Stasi watched closely as West German students infected East German youth with their "dekadente moralisch-ethische Einstellung" (decadent, moral-ethical attitude, 117) and the "Bazillus der Aufsässigkeit" (bug of rebelliousness, 150). The regime's response was twofold: the imprisonment of active "troublemakers" (more than 1,000 protesters were arrested following a variety of protests against the Warsaw Pact intervention, more than 380 stood trial for "staatsfeindliche Hetze" [antistate rabble-rousing propaganda, 169]) and the invention of an "Ersatzprotestkultur" (substitute protest culture, 234), for example through the Festival des politischen Liedes (Festival of the Political Song) in 1970. Wolle concludes that both rebellions effected unintended change:

> The 68ers in the West dreamed of the revolution and effected an evolutionary change of the system. By their own biographies, they demonstrated the very fact that they had wanted to deny, namely, the essential reformability of the civil society. The 68ers in the East, on the other hand, wanted to reform socialism and caused—21 years later, and to a certain extent against their will—a revolution that led to the annihilation of the socialist system. The revolt that was missed in 1968 could not be made up for later in the GDR. From a historical perspective, Germany experienced two failures which cancelled each other out. West and East found themselves in a society whose demise they had often prognosticated, but where it was obviously good to live. (238–39)

While this interpretation posits that the East German revolution of 1989 was conceived and carried out by permanently disaffected East German "68ers," it lacks sufficient evidence. As far as the process of construction of "1968" in unified Germany is concerned, it is interesting to see Wolle use the words "versäumte Revolte" (missed revolt), which suggests that had the East German regime responded differently to the protests, then 1989 might never have happened.

Anna von der Goltz has recently challenged the view that 1968 in East Germany was the moment when many young people and intellectuals lost any hope of transforming socialism for the better and withdrew into resignation and apathy until 1989 gave them the opportunity to overthrow their uncompromising rulers. Her oral history project reveals important differences in the forms of opposition in the wake of the Warsaw Pact's invasion of Czechoslovakia, ranging from fundamental opposition, imprisonment, and expulsion on the one hand to pursuing change from within official structures on the other. She concludes that not only the West German but also the East German "1968" continues to be the object of active reinterpretation:

> Much as the notion of the Western 1968 as a "cultural revolution" strips the Western protests of their political significance [. . .], narratives that promote the Eastern 1968 as evidence of an East German "civic culture" that foreshadowed the "peaceful revolution" of 1989 isolate those elements that continued to see in 1968 the promise of a more perfect Socialism.[19]

Other *Zaungäste*

With the historicization of "1968," the perspective from which we view the era has changed. It is not only the number of self-declared "68ers" that has grown in recent years; there is also an increased number of *Zaungäste*, those who feel, for better or worse, a connection with the 68ers.

The title of Detlef Hohn's account of the riots in Hamburg following the attempted assassination of Rudi Dutschke couldn't be clearer: *Auch wir waren dabei* (We Were There, Too, 2013).[20] The retired police officer, who, together with thousands of his colleagues in West Germany's major cities and university towns, had been ordered to contain the rage of the protesters, shows a lot of sympathy for the students. Forty-five years after the events, he accepts that their analysis of the "authoritarian character" and the fact that West German institutions had failed to learn the lessons of the past was actually an accurate reflection of his own profession at the time:

> For those who looked closer, the Republic was only technically a democratic state. Democracy had, as is well known, been announced and decreed by the victorious powers of the Second World War. [. . .] It was also technical in the sense that West German society had to a large extent adopted the norms and values of the Empire, the Weimar Republic and the Nazi period. (6)

The title of Claus Leggewie's recent book is equally indicative.[21] In *Politische Zeiten: Beobachtungen von der Seitenlinie* (Political Times: Observations from the Sidelines, 2015), the prominent political scientist takes stock of his life as a "sideline"-68er who had focused on his studies while his more radical contemporaries were busy preparing for the revolution. In interviews at the Leipzig Book Fair in March 2015 and with *Der Spiegel*,[22] Leggewie argued for a reevaluation of the 68ers since they had been much more politically active than following generations, a quality that was sorely needed at a time of urgent geopolitical and environmental problems.

Another group of *Zaungäste* is made up of the children of the 68ers. I have mentioned Bettina Röhl (chapter 1) and Sophie Dannenberg (chapter 3). The list of literary portraits of "1968" through the eyes of those born in the late 1960s and early 1970s could be extended considerably, and these individuals and their accounts have also become part of the discourse on"1968."[23] Jess Jochimsen gently satirizes his upbringing in a "typical" 68er household in *Das Dosenmilch-Trauma* (The Condensed-Milk Trauma, 2000),[24] while Katharina Wulff-Bräutigam expressed her rage about growing up in communes in her book *Bhagwan, Che und ich: meine Kindheit in den 70ern* (Bhagwan, Che and I: My Childhood in the 70s, 2005).[25]

And even those who were not born into a 68er world were clearly influenced by the all-pervasive cultural presence of "1968." Both Sven Regner in his *Herr Lehmann* trilogy (*Herr Lehmann* [Mr. Lehmann, 2001], *Neue Vahr Süd* [2004], *Der kleine Bruder* [The Little Brother, 2008]) and Gerhard Henschel in his *Martin Schlosser* novels regularly reference their antiauthoritarian heroes. In Henschel's *Bildungsroman* (2014), for example, the protagonist is acutely aware of the political vacuum the 68ers left behind when he moves to West Berlin in 1984:

> On the way home I passed the Audimax. There, Rudi Dutschke and his comrades had once given their grand speeches in front of a revolutionary-minded student body. Where had it gone?[26]

Judging from the stream of media stories, scholarly articles, television programs, and interviews, the question of what happened to the 68ers continues to fascinate audiences in Germany. In the following chapter, I explore the voices of the "forever young" generation as they move from cultural hegemony to the great gig in the sky.

9: Not Dark Yet: The 68ers at Seventy

THE 68ERS IN GERMANY are increasingly cast as a generation that has overstayed its welcome. Rebels who once coined the slogan "Trau keinem über 30" (Don't trust anyone over 30) must now face the inconvenient truth of their own aging. With the depiction of their increasing infirmity (of body if not of mind) comes a general disassociation with their former ideals and radical political agenda. The revolution has not taken place, certainly not in the way they had imagined. What was once perceived as dangerous and strangely attractive to broad sections of German youth has become, at least in media representations, a bit embarrassing, distinctly old-fashioned, and, in spite of occasional sympathetic portrayals, almost inexplicable to later generations.

A good example of how this perception is constructed is the cover of *Der Spiegel* 44/2007 with the headline "Gnade für die 68er" (Mercy/Clemency for the 68ers). It shows two aging hippies, smiling inanely, with the paraphernalia we associate with the late sixties: afghan coat, John Lennon eyeglasses, "Make Love Not War" badges, joint in hand, megaphone, sitar, and posters of Che Guevara, Mao, Marx, Lenin and Ho Chi Minh. The pair resemble former communard Rainer Langhans and rock singer Janis Joplin, but it is clear that they are meant to represent all 68ers. Above them is a banner with the words "Es war nicht *alles* schlecht" (It wasn't *all* bad; emphasis in the original). The title of the feature story itself, "Bürgerlich bis in die Knochen" (Bourgeois to the Core),[1] gives the impression that *Der Spiegel* has joined its conservative competitors in ridiculing the 68ers. This is not the case, however: the article itself is an excerpt from the book *I can't get no: 68er treffen sich wieder und rechnen ab* by WDR journalist Irmela Hannover and *Spiegel* editorial director Cordt Schnibben. The introduction makes clear that the political and cultural climate has changed in 2007, with high-profile figures like former *Tagesschau* anchor Eva Herman and *Bild* editor in chief Kai Diekmann roundly declaring that the 68ers are responsible for everything that is wrong with Germany. To counter these attacks, Hannover and Schnibben had invited sixteen former 68ers for a weekend to discuss whether their *Aufbruch* (departure, setting out) still meant anything to them. While opinions were predictably divided, the participants painted a broadly positive picture of their rebellion and how it had shaped political culture and everyday life in Germany.

The authors argue that the "68ers" as a homogenous group never existed—those who were active in 1968 had a myriad of positions and have, since the heady days of the rebellion, become successfully integrated citizens in all walks of life:

> The power of the 68ers is a projection in the heads of its critics: the imagined hegemony of a caste of like-minded people. In reality the inhabitants of this fortress have long ago climbed down from the heights of the "correct" world view and arrived in the valley of life where they shake their heads when they see ever new troops leading the attack against something that is assumed to be their legacy. (76)

This point was emphasized by the title of the article and the illustrations that showed, in equal measure, the participants in 1968 and in 2007, and stock photos of the time. The message was that "1968" may have been colorful and eventful, but that the activists had become middle-aged and decidedly harmless. The cover image and the headline "Gnade für die 68er," however, went far beyond that message. They suggested to the wider public—who may not have bothered to read the article—that one did not need to fight the 68ers any longer but should rather tolerate their quirky ways, as one would with an aging relative who has become a bit eccentric.

Anyone expecting the 68ers to go quietly into the night may be disappointed, though. The members of the baby boom generation (eight million Germans, one in ten, were born between 1940 and 1950) have a great appetite to enjoy their retirement. They tend to have more disposable income than their children[2] and, ironically, also have inherited considerable sums from the generation that rebuilt postwar Germany.[3] According to the report of the parliamentary commission on demographic change, they will use their influence to continue to shape public debates:

> Following this demographic change, the older generation in society represents an ever increasing power potential. They represent an increasing proportion of those entitled to vote, and an increasing minority in large associations like the unions. In addition, they increasingly set up their own organizations and are active in political parties and senior advisory boards.[4]

Some expect the 68ers to radically transform the way senior citizens live their lives,[5] though reliable studies on actual change in the behavior patterns of the 68er generation (*Alters-WGs* [senior citizens sharing a house or apartment], political and social activism, volunteering, lifelong learning, etc.) do not yet exist. Meanwhile, well-known representatives of the era are either passing away (e.g., communard Fritz Teufel, *taz* writer Christian Semler, or the author Peter-Paul Zahl), stepping down (e.g., Grips director Detlef Michel, the hosts of the *Philosophische Quartett* Peter Sloterdijk and Rüdiger Safranski), or redefining themselves to such an extent that their past as student activists or street fighters does not dominate the public's perception of them anymore. A case in point is Joschka Fischer, who has become an international policy advisor and runs his own consultancy firm. Seeing him walk through the museum of his own history in Pepe Danquart's documentary film *Joschka und Herr Fischer: Eine Zeitreise durch 60 Jahre Deutschland* emphatically illustrates the effect of the passage of time and the increasing difficulties in connecting the concerns of a militant firebrand in his twenties with those of a seasoned politician in his sixties.

While its presence in the media has somewhat lessened after the plethora of books, scholarly articles, exhibitions, and television programs in 2008, "1968" has not disappeared from the public sphere: especially the literary construction continues unabated. To illustrate this latest stage, I will take a brief look at Peter Schneider's *Rebellion und Wahn* (Rebellion and Delusion, 2008), Erasmus Schöfer's *Winterdämmerung* (The Twilight of Winter, 2008), Jochen Schimmang's *Das Beste, was wir hatten* (The Best We Had, 2008), Uwe Timm's *Freitisch* (Free Meals, 2011) and *Vogelweide* (Bird Meadow, 2013), Friedrich Christian Delius's *Als die Bücher noch geholfen haben* (When Books Were Still Helpful, 2012), Bernd Cailloux's *Gutgeschriebene Verluste* (Credited Losses, 2012), and Hans Magnus Enzensberger's *Tumult* (Tumult, 2014). These writers have been involved in the construction of "1968" over decades. Their work continues to attract broad attention, as evidenced by sales, book reviews, and longlisting to the German Book Prize (*Gutgeschriebene Verluste*; *Vogelweide*), as well as academic books and articles written about them and their work. I argue that these tale spinners remain committed to the cause: the project of Germany's *politische Alphabetisierung* and an aesthetic that evolved out of the spirit of "1968."

Between Rebellion and Delusion

With *Skylla* (2005), Peter Schneider had published a novel that showed a former 68er confronted with his past and the fatal consequences of his fiery speeches. In the "autobiographical narrative" *Rebellion und Wahn* (2008),[6] the author sheds further light on his own role in the movement, focusing on his life as writer, activist, and lover of a woman simply referred to as "L." who eventually joined the terrorist organization Bewegung 2. Juni. Schneider bases his reflections on the diaries he kept in the late 1960s. Reading through them, he finds himself confronted by someone who is both familiar and a total stranger. He feels a sense of superiority, seeing how naive and impulsive he used to be. Characterizing his younger self as "beschwipst" (intoxicated), "irrwitzig" (mad), and "übermütig" (full of beans/hyper), he nevertheless wants to do justice to "1968" and the historical moment:

> But I would not do justice to us and the mood at the time if I didn't talk about the euphoria of those months that blew like an intoxicating wind through the streets of Berlin. In those days, everything seemed possible, especially the impossible—and we, who were carried along by this wind, felt that history itself had chosen us to build a new society with new rules. It was a trip without drugs, the high of a "historically necessary" and "scientifically founded" utopia which had taken control of our brains and our hearts. (11)

Again and again, though, he returns to the question whether the 68ers' flirtation with violence was really justified. He admits that the "antifascist impulse" of the movement was based more on emotions than on hard facts (124) and worries that the "dreadful aberration of perhaps one hundred desperados" is the only aspect of his generation that will remain in our collective memory (177). Reflecting on his personal responsibility for the escalation of violence, Schneider returns to his *konkret* article "Gewalt in den Metropolen" from 1968, in which he had argued that it was acceptable to use "all available means"[7] to achieve the aims of the revolt. The article now appears to him as "the work of a delirious man" (272), who used a linguistic sleight of hand to convince the readers of *konkret* that direct action was justified in the face of the "latent violence"[8] the rebels allegedly encountered every day. He tries to rationalize his former radical position (Springer had never shown any remorse; he had been hopelessly in love with the radical L.; he does not feel shame for supporting the militant revolt in Detroit), but in the end the only explanation he can find for his "delusion" is that he had been the victim of a collective "intellectual contamination":

> I was then, I think, not more stupid than I am now. The metamorphosis that has to be depicted here is a collective process of mutual intellectual contamination, of manipulation and self-manipulation—not dissimilar to the type employed by political, but also religious sects of any kind. (273)

It is worth looking at this passage in some detail. Schneider initially accepts that he was compos mentis in 1968. But then, with a the air of a psychologist giving an expert witness statement in a murder trial, he exonerates himself by suggesting that he was the victim of a collective process of external and self-manipulation, akin to the brainwashing methods used by political and religious sects. Up to this point, the reader could be forgiven for believing that the author has joined renegades like Gerd

Koenen or Götz Aly.⁹ Interestingly, though, Schneider then allows his former self the right to reply, and the response is a withering indictment of his rationalizations:

> Where do you get the right to judge, what do you have to offer? Forget for one moment your explanations for my "delusion" and answer me this one question: Weren't those two years—the time when you and your careful considerations did not yet exist—even with all their horrors—the most important time of your life? Why do you constantly talk about them, why these tons of paper in the libraries, these weeks of expensive screen time, these endless kilometers of film about a small—and "failed"—student rebellion? (281)

In the end, readers will have to decide for themselves. Schneider now sees his former self as part of "the specifically German delusion of a global revolution" (278), "a frightening revolutionary" whose main motivation was to impress his then girlfriend L. (280–81). By juxtaposing innocence and experience, he shows us that neither the eager young activist nor the sage graybeard has a monopoly on the interpretation of "1968," but that, by turning the political into the private, we may arrive at a dialectic point where opposites are equally true.¹⁰

The Twilight of Winter

With *Winterdämmerung*, Erasmus Schöfer completed his tetralogy *Die Kinder des Sisyfos*, which charts the lives and struggles of a number of communists from the heady days of the Extraparliamentary Opposition in the late 1960s to New Year's Eve 1989. The fight against a third runway at Frankfurt Airport and the campaign of the workforce to keep open the Krupp works in Duisburg-Rheinhausen are ultimately unsuccessful, just as the attempt to establish a socialist society in Germany. But Schöfer is not despondent, nor are his protagonists Viktor Bliss, Martin Anklam, and Armin Kolenda, who continue to believe that an alternative to the capitalist system is possible even though they are at a loss how this could happen after the implosion of the GDR. Nevertheless, the tight-knit groups of rebellious workers, intellectuals, union officials, journalists, and dreamers continue to offer solidarity to each other, and the ideas of "1968" are never far away. The novel's key sentence occurs when a left-wing journalist reflects on the *Historikerstreit* (historians' quarrel) and German war guilt, a sentence that could be equally applied to the 68ers:

> If a past is contested to such an extent in the political present of a country, what can it mean other than that it is, on the one hand, unfinished and reversible, and, on the other hand, effective?¹¹

Schöfer's final part of the tetralogy can be interpreted in a number of ways. Left-leaning reviewers were missing a stronger message of hope. The book, ending with a worker hoisting the red flag on a tower of the decommissioned steel works while the protagonists gather to celebrate the end of another bruising decade, does indeed convey the sense of defeat. But there is no grand finale as in Richard Wagner's *Götterdämmerung* (Twilight of the Gods), with fire, water, and the demise of the gods. Instead, as the title of the book suggests, there is a muted sound of hope that at the end of a long, cold winter, a new spring will arrive.

The Best That We Had

In *Das Beste, was wir hatten*,[12] Jochen Schimmang, the author of *Der schöne Vogel Phönix*, tells the story of Leo Münks and Gregor Korff, two friends who had been left-wing radicals in West Berlin in the late sixties and since then have been swallowed up by the institutions they had set out to change on their Long March. Leo works for "das Amt" (the office), the Bundesverfassungsschutz (Germany's national intelligence agency), while Gregor has become special advisor to the conservative minister of the interior following Helmut Kohl's rise to power in 1982. While Leo's path was fairly linear (he had started spying on his fellow students while still at university), Gregor's journey was more complex: he spent two years in a Maoist group, then wrote his PhD thesis on the political theorist Carl Schmitt and finally taught administrative sciences at a backwater university before entering the corridors of power, "loyal, but without faith" (41).[13]

Imperceptibly, Gregor begins to feel in tune with the country he used to reject. He gets quite sentimental, and almost biblical, about the old Federal Republic—"This is my country, in which I am well pleased" (49)—and breathes in the "normality" and nonbelligerent quality of the Bonn republic that had allowed even a former radical like himself the chance to feel at home:

> The streets he walked every evening on his way home, with their friendly houses dating from the Wilhelminian era, were for him an ideal representation of the greatest possible happiness. [. . .] These houses drove away with their friendliness any frightening memories of his years in the training committee and in front of the factory gates, distributing flyers. All in all, they stood for a feeling of having gone through tough times and come out alive, not just in his own case, but for the whole country, at least the Western part. (88)

When the wall comes down, he realizes that the old Federal Republic of Germany had held many of the utopian attributes that he had been looking for in his youth, and that he actually loved this country. The irony, of course, is that this realization is cut short by German unification, which puts paid to this comfortable existence of driving along the Rhine in his Borgward Isabella and "blessing the country unawares" like a latter-day romantic.

Within the new political constellation, Gregor and Leo rediscover their rebel identity. They free Carl Schelling, a former comrade who had planned to blow up the Niederwald memorial near Rüdesheim,[14] and Gregor throws a couple of paint bombs during a podium discussion on "Wertewandel oder Werteverlust" (changing values or loss of values) at the thinly veiled fictional versions of the historian Michael Stürmer (who started on the Left in the late 1960s and later became an advocate of the Right, especially in the *Historikerstreit* of 1986/1987) and Peter Schneider (whom Gregor—and, presumably, Schimmang—regards as a renegade). When Gregor tells his mother what Carl had planned, she observes drily that no one should be arrested for blowing up the memorial; they should be given a medal instead (246).

Gregor and Leo attend a Bob Dylan concert and find themselves part of a large middle-aged audience who share a history of protest. They know that their time is over, but that doesn't mean that it didn't count:

> Most of the tears, however, remained hidden behind sunglasses. For many, they were surely shed in memory of the fact that one had once lived the original version, so to say. Of course, this time was irretrievably lost, but all those who stood there also knew that it could not be taken away from them. (254)

Das Beste, was wir hatten was enthusiastically reviewed.[15] Stephan Wackwitz declared that Schimmang's central thesis, that with the fall of the wall not only the GDR but also the old Federal Republic had come to an end, had not yet been widely acknowledged.[16] At the same time, Schimmang's story line of a postunification guerrilla who did not exist in reality indicated that the author had not written a history of the old Federal Republic but one as it could have, or perhaps even ought to have been. Volker Hage, in his review in *Der Spiegel*, went so far as to suggest that the novel was, if not a contender for the much anticipated *Wenderoman*, certainly a frontrunner for the best book about the vanishing of the old Federal Republic.[17]

Schimmang's novel, a meditation on the difference between state and nation, and the long and painful journey the 68ers took to come to terms with their complicated fatherland, is more than an elegy. It contributes to the construction of a master narrative that allocates them a significant role in the history of the Federal Republic, just as much as the old Federal Republic, for better or worse, is their spiritual home. Just as in *Winterdämmerung*, the monumental shift of German unification has upset the carefully achieved equilibrium, the truce between the 68ers and the state they once despised. But Schimmang sees perhaps more of a silver lining for the aging 68ers in unified Germany. Where Schöfer relies on a much shaken belief in the scientific accuracy of Marxist philosophy that expects the capitalist system to eventually collapse, Schimmang strikes a subtle balance between a belief in decisionist activism and the healing power of romantic imagination that allows his protagonists to approach their demise with some equanimity.

A Short Summer of Anarchy

In his 2011 novella *Freitisch*,[18] Uwe Timm revisits Ulrich Krause, the protagonist of his seminal 68er novel *Heißer Sommer* who also played a bit part in his magnum opus *Rot*. Still living in Anklam, a small town in Mecklenburg-Vorpommern near the Baltic Sea, he is now retired with two grown-up sons who "make money," tending a flower garden and his APO archive stocked with first editions of the revolutionary texts that had inspired the student movement. One day, he chances upon Euler, a friend from his early university days who is visiting the town. In the early 1960s, they were part of a group of four who were given a free meal each day in the staff canteen of a Munich insurance firm (the "Freitisch" of the title). Euler is a specialist in waste management and is scouting a site for a treatment plant of contaminated waste right where Ulrich and his wife have created a refuge from the world and live out their days in a "Hermann und Dorothea"-like idyll.

While the "unerhörte Begebenheit" (an unheard-of event; Goethe's definition of a novella) ostensibly refers to a pilgrimage Krause and Euler once made to the house of the writer Arno Schmidt—whom they all revered (and were deeply disappointed by when they met him in person)—the actual unheard-of event is the encounter between the two, forty-five years after their student days. Euler's visit to the town is strictly business, but on meeting Krause, they spend the day in a café reminiscing about the old days and catching up. Euler is initially reluctant to talk about what he calls their "Jugendsünden" (sins of youth, 14) but, warming to the subject, declares that life, and sex before the pill, used to be more intense in the sixties:

> I am convinced, Euler said abruptly, that our passions were more intensive, crazier and wilder in those days. [. . .] To let yourself go was a risk: a determination, blindness, an implosion of reason, a rapturous whirl. (32–33)

Krause agrees: "Yes, it really was a brief summer of anarchy" (36). Given that Timm wrote his requiem for "1968" in the novel *Rot* and the autobiographical narrative *Der Freund und der Fremde*, there is no reason to expect a radically different take on the era or major personal revelations. What *Freitisch* does is fill in the blanks in Ulrich Krause's life.[19] What used to be a rather two-dimensional character in *Heißer Sommer* who mainly served to exemplify a "typical" student rebel, turns out to have an interesting backstory, much like "1968" itself, which, according to the consensus among historians, can only be properly understood in the context of the "long 1960s" (see chapter 2). But we also get a glimpse of the life of a 68er in retirement: Krause gives (free) private tuition to local kids who have difficulties in school and involves himself in local initiatives. Euler's response is noncommittal, but we sense, through the narrator, that he is unimpressed by what became of Krause's "großer Aufbruch" (grand departure) all those years ago:

> Ah well. You used to support them in the old days. He smiled, not in a nasty way, and yet one could see in his face what he was thinking: So that's what has become of the revolutionary project of a new society—private lessons after school. (116)

The question whether Uwe Timm continues to support the ideas of "1968" at a time when they seem to be completely out of synch with the policies of a conservative-led government in Berlin and the triumph of global capitalism is hotly debated. I have argued elsewhere that *Rot*, in spite of outward appearances, does not discard the idealistic intentions of the 68ers together with its ideological baggage.[20] More recently, Peter Mohr has suggested that Timm has developed an "ever more distant relationship to the Student Movement and its left-wing romantics,"[21] referring to the long list of "gescheiterte Existenzen" (failed individuals)[22] in Timm's novels. Monika Albrecht disagrees, pointing to the author's continuing interest in, and commitment to, mutual and practical solidarity as exemplified by Krause first moving to the former East Germany, cutting his hours to give newly qualified teachers a chance, and, following his retirement, helping disadvantaged kids with their homework.[23]

While Timm may subversively continue to write the revolution, he is also well aware that society and reality have moved in a different direction. This becomes painfully clear in his novel *Vogelweide*. In this skillfully composed and layered novel, the protagonist Christian Eschenbach, another "gescheiterte Existenz," performs the duties of a bird warden on an island in the North Sea following the collapse of his business and the end of a passionate relationship that fundamentally altered the lives of two couples. While the allusions to Goethe's *Wahlverwandtschaften* (Elective Affinities) are most obvious, the novel also explores whether the sexual revolution and the 68ers' pursuit of individual fulfilment has not caused undue collateral damage. Most significant for our enquiry into the construction of "1968" and the aging of the 68ers is Timm's characterization of Eschenbach's parents. These are former revolutionaries and cofounders of the Republikanischer Club who now live in a "Rentnerparadies" (pensioners' paradise) in Munich with two other couples.[24] Eschenbach holds a grudging respect for his father, who clings to his ideals:

> He liked the old man, even though, or maybe because, he could not share his rage and tough persistence, and especially not his faith that one could radically change society and the individual. (247)

His daughter Sabrina, who works in finance, has no such sentimental sympathies. She cannot stand their grandparents' constant talk about "Gerechtigkeit" (justice, 266):

> The revolution. That's what the old man keeps saying in his comfortably furnished pensioners' commune. The revolution will come. It will be those who see through things. Not those who have nothing. The system has reached its limits. It creaks and groans. (267)

Timm revels in the irony that the 68ers who once declared that they would rather die than grow old are now as out of kilter with their children and grandchildren as the Nazi-generation was with them. When they talk about "Konsumterror" (terror of consumerism), both son and granddaughter think it is "a word from the political stone-age" (268) and Sabrina comments: "Opi has gone completely cuckoo" (270).

Toward the end of the book, when Anna, Eschenbach's former lover, visits him on his island, they talk about his parents, "a commune of old people, sitting on their balcony." In a seemingly inconsequential exchange that prefigures their brief reunion (the next day, Anna will return to her life in Los Angeles, her children, and a grueling course of chemotherapy), we can see a wistful acceptance of life passing but also the realization that desire can be rekindled, that a "magic moment" may return:

> Even our desires age, she said.
>   Perhaps they grow strong again and become, how shall I put it, viral, when forgetting sets in, and our control mechanisms are lowered or switched off. (323)

It is up to the reader to decide whether or not this is Timm hinting that the essence of "1968," in spite of the ridiculousness and "Unzeitmäßigkeit" (untimeliness, 267) of the 68ers, can survive the buffeting of our postpostmodern ways. The fact that he continues to mix in the central themes of the movement into his works, juxtaposing them with an ever-changing reality, suggests that the author hasn't yet given up on his own long-term project, which I would describe, with a nod to Hans

Magnus Enzensberger, as the *emotionale Alphabetisierung Deutschlands* (emotional alphabetization of Germany).

When Books Were Still Helpful

In *Als die Bücher noch geholfen haben,* Friedrich Christian Delius's collection of autobiographical essays, the author of *Amerikahaus, oder der Tanz um die Frauen* and *Mein Jahr als Mörder* returns to some of the key moments of his life. On the one hand, he declares that he is well and truly sick of the era: "Von 1968 habe ich, offen gesagt, die Schnauze voll" (To be frank, I've had it with 1968).[25] On the other hand, as the recipient of the prestigious Georg Büchner Prize in 2011, he does his level best to keep "1968" in the public sphere by using his considerable literary capital. He is well placed to shed light on the era and modify, even if only by degrees, the established image of "1968": as a promising young author he was invited to join the Gruppe 47; he worked as a Lektor at the Wagenbach Verlag, got into a protracted legal wrangle with the Siemens company over his satire *Unsere Siemens-Welt* and was instrumental in bringing Peter Schneider's *Lenz* to publication at the Rotbuch Verlag.

A shy and reticent student, he never belonged to the inner circle of the Extraparliamentary Opposition (he describes himself as "kein guter Linker" [not a good leftist, 70]), but he certainly felt part of the imaginative and playful antiauthoritarian movement in 1966/67, before language and action became radicalized. Looking back, he acknowledges that there was peer pressure to conform but equally the freedom to go one's own way (73). It is the independent thinkers within the movement that have his sympathy, precisely because they did not get the media attention:

> The images, reports and documents from those days do not lie, and yet they do. They show the people in the first few rows, the wildest faces, the most naked communards, the boldest posters, the most untidy flats, the reddest flags, the most spectacular actions. What gets quoted tends to be the most belligerent speeches, the most outrageous political gibberish and the most euphoric—instead of the most skeptical—voices. (78)

In hindsight, he feels that "1968" is not just a product of the media but the victim of its own hype—of being on the right side, of being able to change the world:

> No political movement other than the 68ers has ever been taken in to such an extent by its own myths and clichés. Most of these clichés are not even wrong. And yet, I say: everything was different, more contradictory, more ambiguous, and more playful. (79)

Credited Losses

Bernd Cailloux, the author of *Das Geschäftsjahr 1968/69*, picks up the story of his alter ego in *Gutgeschriebene Verluste*. Suffering from chronic hepatitis (contracted in his drug-fueled youth), he spends his days at the "Cafe der Übriggebliebenen" (Café of Those Left Behind),[26] where he meditates on aging, the long-term effects of substance abuse held at bay by expensive drugs, his unsatisfactory relationships, and whether the late sixties or the hedonistic eighties in Berlin were the best years of his life. By turns ironic, melancholic and depressed, he reflects that it is slightly embarrassing for anyone of his generation, no matter whether they had succumbed to the armed struggle or drug addiction, to still be alive:

> Some were driven out of their socialist utopia, others out of their artificial paradise; when they woke up, both were left with a hangover. This doesn't stop them from feeling a twinge of embarrassment for still being alive, given that all the many really significant figures have kicked the bucket. (176–77)

As Jochen Schimmang has noted,[27] Cailloux is at his best when he observes his fellow 68ers and the way some of them have turned their youthful escapades into a career. For example, the protagonist gets invited to a podium discussion on "1968 and its legacy" in Zurich in his capacity as coinventor of the strobe light that illuminated the psychedelic music of the time. Ironically, neither he nor a former SDS leader—who is proud "to have stood on the right side at least once in his life" (211)—is the star of the event, but a former RAF terrorist (now residing in Tuscany) who is treated with reverence by the fawning academics and the audience. The protagonist, who can't think of much to say other than the bon mot "Sixty-Eight must not die"[28] feels like an outsider in his own generation:

> Such encounters unsettled me every time. What humiliation for a member of my generation not to have been at the center of the student movement, what an affront given that others had experienced such exclusivity! To have carried Dutschke's bag for him at least once, to have fought over the text of flyers for a year or two with a future TV-philosopher in a Maoist group, that was the minimum price of membership. Someone like me, coming from what was at best a semi-political subculture, was destined to listen rather than talk. (205)

Tumult

It seems appropriate to end this chapter with the author who initiated the writers' quest for the "politische Alphabetisierung Deutschlands" in his

Kursbuch in 1968.[29] In the autobiographical text *Tumult*, Hans Magnus Enzensberger delves deep into his diaries and notebooks. While he covers his literary and personal journeys of discovery to the Soviet Union, the United States, and Cuba, the focus is clearly on "1968," the era the book's title refers to. Like Peter Schneider in *Rebellion und Wahn*, he imagines a dialogue with his former self who has become a stranger to him:

> This "I" was someone else. I saw only one way in which I could approach him: in a dialogue with a double (Doppelgänger), who seemed like a younger brother to me, a brother I hadn't thought of for a long time. I decided to ask him many questions.[30]

In the chapter "Erinnerungen an einen Tumult (1967–1970)," Enzensberger expands significantly on his previously published "Erinnerungen an einen Tumult: Zu einem Tagebuch aus dem Jahre 1968" (Memories of a Tumult: On a Diary from the Year 1968, 1985) and manages to erase himself almost completely out of the picture, as someone who stayed "in der Kulisse" (backstage, 152), and can only accept a "Rest von Komplizentum" (a remnant of responsibility as an accomplice, 265) for simply having lived through the era.[31] He claims to be surprised at how much had been going on in those three years, given that he was often elsewhere (e.g., at the time of the Vietnam Congress he was in Berkeley). However, his verdicts on the impact of the German student movement prove that he has paid, and continues to pay, close attention to the ongoing construction of "1968" and is well aware of his own role in it. In a sardonic broadside at the extraordinary flexibility with which German capital and consumer society have adapted to the challenge of the 68ers, he describes the Kommune I as

> the very first who were serious about the removal of the private sphere. Most likely they had no clue what they had done. An entire industry has followed them on this path. Private television, a medium that does not allow any form of private life, copied their formula and makes enormous profits with its various shows. Since then, no voyeur or exhibitionist has to go and visit a run-down flat in Berlin any more. Just switch on the telly. (116–17)

His alter ego is visibly exasperated by the author's obfuscation and challenges him to say something concrete about "1968," but Enzensberger stays true to his image as "harlequin at the court of the would-be revolutionaries" (Habermas) who cannot be tied down to a single position:

> *Is that all you have to say?*
> No. 1968, is no more than an imaginary number, a milling mass of reminiscences, self-delusions, generalizations and projections that

have replaced what actually happened in those few years. The experiences lie buried beneath the dung heap of the media, of the archival materials, the podium discussions, the stylization of veteran experiences which have become unimaginable by now. (236–37, italics in original)

These experiences, the reader is led to deduce, are valid, important, and potentially still instructive, especially the liberating and emancipating moments of antiauthoritarian action. But apparently they lie "buried" beneath the detritus of representations, to which, ironically, the author has now added another layer. Even at the age of eighty-five, Hans Magnus Enzensberger remains one of the most perceptive and skillful manipulators of the written word. At one point, the author who had once claimed that West Germany's political system was "quite beyond repair" suggests that the "politische Alphabetisierung" may have worked after all:

To my surprise, it became apparent that our wasted country had inadvertently, almost behind our backs, become more and more habitable. [. . .] There are signs and miracles happening in Germany. One might even think the Republic was on the way to civilization. (243)

But we need to read carefully: the qualification "might" signals that optimism may well be misplaced and that, once again, the establishment, the political elites, the media, and the "Bewußtseinsindustrie" have prevailed. The victories that the 68ers and their "Systemopposition" (opposition to the system) might claim to have won, for example the modernization of institutions like kindergardens and universities, were, Enzensberger suggests, merely minor concessions of a quick-learning capitalist society (269).

Summary

Once more the veteran writers of the revolution evoke what the media (condescendingly) and publishers (with an eye to their aging readership) have come to call "der Aufbruch einer Generation" (the departure or setting out of a generation), but now with an awareness of time slipping away and a wistful focus on the unfulfilled promise of "1968." An elegiac quality has entered their work, which we could term "late style,"[32] were it not for their stubborn insistence on the continuing validity of their quest and their youthful spirit. Their writing is deeply reflective and self-aware, especially of being strangers in a (father-)land they had only belatedly come to accept as theirs. The generation that hoped to die before they got old has left its *Prominenzphase* (era of their greatest visibility and influence) and entered uncharted waters, a stage in life when one has one last chance to admit mistakes, to forgive if not forget, to remember (if one can), and to evaluate one's defining moments in the light of a lifetime's experience.[33] This may sound sentimental, but it also points to an affinity to romantic thought that accompanied the German student movement from the outset. In the following chapter, I explore whether the construction of "1968" is the consequence of a romantic relapse or whether other, hitherto ignored factors play a role in this narrative.

10: Romantic Relapse or Modern Myth?

Looking at the construction of "1968" by historians, novelists, and the media over the past five decades, this study has revealed two important points that need to be borne in mind when discussing its "afterlives." The first one is that this building work is not happening randomly but consciously, overseen by a relatively small number of determined writers who have a clear (though often not declared) objective in mind.[1] There may be several objectives, which can amplify each other or cancel each other out. An example for this phenomenon would be the claim that "1968" has freed Germans from their "authoritarian character" versus the claim that "1968" has undermined "secondary virtues" like diligence, obedience, sense of duty, and discipline.

The second point is that we need to distinguish the aims and objectives of the German student movement from its subsequent construction in history books, literature, and the media. While some of the people active in the movement have become interpreters of their own history, others have come to writing about "1968" for a variety of reasons, often in response to sociopolitical developments that they see in some way connected to the German student movement (or which can be blamed on them). An example for this would be the recurring reference made to antiauthoritarian practices in primary and secondary education and their alleged disastrous impact on the attitudes and performance of school leavers.[2] We should also note that different political constellations in the past five decades have repeatedly changed the trajectory of the discourse over the legacy of "1968," for example the "German Autumn" in 1977, German unification in 1989/90, the coming to power of the red–green government in 1998, the terrorist attacks in September 2001, or the global financial crisis in 2008.

A third point that needs to be made is that the German student movement has, right from the start, invited an association with a number of cultural reference points that have, for better or worse, influenced the course of German history and continue to shape German identity debates in the present. In this chapter, I explore two interpretative paradigms that help explain the longevity and intensity of the debate in Germany. Via processes of nostalgic memorialization, utopian projection, and aesthetic reimagination, the student movement has been, and continues to be, cast as a "romantischer Rückfall" (romantic relapse) and a "Gründungsmythos" (foundation myth), powerful constructions that shape our perception of "1968."

"1968" and the Romantic Imagination

The German student movement has long been suspected of romantic affinities, and repeatedly described as a well-meaning but essentially irrational and impractical attempt by a group of oversensitive malcontents to reconfigure consensus reality. A number of historians, critics, and journalists have adopted this paradigm in one form or another, as the following examples will illustrate.

In January 1968, Marion Gräfin Dönhoff analyzed the "Rebellion der Romantiker" as an explosive mix of idealistic utopianism and agnostic realism:

> What ails them is the alienation, the sense of being defenceless against the power of anonymous bureaucracies, the hypocrisy of a society whose moral maxims have become clichés. Believing in miracles like the Romantics, these young moralists expect salvation from "consciousness-raising." They believe that they are already on the long march that leads to an ideal society without an establishment, without lies and deceit, where bureaucracy has no power, money is irrelevant, and where students know more than professors. It seems to be a new type of charismatic redemption.[3]

In 1970, Richard Löwenthal interpreted the radical students' contempt of West Germany's young democracy as a "romantischer Rückfall."[4] He claimed that they showed a complete refusal to accept the reality (and rules) of the modern industrialized world. By attempting to destroy its institutions instead of humanizing them, and negating all values instead of reformulating them, the intellectual leaders of the movement had therefore given in to a "romantic nihilism" that preferred romantic utopia over any reform. Although the revolt was, in his view, politically inconsequential in the short term, Löwenthal feared that their "Glaubenssucht" (addiction to something to believe in, 36) would make the followers of the movement easy prey for totalitarian ideologies, just as their parents had followed the Nazis.

In *The Germans*, the historian Gordon A. Craig pointedly linked his chapters on German Universities and on German romanticism.[5] The romantic movement, he argued, was essentially a youth and protest movement, searching for a world of imagination and wonder. The German students in the second half of the 1960s had formed a similar movement, characterized by cultural pessimism and a rejection of consumerism and commercialized culture. What the various countercultural groups had in common, according to Craig, was a retreat from reality into a self-created subculture and their lack of clear visions of what they wanted their new society to be.

Building on the work of social psychologist Peter Brückner, Lothar Voigt has argued that a "säkularisierte Erlösungshaltung" (a secularized hope for redemption) had determined the students' actions:

> During the so-called "hot" phases of the movement, when their actions where most visible, the activists began to believe that their search was almost over. They expected redemption in the form of revolution, most commonly world revolution. The activists had no doubt that it would happen. This chiliastic state of mind sits outside normal reality, it exists in a community of like-minded believers, united in their determination to radically change the status quo. There is no need to talk about this way of thinking, it is felt.[6]

Alois Prinz suggested in his study on the relationship between social movements and literature that the world view of the student movement had a profound influence on the literature representing it. It had the same aesthetic and political concepts as the romantic movement, only the form of realization was different. Thus, a romantic counterworld was created to convey the subjective "Anspruch auf Glück" (claim to happiness).[7]

Even Wolfgang Kraushaar eventually accepted the paradigm. In *Achtundsechzig: Eine Bilanz* (Sixty-Eight: An Assessment, 2008), he devotes a brief chapter to the "romantische Revolte" (romantic revolt):[8]

> Above "1968" floated a gigantic romantic cloud. It floated above all the enthusiasm for any kind of alternative to existing society: for anormality, adventure, intoxication and celebration; for action, discussion, introspection and endless talking; for the dream, imagination, and utopia; for far away exotic countries and peoples, no matter whether in Latin America, Africa or Asia. And it was no accident that, at least for a short while, so-called marginalized groups were considered to be the only remaining revolutionary subjects. (259)

Kraushaar argues that the 68ers—unconsciously—copied the German romantic movement by fomenting "a revolution in spirit" (261):

> Since the revolution did not take place in social reality, it could only be articulated in cultural terms, as a poetic figure in a world of the imagination, in the form of as-if-it-had-happened. The desire for freedom could only be lived out in the spiritual arena, in literature, in the theatre, in music, in conversation and correspondence. It remained a subjective figure, a desire that lacked the political strength to achieve social change. The romantic revolt was therefore necessarily a phenomenon that could only express itself in the medium of aesthetics. (261)

The question we need to ask, though, is this: what does it mean if we read "1968" as a romantic project? In a German context, we are immediately confronted with a myriad of connotations and associations, ranging from Novalis's dictum "Die Welt muß romantisiert werden" (the world must be romanticized),[9] Schlegel's demand to overcome the man-made barriers of ideology and theory in order to reconcile man and nature via the creative self, Richard Wagner's *Ring Cycle*, the Nazi myth of the "Tausendjährige Reich" (the Thousand Year Reich), to the *Heimatfilme* of the 1950s that harked back to a simpler past that never really existed.

But we need to be very careful. The romantic mindset characterized by Lothar Pikulik as an "Ungenügen an der Normalität" (dissatisfaction with normality, 1979), has come under fire from the Right as well as from the Left and used as a label for apolitical daydreaming, while it originally represented an effort by disenfranchised Germans to envisage ways of escaping oppression. On its own, the characterization of a protest movement as a "romantische Revolte" can be understood as a critique of an irrational response to the sadly but necessarily suboptimal conditions of life, or as praise for an emancipatory project that challenges the arbitrarily set rules of the establishment. By interpreting "1968" as a "romantischer Rückfall," though, the utopian impulse of the rebelling students is constructed specifically as a potentially dangerous and ultimately futile attempt, since history (with references to Germany's failed revolutions in 1848 and 1918, as well as the disaster of the so-called national socialist revolution in 1933) tells us that no good can come out of an attempt to change the status quo.[10]

If the characterization of "1968" as a "romantic relapse" seems somewhat unfair, then the 68ers and those who keep their memory alive have certainly helped to make the label stick, by nostalgically imbuing the period with "magic moments," epiphanies, and a diffuse set of emotions balancing a sense of loss and a sense of expectation. For example, Peter Mosler's stylization of the 68ers as a romantically doomed generation could easily be mistaken for a portrait of the romantics:

> They are different from their fathers because of their sensitivity, which the unhappy awareness of society forces upon them. It is a situation where the old is without strength, but the new without contours; even the awareness of the not-yet is rare, instead there is a sense of no-more, even mourning.[11]

Barbara Sichtermann, writing in the Wagenbach-anthology *Die Früchte der Revolte* (The Fruits of the Revolt), which was published on the twentieth anniversary of "1968," underlines the symbolic significance of the 68ers' insistence on the dominance of subjective experiences, which was one of the key tenets of German romanticism and which stood in direct opposition to the experience of their parents and their teachers (as well as the type of Socialism practiced in the GDR):

> The greatest achievement of 1968 is on the one hand the subjective experience of an entire generation: "If we stand up, the whole world will notice us"—and we the world. However, 1968 is misunderstood without the symbolic content of subjectivity, the experience of uprising and discovery: without it, this year and its emphatic attitude appears as a broken promise, a plan never realized, and of course this is how people like to see it. But, right from the beginning, the promise was too big to keep, the plan too daring to turn into reality overnight, but this realization wasn't really the point, at least not entirely. The promise meant that it was possible to conceive of revolution, change, praxis—a lot, even though, measured against the criteria of the revolt, not enough. The possibility of revolution was suddenly in the world, perhaps for the last time, and that is the second great achievement of 1968.[12]

One could go on. When Jochen Schimmang nostalgically describes the late 1960s as a time "als die Welt noch in Ordnung war" (when the world was still ok)[13] or when the *taz*, on occasion of the fortieth anniversary, dejectedly asks, "War unser Traum ein Hirngespinst?" (Was our dream just a fantasy?),[14] "1968" emerges as a golden age that has vanished and is unlikely to be recovered. The sense of loss conveyed in these headlines is all-pervasive. But loss can be mourned and worked through, or it can cloud our judgement and take us into dark places. In the following excursion, I highlight one specific way in which "1968" has tapped into a romantic legend that has been used for sinister purposes.

In contrast to the Arthurian legend, where the heroes gather around the roundtable between quests for the common good (at least according to T. H. White), and the return of a golden age is a legitimate hope,[15] the German romantic tradition is inextricably linked with the much darker *Nibelungenlied*, a medieval epic poem that was reconstructed by patriotic Germanists in the nineteenth century as a *Nationalepos* (national epic), a blueprint for a national character that had yet to be built. Here, we have an emphasis on *triuwe* (unconditional support, based on the binding relationship between a ruler and his subjects) to the bitter end, often in full awareness that the leader's objectives are morally and ethically wrong.

In July 1914, following the assassination of Crown Prince Franz Ferdinand, Emperor Wilhelm II declared that the German Empire stood "in Nibelungentreue" (unswerving loyalty) with its Austro-Hungarian ally. Under National Socialism, the *Nibelungentreue* was referenced exhaustively. The SS motto was "Meine Ehre heißt Treue" (My honor lies in my loyalty), and Hermann Göring compared the fate of the German soldiers in Stalingrad with the Burgundian knights who were slaughtered in King

Etzel's hall. The 68ers were well aware of this tradition through their school curriculum, and, while it seems paradoxical that they would condone or copy behavior patterns that they had criticized in their parents' generation, they nevertheless, consciously or unconsciously, displayed similar traits in their practice. While I would not go as far as Götz Aly, who suggested in *Unser Kampf* that the 68ers had internalized their parents' values, the strong sense of *duty* cultivated by the radical students ("Die Pflicht jedes Revolutionärs ist es, die Revolution zu machen" was the slogan chosen for the huge banner at the International Vietnam Conference), the emphasis on unconditional *solidarity* (often expected for the support of imprisoned comrades, Third World guerrillas, and later RAF terrorists), and the sense of a collective *mission* (Dutschke's strategy of the Long March) indicate that the motivations behind "1968" were more deeply rooted in German romanticism than generally acknowledged.

We can find plenty of evidence for the enduring lure of the *Nibelungen* saga and its behavior codex in the literary representations of "1968": In *Vesper, Ensslin, Baader: Urszenen des deutschen Terrorismus* (primal scenes of terrorism, 2003), Gerd Koenen explores Bernward Vesper's tortuous but ultimately futile attempts to destroy his "faschistischer Charakterpanzer" (fascist character armour). while Peter Schneider's choice of the word "Wahn" (delusion) in his 2008 autobiography indicates an intimate acquaintance with Wagner's *Ring Cycle*. Similarly, Uwe Timm's depiction of the symbolic killing of the dragon by St. George in the novel *Rot* (a reproduction of Paolo Uccello's *St George and the Dragon* hangs in Aschenberger's apartment) and extensive allusions to Richard Wagner (who himself started off as a fervent revolutionary) signal that German romantic iconography has a firm hold on the imagination of the 68ers and their tale spinners.[16] Again, one could go on. Uwe Timm has in recent years consistently referenced German medieval literature (e.g., in *Der Freund und der Fremde*, when he places his friend Benno Ohnesorg in a posture famously adopted by the Minnesang poet Walter von der Vogelweide, or when he gives the protagonist in *Vogelweide* the name of the medieval poet Wolfram von Eschenbach), while Erasmus Schöfer's *Winterdämmerung* evokes the twilight of the gods in Wagner's *Ring Cycle*.

The effect of associating "1968" with romantic thought and imagery, whether in a positive (golden age, utopian dream) or negative (romantic relapse) sense, is significant for our discussion of its construction. In the tradition of German romanticism, men and women of letters continue to shape public opinion, taste, ideologies, and political programs. By comparing life as it is with life as it might be, either in an imagined past or a utopian future, present reality appears wanting.

What is often overlooked by those who see the 68ers as latter-day romantics is that the utopian impulse that fueled the student movement was not limited to the widening of subjective perception and individual consciousness but also contained a strong pragmatic element: the realization that the liberation of the individual had to go hand in hand with a recognition of the need for these individuals to join in collective action in order to change the status quo, human nature, and reality:

> The notion that happiness is an objective condition which demands more than subjective feelings has been effectively obscured; its validity depends on the real solidarity of the species "man," which a society divided into antagonistic classes and nations cannot achieve. As long as this is the history of mankind, the "state of nature," no matter how refined, prevails: a civilized *helium omnium contra omnes*, in which the happiness of the ones must coexist with the suffering of the others.[17]

By labeling the students' utopian vision of a better world without war, hunger, oppression, and exploitation as a romantic, that is, unobtainable and futile daydream, it is denigrated as a puerile fantasy, regarded by those who are interested in maintaining the status quo with what Herbert Marcuse would have described as "repressive Toleranz" (repressive tolerance).[18] The alternative to seeking this radical change is the view that we already live in the best possible world, and that, given that we have reached a stage in human civilization where socialism has failed and capitalism has triumphed, there is no more history to come.[19] This is where the discourse of "1968 as myth" comes in.

"1968" between Myth and Reality

Closely related to the ongoing construction of "1968" as a romantic relapse is its construction as a foundational myth. Here, the German student movement is painted not only as a nostalgically remembered point in time that one may or may not be able to recreate through the romantic imagination but also as a crucial moment that has altered the course of West German history (see chapter 2). The tenacity with which the 68ers insist on the uniqueness of their revolt and with which critics have asserted its significance for Germany's "Fundamentalliberalisierung,"[20] has, over time, solidified the narrative into a myth: there once was a time when brave young students challenged the might of government, business, police, and press with their demands for a radically different reality, one that would break with the country's authoritarian past. By doing so, the myth asserts, they effected a second founding of the Federal Republic of Germany.[21]

As with the discourse on the "Rebellion der Romantiker," however, there is a different way to interpret the "myth of 1968": if we define a myth not as a foundational narrative that carries important truths for a collective, but as a narrative based on wishful thinking, or one that is told with the intention to manipulate, mislead, and omit the unflattering mistakes made along the way, then the *Mythos 1968* (myth of 1968) acquires very different connotations. Ironically, the rebellion of the 68ers against unquestioned (master-)narratives has opened up their own "story" to challenge and ridicule, resulting in a distinctly battered image and a permanently contested legacy.

The historians, writers, and journalists discussed in this book have been the main producers of the *Mythos 1968*, by asserting that the German student movement with its intense experiences, notable individuals, and collective actions contained a wealth of meanings that should not be forgotten. By the thirtieth anniversary, an awareness spread that a myth had been created, and a more critical reaction set in: Arthur Marwick talked about "nostalgic mythologizing,"[22] while Ingrid Gilcher-Holtey included Robert Frank's essay "1968: Ein Mythos?" (1968: A Myth?, 1998) in her volume on the historicization of the era.[23] In 2000, Wolfgang Kraushaar published his influential *1968 als Mythos, Chiffre, und Zäsur*, which purported to critically engage with the mythicization of the German student movement: "Wer dem 'Mythos 68' nicht aufsitzen will, dem bleibt nichts anderes übrig, als die damalige Jugendbewegung zu historisieren" (If we don't want to be hoodwinked by the myth of "1968," then we have to historicize the erstwhile youth movement).[24] Ultimately, though, he added to the myth by means of a seemingly innocent observation printed on the dust cover:

> The question remains [steht im Raum] whether a fundamental transformation of mentalities, lifestyles and life plans, the creation of norms for a civil society, and the fundamental liberalization of the new middle classes would have even been conceivable without the thrust created by the antiauthoritarian movement.[25]

Even if we ignore the fact that hardly anyone actually asked the question (and certainly not in this suggestive way), this statement cunningly asserts two aspects that are key to the mythicization of "1968": First, that the antiauthoritarian movement was responsible for a fundamental change in the mentality, lifestyles, life plans, as well as the development of a civic society and the fundamental liberalization of the new middle classes in West Germany. Second, that all these changes would not even have been *conceivable* without the impetus from the rebelling students.

In his discussion of the concept of myth, its political function, and its relationship to nation, religion, ideology, cult, and democracy, Matthias Waechter has pointed out that the term "myth" is often juxtaposed with "reality" or "truth."[26] This is certainly the case when we encounter the *Mythos 1968* outside academic circles: the press and countless chat shows never tire of asking the question whether "1968" wasn't just a chimera, and openly challenge the dominance of the narrative that sees "1968" in a broadly positive light.[27] What they tend to overlook is the fact that a myth works on an emotional level, and by endlessly repeating the narrative, the myth emerges even stronger as it is publically acknowledged that it was an event of great significance. I would add that these articles and television programs can also have a compensatory and comforting function: they can signal that while history has taken a different turn, the actions of the 68ers in the past have not been in vain. That way, former activists (as implied audience) can feel accepted by the collective, though their demands have been rejected.

Even when established academics engage directly with the mythicization of "1968," they cannot seem to escape its gravitational pull. Thus Hubert Kleinert sets out to critically engage with the *Mythos 1968* in the respected *Aus Politik und Zeitgeschichte* published by the Bundeszentrale für politische Bildung, only to conclude with the core tenet of the myth itself: "68 has brought about the fundamental liberalization of society, as well as the democratization of all areas of life."[28] The sociologist Rudi Schmidt manages to escape the vortex, but only by artificially distinguishing between the "myth," which he describes as "erfahrungs- und aufklärungsresistent" (resistant to experience and critique),[29] and the "cypher," which is a shorthand for whatever observers want to associate with "1968." Schmidt assigns the mythical elements to the *intentions* of the movement:

> "68" is a myth because the aim was, in one all-encompassing gesture, to do away with nothing less than "the domination of man over man"; because the exciting unity of thinking, action and feeling, of national and international perspectives, caused, at least for a few months, a complete blindness towards social background, religious beliefs and gender; and because it was initially easy (at least in the early anti-authoritarian phase) to claim one's moral superiority over the guilt-ridden father-generation. "68" became a myth because of its overbearing utopian message, its claimed reconciliation of absolute freedom and equality, its transcendence of the performance principle into the pleasure principle, and because of the immediacy of a de-sublimated sex-drive.[30]

In contrast, he assigns the cypher "1968" a more flexible role in political and cultural debates about the *consequences* of the revolt:

> In public rhetoric, "68" generally functions as a cypher for revolution, radical change, etc., either in positive connotations [. . .], or as pure destruction. [. . .] In the confrontational battle between political camps, "68" serves mainly as a destructive event, so that its long-term effects can be blamed on the initiators, that is, the "68ers."

In a cultural context, on the other hand, the cypher stands for an irreversible liberalising push in everyday life, for the definitive arrival of German society in the modern world.

Whatever the niceties of definition, the concept of "1968 as myth" has become commonplace in recent years. As a consequence, the editors of the journal *The Sixties* believe that rather than ignoring the mythicization we should accept and creatively engage with it by exploring its relationship to the historicization of the era:

> One may already feel so inundated with all things Sixties that it is tempting to pit history against memory and try to rescue the Sixties *as a period*, accessed through careful research, from "the Sixties" as a *popular mythology*, spun largely by mass entertainments, middlebrow commentary, commercial bromides, and pedagogic clichés. Though we certainly champion rigorous inquiry, this is a temptation worth at least partially resisting. Above all, it is neither easy nor even advisable to separate history categorically from myth, let alone the past from its representation. Far more fruitful is to explore their dialectic—the means by which history converts to myth, as well as how the past itself may resist certain forms of mythmaking.[31]

Whether the mythicization of "1968" is always treated with critical rigor is doubtful, though. Given its prominent place in publications like Etienne François and Hagen Schulze's *Deutsche Erinnerungsorte* (Places of Memory, 2001), Herfried Münkler's *Die Deutschen und ihre Mythen* (The Germans and Their Myths, 2009), or Stephanie Wodianka and Juliane Ebert's *Metzler Lexikon moderner Mythen* (Metzler Lexicon of Modern Myths, 2014), we risk "buying into" the narrative that the era holds a particular significance for the collective.[32]

One aspect that has been stressed recently is that the myth does not only look backward but also provides perspectives for the present and hope for the future. Claus Leggewie talks about "the living myth of '68," which feeds a sense of possibility,[33] while Uwe Timm devotes a highly personal essay on the power of "Gründungsmythen" which, he believes, contain within them a promise of hope and permanence.[34] Timm regards a myth as "einen Erzählmodus hochverdichteter Sinndeutung" (a narrative mode with highly compressed interpretations, 40). As such, the myth of "1968" contains a myriad of individual moments, derring-do and epiphanies that began with the death of Benno Ohnesorg:

> It was the beginning of the rebellion of the young against their fathers, against the establishment with the great and the good, among them many judges, policemen, government officials who had previously served the NS state. Even if the protest started because of the authoritarian actions of the economic and political establishment,

it wasn't just about co-determination in universities, editorial offices, theatres or publishing houses. Rather, it was about the desire for a different form of life, and also a different self. What was needed was sensitivity, a distinctive perception of the mechanisms of power, of injustice, of open and hidden use of violence, also between the sexes. The desire for equality, for free and open relationships. Play. Sensuality. Challenge. Having a say in one's work, for whom and on what. The point, as Herbert Marcuse put it, was to turn reason into liberating action. A concrete utopia. The myth was the *action*, was political praxis that did not allow anything personal. Yes to theory, but no to aesthetics, unless it was the aesthetics of enlightenment and propaganda. Literature was declared dead as it was considered incapable of change. Where everything was explained in terms of the class antagonism, disinterested pleasure was suspicious. Thus, we have very little myth-forming literature from this period of revolt, even though, and this is the punch line, the era was full of myths like no other, of *lived* myths. (55–56, italics in original)

It would be easy to accuse Timm of simply repeating and reaffirming the familiar 68er narrative in an obvious attempt to manipulate the reader, were it not for the direction he now takes. Just as with his personal family myth which, over time, had become embellished and smoothed out to replace sobering reality, so the myth of "1968" has become the victim of nostalgic projection. The reality, Timm admits, was very different: the revolution and the hoped-for support from the working class were simply "Wunschbilder" (wishful thinking, 58). For him, the myth only retains its meaning through the experience and promise of the revolt as a lived experiment of emancipation:

The revolution with its borrowed images of guns and spanners held high has failed. What hasn't failed is the project of a life praxis which incorporates something that is living, sensual and incomplete, something which Jacques Derrida described as the emancipatory promise. (58)

Summary: "1968" as Aesthetic Reimagination

The processes of romanticization and mythicization of "1968" share a number of characteristics. They are both engaged in the aesthetic construction of reality, they require constant updating to match an increasingly distant past with an ever-changing present, and they oscillate between a nostalgic backward glance and a defiant hope directed toward the future. Together, they create a "virtual past," of which the British novelist David Mitchell wrote:

The actual past is brittle, ever-dimming + ever more problematic to access + reconstruct: in contrast, the virtual past is malleable, ever-brightening + ever more difficult to circumvent/expose as fraudulent.

The present presses the virtual past into its own service, to lend credence to its mythologies + legitimacy to the imposition of will. Power seeks + is the right to "landscape" the virtual past. (He who pays the historian calls the tune.)[35]

We should however allow for the possibility to escape the myth, to detach ourselves from the script. The cultural critic Martin Burckhardt has done just that in his *68: Die Geschichte einer Kulturrevolution* (68: The History of a Cultural Revolution, 2009). Readers expecting another version of the myth were in for a surprise, for Burckhardt frees himself from what he regards as "Pfadfinderträume" (scout dreams, 9) and "Selbstermächtigungsphantasie" (self-empowerment fantasy, 10) of the 68ers. He acknowledges the power of political romanticism but suggests that the real cultural revolution in 1967/68 took place elsewhere: in the "separation of the head from the body"[36] (for example with the first heart transplantation and discovery of antibodies, the development of hardware and software that anticipated the Internet, and the introduction of the free-floating dollar). In this way, the "Epochenriss" (epochal rupture, 176) of "1968" is no longer defined by the caesura of a student protest that after all occurred in all modern societies, but a genuine "Nullpunkt der Geschichte" (point zero of history, 175) where the foundations of our reality were moved in a much more profound way.

Nevertheless, the construction, deconstruction, and subsequent reconstruction of the *Mythos 1968* have produced a master narrative that has certain similarities to foundational myths like the American War of Independence, the French Revolution or the *Stunde Null* (zero hour). The tale spinners producing the myth all have their role to play: the historians provide the detail, the media adds color, while the literary imagination attempts to give us an insight into the protagonists. As the layers of autobiographical, sensational, nostalgic, vitriolic, and analytical writing accumulate, they turn into something else: a cultural memory, an entertainment, a red rag, or a call to action.

Conclusion

THIS BOOK SET out to answer three closely related questions:

1) How can a relatively small number of individuals maintain control over the cultural memory of a generation?
2) How has the representation of "1968" changed in response to political events over the last five decades?
3) To what extent has "1968" become the master narrative of a nostalgically commemorated West Germany?

The discussion has shown that the perseverance of a cultural elite made up of novelists, academics, and journalists has indeed created, maintained, and defended a concept of "1968" that is now very difficult to alter, at least in its key elements. If it is true that history is written by the victors, then the 68ers—and their tale spinners—seem not to have heard the news. In spite of the students' failure to achieve their key objectives, "1968" is seen today as a crucial moment in postwar German history that "changed everything": attitudes to authority, sexuality, democracy, history, traditions, and cultural practice. Over five decades the student revolt has been historicized, memorialized, sensationalized, romanticized, analyzed, mythicized, theorized, dramatized, aestheticized, vilified, and glorified. Through a process of construction, deconstruction, and reconstruction, former activists, writers, academics, and the media have fashioned a complex narrative if not for a nation, then certainly for the old Federal Republic. In doing so, they created a collective consciousness that continues to shape political and cultural identities in united Germany.

What has become clear is that "1968" isn't just a narrative produced by 68ers: it has become a screen onto which a small but vocal group of historians, political scientists, sociologists, novelists, political pundits, media professionals, and activists from the Left and Right project their political opinions and private fantasies. Almost fifty years on, "1968" in Germany is not primarily about historicization or impact or cultural memory, though these aspects are all important. The initial impetus for writing about "1968" was a desire to continue the revolt by other means when it had failed in the streets. Yet the main motivation for the continued and sustained production of narratives by subsequent generations of writers is a widely shared, diffuse sense of unfinished business: a feeling that the 68ers started something that needs to be concluded or rejected. Frustratingly for both sides, though, the political constellations and cultural reference points have shifted to such an extent that neither option is a possibility any more. This means that the "spirit of 1968" has become both a holy grail and an object of loathing.

In the eyes of those who are sympathetic to the rebellion of the students and their analysis of the evils of modern capitalism, there exists a void at the center of a pragmatic, materialistic, and technocratic society, a void into which they project the image of a radically different political, social, and economic order, a nostalgic *nicht mehr* (not anymore) that they skillfully transform into a utopian *noch nicht* (not yet) in the sense of Ernst Bloch's *Das Prinzip Hoffnung* (The Principle of Hope, 1954–59). Unencumbered by the need to declare a game plan or by the reality that the students' idealistic model has been confined to the alternative milieus that sprang up in the wake of "1968," driven by the romantic vision of what might have been (had the students won the day), and what therefore could exist in the future, they created a myth-making motor of enduring potency. The heroic, quixotic, and iconoclastic attributes of "1968" fire the imagination through the (endlessly recycled) memories of a romanticized "magic moment," and the dream of its realization:

> It is an imaginary reality which draws a line between a society which we desire and one that we reject. It is comprised of images which have the ability to unleash their immense power and cause us to act because we submit to these images, images of our own making.[1]

Those who reject the students' analysis and challenge the myth of "1968" have added to the narrative. Renegades and critics of the movement have for decades stoked the fear of a fifth column working its way through the institutions, suggested a direct link between the 68ers and the RAF (and the Nazis as well as the GDR/Stasi), denounced the "red–green project" as a conspiracy, and, in recent years, ridiculed the aging 68ers for growing old. By harking back to a time of certainties, higher educational standards, stricter morals, and adherence to "national" traditions, they have created their own myth and inadvertently put the spotlight on the cataclysmic changes effected by the antiauthoritarian revolt, changes that even the Springer newspapers acknowledge to have been vital for "das Selbstverständnis unserer Nation" (the self-conception of our nation).[2] Frustrating for the most vociferous critics of the 68ers is the fact that, while living in a pluralistic, constantly arguing, and multiculturally diverse society represents its own challenges, very few people seem to actually want to return to the status quo ante.

This study has shown that writing about "1968" happens in segregated communities. Historians tend to ignore the insights afforded by the empathetic imagination in fiction, though they create their own imaginaries when they do not declare their interest. Novelists tend to keep their distance from historians for fear of putting their creativity in a straitjacket. Journalists show little interest in the differentiated studies of historians, even though the media have an important role in educating the public about the past. Political and cultural institutions, such as the Bundeszentrale für politische Bildung, public broadcasters, museums, libraries, archives, publishers, theaters, and galleries, dutifully observe the anniversary celebrations but rarely dig beneath the surface.

Given their different objectives, their collective and cumulative impact has until now not been understood as what I have shown it to be: a *Gesamtzusammenhang* that encompasses all three types of writing about "1968." Only by acknowledging this wider context can we critique the power of a narrative that now carries meaning across generations and is accessed via a myriad of triggers, be it dates (June 2, 1967), sounds ("Street Fighting Man" by the *Rolling Stones*), images (water cannons against demonstrating students), ideas (the Long March), slogans ("Unter den Talaren, Muff von tausend Jahren"), names (Rudi Dutschke), or fashions (parka). By turns foundational narrative, utopian dream, collective memory and cautionary tale, this "grand narrative" exerts its influence on political decision making, social behavior and moral judgements.

To give an example: Laurence Rickels recently observed that Germany's decision to disinvest in nuclear energy following "the mishap in Japan" was "too sudden and total to be rational." He posits that this decision has much to do with its history of *Gleichschaltung*: "the ability of an entire nation to close rank [. . .] which [. . .] makes Germans good subjects but not necessarily good leaders."[3] I would argue that the decision, though politically opportunistic, given that public opinion had been against nuclear power for a long time, owes much more to the lessons Germans have learnt from the Nazi period, the countless citizens' initiatives that emerged in the wake of "1968," and the channeling of the students' antiauthoritarian mindset into ecological pressure groups. In short, rather than being mindless sheep following their leader, autonomous individuals used their collective strength to achieve change. As such, Germany's reaction to Fukushima in 2011 is more in line with the country's refusal to join the US-led coalition in the Second Iraq War in 2003.

While the veracity of either argument is impossible to determine conclusively, the example sheds light on the elasticity and reach of "1968" as a measure of political values and moral judgments. Crucially, a new battle over the political and cultural legacy of the German student movement has taken place in the last two decades, when a growing number of individuals began to write (about) the revolution. While Joschka Fischer could look back to "1968" in 1998 and describe the era and the movement as a catalyst for change as well as the legitimate object of historicization, it is no longer the events themselves or the initial *Wertewandel* caused by them that we are concerned with today. It is, rather, the loading of utopian hopes and dystopian fears onto a vehicle that is strong and big enough to accommodate a broad range of passengers.

Nostalgia for "1968" isn't just about the fashion and the music, perhaps not even about the students' challenge to the capitalist system (though the Occupy movement saw itself walking in their footsteps). It is a yearning for the energy with which the students demanded change, the energy that subsequent generations, unhappy with their lot, apparently failed to organize, mobilize, and channel to fight for their issues.[4] "1968" retains its mythical status, constantly reaffirmed in public discourse by its literary and cultural representations, as well as in political debates. Thus, it was no surprise when the majority of the German public accepted Joschka Fischer's militant past in 2001—he was seen as someone who had once possessed and wielded that energy, an "aura" that is still associated with the 68er generation.[5]

With each passing year, "1968" gains new layers of meaning that reflect major global events, the prevailing political climate in Germany, and fresh research paradigms. German unification (was Rudi Dutschke a nationalist?), the red–green government (had the 68ers succeeded in their Long March by "normalizing" the country?), 9/11 (were the 68ers responsible for terrorism?), globalization (the German student movement as part of a transnational protest movement?), migration (are Germans more tolerant and empathetic because of "1968"?), and the aging of Germany's population (will the 68ers revolutionize life in retirement?) have all influenced the way "1968" is perceived and written about. Scholars, journalists, and not least novelists have responded to these shifts in public perception with a surprising range of imaginative and innovative approaches. Moreover, their productive basis has broadened: while twenty years ago it would have been correct to describe the construction of "1968" as dominated by white middle-aged men, today we find men and women, West and East Germans, Left and Right, Germans and non-Germans adding their voices and perspectives to the mix.

What unites them is the problem of how to convey to the reader the intensity of the "magic" moment, to (re-)construct a unique experience that appears infinitely desirable, but also to come to terms, like the knight Parzival in Wolfram von Eschenbach's medieval romance, with the 68ers' failure to seize the grail when it was in their grasp. This literary topos continues to tempt former activists, established writers and newcomers alike. To make matters more complicated, the intense debate about the impact of "1968" has itself changed the impact—the student revolt is accorded a mythical status and historical significance because it holds the interest of the media and, because of its multifacetted nature, has become a rich field for academic research. While we are trying to analyze the impact, we contribute to the impact, and can no longer separate this additional layer from the initial status.

There are many reasons to keep writing about "1968." There is a sense of envy, but also grudging admiration, that the 68ers managed to achieve something that later generations have fallen short of. They were the first to challenge, in large numbers and with the vehemence of youth, the political and moral compromises on which West Germany had been built. They set a benchmark for subsequent social movements, which they influenced in terms of ideology, forms of protest and membership. They believed that they could "make history" and create a critical public sphere. As time passes, the motives to write about "1968" change: there is a growing curiosity about a very different mindset but also a bundle of more prosaic reasons: the obvious financial returns in a market still hungry for news about the 68ers, the chance to establish an academic or literary reputation, and, rarely admitted but always present, the desire to share, however remotely, in a utopian dream.

What Next?

There is no sign that academic or public interest in "1968" will abate anytime soon. The lost utopian dream, the myth of a golden age that may come again, the revolutionary fight for freedom and justice—these elements will always make for a good story. The fiftieth anniversary in 2018 offers an opportunity for scholars around the world to revisit "1968" and discuss the constructedness of "1968" in a global context, for example by comparing its historiography, media, and literary representations across continents and by challenging the dominant discourse, which, as in Germany, is controlled by a relatively small number of individuals.

It is easy to predict another spike in interest in Germany, produced by the media and publishing industry who know that sex (Kommune I!), crime (the RAF!), drugs (Haschrebellen!), and rock and roll *(Beat-Club!)* sell to an audience that increasingly knows only the materialistic here and now of the Merkel years, but also by former activists who will seize this opportunity to share their experiences and control their story. The interesting question is what turn the research agenda will take next. Following a problematic and perhaps premature attempt at the historicization of "1968," a largely successful campaign to set the German "1968" into a transnational and global context, investigations into its character as a social movement, as a media phenomenon and as a countercultural revolution, as well as promising recent research into the impact of "1968" on pedagogy, my expectation is that there will be a fierce interest in the long-term impact of the "ideas of 68" (and their representations) on Germany's political decision making, both domestic and foreign.

In July 2015, when the eurozone agreed on a third bailout for Greece with very harsh terms, Jürgen Habermas, onetime mentor of the German students and still one of Germany's most influential intellectuals, asserted that Chancellor Angela Merkel and her grand coalition had "gambled away in one night all the political capital that a better Germany had accumulated in half a century."[6] He clarified that by "better Germany" he meant a country "characterized by greater political sensitivity and a post-national mentality." We can infer that he wanted a significant portion of this achievement to be attributed to "1968." And so the construction continues . . .

Notes

Preface

[1] I distinguish between the year 1968 and the accumulation of events, actors, associations with and representations of, the German student movement. For the latter, I use the shorthand "1968."

[2] A point made in Robert Redford's film *The Company You Keep* (2012) where history professor Jed Lewis accuses former members of the *Weather Underground* of having splintered the antiwar left.

[3] Ingo Cornils and Sarah Waters, eds., *Cultural History and Literary Imagination*, vol. 16, *Memories of 1968: International Perspectives* (Oxford: Peter Lang, 2010).

Introduction

[1] Mark Kurlansky, *1968: The Year That Rocked the World* (London: Jonathan Cape, 2004); Wolfgang Kraushaar, *1968: Das Jahr, das alles verändert hat* (Munich: Piper, 1998).

[2] Immanuel Wallerstein, "1968: Revolution in the World-System," *Theory and Society* 18, no. 4 (1989): 431–49; see chapter 2.

[3] Cf. Ingo Cornils, "Successful Failure? The Impact of the German Student Movement on the Federal Republic of Germany," in *Recasting German Identity: Culture, Politics and Literature in the Berlin Republic*, ed. Stuart Taberner and Frank Finlay (Rochester, NY: Camden House, 2002), 105–22.

[4] Claus Leggewie, "1968 ist Geschichte," *Aus Politik und Zeitgeschichte* B 22–23 (2001): 3–6, http://www.bpb.de/apuz/26234/1968-ist-geschichte.

[5] Ingrid Gilcher-Holtey, ed. *1968: Vom Ereignis zum Gegenstand der Geschichtswissenschaft* (Göttingen: Vandenhoeck & Ruprecht, 1998).

[6] Gerd Koenen, *Das rote Jahrzehnt: Unsere kleine Kulturrevolution 1967–1977* (Cologne: Kiepenheuer & Witsch, 2001).

[7] Götz Aly, *Unser Kampf 1968: Ein irritierter Blick zurück* (Frankfurt am Main: Fischer, 2008).

[8] Not to be confused with the American SDS, the Students for a Democratic Society.

[9] Richard von Weizsäcker, Ansprache beim Staatsakt zum "Tag der deutschen Einheit," Berlin, October 3, 1990, http://www.bundespraesident.de/SharedDocs/Reden/DE/Richard-von-Weizsaecker/Reden/1990/10/19901003_Rede.html.

¹⁰ See Paul Bermann, *Power and the Idealists, or The Passion of Joschka Fischer, and Its Aftermath* (Berkeley: Soft Skull Press, 2005).

¹¹ "Nachgefragt: Fischer soll bleiben," *Der Spiegel* 3/2001, January 15, 2001, http://www.spiegel.de/spiegel/print/d-18257203.html.

¹² Anne Fuchs, Mary Cosgrove, and Georg Grote, eds., *German Memory Contests: The Quest for Identity in Literature, Film, and Discourse since 1990* (Rochester, NY: Camden House, 2006), 2. See also Sarah Waters, "Introduction: 1968 in Memory and Place," in *Memories of 1968: International Perspectives*, ed. Ingo Cornils and Sarah Waters (Bern: Peter Lang, 2010), 1–21; Elizabeth Pfeifer, "1968 in German Political Culture, 1967–1993: From Experience to Myth," PhD diss., University of North Carolina at Chapel Hill, 1997.

¹³ Habermas, interview. See chapter 2, note 4.

¹⁴ Albrecht von Lucke, *68 oder neues Biedermeier: Der Kampf um die Deutungsmacht* (Berlin: Wagenbach 2008), 15.

¹⁵ Susan McManus, *Fictive Theories: Towards a Deconstructive and Utopian Political Imagination* (Basingstoke: Palgrave Macmillan, 2005), 3.

¹⁶ "Erinnerung an etwas, das irgendwann seine Realität verloren hatte und wieder zu holen war." Herbert Marcuse, *Kultur und Gesellschaft I* (Frankfurt am Main: Suhrkamp, 1965), 11.

¹⁷ Nick Thomas, *Protest Movements in 1960s West Germany: A Social History of Dissent and Democracy* (Oxford: Berg, 2003), 5.

¹⁸ Timothy Garton Ash, "This Tale of Two Revolutions and Two Anniversaries May Yet Have a Twist," *Guardian*, May 8, 2008.

¹⁹ Wolfgang Kraushaar, *1968 als Mythos, Chiffre und Zäsur* (Hamburg: Hamburger Edition, 2000).

²⁰ Hans Magnus Enzensberger, "Erinnerungen an einen Tumult: Zu einem Tagebuch aus dem Jahr 1968," *text + kritik* 49, ed. Heinz Ludwig Arnold (January 1985): 6–9.

²¹ Klaus Briegleb, *1968: Literatur in der antiautoritären Bewegung* (Frankfurt am Main: Suhrkamp, 1993).

²² Wolfgang Kraushaar, "Der Zeitzeuge als Feind des Historikers? Neuerscheinungen zur 68er Bewegung," *Mittelweg 36* 8, no. 6 (1999–2000): 49–72.

²³ Etienne Francois and Hagen Schulze, eds., *Deutsche Erinnerungsorte*, vol. 2 (Munich: C. H. Beck, 2001).

²⁴ Peter L. Berger and Thomas Luckmann, *Die gesellschaftliche Konstruktion der Wirklichkeit: Eine Theorie der Wissenssoziologie* (1966; Frankfurt am Main: Fischer, 1977).

²⁵ John R. Searle, *The Construction of Social Reality* (London: Penguin, 1995).

²⁶ Dave Elder-Vass, *The Reality of Social Construction* (Cambridge: Cambridge University Press, 2012), 46.

²⁷ Karin Bauer, "Questioning the RAF: The Politics of Culture," *Seminar: A Journal of Germanic Studies* 47, no. 1 (2011): 2–3.

²⁸ Jan Assmann, "Communicative and Cultural Memory," in *Cultural Memory Studies: An International and Interdisciplinary Handbook*, ed. Astrid Ertl and Ansgar Nünning (Berlin: 2008), 109–18.

²⁹ Harald Welzer, *Das kommunikative Gedächtnis: Eine Theorie der Erinnerung* (Munich: C. H. Beck, 2011), 233.

³⁰ While I am reluctant to adopt Michael Rothberg's term "multidirectional memory" for this process, the memory of "1968" is no doubt "subject to ongoing negotiation, cross-referencing, and borrowing." Michael Rothberg, *Multidirectional Memory: Remembering the Holocaust in the Age of Decolonialisation* (Stanford: Stanford University Press, 2009), 3.

³¹ Deutscher Bundestag, Bericht der Enquete-Kommission "Aufarbeitung von Geschichte und Folgen der SED-Diktatur in Deutschland," Drucksache 12/7820, May 31, 1994, http://dipbt.bundestag.de/dip21/btd/12/078/1207820.pdf.

³² The Stasi Records Agency. http://www.bstu.bund.de/EN/Agency/TasksOfBStU/_node.html.

³³ Alexandra Senfft, "Kollidierende Gedächtnisse," *taz*, October 11, 2013, http://www.taz.de/!5057429/.

³⁴ Aleida Assmann, *Das neue Unbehagen an der Erinnerungskultur: Eine Intervention* (Munich: C. H. Beck, 2013), 13–14.

Chapter One

¹ Hilke Schlager, "Der Kongreß in Hannover," *Die Zeit*, June 16, 1967, http://www.zeit.de/1967/24/der-kongress-in-hannover/komplettansicht.

² Cf. Roman Brodman, dir., *Der Polizeistaatsbesuch: Beobachtungen unter deutschen Gastgebern*, Süddeutscher Rundfunk, 1967.

³ Siegward Lönnendonker, Bernd Rabehl, and Jochen Staadt, *Die antiautoritäre Revolte: Der Sozialistische Studentenbund nach der Trennung von der SPD*, vol. 1, *1960–1967* (Wiesbaden: Westdeutscher Verlag, 2002), 331.

⁴ Uwe Wesel, *Die verspielte Revolution: 1968 und die Folgen* (Munich: Blessing 2002), 51.

⁵ The open letter was printed in *Der Spiegel* 27/1967, June 26, 1967.

⁶ Kraushaar, *1968 als Mythos*, 253.

⁷ Uwe Timm, *Heißer Sommer* (Königstein, 1974), 37–38.

⁸ Ibid., 41.

⁹ Ingo Cornils, "Folgenschwere Schüsse: Die Kugeln auf Benno Ohnesorg und Rudi Dutschke im Spiegel der deutschen Literatur," *Jahrbuch für Internationale Germanistik* 35, no. 2 (2003): 55–73.

¹⁰ Leander Scholz, *Rosenfest* (Munich: Hanser, 2001), 19–20.

¹¹ Scholz, *Rosenfest*, 18.

¹² Ibid., 23.

¹³ Ibid., 120.

14 Uwe Timm, *Der Freund und der Fremde* (Cologne: Kiepenheuer und Witsch, 2005).

15 See Gerrit Bartels, "Spürbares Bewegtsein," *taz*, September 17, 2005.

16 The image is part of the permanent exhibition in the German Historical Museum in Berlin.

17 "Zu Protokoll," *ARD*.

18 "Der lange Marsch," *Der Spiegel* 51/1967, December 11, 1967, http://www.spiegel.de/spiegel/print/d-46209544.html.

19 Michael Ruetz, *Sichtbare Zeit: Fotographien, 1965–1995; Time Unveilled* (Frankfurt am Main: Zweitausendeins, 1995), 251.

20 Jürgen Miermeister, ed., *Rudi Dutschke, Geschichte ist machbar: Texte über das herrschende Falsche und die Radikalität des Friedens* (Berlin: Wagenbach, 1980), 182, 184.

21 Rudi Dutschke, *Mein langer Marsch: Reden, Schriften und Tagebücher aus zwanzig Jahren*, ed. Gretchen Dutschke-Klotz, Hellmut Gollwitzer, and Jürgen Miermeister (Reinbek: Rowohlt, 1980).

22 Cf. Reinhard Mohr, "Die Achtziger unter Kohl: Birne im Freizeitpark," *Der Spiegel*, March 26, 2010, http://www.spiegel.de/kultur/gesellschaft/die-achtziger-unter-kohl-birne-im-freizeitpark-a-685811.html.

23 Rudi Dutschke, *Die Revolte: Wurzeln und Spuren eines Aufbruchs*, ed. Gretchen Dutschke-Klotz, Jürgen Miermeister, and Jürgen Treulieb (Reinbek: Rowohlt, 1983), 2.

24 Jürgen Miermeister, *Rudi Dutschke* (Reinbek: Rowohlt, 1986).

25 Ulrich Chaussy, *Die drei Leben des Rudi Dutschke: Eine Biographie* (Berlin: Links, 1993), 335.

26 Gretchen Dutschke, *Wir hatten ein barbarisches, schönes Leben; Rudi Dutschke: Eine Biographie* (Cologne: Kiepenheuer & Witsch, 1996); Jürgen Miermeister, *Ernst Bloch, Rudi Dutschke* (Hamburg: EVA, 1996).

27 Miermeister, *Ernst Bloch*, 147.

28 Hans Halter, "Herz der Revolte," *Der Spiegel* 34/1996, August 19, 1996, 94–96.

29 Gretchen Dutschke, ed., *Rudi Dutschke; Jeder hat sein Leben ganz zu leben: Die Tagebücher 1963–1979* (Kiepenheuer & Witsch, 2003).

30 Michaela Karl, *Rudi Dutschke: Revolutionär ohne Revolution* (Frankfurt am Main: Neue Kritik, 2003).

31 Bernd Rabehl, *Linke Gewalt: Der kurze Weg zur RAF* (Schnellroda: Edition Antoios, 2006), 59.

32 Unfried Knott and Asmuth Knott, "Die Dutschke-Straße kommt," *taz*, April 21, 2008, http://www.taz.de/!16172/.

33 Hans-Jörg Vehlewald, "Mythos Rudi Dutschke: Was ist dran am linken Helden der 68er?," *Bild-Zeitung*, April 28, 2010, http://www.bild.de/politik/2010/was-ist-dran-am-linken-helden-der-68er-12347364.bild.html.

34 Helmut Reinicke, Bibliothek des Widerstands, vol. 12, *Rudi Dutschke: Aufrecht gehen; 1968 und der libertäre Kommunismus* (Hamburg: Laika, 2012). The book contains a DVD with four films about Rudi Dutschke: Helga Reidemeister, *Aufrecht gehen* (1988); Jürgen Miermeister, *Dutschke, Rudi, Rebell* (1998); Wolfgang Venohr, *RD: Sein jüngstes Portrait* (1968); Günter Gaus, *RD: Zu Protokoll* (1967).

35 Jochen Schimmang, *Der schöne Vogel Phönix: Erinnerungen eines Dreißigjährigen* (Frankfurt am Main: Suhrkamp, 1979), 14.

36 Erasmus Schöfer, *Ein Frühling irrer Hoffnung* (Berlin, Dittrich Verlag 2001), 130. http://www.erasmusschoefer.de/ganz-oben/ein-fruehling-irrer-hoffnung/.

37 Uwe Timm, *Rot* (Cologne: Kiepenheuer & Witsch, 2001), 378.

38 Gerard DeGroot. *The 60s Unplugged: A Kaleidoscopic History of a Disorderly Decade* (London: Macmillan, 2008), 340.

39 "You have to make the case. And to make the case in a democracy you must convince by yourself. Excuse me, I am not convinced. This is my problem. And I cannot go to the public and say, 'Oh, well, let's go to war because there are reasons,' and so on, and I don't believe in them." Quoted in Paul Bermann, *Idealisten an der Macht: Die Passion des Joschka Fischer* (Munich: Siedler, 2006), 134.

40 Sibylle Krause-Burger, *Joschka Fischer: Der Marsch durch die Illusionen* (Reinbek: Rowohlt, 2000), 225.

41 Wolfgang Kraushaar, *Fischer in Frankfurt* (Hamburg: Hamburger Edition, 2001).

42 Joschka Fischer, "Ein magisches Jahr," *Spiegel Special* 9/1998, September 1, 1998, http://www.spiegel.de/spiegel/spiegelspecial/d-7518979.html.

43 For a discussion of the significance of St. George and the Dragon in Uwe Timm's *Rot* see my "Uwe Timm, der heilige Georg und die Entsorgung der Theorie," in *(Un-) Erfüllte Wirklichkeit: Neue Studien zu Uwe Timm*, ed. Frank Finlay and Ingo Cornils (Würzburg: Königshausen & Neumann, 2006), 55–71.

44 Fischer, "Ein magisches Jahr."

45 Matthias Lohre, "Helmut Schmidt junior," *taz*, February 17, 2011.

46 Kraushaar, *Fischer in Frankfurt*, 34–35.

47 Daniel Cohn-Bendit, "Ich bin ein Held," *Frankfurter Rundschau*, April 29, 2008, http://www.fr-online.de/zeitgeschichte/daniel-cohn-bendit-ich-bin-ein-held,1477344,2795836.html; see also Daniel Cohn-Bendit, *Forget 68* (Paris: Editions de l'Haube, 2009).

48 Daniel Cohn-Bendit, *Wir haben sie so geliebt, die Revolution* (French original 1986; Berlin: Philo, 2001) (preface to the German edition), 8, 16.

49 Daniel Cohn-Bendit and Ruediger Dammann, eds., *1968: Die Revolte* (Frankfurt am Main: Fischer, 2007), 15.

50 Ibid., 16–17.

51 Alice Schwarzer, "Daniel Cohn-Bendit & die Kinder," *Emma*, May/June 2001, http://www.emma.de/artikel/daniel-cohn-bendit-der-vergangenheit-liegt-die-gegenwart-265010.

52 Daniel Cohn-Bendit, "Wir müssen den Geist von 1968 verteidigen," *Die Welt*, January 8, 2015, http://www.welt.de/136172915.

53 It should be noted that the SDS publically distanced itself from the arson attack: "The SDS is appalled that there are people in the Federal Republic of Germany who believe that they can express their opposition to political and social conditions in this country by means of terrorist action." Quoted in Stefan Aust, *Der Baader-Meinhof-Komplex* (Hamburg: Hoffmann & Campe, 1985), 67.

54 Ulrike Meinhof, "Warenhausbrandstiftung," *konkret* 14 (1968): 5, http://www.infopartisan.net/archive/1967/266785.html.

55 See Julian Preece, "The Lives of the RAF Revisited: The Biographical Turn," *Memory Studies* 3, no. 2 (2010): 151–63.

56 See Clare Bielby, *Violent Women in Print: Representations in the West German Print Media of the 1960s and 1970s* (Rochester, NY: Camden House, 2012).

57 Sarah Colvin, *Ulrike Meinhof and West German Terrorism: Language, Violence, and Identity* (Rochester, NY: Camden House, 2009).

58 Karin Bauer, *Everybody Talks about the Weather . . . We Don't: The Writings of Ulrike Meinhof* (New York: Seven Stories Press, 2008).

59 Bettina Röhl, *So macht Kommunismus Spass! Ulrike Meinhof, Klaus Rainer Röhl und die Akte Konkret* (Hamburg: EVA, 2007).

60 Bauer, *Everybody Talks*, 263.

61 Alois Prinz, *Lieber wütend als traurig: Die Lebensgeschichte der Ulrike Marie Meinhof* (Weinheim: Beltz, 2003), 13.

62 Butz Peters, *Tödlicher Irrtum: Die Geschichte der RAF* (Frankfurt am Main: Fischer, 2007), 81.

63 Caroline Harmsen, Ulrike Seyer, and Johannes Ullmaier, eds., *Gudrun Ensslin / Bernward Vesper: "Notstandsgesetze von deiner Hand"; Briefe 1968/1969* (Frankfurt am Main: Suhrkamp, 2009), 285.

64 A photograph by Michael Ruetz shows her, with then husband Bernward Vesper and son Felix in his baby carriage, at a demonstration against the Vietnam War at the Berlin airport.

65 Most notable: Margarete von Trotta, dir., *Die bleierne Zeit* (1981; in English as *Marianne and Juliane*, 1981); Gerd Koenen, *Vesper, Ensslin, Baader: Urszenen des deutschen Terrorismus* (Cologne, K&W, 2003).

66 Jullian Becker, *Hitler's Children* (New York: Lippincott, 1977), 88; Aust, *Baader-Meinhof-Komplex*, 54.

67 E.g., Richard Huffman, "June 2 1967 West Berlin," http://www.baader-meinhof.com/june-2-1967-berlin/; Michael Sontheimer, "High sein, frei sein," *Der Spiegel* 39/2007, September 24, 2007.

68 See Susanne Bressen and Martin Jander, "Gudrun Ensslin," in *Die RAF und der linke Terrorismus*, vol. 1, ed. Wolfgang Kraushaar (Hamburg: Hamburger Edition, 2006), 390–429, here: 406; Wolfgang Kraushaar, "Hitler's Children? The German 1968 Movement in the Shadow of the Nazi Past," in Cornils and Waters, *Memories of 1968*, 79–102, here: 84.

⁶⁹ Aribert Reimann, *Dieter Kunzelmann: Avantgardist, Protestler, Radikaler*, Kritische Studien zur Geschichtswissenschaft 188 (Göttingen: Vandenhoeck & Ruprecht, 2009); Rainer Langhans, *Ich bin's: Die ersten 68 Jahre* (Munich: Blumenbar, 2008); Marco Carini, *Fritz Teufel: Wenn's der Wahrheitsfindung dient* (Hamburg: Konkret Literatur Verlag, 2008).

⁷⁰ Gerd Conradt, *Starbuck—Holger Meins: Ein Portrait als Zeitbild* (Berlin: Espresso, 2001).

⁷¹ For example in Elfriede Jelinek, *Ulrike Marie Stuart* (Premiere October 28, 2006, Thalia Theater Hamburg, dir. Nicolas Stemann).

Chapter Two

¹ Jay Winter, *Dreams of Peace and Freedom: Utopian Moments in the 20th Century* (New Haven, CT: Yale University Press, 2006), 2.

² Friedrich Mager and Ulrich Spinnarke, *Was wollen die Studenten?* (Frankfurt am Main: Fischer, 1967), 151.

³ Jürgen Habermas, "Die Scheinrevolution und ihre Kinder," *Frankfurter Rundschau*, June 5, 1968.

⁴ Jürgen Habermas, *Protestbewegung und Hochschulreform* (1969; Frankfurt am Main: Suhrkamp, 2008), 28. By 1988, Habermas credited the movement with West Germany's "Fundamentalliberalisierung" (Jürgen Habermas, "Der Marsch durch die Institutionen hat auch die CDU erreicht," *Frankfurter Rundschau*, March 11, 1988).

⁵ Peter Mosler, *Was wir wollten, was wir wurden: Studentenrevolte—zehn Jahre danach* (Reinbek: Rowohlt 1977), 8.

⁶ Frank Wolff and Eberhard Windaus, eds., *Studentenbewegung 1967–69: Protokolle und Materialien* (Frankfurt am Main: Roter Stern, 1977), 11.

⁷ Klaus Große Kracht, *Die zankende Zunft: Historische Kontroversen in Deutschland nach 1945* (Göttingen: Vandenhoeck & Ruprecht, 2011), esp. chapter 2, "'Achtundsechzig': Geschichte in der Defensive, 69–90.

⁸ Klaus Hartung, "Fehler der antiautoritären Bewegung: Versuch, die Krise der antiautoritären Bewegung zur Sprache zu bringen," *Kursbuch* 48 (1977): 14–44; Klaus Hartung, "Über die langandauernde Jugend im linken Ghetto: Lebensalter und Politik—Aus der Sicht eines 38jährigen," *Kursbuch* 54 (1978): 174–88.

⁹ Silvia Bovenschen, "Die Generation der Achtundsechziger bewacht das Ereignis: Ein kritischer Rückblick," *Frankfurter Allgemeine Zeitung*, December 3, 1988; reprinted in: *Frankfurter Schule und Studentenbewegung: Von der Flaschenpost zum Molotowcocktail 1946–1995*, vol. 1, *Chronik*, ed. Wolfgang Kraushaar (Hamburg: Rogner & Bernhard, 1998), 232–38, here: 232.

¹⁰ Dany Cohn-Bendit and Reinhard Mohr, *1968: Die letzte Revolution, die noch nichts vom Ozonloch wußte* (Berlin: Wagenbach, 1988), 112–13.

¹¹ Heinz Bude, *Das Altern einer Generation: Die Jahrgänge 1938–1948* (Frankfurt am Main: Suhrkamp, 1995), 41.

[12] Heinz Bude, "Achtundsechzig," in Francois and Schulze *Deutsche Erinnerungsorte*, 122–34, here: 122.

[13] Axel Schildt, "Überbewertet? Zur Macht objektiver Entwicklungen und zur Wirkungslosigkeit der '68er,'" in *Reform und Revolte: Politischer und gesellschaftlicher Wandel in der Bundesrepublik Deutschland vor und nach 1968*, ed. Udo Wengst (Munich: Oldenbourg, 2011), 89–102, here: 92–93.

[14] Lutz Niethammer, "Die letzte Gemeinschaft: Über die Konstruierbarkeit von Generationen und ihre Grenzen," in Bernd Weisbrod, *Historische Beiträge zur Generationenforschung* (Göttingen: Wallstein, 2009), 13–38.

[15] Joe Queenan, *Balsamic Dreams: A Short but Self-Important History of the Baby Boomer Generation* (London: Picador, 2006).

[16] Cf. Ronald Fraser, *1968: A Student Generation in Revolt* (London: Chatto & Windus, 1988); David Farber, *The Sixties: From Memory to History* (Chapel Hill: University of North Carolina Press, 1994); Mark Kurlansky, *1968: The Year That Rocked the World* (London: Jonathan Cape, 2004).

[17] Anna von der Goltz, ed., *"Talkin' 'bout my generation": Conflicts of Generation Building and Europe's "1968"* (Göttingen: Wallstein, 2011).

[18] Anna von der Goltz, "Generations of 68ers: Age-Related Constructions of Identity and Germany's '1968,'" *Cultural and Social History* 8, no. 4 (2011): 473–90, here: 485.

[19] Linda Shortt, *German Narratives of Belonging: Writing Generation and Place in the Twenty-First Century* (London: Legenda, 2015), 12.

[20] The most iconic poster of "1968" in Germany is "Alle reden vom Wetter. Wir nicht." A parody of a poster of the German railways, it depicts the heads of Marx, Engels, and Lenin over a red background.

[21] Tilman Fichter and Siegward Lönnendonker, *Kleine Geschichte des SDS: Der Sozialistische Deutsche Studentenbund von 1946 bis zur Selbstauflösung* (Berlin: Rotbuch, 1977), 182.

[22] Tilman Fichter and Siegward Lönnendonker, "Berlin: Hauptstadt der Revolte," in Michael Ruetz, *"Ihr müßt diesen Typen nur ins Gesicht sehen": Die APO Berlin 1966–69* (Frankfurt am Main: Zweitausendeins, 1980), 160–68, here: 168.

[23] Siegward Lönnendonker, Tilman Fichter, and Jochen Staadt, eds., *Hochschule im Umbruch; Teil V: Gewalt und Gegengewalt (1967–1969)* (Berlin: Freie Universität Berlin, 1983), 174.

[24] Ibid., 184.

[25] Ibid., 6.

[26] Lönnendonker, Rabehl, and Staadt, *Die antiautoritäre Revolte*, ix.

[27] Tilman P. Fichter and Siegward Lönnendonker, *Dutschkes Deutschland: Der Sozialistische Deutsche Studentenbund, die nationale Frage und die DDR-Kritik von links (Eine deutschlandpolitische Streitschrift mit Dokumenten von Michael Mauke bis Rudi Dutschke)* (Essen: Klartext Verlag, 2011).

[28] Michael Naumann and Wolfgang Kraushaar, "Wie wir uns befreiten," *Zeit Geschichte* 2/2007, http://www.zeit.de/zeit-geschichte/naumann.

²⁹ The HIS library holds extensive collections in the areas of social movements and protest movements, while the archive has one of the largest collections of German-language documents on protest, resistance, and utopia in the Federal Republic of Germany (http://www.his-online.de).

³⁰ Wolfgang Kraushaar, "Autoritärer Staat und antiautoritäre Bewegung: Zum Organisationsreferat von Rudi Dutschke und Hans-Jürgen Krahl auf der 22. Delegiertenkonferenz des SDS in Frankfurt (September 1967)," in *Revolte und Reflexion: Politische Aufsätze 1976–87* (Frankfurt am Main: Neue Kritik, 1990), 57–80.

³¹ Wolfgang Kraushaar, ed., *Frankfurter Schule und Studentenbewegung: Von der Flaschenpost zum Molotowcocktail 1946–1995* (Hamburg: Rogner & Bernhard, 1998).

³² Kraushaar, *1968: Das Jahr*.

³³ Tariq Ali and Susan Watson, *1968: Marching in the Streets* (London: Bloomsbury, 1998); Mark Kurlansky, *1968*.

³⁴ Kraushaar, "Der Zeitzeuge, 49–72, here: 70.

³⁵ Kraushaar, *1968 als Mythos*, 12.

³⁶ Wolfgang Kraushaar, "Zur Historisierung der 68er-Bewegung," *Forschungsjournal NSB* 14, no. 2 (2001): 13–22.

³⁷ Wolfgang Kraushaar, "Denkmodelle der 68er-Bewegung," *Aus Politik und Zeitgeschichte*, no. B 22–23 (2001): 14–27.

³⁸ Wolfgang Kraushaar, "'Die Revolte der Lebenstriebe': Marcuse als Mentor gegenkultureller Bewegungen," in Herbert Marcuse, *Nachgelassene Schriften*, vol. 4, *Die Studentenbewegung und ihre Folgen*, ed. Peter-Erwin Jansen (Springe: zu Klampen, 2004), 15–25.

³⁹ Wolfgang Kraushaar, "Rudi Dutschke und der bewaffnete Kampf," in *Rudi Dutschke, Andreas Baader und die RAF*, ed. Wolfgang Kraushaar, Karin Wieland, and Jan Philipp Reemstma (Hamburg: Hamburger Edition, 2005), 13–50.

⁴⁰ Wolfgang Kraushaar, "Rezension Gerd Koenen: Das rote Jahrzehnt," *H-Soz-u-Kult* 27 (2002), www.hsozkult.de/publicationreview/id/rezbuecher-850.

⁴¹ "Die Rote Armee Fraktion leugnet im Unterschied zu den 'proletarischen Organisationen' der Neuen Linken ihre Vorgeschichte als Geschichte der Studentenbewegung nicht, die den Marxismus-Leninismus als Waffe im Klassenkampf rekonstruiert und den internationalen Kontext für den revolutionären Kampf in den Metropolen hergestellt hat." (In marked difference to the "proletarian organizations" of the New Left the RAF does not deny its roots in the history of the student movement, which reconstructed Marxism-Leninism as a weapon in class struggle and provided the international context for the revolutionary struggle in the metropoles.) Ulrike Meinhof / Rote Armee Fraktion, "Das Konzept Stadguerilla," May 1971, https://www.hdg.de/lemo/bestand/objekt/dokument-das-konzept-stadtguerilla.html.

⁴² This view is supported by Dutschke's famous first encounter with Ernst Bloch. Speaking in Bad Boll on February 8, 1968, Dutschke distanced himself from politically motivated violence: "Im Spätkapitalismus ist unter unseren heutigen

Bedingungen Gewalt gegen Menschen nicht mehr als revolutionäre Gewalt zu legitimieren" (In late capitalism and under our current conditions violence against people can no longer be legitimized as revolutionary violence). Walter, "In Bad Boll ein Butzemann?," http://www.ev-akademie-boll.de/fileadmin/res/otg/misc/butzemann.pdf.

43 "Terrorismus ist entgegen der sozialistischen Ethik," quoted in Kraushaar, "Rudi Dutschke," 47.

44 Stefan Reinecke, "Kein Dämon, kein Heiliger," *taz*, December 24, 2004, http://www.taz.de/1/archiv/?dig=2004/12/24/a0117.

45 Ibid.

46 Stephan Schlak, "Der Nicht-Anschlußfähige," *taz*, March 30, 2005, argued that Negt had attempted this in his speech "die linke Unschuld vor der RAF zu retten" (to save left-wing innocence from the RAF), but Peter O. Chotjewitz, "Nicht versöhnt," *Der Stern*, February 18, 2004, believes that even this critical interpretation is too convenient: "Die Linke hatte sich von der RAF verabschiedet. Vergessen, wie viele noch die Angriffswelle im Frühjahr 1972 begrüßt hatten." (The Left had said good-bye to the RAF. Forgotten, how many had still welcomed the wave of attacks in the spring of 1972.)

47 Klaus Meschkat, "Fantasievolle Überraschungen," *taz*, March 1, 2005.

48 Wolfgang Kraushaar, "Der Eskalationsstratege," *taz*, March 8, 2005.

49 Isolde Charim, "Kampf um die Sehnsüchte," *taz*, April 13, 2005.

50 Claus Leggewie, "Entmystifiziert euch!," *taz* May 3, 2005. Cf. Klaus Weinhauer, "Terrorismus in der Bundesrepublik der Siebzigerjahre: Aspekte einer Sozial- und Kulturgeschichte der Inneren Sicherheit," *Archiv für Sozialgeschichte* 44 (2004): 221 and 230.

51 Wolfgang Kraushaar, *Achtundsechzig: Eine Bilanz* (Berlin: Propyläen, 2008).

52 Historians in the United States started earlier. Cf. Farber, *The Sixties*.

53 Ingrid Gilcher-Holtey, *Die 68er Bewegung: Deutschland—Westeuropa—USA* (Munich: Beck, 2001), 115.

54 Ingrid Gilcher-Holtey, ed., *"1968"—Eine Wahrnehmungsrevolution? Horizont-Verschiebungen des Politischen in den 1960er und 1970 Jahren* (Munich: Oldenbourg, 2013), 8.

55 "Die Revolution muß gleichzeitig eine Revolution der Wahrnehmung sein." (Herbert Marcuse, *Versuch über die Befreiung* [Frankfurt am Main: Suhrkamp, 2008], 61).

56 Ingrid Gilcher-Holtey, ed., *A Revolution of Perception? Consequences and Echoes of 1968* (New York: Berghahn, 2014), 11.

57 Cf. Wolfgang Kraushaar, *Der Aufruhr der Ausgebildeten: Vom Arabischen Frühling zur Occupy-Bewegung* (Hamburg: Hamburger Edition, 2012).

58 Sabine von Dirke, *"All Power to the Imagination!": The West German Counterculture from the Student Movement to the Greens* (Lincoln: University of Nebraska Press, 1997), 2.

[59] Axel Schildt, Detlef Siegfried, and Karl Christian Lammers, eds., *Dynamische Zeiten: Die 60er Jahre in den beiden deutschen Gesellschaften* (Hamburg: Christians, 2000), 50–51.

[60] Christina von Hodenberg and Detlef Siegfried, eds., *Wo "1968" liegt: Reform und Revolte in der Geschichte der Bundesrepublik* (Göttingen: Vandenhoeck & Ruprecht, 2006), 11.

[61] Detlef Siegfried, *Time Is on My Side: Konsum und Politik in der westdeutschen Jugendkultur der 60er Jahre* (Göttingen: Wallstein, 2008), 21–22.

[62] Sven Reichardt, *Authentizität und Gemeinschaft: Linksalternatives Leben in den siebziger und frühen achtziger Jahren* (Berlin: Suhrkamp, 2014).

[63] Arthur Marwick, *The Sixties: Cultural Revolution in Britain, France, Italy, and the United States, c.1958-c.1974* (Oxford: Oxford University Press, 1998). The omission of West Germany was rectified by Thomas, *Protest Movements*.

[64] Ingo Juchler, *Die Studentenbewegungen in den Vereinigten Staaten und der Bundesrepublik Deutschland der sechziger Jahre: Eine Untersuchung hinsichtlich ihrer Beeinflussung durch Befreiungsbewegungen und -theorien aus der dritten Welt* (Berlin: Duncker & Humblot, 1996).

[65] Michael Kimmel, *Die Studentenbewegungen der 60er Jahre: BRD, Frankreich, USA; Ein Vergleich* (Vienna: WUV, 1998).

[66] Carole Fink, Philipp Gassert, and Detlef Junker, eds., *1968: The World Transformed* (Cambridge: Cambridge University Press, 1998), 2.

[67] Immanuel Wallerstein, "1968," 431–49; George Katsiaficas, *The Imagination of the New Left: A Global Analysis of 1968* (Boston: South End Press, 1987).

[68] The International Centre for Protest Research seeks to offer a central virtual platform for presenting research projects associated with the center's theme: http://www.protest-research.org.

[69] Martin Klimke and Joachim Scharloth, *1968 in Europe: A History of Protest and Activism, 1956–1977* (New York: Palgrave, 2008), vii.

[70] Cf. Martin Klimke, "1968 als transnationales Ereignis," *Aus Politik und Zeitgeschichte* 14–15 (2008): 7.

[71] Philipp Gassert and Martin Klimke, eds., *1968: Memories and Legacies of a Global Revolt*, Bulletin, Supplement 6 (Washington, DC: German Historical Institute, 2009), 9, http://ghi-dc.org/index.php?option=com_content&view=article&id=1041&ItemId=932&Itemid=16.

[72] Martin Klimke, *The Other Alliance: Student Protest in West Germany & the United States in the Global Sixties* (Princeton, NJ: Princeton University Press, 2010).

[73] Timothy Scott Brown, *West Germany and the Global Sixties: The Antiauthoritarian Revolt, 1962–1978* (Cambridge: Cambridge University Press, 2013), 366.

[74] Timothy Scott Brown, "1968 in West Germany: The Anti-Authoritarian Revolt," *The Sixties: A Journal of History, Politics and Culture* 7, no. 2 (2015): 4–5.

[75] Edgar Wolfrum, "'1968' in der gegenwärtigen deutschen Geschichtspolitik," *Aus Politik und Zeitgeschichte* 49, no. B 22–23 (2001): 28–36.

76 Cf. Paul Hockenos, "Germany Year 1968: Democratic Turning Point or Annus Terribilis? Germany's Debate over the Rebellious Sixties Has Everything to Do with the Present," *Logos: A Journal of Modern Society & Culture* 8, no. 1–2 (2009), http://logosjournal.com/2011/hockenos/.

77 Edgar Wolfrum, *Die geglückte Demokratie: Geschichte der Bundesrepublik Deutschland von ihren Anfängen bis zur Gegenwart* (Stuttgart: Klett-Cotta, 2006), esp. "Die 68er-Bewegung zwischen Protest und Gewalt," 261ff.

78 Edgar Wolfrum and Günther R. Mittler, "Das Jahr 1968: Vom Politikereignis zum Geschichtsereignis," *Forschungsjournal: Neue Soziale Bewegungen* 21, no. 3 (2008): 16–24.

79 Angela Merkel, "60 Jahre CDU," Berlin, June 16, 2005, http://www4.dr-rath-foundation.org/THE_FOUNDATION/peoples_europe/pdf/Merkel_60_Jahre_CDU_2005_June_16.pdf.

80 Kristin Ross, *May '68 and Its Afterlives* (Chicago: University of Chicago Press, 2002), 2.

81 Oskar Negt, *Achtundsechzig: Politische Intellektuelle und die Macht* (Göttingen: Steidl, 1995), 13.

82 Oskar Negt, "Demokratie als Lebensform: Mein Achtundsechzig," *Aus Politik und Zeitgeschichte* 14–15 (March 2008): 5.

83 Gerhard Fels, *Der Aufruhr der 68er: Zu den geistigen Grundlagen der Studentenbewegung und der RAF* (Bonn: Bouvier, 1998), 278.

84 Michael Watts, "1968 and All That . . .," *Progress in Human Geography* 25, no. 2 (2001): 157–88, here: 177.

85 Norbert Frei, *1968: Jugendrevolte und globaler Protest* (Munich: DTV, 2008), 210.

86 Stefan Bollinger, *1968: Die unverstandene Weichenstellung* (Berlin: Dietz, 2008), 126.

87 Hans Kundnani, *Utopia or Auschwitz: Germany's 1968 Generation and the Holocaust* (New York: Columbia University Press, 2009), 11.

88 Richard Langston, "Palimpsests of '68: Theorizing Labor after Adorno," in *The Long 1968: Revisions and New Perspectives*, ed. Daniel J. Sherman, Ruud van Dijk, Jasmine Alinder, and A. Aneesh (Bloomington: Indiana University Press, 2013), 49–72, here: 49.

89 Fraser, *1968*, 5.

90 Werner Pieper, ed., *Alles schien möglich: 60 Sechziger über die 60er Jahre und was aus ihnen wurde* (Löhrbach: Grüne Kraft, 2007), 247.

91 Jeremy Varon, Michael S. Foley, and John McMillian, "Time Is an Ocean: The Past and Future of the Sixties," *The Sixties: A Journal of History, Politics and Culture* 1, no. 1 (2008): 1–7, here: 4.

92 Frei, *1968*, 211.

93 Joachim Scharloth, *1968: Eine Kommunikationsgeschichte* (Munich: Fink, 2011), 28.

⁹⁴ A term used by the historian Udo Wengst in a review of books on "1968": Udo Wengst, review, *sehepunkte* 9 (2009), http://www.sehepunkte.de/2009/01/14414.html.

⁹⁵ Brown, *West Germany*, 2.

⁹⁶ Silja Behre, "Horizont-Ende? Kämpfe um die Erinnerung der 68er-Bewegung: Eine deutsch-französische Perspektive," in Gilcher-Holtey, *"1968"—Eine Wahrnehmungsrevolution?*, 95–110, here: 106.

⁹⁷ Klimke and Scharloth, *1968 in Europe*, 330.

⁹⁸ Siegfried, *Time*, 830.

⁹⁹ Philipp Gassert, "Das kurze '1968' zwischen Geschichtswissenschaft und Erinnerungskultur: Neuere Forschungen zur Protestgeschichte der 1960er-Jahre," *H-Soz-u-Kult*, April 30, 2010, http://hsozkult.geschichte.hu-berlin.de/forum/2010-04-001.

¹⁰⁰ Ibid.

Chapter Three

¹ E.g., Terence Blacker, "Everything Bad in the World Today Is the Fault of the 1960s," *Independent*, August 26, 2013, http://www.independent.co.uk/voices/comment/everything-bad-in-the-world-today-is-the-fault-of-the-1960s-8784843.html; Simon Heffer, "Wish You Were Living in the Sixties? You Must Be Mad. It Was a Ghastly Decade," *The Daily Mail*, October 1, 2014, http://www.dailymail.co.uk/debate/article-2775837/SIMON-HEFFER-Wish-living-Sixties-You-mad-It-ghastly-decade.html.

² Joe Queenan, *Balsamic Dreams: A Short but Self-Important History of the Baby Boomer Generation* (London: Picador, 2006), vii.

³ DeGroot, *60s Unplugged*, 1–2.

⁴ Jürgen Habermas, "Scheinrevolution unter Handlungszwang," *Der Spiegel* 24/1968, June 10, 1968, http://www.spiegel.de/spiegel/print/d-46020971.html.

⁵ Richard Löwenthal, *Der romantische Rückfall* (Stuttgart: Kohlhammer, 1970).

⁶ Franz Schneider, ed., *Dienstjubiläum einer Revolte: "1968" und 25 Jahre* (Munich: von Hase & Koehler, 1993), 9.

⁷ Gerd Langguth, *Protestbewegung: Entwicklung, Niedergang, Renaissance; Die Neue Linke seit 1968* (Cologne: Verlag Wissenschaft und Politik, 1983).

⁸ Gerd Langguth, *Mythos '68: Die Gewaltphilosophie von Rudi Dutschke; Ursachen und Folgen der Studentenbewegung* (Munich: Olzog, 2001).

⁹ Deutscher Bundestag, 14. Wahlperiode—142. Sitzung, Berlin, Mittwoch, den 17. Januar 2001, 13909, http://dip21.bundestag.de/dip21/btp/14/14142.pdf.

¹⁰ Michael Klonovsky, "Demokraten wider Willen," *Focus* 31 (2005): 46–50, http://www.michael-klonovsky.de/artikel/item/91-demokraten-wider-willen.

11 Kai Diekmann, *Der große Selbstbetrug: Wie wir um unsere Zukunft gebracht werden* (Munich: Piper, 2007).

12 Cf. Paul Münch, ed., *Ordnung, Fleiß und Sparsamkeit: Texte und Dokumente zur Entstehung der "bürgerlichen Tugenden,"* Munich: DTV, 1984.

13 Bernhard Vogel and Matthias Kutsch, eds., *40 Jahre 1968: Alte und Neue Mythen; Eine Streitschrift* (Freiburg: Herder, 2008).

14 Wolf Wetzel, "Ein Staatsbegräbnis für '68', oder: Ihr Scheitern als Erfolgsstory," in *Die Hunde bellen ... Von A bis RZ: Eine Zeitreise durch die 68er Revolte und die militanten Kämpfe der 70er bis 90 Jahre*, ed. Autonome L.U.P.U.S. Gruppe (Münster: Unrast Verlag, 2001), 13–28.

15 Wesel, *Die verspielte Revolution*.

16 Matthias Berninger, "Die 68er im Wahljahr 1998," in *Die 68er: Warum wir Jungen sie nicht mehr brauchen*, ed. Stiftung für die Rechte zukünftiger Generationen (Freiburg: Kore, 1998), 33–53, here: 40.

17 Sophie Dannenberg, *Das bleiche Herz der Revolution* (Munich: DVA, 2004), 64.

18 Sophie Dannenberg, "Generationenkonflikt: 'Ich habe nie geglaubt, dass die 68er Antifaschisten waren,'" *Spiegel Online*, November 18, 2004, http://www.spiegel.de/kultur/literatur/generationenkonflikt-ich-habe-nie-geglaubt-dass-die-68er-antifaschisten-waren-a-327028.html.

19 Ursula März, "Immer wieder Kinderläden: Die unendliche 68-Diskussion," *Frankfurter Rundschau*, October 29, 2004.

20 Katrin Hillgruber, "Ein Kommunist braucht kein Deodorant," *Frankfurter Rundschau*, September 1, 2004.

21 Robin Detje, "Der Teufel trug Birkenstock," *Literaturen*, no. 12 (2004).

22 Hartmuth Becker, Felix Dirsch, and Stefan Winkler, eds., *Die 68er und ihre Gegner: Der Widerstand gegen die Kulturrevolution* (Graz: Stocker, 2003).

23 Torsten Mann, *Rot-Grüne Lebenslügen: Wie die 68er das Land an die Wand gefahren haben* (Rottenberg: Kopp Verlag, 2005).

24 Rolf Kosiek, *Die Machtübernahme der 68er: Die Frankfurter Schule und ihre zersetzenden Auswirkungen* (Tübingen: Hohenrain, 2009), http://www.zeitreisen-verlag.de/Enthuellungen/Politik/Rolf-Kosiek-Die-Machtuebernahme-der-68er.html.

25 Holger Pinter, *Die 68er-Verschwörung: Die Herrschaft der Unfähigen* (Siegburg: Edition Esoterick, 2010), https://www.neobooks.com/ebooks/holger-pinter-die-68er-verschworung-ebook-neobooks-32794.

26 Markus Willinger, *Die identitare Generation: Eine Kriegserklaerung an die 68er* (Arktos Media, 2013), http://www.arktos.com/markus-willinger-die-identitare-generation.html.

27 Ibid.

28 Klaus Rainer Röhl, *Fünf Finger sind keine Faust: Eine Abrechnung* (1974; Munich: Universitas, 1998), 214.

29 Klaus Rainer Röhl, *Linke Lebenslügen: Eine überfällige Abrechnung* (Berlin: Ullstein, 1995), 53.

30 Bettina Röhl, *So macht Kommunismus Spass!*

31 E.g., Kay Schiller, "Political Militancy and Generation Conflict in West Germany during the 'Red Decade,'" *Debatte: Journal of Contemporary Central and Eastern Europe* 11 (2003): 19–38.

32 Koenen, *Das rote Jahrzehnt*, 45.

33 Koenen, *Vesper*.

34 Wolfgang Kraushaar, "1968 und die RAF: Ein umstrittenes Beziehungsgeflecht," *Vorgänge*, no. 3–4 (2005): 208–20, here: 218.

35 Gerd Koenen, "Mein 1968," in Gerd Koenen and Andres Veiel, *1968: Bildspur eines Jahres* (Cologne: Fackelträger, 2008), 6.

36 Götz Aly, *Unser Kampf*, 7.

37 Wolfgang Kraushaar, "Hitlers Kinder? Eine Antwort auf Götz Aly: Die 68er-Bewegung im Schatten der NS-Vergangenheit; Zur Analogiekonstruktion des NS-Historikers Götz Aly." *Perlentaucher.de*, March 25, 2009, http://www.perlentaucher.de/essay/hitlers-kinder-eine-antwort-auf-goetz-aly.html; English version: Kraushaar, "Hitler's Children," 79–102.

38 Werner Olles, "Zur Rechten Gottes," in *Bye-bye '68 . . .: Renegaten der Linken, APO Abweichler und allerlei Querdenker berichten*, ed. Claus-M. Wolfschlag (Graz: Stocker, 1998), 10–28, here 23.

39 Peter Schütt, "1968: Ein persönlicher und politischer Rückblick," in *Bye-bye '68 . . .: Renegaten der Linken, APO Abweichler und allerlei Querdenker berichten*, ed. Claus-M. Wolfschlag (Graz: Stocker, 1998), 88–98, here: 93.

40 Klaus Hartung, "Selbstkritische Überlegungen und Überlegungen zur Selbstkritik nach 40 Jahren," *Ästhetik & Kommunikation* 39, no. 140–14 (2008): 95–112, http://www.aesthetikundkommunikation.de/?artikel=359.

41 Kraushaar, *1968: Das Jahr*, 313.

Chapter Four

1 Kraushaar, *1968 als Mythos*, 52.

2 E.g., Rolf Dieter Brinkmann, Heinrich Böll, Inga Buhmann, Michael Buselmeier, Bernd Cailloux, Peter O. Chotjewitz, Sophie Dannenberg, F. C. Delius, Hubert Fichte, Gerd Fuchs, Christian Geissler, Günter Grass, Urs Jaeggi, Hermann Kinder, Alexander Kluge, Roland Lang, Peter Mosler, Sten Nadolny, Judith Offenbach, Hanns-Josef Ortheil, Emine Sevgi Özdamar, Elisabeth Plessen, Hazel Rosenstrauch, Jochen Schimmang, Bernhard Schlink, Peter Schneider, Erasmus Schöfer, Leander Scholz, Friederike Schwab, Gerhard Seyfried, Andreas Siekmann, Franz-Maria Sonner, Karin Struck, Uwe Timm, Bernward Vesper, Fred Viebahn, Matthias Wahl, Ulrich Woelk, and Michael Zeller.

3 It should come as no surprise that these authors are white and male. In chapter 5, I discuss the contribution by female authors.

4 Stephen Spender, *The Year of the Young Rebels* (London: Weidenfeld and Nicolson, 1969). Deeply impressed but also perturbed by his conversations with

West German students, Spender noted, "The students are isolated and they are resented, not just on account of their violence, but because they are reminders. As well as having the look of the unprecedented new young, they also have the look of ghosts risen from hastily covered graves" (95).

[5] Cees Nooteboom, *Paris, Mai 1968* (Frankfurt am Main: Suhrkamp, 2003; Dutch original 1968), 14–15. Even in a postscript from 1977, Noteboom expressed "Heimweh" (homesickness/yearning) for this moment in time: "For this strange, inexplicable electric feeling, the almost tangible expectation, the complete and touching openness of all towards everyone, the mixture of hope, naivety, tactics and honesty, for everything that, now that the world has returned to look like the world, has become invisible" (90).

[6] Keith Bullivant, *After the Death of Literature: West German Writing in the 1970s* (Oxford: Berg, 1989).

[7] W. Martin Lüdke, ed., *Nach dem Protest: Literatur im Umbruch* (Frankfurt am Main: Suhrkamp, 1979).

[8] Andrew Plowman, *The Radical Subject: Social Change and the Self in Recent German Autobiographies* (Bern: Peter Lang, 1998).

[9] Ingeborg Gerlach, *Abschied von der Revolte: Studien zur deutschsprachigen Literatur der siebziger Jahre* (Würzburg: Königshausen & Neumann, 1994), 9.

[10] Ralf Schnell, *Geschichte der deutschsprachigen Literatur seit 1945* (Stuttgart: Metzler 1993), 420.

[11] Gerlach, *Abschied von der Revolte*, 15.

[12] Mary Fulbrook and Martin Swales, *Representing the German Nation* (Manchester: Manchester University Press, 2000), 16.

[13] Ingo Cornils, "Long Memories: The German Student Movement in Recent Fiction," *German Life and Letters* 56, no. 1 (2003): 89–101.

[14] Hermann Peter Piwitt, "Rückblick auf heiße Tage: Die Studentenrevolte in der Literatur," in *Literaturmagazin 4: Die Literatur nach dem Tod der Literatur; Bilanz der Politisierung*, ed. Hans-Christoph Buch (Reinbek: Rowohlt, 1975), 35–46, here: 37.

[15] Briegleb, *1968*; see also Helmuth Kiesel, "Literatur um 1968: Politischer Protest und postmoderner Impuls," in *Protest! Literatur um 1968*, ed. Ulrich Ott and Friedrich Pfäfflin (Marbach: Deutsche Schillergesellschaft, 1998), 593–640.

[16] Cf. Marcel Reich-Ranicki, *Mein Leben* (Munich: DTV, 2000), 463.

[17] "Heiß gekocht," *Der Spiegel* 44/1967, October 23, 1967, http://www.spiegel.de/spiegel/print/d-46197113.html.

[18] ASTA Uni HH + Kollektiv Literaturtheorie, eds., *Literatur und Literaturwissenschaft im Zeitalter des Kapitalismus*, 69–70, Sondersammlung "Protest, Widerstand und Utopie in der Bundesrepublik Deutschland," ASTA Dokumente XV, Hamburger Institut für Sozialforschung.

[19] Cf. Susanne Rinner, *The German Student Movement and the Literary Imagination: Transnational Memories of Protest and Dissent* (New York: Berghahn, 2013).

[20] Nicolaus Born, *Literaturmagazin 3: "Die Phantasie an die Macht"; Literatur als Utopie* (Reinbek: Rowohlt, 1975), 9–10.

21 Peter Weiss, *The Aesthetics of Resistance*, vol. 1, translated by Joachim Neugroschel, with a foreword by Frederic Jameson (Durham, NC: Duke University Press, 2005), vii.

22 Hans Magnus Enzensberger, "The Writer and Politics," *Times Literary Supplement*, September 28, 1967.

23 Ibid.

24 "Ist Revolution unvermeidlich?," *Der Spiegel* 15/1968, April 8, 1968, 60–73.

25 The title "Kursbuch" signaled Enzensberger's intention to show the direction of travel for the protest movement.

26 Hans Magnus Enzensberger, "Gemeinplätze, die Neueste Literatur betreffend," *Kursbuch* 15 (1968): 187–97.

27 Ibid., 197. The original German reads:

> Die politische Alphabetisierung Deutschlands ist ein gigantisches Projekt. Sie hätte selbstverständlich, wie jedes derartige Unternehmen, mit der Alphabetisierung der Alphabetisierer zu beginnen. Schon dies ist ein langwieriger und mühseliger Prozeß. [. . .] Der Schriftsteller, der sich auf sie einläßt, verspürt plötzlich eine kritische Wechselwirkung, ein feedback zwischen Leser und Schreiber, von dem er sich als Belletrist nichts konnte träumen lassen. [. . .] Vielleicht erreicht der Alphabetisierer eines Tages sogar, was ihm versagt bleiben mußte, solange er auf Kunst aus war: daß der Gebrauchswert seiner Arbeit ihrem Marktwert über den Kopf wächst.

28 Ingrid Gilcher-Holtey, "Die APO und der Zerfall der Gruppe 47," *Aus Politik und Zeitgeschichte* 25 (2007): 19–24, http://www.bpb.de/apuz/30417/die-apo-und-der-zerfall-der-gruppe-47.

29 Jürgen Habermas, *Protestbewegung und Hochschulreform* (Frankfurt am Main: Suhrkamp, 1969), 196.

30 F. C. Delius, "Wie scheintot war die Literatur? *Kursbuch* 15 und die Folgen," www.fcdelius.de/widerreden/wider_kursbuch_15.html.

31 Wolfgang Kraushaar, "Vexierbild: Hans Magnus Enzensberger im Jahre 1968," *Mittelweg 36* 5 (2009): 52–70, http://www.eurozine.com/articles/2009-11-03-kraushaar1-de.html.

32 Hans Magnus Enzensberger, *Der kurze Sommer der Anarchie: Buenaventura Durrutis Leben und Tod* (Frankfurt am Main: Suhrkamp, 1972), 13.

33 Hans Magnus Enzensberger, *Der Untergang der Titanic: Eine Komödie* (Frankfurt am Main: Suhrkamp, 1978), 14–15.

34 Henning Marmulla, *Enzensbergers Kursbuch: Eine Zeitschrift um 68* (Berlin: Matthes & Seitz, 2011).

35 Habermas, Protestbewegung und Hochschulreform, 148.

36 There was certainly a medium and long-term demand for the magazine: in 1976, the Zweitausendeins Verlag published all *Kursbuch* issues from 1965–1970 in a two-volume edition, and in 2008 the Suhrkamp Verlag reissued the *Kursbuch* issues from 1968 in one volume.

37 Peter Schneider, "Wir haben Fehler gemacht," speech held on May 5, 1967, http://www.glasnost.de/hist/apo/fehler.html.

38 Kraushaar, *Achtundsechzig*, 82–83.

39 Peter Schneider, "Bild macht dumm," *konkret* 3 (March 1968): 14–17.

40 Anonymes Autorenkollektiv, "Gewalt in den Metropolen."

41 Peter Schneider, "Die Phantasie im Spätkapitalismus und die Kulturrevolution," *Kursbuch* 16 (March 1969): 1–37.

42 Cf. "Vorbild Mao tse-Tung: Kunstpreisträger Peter Schneider über die Literatur in der Kulturrevolution," *Der Spiegel* 15/1969, April 7, 1969.

43 Peter Schneider, *Lenz* (Berlin: Rotbuch Verlag, 1973), 88.

44 Oliver Sill, *Zerbrochene Spiegel: Studien zu Theorie und Praxis modernen autobiographischen Erzählens* (Berlin: de Gruyter, 1991), 287.

45 Thomas J. A. Krüger, "From the 'Death of Literature' to the 'New Subjectivity': Examining the Interaction of Utopia and Nostalgia in Peter Schneider's *Lenz*, Hans Magnus Enzensberger's *Der kurze Sommer der Anarchie*, and Bernward Vesper's *Die Reise*" (PhD thesis, McGill University, Montreal, 2008), 254, http://digitool.library.mcgill.ca/R/?func=dbin-jump-full&object_id=32407&local_base=GEN01-MCG02.

46 Peter Schneider, "Über den Unterschied von Literatur und Politik," in "Das Vergehen von Hören und Sehen: Aspekte der Kulturvernichtung," ed. Hermann Peter Piwitt and Peter Rühmkorf, special issue, *Literaturmagazin* 5 (1976), 188–98.

47 For an account of his continuing feud with the Springer-Verlag, see chapter 6; for a discussion of Peter Schneider, *Rebellion und Wahn: Mein '68* (Cologne: Kiepenheuer & Witsch, 2008), see chapter 9.

48 Peter Schneider, *Skylla* (Berlin: Rowohlt, 2005), 125.

49 Ibid., 207.

50 "Wider die Kultur des Gehorsams: Der Schriftsteller Peter Schneider über die 68er, seinen neuen Roman und sein Leben," *Märkische Allgemeine*, April 20, 2005.

51 Ironically, while Ullrich is unable to finish a seminar paper on the German romantic poet Hölderlin in Munich, his poem *Die Liebe* (1800), which reflects the poet's fascination with the French Revolution as well as its idealistic romanticization, later gives Ullrich's naive protest a voice: "Sprache der Liebenden // sei die Sprache des Landes, // Ihre Seele der Laut des Volks!' (HS, 340).

52 Timm, *Heißer Sommer*, 117–33.

53 Cf. Helene Heise, "Das Ende der Talare," *Spiegel Online*, November 8, 2007, http://www.spiegel.de/einestages/das-ende-der-talare-a-948827.html.

54 "Muff im Talar," *Der Spiegel* 48/1967, November 20, 1967, 84, http://www.spiegel.de/spiegel/print/d-46196225.html.

55 See my "Denkmalsturz: The German Student Movement and German Colonialism," in *German Colonialism and National Identity*, ed. Michael Perraudin and Jürgen Zimmerer (New York: Routledge, 2010), 197–212.

[56] It should be noted that Timm is not completely straight with his readers. While the quote is taken verbatim from Herbert Marcuse's essay "Ethik und Revolution" (in Herbert Marcuse, *Kultur und Gesellschaft 2* [Frankfurt am Main: Suhrkamp, 1966], 130–46, here: 134), Marcuse is in fact paraphrasing Robespierre and goes on to discuss the ethics of violence in a revolution. He concludes that the relationship between the means and the ends is a dialectical one.

[57] Uwe Timm, "Die Rotts und die Rothschilds: Von einem, der glaubte, ohne zu arbeiten, gut leben zu können," *Deutsche Volkszeitung: Wochenzeitung für demokratischen Fortschritt*, November 30, 1972.

[58] Martin Hielscher, *Uwe Timm* (Munich: DTV, 2007), 73.

[59] Uwe Timm, *Deutsche Kolonien*, AutorenEdition (1981) (Cologne: Kiepenheuer & Witsch, 2001), 10.

[60] Uwe Timm, *Kerbels Flucht* (Munich: DTV, 2000), 12.

[61] Timm, *Rot*, 211.

[62] Ulrich Greiner, "Der Wiedergänger," *ZEITLiteratur* (Sonderbeilage), *Die Zeit*, October 4, 2001, 3–4.

[63] Ursula März, "Archiv in der Zeitfalte," *Frankfurter Rundschau*, October 10, 2001.

[64] Friedrich Christian Delius, *Amerikahaus und der Tanz um die Frauen* (Reinbek: Rowohlt, 1997), 69–70.

[65] Friedrich Christian Delius, *Mein Jahr als Mörder* (Berlin: Rowohlt, 2004), 9.

[66] Cf. Anne Fuchs, "F. C. Delius's *Mein Jahr als Mörder* (My Year as a Murderer)," in *The Novel in German since 1900*, ed. Stuart Taberner (Cambridge: Cambridge University Press, 2011), 226–40.

[67] Schöfer, *Ein Frühling irrer Hoffnung*, 281.

[68] Ibid., 86.

[69] Cf. Thomas Hecken, *1968: Von Texten und Theorien aus einer euphorischen Zeit* (Bielefeld: transcript, 2008), 59.

[70] In part three of the tetralogy, *Sonnenflucht* (Berlin 2005, previously published as *Tod in Athen* [Dortmund: 1986]), Viktor sustains serious burns when he attempts to rescue hospital patients in a forest fire near Athens.

[71] Harald Jähner, "Gudrun, jetzt muß die Knarre sprechen: Drei Romane über 1968," *Berliner Zeitung*, March 20, 2001.

[72] Erasmus Schöfer, *Zwielicht* (Berlin: Dittrich, 2004), 248.

[73] Volker Dittrich, ed., *Unsichtbar lächelnd träumt er Befreiung: Erasmus Schöfer unterwegs mit Sisyfos* (Berlin: Dittrich Verlag, 2006), 16.

[74] Schöfer, *Ein Frühling irrer Hoffnung*, 7.

[75] Schimmang, *Der schöne Vogel Phönix*, 123.

[76] Bernd Cailloux, *Das Geschäftsjahr 1968/69* (Frankfurt am Main: Suhrkamp, 2005), 58.

[77] Ibid., 60.

[78] Günter Grass, "Die angelesene Revolution: Rede auf einer Veranstaltung des Sozialdemokratischen Hochschulbundes in Bochum," in Günter Grass, *Werkausgabe in zehn Bänden*, vol. 9, *Essays, Reden, Briefe, Kommentare*, ed. Daniela Hermes (Darmstadt: Luchterhand, 1987), 297–311, here: 298.

[79] Günter Grass, *örtlich betäubt* (1969; Munich: DTV, 1995).

[80] Horst Krüger, "Kein Geschmack für Ort und Augenblick," *Die Zeit*, August 22, 1969.

[81] Marcel Reich-Ranicki, "Eine Müdeheldensoße; Zum zweitenmal: Der neue Roman von Günter Grass," *Die Zeit*, August 29, 1969.

[82] Anatole Broyard, "Günter Grass Demonstrates That Fiction Is Not Only Alive but Healthier Than Ever," *New York Times*, March 29, 1970, https://www.nytimes.com/books/99/12/19/specials/grass-local.html.

[83] *Time* cover Günter Grass, April 13, 1970, http://content.time.com/time/covers/0,16641,19700413,00.html.

[84] "The Dentist's Chair as an Allegory in Life," *Time Magazine*, April 13, 1970, 68, 69; see also Siegfried Mews, *Günter Grass and His Critics: From the Tin Drum to Crabwalk* (Rochester, NY: Camden House, 2009), 103–19.

[85] Günter Grass, *Kopfgeburten, oder Die Deutschen sterben aus* (Darmstadt: Luchterhand, 1980), 168.

[86] Günter Grass, *Mein Jahrhundert* (Göttingen: Steidl, 1999), 252.

[87] Günter Grass and Pierre Bourdieu, "The 'Progressive' Restoration: A Franco-German Dialogue," *New Left Review*, no. 14 (2002): 63–77, here: 73.

[88] Monika Shafi, "Talkin' 'bout My Generation: Memories of 1968 in Recent German Novels," *German Life and Letters* 59, no. 2 (2006): 201–16, here: 205.

[89] Manuel Gogos and Andreas Pflitsch, "Die Literatur ist tot, es lebe die Literatur: Schreiben um 1968," in *Die 68er: Kurzer Sommer—lange Wirkung; Ein literarisches Lesebuch* (Begleitbuch zur Ausstellung des Historischen Museums in Frankfurt am Main), ed. Andreas Schwab, Beate Schappach, and Manuel Gogos (Frankfurt: DTV, 2008), 378–79.

[90] Susanne Rinner, *The German Student Movement and the Literary Imagination: Transnational Memories of Protest and Dissent* (New York: Berghahn, 2013), 11.

[91] Susanne Komfort-Hein, *"Flaschenposten und kein Ende des Endes"; 1968: Kritische Korrespondenzen um den Nullpunkt von Geschichte und Literatur* (Freiburg: Rombach, 2001), 339.

[92] Julian Preece, *Baader-Meinhof and the Novel: Narratives of the Nation / Fantasies of the Revolution, 1970–2010* (New York: Palgrave, 2012), 2.

[93] Kraushaar, "Vexierbild," 65.

[94] Piwitt, "Rückblick," 37.

[95] As seen on the massive poster hanging on the wall behind the podium in the Audimax of the Technical University Berlin, where the International Vietnam Congress took place in February 1968.

Chapter Five

[1] According to K. D. Wolff, "Geschlechterrollen bei der 68ern: Kurzer Sommer, lange Wirkung—eine virtuelle Gesprächsrunde," Bundeszentrale für politische Bildung, 2008, http://www.bpb.de/mediathek/190167/geschlechterrollen-bei-den-68ern.

[2] Michael Ruetz, *1968: Ein Zeitalter wird besichtigt* (Frankfurt am Main: Zweitausendeins, 1997), 202–6; see also http://www.deutschefotothek.de/documents/obj/71400647.

[3] Sheila Rowbotham, *Promise of a Dream: Remembering the Sixties* (London: Allen Lane, 2000), xii.

[4] Kolja Mensing, "Auf der richtigen Seite," *taz*, June 2, 2007, http://www.taz.de/1/archiv/?id=archivseite&dig=2007/06/02/a0007.

[5] "Aktion Blanker Busen," *Spiegel Online*, October 16, 2007, http://www.spiegel.de/einestages/achtundsechzig-aktion-blanker-busen-a-949905.html.

[6] "Und wir zeigen unsere Brüste für jeden," *Der Spiegel* 51/1968, December 16, 1968, 24, http://magazin.spiegel.de/EpubDelivery/spiegel/pdf/45865104; Sepp Binder, "Barbusig vor der Barriere: Weibliche Wunderwaffen besiegen einen Hamburger Richter," *Die Zeit*, December 20, 1968, 13, http://pdfarchiv.zeit.de/1968/51/barbusig-vor-der-barriere.pdf.

[7] Erica Fischer, "Vom Tomatenwurf zum Paradiesgarten: Zu Besuch bei Sigrid Fronius in Bolivien," radio feature, SFB RadioKultur, April 1, 2003, http://www.erica-fischer.de/texte/frauen/bolivien.html.

[8] Silvia Bovenschen, "Sexuell befreite Spiesser," interview by Heide Oestreich, *taz*, December 29, 2007, http://www.taz.de/1/archiv/digitaz/artikel/?ressort=sp&dig=2007%2F12%2F29%2Fa0048&src=GI&cHash=5443435af7.

[9] Maren Keller, "Golden Girls in weißer Villa," *Der Spiegel*, August 5, 2013, http://www.spiegel.de/kultur/literatur/das-buch-von-silvia-bovenschen-nur-mut-a-914575.html.

[10] Oliver Tolmein, *"RAF—Das war für uns Befreiung": Ein Gespräch mit Irmgard Möller über den bewaffneten Kampf, Knast und die Linke* (Hamburg: Konkret, 1997).

[11] Waltraud Schwab, "Die letzte aus der Dutschke-WG," *taz*, March 7, 2005, http://www.taz.de/1/archiv/?dig=2005/03/07/a0247.

[12] Severin Weiland, "Nazi-Jäger: Gauck zeichnet Beate und Serge Klarsfeld aus," *Der Spiegel*, May 13, 2015, http://www.spiegel.de/politik/deutschland/ns-aufarbeitung-gauck-zeichnet-ehepaar-klarsfeld-aus-a-1033660.html.

[13] The magazine *Der Spiegel* published excerpts as a miniseries. "Ich Kobold, du Halbgott," *Der Spiegel* 34/1996, August 19, 1996, 98–108, and *Der Spiegel* 35/1996, August 26, 1996, 108–19.

[14] Alice Schwarzer, *Lebenslauf* (Cologne: Kiepenheuer & Witsch, 2011).

[15] Alice Schwarzer, "Zur Person: Alice Schwarzer erzählt ihr Leben," October 1, 2011, http://www.aliceschwarzer.de/artikel/alice-schwarzer-erzaehlt-ihr-leben-311561.

[16] Mick Fleetwood and John McVie of the band Fleetwood Mac recall that Obermaier was the "bait" to lure their then guitarist Peter Green to the party in Munich where he "took some more drugs and never really came back from that." Their manager Clifford Davis claims that this was the night that Green became "seriously mentally ill": "Peter Green: The Munich LSD Party Incident," YouTube video, August 12, 2012, https://www.youtube.com/watch?v=mcZJCLce1cY.

[17] Uschi Obermaier, "Zum Frühstück gab's bei mir Apfelsaft, Heroin und Sex," *Bild*, January 10, 2007, http://www.bild.de/leute/2007/obermaier-serie-fruehstueck-se-x-1242608.bild.html.

[18] Sabine Reichel, "Uschis Märchenstunde," *Berliner Zeitung*, January 21, 2007, www.berliner-zeitung.de/archiv/nackter-diebstahl-und-ein-bisschen-verrat--wie-das-sexsymbol-obermaier-die-bewegung-der-68er-vermarktet--zur-freude-der-deutschen-uschis-maerchenstunde,10810590,10451276.html; see also Tony Paterson, "Uschi: Groupie, Addict and Heroine of the Left," *Independent*, February 2, 2007, http://www.independent.co.uk/news/world/europe/uschi-groupie-addict-and-heroine-of-the-left-434740.html.

[19] Helke Sander, "Rede des 'Aktionsrates zur Befreiung der Frauen' bei der 23. Delegiertenkonferenz des Sozialistischen deutschen Studentenbundes (SDS) im September 1968 in Frankfurt," in *1968: Eine Enzyklopädie*, ed. Rudolf Sievers (Frankfurt am Main: Suhrkamp, 2004), 372–78.

[20] Ulrike Meinhof, "Die Frauen im SDS, oder: in eigener Sache," in *Die Würde des Menschen ist antastbar: Aufsätze und Polemiken* (Berlin: Wagenbach, 1994), 149–52.

[21] Cf. Julia Paulus, "Juni 1969: Die kulturelle Revolution der Frau," in Internet-Portal "Westfälische Geschichte," http://www.westfaelische-geschichte.de/web605. See also Dagmar Herzog, *Sexuality in Europe: A Twentieth-Century History* (Cambridge: Cambridge University Press, 2011), 162.

[22] Cf. Kraushaar, *Achtundsechzig*, 226–30.

[23] Ute Kätzel, *Die 68erinnen: Portrait einer rebellischen Frauengeneration* (Berlin: Rowohlt, 2002).

[24] Erica Fischer, "Vorkämpferinnen der Generation 'Ally': Ein Buch über die 68erinnen füllt eine wichtige Lücke," http://www.erica-fischer.de/texte/rezensionen/68erinnen_Rezension.html.

[25] Kristina Schulz, "Bräute der Revolution: Kollektive und individuelle Interventionen von Frauen in der 68er-Bewegung und ihre Bedeutung für die Formierung der neuen Frauenbewegung," *Westfälische Forschungen: Zeitschrift des Westfälischen Instituts für Regionalgeschichte des Landschaftsverbandes Westfalen-Lippe* 48 (1998): 97–116; Kristina Schulz, *Der lange Atem der Provokation: Die Frauenbewegung in der Bundesrepublik und in Frankreich (1968–1976)* (Frankfurt am Main: Campus, 2002); Kristina Schulz, "Frauen in Bewegung: Mit der neuen Linken über die Linke(n) hinaus," in *Handbuch 1968 zur Kultur- und Mediengeschichte der Studentenbewegung*, ed. Martin Klimke and Joachim Scharloth (Stuttgart: Metzler, 2007), 247–58; Kristina Schulz, "Ohne Frauen keine Revolution: 68er und neue Frauenbewegung," http://www.bpb.de/LIBTTI.html, March 6, 2008.

²⁶ Belinda Davis, "The Personal Is Political: Gender, Politics, and Political Activism in Modern German History," in *Gendering Modern German History: Rewriting Historiography*, ed. Jean Quataert and Karen Hagemann (New York: Berghahn, 2007), 107–27.

²⁷ Ingrid Bauer and Hana Havelková, eds., "Gender & 1968," special issue, *L'Homme: Europäische Zeitschrift für Feministische Geschichtswissenschaft* 20, no. 2 (2009).

²⁸ Susanne Maurer, "Gespaltenes Gedächtnis? '1968 und die Frauen' in Deutschland," in Bauer and Havelková, "Gender," 118.

²⁹ Elisabeth Plessen, *Mitteilung an den Adel* (Zurich: Benzinger, 1976), 101.

³⁰ Christian Schulz-Gerstein, "Das Fräulein Tochter meutert," *Der Spiegel* 46/1976, November 8, 1976, 225–27.

³¹ Inga Buhmann, *Ich habe mir eine Geschichte geschrieben* (1977; Frankfurt, 1998).

³² Judith Offenbach, *Sonja: Eine Melancholie für Fortgeschrittene* (Frankfurt am Main: Suhrkamp, 1980).

³³ Sabine Reichel, *What Did You Do in the War, Daddy? Growing up German* (New York: Hill and Wang, 1989), 4.

³⁴ Emine Sevgi Özdamar, *Die Brücke vom goldenen Horn* (Cologne: Kiepenheuer & Witsch, 1998); see also Ernest Schonfield, "1968 and Transnational History in Emine Sevgi Özdamar's *Die Brücke vom goldenen Horn*," *German Life and Letters* 68, no. 1 (2015): 66–87.

³⁵ Ulrike Heider, *Keine Ruhe nach dem Sturm* (Hamburg: Rogner und Bernhard bei Zweitausendeins, 2001).

³⁶ Heide Platen, "Brötchen mit Adorno," *taz*, March 5, 2002, http://www.taz.de/1/archiv/?dig=2002/03/05/a0162; Sabine Peters, "Angst vor dem Chaos," *der freitag*, August 16, 2002, https://www.freitag.de/autoren/der-freitag/angst-vor-dem-chaos.

³⁷ Cf. Meike Sophia Baader, "Das Private ist politisch: Der Alltag der Geschlechter, die lebensformen und die Kinderfrage," in *"Seid realistisch, verlangt das Unmögliche!": Wie 1968 die Pädagogik bewegte*, ed. Meike Sophia Baader (Weinheim: Beltz, 2008), 153–72.

Chapter Six

¹ Christina von Hodenberg has pointed out that press and broadcasting heavily recruited from the humanities and social sciences in the 1970s and was not subject to the "decree concerning radicals" that blocked entry to the civil service: "The field of mass media offered candidates with a political mission and the will to change things opportunities for social impact." Christina von Hodenberg, "Der Kampf um die Redaktionen: '1968' und der Wandel der westdeutschen Massenmedien," in *Wo "1968" liegt: Reform und Revolte in der Geschichte der Bundesrepublik*, ed. Christina von Hodenberg and Detlef Siegfried (Göttingen: Vandenhoeck & Ruprecht, 2006), 145; see also Uwe Krüger, *Meinungsmacht:*

Der Einfluss von Eliten auf Leitmedien und Alpha-Journalisten—eine kritische Netzwerkanalyse (Cologne: Van Halem, 2013).

[2] Alison Landsberg, *Prosthetic Memory: The Transformation of American Remembrance in the Age of Mass Culture* (New York: Columbia University Press, 2004).

[3] Wolfgang Kraushaar, ed., *Die Protest-Chronik 1949–1959: Eine illustrierte Geschichte von Bewegung, Widerstand und Utopie* (Hamburg: Rogner & Bernhard, 1996).

[4] Lutz Korndörfer, *1968 im Spiegel der Presse: Die divergierenden Reaktionen deutscher und amerikanischer Printmedien auf die deutsche Protestbewegung und die Bürgerrechtsbewegung in den USA* (Berlin: Lit Verlag, 2014).

[5] Mathias Döpfner, "Sieg der Achtundsechziger," *Die Welt*, September 28, 1998.

[6] Bernd Rabehl, "Medien," in *'68 und die Folgen: Ein unvollständiges Lexikon*, ed. Christiane Landgrebe and Jörg Plath (Berlin: Argon, 1998), 69–74, here: 74.

[7] Shafi, "Talkin' 'bout My Generation," 204.

[8] Barbara Zelizer, "Why Memory's Work on Journalism Does Not Reflect Journalism's Work on Memory," *Memory Studies* 1 (2008): 79–87.

[9] Enzensberger, "Erinnerungen an einen Tumult."

[10] Klaus Hartung, "Das große Gefühl," *Der Tagesspiegel*, April 11, 2008, http://www.tagesspiegel.de/kultur/1968-das-grosse-gefuehl/1208548.html.

[11] Quinn Slobodian, "The Axe of the Event: In and Out of the Echo Chamber of West Germany's 1968," *The Sixties: A Journal of History, Politics and Culture* 7, no. 2 (2014): 178–83.

[12] Kathrin Fahlenbrach, *Protest-Inszenierungen: Visuelle Kommunikation und kollektive Identitäten in Protestbewegungen* (Wiesbaden: Westdeutscher Verlag, 2002), 132.

[13] Ibid., 165–236.

[14] Kathrin Fahlenbrach, "Protestinszenierungen: Die Studentenbewegung im Spannungsfeld von Kultur-Revolution und Medien-Evolution," in Klimke and Scharloth, *1968: Handbuch zur Kultur- und Mediengeschichte*, 11.

[15] Klimke and Joachim, *1968*, 14.

[16] Katrin Fahlenbrach, "Zwischen Faszination, Grauen und Vereinnahmung: Die wechselvolle Resonanz der Massenmedien auf die Proteste von '68," February 6, 2008, http://www.bpb.de/geschichte/deutsche-geschichte/68er-bewegung/51830/68-und-die-medien.

[17] Kathrin Fahlenbrach, Erling Sivertsen, and Rolf Werenskjold eds., *Media and Revolt: Strategies and Performances from the 1960s to the Present* (New York: Berghahn, 2014).

[18] "Das ist Terror!" *Berliner Zeitung*, June 3, 1967, 3.

[19] "Wir fordern die Enteignung Axel Springers," *Der Spiegel*, July 10, 1967, 30–33.

[20] *Berliner Extra-Dienst* 64/1967, December 29, 1967, http://www.infopartisan.net/archive/1967/266741.html.

21 The "tribunal" took place on February 1, 1968, at Technische Universität in West Berlin. Holger Meins presented his 3-minute film "Wie baue ich einen Molotov-Cocktail?" which, at the end, showed the Springer headquarters in Kochstraße as the obvious target. See Gerd Conradt, *Starbuck—Holger Meins: Ein Portrait als Zeitbild* (Berlin: Espresso, 2001).

22 Peter Schneider, "*Bild* macht dumm."

23 Chaussy, *Die drei Leben*, 283.

24 Wolf Biermann, *Mit Marx- und Engelszungen* (Berlin: Wagenbach, 1968).

25 Wolfgang Kraushaar, "Kleinkrieg gegen einen Großverleger: Von der Anti-Springer-Kampagne der APO zu den Brand- und Bombenanschlägen der RAF," in *Die RAF und der linke Terrorismus*, ed. Wolfgang Kraushaar (Hamburg: HIS, 2006), 1075–116; see also Daniel de Roulet, *Ein Sonntag in den Bergen* (Zurich: Limmat, 2006).

26 Heinrich Böll, *Die verlorene Ehre der Katharina Blum* (Cologne: Kiepenheuer & Witsch, 1974); Günter Wallraff, *Der Aufmacher: Der Mann, der bei "Bild" Hans Esser war* (Cologne: Kiepenheuer & Witsch, 1977).

27 Hans-Peter Schwarz, "Die eigentlichen Helden," *Die Welt*, September 6, 1997.

28 "Wir Deutschen sind unberechenbar: Spiegel Streitgespräch mit Springer Vorstandschef Mathias Döpfner and Literaturnobelpreisträger Günter Grass," *Der Spiegel* 25/2006, 156–63. It was published in book form later in the year: Günter Grass and Mathias Döpfner, *Die Springer Kontroverse: Ein Streitgespräch über Deutschland*, ed. Manfred Bissinger (Göttingen: Steidl, 2006).

29 Thomas Schmid, "Die 68er: Es gab kein 'rotes Jahrzehnt,'" *Die Welt*, December 30, 2007, http://www.welt.de/politik/article1505116/Die-68er-Es-gab-kein-rotes-Jahrzehnt.html.

30 Ibid.

31 Ibid.

32 Ibid.

33 E.g., Klaus Raab, "Mann von Welt," *taz*, May 7, 2008, http://www.taz.de/!16936/.

34 Michael Ludwig Müller, *Berlin 1968: Die andere Perspektive* (Berlin: Berlin Story Verlag, 2008).

35 Sven Felix Kellerhoff, "1968 und die Medien," in *40 Jahre 1968: Alte und neue Mythen; Eine Streitschrift*, ed. Bernhard Vogel and Matthias Kutsch (Freiburg: Herder Verlag, 2008), 86–109.

36 Hans-Peter Schwarz, *Axel Springer: Die Biographie* (Berlin: List, 2008).

37 Reinhard Mohr, "Kampf um Meinungsmacht: Springer lädt 68er zum Tribunal," *Spiegel Online*, July 2, 2009, http://www.spiegel.de/kultur/gesellschaft/kampf-um-meinungsmacht-springer-laedt-68er-zum-tribunal-a-633924.html.

38 "Springer-Tribunal fällt aus," *Spiegel Online*, August 22, 2009, http://www.spiegel.de/kultur/gesellschaft/68er-gespraech-springer-tribunal-faellt-aus-a-644461.html.

39 Thomas Schmid, "Der ganz freie Diskurs," *Die Welt*, August 22, 2009, http://www.welt.de/welt_print/politik/article4379213/Der-ganz-freie-Diskurs.html.

40 "Springer hat die Idee einer Aussprache selbst begraben," *Spiegel Online*, August 23, 2009, http://www.spiegel.de/kultur/gesellschaft/abgesagtes-tribunal-mit-68ern-springer-hat-die-idee-einer-aussprache-selbst-begraben-a-644510.html.

41 Peter Schneider, "Vergessen, was Manipulation ist," *Frankfurter Rundschau*, September 3, 2009.

42 Mathias Döpfner, "Editorial zum Medienarchiv68," http://www.medienarchiv68.de/.

43 Ibid.

44 "Pressespiegel: A chronological list of reactions to the Medienarchiv68," Springer SE 2010, http://www.medienarchiv68.de/artikel/Pressespiegel_1049602.html.

45 Georg Altrogge, "Nur einer kann gewinnen," January 12, 2010, http://meedia.de/2010/01/12/68er-archiv-nur-einer-kann-gewinnen/.

46 Sven Felix Kellerhoff, "Das Archiv zur Revolte," *Die Welt*, January 18, 2010.

47 M. L. Müller, "Eine Waffe in den Händen der SDS-'Revolutionäre,'" *Berliner Morgenpost*, November 5, 1967, http://medienarchiv68.de/dl/203807/1374.jpg.pdf.

48 Steffen Grimberg, "Neues aus der Wagenburg," *taz*, January 12, 2010, http://www.taz.de/!46653/.

49 Jan-Philipp Hein, "Der Versuch einer Korrektur," *Kölner Stadt-Anzeiger*, January 28, 2010, http://www.ksta.de/medien/springer-medienarchiv-der-versuch-einer-korrektur,15189656,12772900.html.

50 Michael Meyer, "Medienhetzer und Politgammler: Springer und die 68er," *Deutschlandradio*, January 18, 2010, http://www.deutschlandfunk.de/medienhetzer-und-politgammler.724.de.html?dram:article_id=99713.

51 Wolf-Sören Treusch, "Ist das sowas wie Aufarbeitung: 100 Tage 'Medienarchiv 68' vom Axel Springer Verlag," *Deutschlandradio*, April 8, 2010, http://www.deutschlandradiokultur.de/ist-das-sowas-wie-aufarbeitung.1001.de.html?dram:article_id=157025.

52 Jochen Staadt, Tobias Voigt, and Stefan Wolle, *Feind-Bild Springer: Ein Verlag und seine Gegner* (Göttingen: Vandenhoeck & Ruprecht, 2009).

53 See Georg von Bönisch and Klaus Wiegrefe, "Ein Abgrund von Lüge," *Der Spiegel* 38/2012, September 17, 2012, http://www.spiegel.de/spiegel/print/d-88656050.html.

54 Rudolf Augstein, "Lex Springer," *Der Spiegel* 32/1966, August 1, 1966, http://www.spiegel.de/spiegel/print/d-46408143.html. It is perhaps ironic that Hans Magnus Enzensberger had accused *Der Spiegel* of being a danger to West German democracy since it was "disorienting" its readers. See Hans Magnus Enzensberger, "Die Sprache des Spiegel," *Der Spiegel* 10/1957, March 6, 1957, http://www.spiegel.de/spiegel/print/d-32092775.html.

55 Rudolf Augstein, "Enteignen?," *Der Spiegel* 40/1967, September 25, 1967, http://www.spiegel.de/spiegel/print/d-46353340.html.

56 "Titelbilder und Heftarchive 1967," *Der Spiegel*, http://www.spiegel.de/spiegel/print/index-1967.html.

57 "Titelbilder und Heftarchive 1968," *Der Spiegel*, http://www.spiegel.de/spiegel/print/index-1968.html.

58 "Die wilden 68er: Die Spiegel-Serie über die Studentenrevolution," *Spiegel Special* 1/1988, http://www.spiegel.de/spiegel/spiegelspecial/index-1988-1.html.

59 Halter, "Herz der Revolte."

60 Cordt Schnibben, "Vollstrecker des Weltgewissens," *Der Spiegel* 23/1967, June 2, 1967, http://www.spiegel.de/spiegel/print/d-8720253.html.

61 Thomas Hüetlin, "Tage der Kommune," *Der Spiegel* 27/1997, June 30, 1997, http://www.spiegel.de/spiegel/print/d-8736657.html.

62 "Generation Ich: Von der Revolte zur Rendite; Die 68er regieren—und ihre Kinder gründen Unternehmen," *Der Spiegel* 22/2000, May 22, 2000, http://www.spiegel.de/spiegel/print/d-21114291.html.

63 Peter Schneider, "Ausbruch aus der Käseglocke," *Der Spiegel* 21/2000, May 22, 2000, http://www.spiegel.de/spiegel/print/d-16466527.html.

64 Meike Vogel, *Unruhe im Fernsehen: Protestbewegung und öffentlich-rechtliche Berichterstattung in den 1960er Jahren* (Göttingen: Wallstein, 2010).

65 "Zu Protokoll: Günter Gaus im Gespräch mit Rudi Dutschke," *ARD*, December 3, 1967; "Retro spezial: 1968 Jahr des Aufstands," *ORF*, *Club 2*, June 13, 1978, https://www.youtube.com/watch?v=8v3bcJLaG6I.

66 "Retro spezial," *ORF*.

67 "Was war links?" is occasionally repeated on cultural channels (such as Phoenix in 2010) but is also available on YouTube. Transcripts of the programs are available on www.waswarlinks.de.

68 3sat Programmarchiv, April 6, 2008, http://www.3sat.de/programm/?viewlong=viewlong&d=20080406.

69 *Kulturzeit extra: Mythos 68; Die Revolte und ihre Archäologen* (Mainz: ZDF, 2008), https://www.youtube.com/watch?v=my9wSKkJQyA.

70 Annette Hinz-Wessels and Regina Haunhorst, "Studentenbewegung und APO," Lebendiges Museum Online, Stiftung Haus der Geschichte der Bundesrepublik Deutschland, http://www.hdg.de/lemo/kapitel/geteiltes-deutschland-modernisierung/bundesrepublik-im-wandel/studentenbewegung-und-apo.html.

71 *Das Gedächtnis der Nation* (Mainz, ZDF), http://www.gedaechtnis-der-nation.de/.

72 Bundeszentrale für politische Bildung, "Was ist unser Auftrag?," http://www.bpb.de/die-bpb/52218/was-ist-unser-auftrag.

73 "Die 68er-Generation," *Aus Politik und Zeitgeschichte*, B 22–23 (2001), http://www.bpb.de/apuz/26231/die-68er-generation.

74 "1968," *Aus Politik und Zeitgeschichte* 14–15 (2008), http://www.bpb.de/apuz/31312/1968.

75 Dossier: Die 68er Bewegung, Bundeszentrale für politische Bildung, http://www.bpb.de/geschichte/deutsche-geschichte/68er-bewegung/.

76 Stephan Trinius, ed., "War 68 eine Revolution? Kurzer Sommer, lange Wirkung—eine virtuelle Gesprächsrunde," Mediathek, Bundeszentrale für politische Bildung, 2008, http://www.bpb.de/mediathek/190170/war-68-eine-revolution.

77 "1968: Myth or Reality?," BBC Radio 4, http://www.bbc.co.uk/radio4/1968/.

78 "Jahre der Rebellion," Dossier: Die 68er-Bewegung," Bundeszentrale für politische Bildung, http://www.bpb.de/geschichte/deutsche-geschichte/68er-bewegung/51790/jahre-der-rebellion.

79 "Die Bedeutung von 1968 heute: Ein Streitgespräch zwischen Eberhard Diepgen und Peter Schneider," Dossier: Die 68er-Bewegung, Bundeszentrale für politische Bildung, January 30, 2008, http://www.bpb.de/geschichte/deutsche-geschichte/68er-bewegung/52052/streitgespraech?p=all.

80 "Transkript: Mythos 68; Streitgespräch zwischen Gerd Langguth und Reinhard Mohr," Dossier: Die 68er-Bewegung, Bundeszentrale für politische Bildung, June 3, 2008, http://www.bpb.de/geschichte/deutsche-geschichte/68er-bewegung/52104/reinhard-mohr-gerd-langguth.

81 "Künstler 68," Dossier: Die 68er-Bewegung, Bundeszentrale für politische Bildung, http://www.bpb.de/geschichte/deutsche-geschichte/68er-bewegung/52062/kuenstler-68.

82 "Links ins Internet," Dossier: Die 68er-Bewegung, Bundeszentrale für politische Bildung, http://www.bpb.de/geschichte/deutsche-geschichte/68er-bewegung/52115/links.

Chapter Seven

1 Berliner SDS-Gruppe "Kultur und Revolution," "Kunst als Ware der Bewußtseinsindustrie," *Die Zeit*, November 29, 1968. The ensuing debate rumbled on for months. See also Peter Schneider, "Die Phantasie.

2 "The 1968 Exhibit: About the Exhibit," Minnesota Historical Society, http://the1968exhibit.org/about-exhibit.

3 "The 1968 Exhibit: 1968 Goals and Standards," Minnesota Historical Society, http://the1968exhibit.org/node/3240.

4 Margrit Hahn, "Rudi Dutschkes Pulli hinter Glass," *Märkische Allgemeine Zeitung*, October 22, 2013, http://www.maz-online.de/Lokales/Teltow-Flaeming/Luckenwalde/Rudi-Dutschkes-Pulli-hinter-Glas. See also "Die Wiege der Revolution," *Der Spiegel* 4/2008 (under the rubric "Legenden": http://magazin.spiegel.de/EpubDelivery/spiegel/pdf/55508015).

5 Rückblick 1. Mai bis 31. August 2008, Die 68er: Kurzer Sommer, lange Wirkung, Historisches Museum Frankfurt, http://www.historisches-museum.frankfurt.de/index.php?article_id=113&clang=0.

6 Andreas Schwab, Beate Schappach, and Manuel Gogos, eds., *Die 68er: Kurzer Sommer—lange Wirkung; Ein literarisches Lesebuch* (Begleitbuch zur Ausstellung des Historischen Museums in Frankfurt am Main) (Munich: DTV, 2008).

⁷ Claus Kröger, "Ausstellungs-Rezension zu *Die 68er: Kurzer Sommer—lange Wirkung.* 01.05.2008–02.11.2008, Historisches Museum Frankfurt am Main," *H-Soz-u-Kult*, August 2, 2008, http://hsozkult.geschichte.hu-berlin.de/rezensionen/id=65&type=rezausstellungen.

⁸ Arno Widmann, "In Frankfurt weltberühmt," *Frankfurter Rundschau*, April 30, 2008, http://www.fr-online.de/zeitgeschichte/-kurzer-sommer---lange-wirkung--in-frankfurt-weltberuehmt,1477344,2796486.html.

⁹ Volker Ludwig, *Grips Chronik* 1969–2009, 21, http://www.grips-theater.de/unser-haus/historie/. See also Gerhard Fischer, *Grips: Geschichte eines populären Theaters (1966–2000)* (Munich: Iudicium, 2002), 275–97.

¹⁰ Barbara Burkhardt, "Eine linke Geschichte," *Theater Heute*, August/September 2002, 102.

¹¹ "Rocky Dutschke '68: Ein Hörspiel von Christoph Schlingensief," (WDR) 1997/50, http://www.schlingensief.com/projekt.php?id=h003.

¹² Peter Laudenbach, "Fröhliche Leichenschändung," *Berliner Zeitung*, May 20, 1996, http://www.berliner-zeitung.de/archiv/-rocky-dutschke--68---christoph-schlingensief-laeuft-amok-froehliche-leichenschaendung,10810590,9126794.html.

¹³ Cf. Chris Homewood, "Have the Best Ideas Stood the Test of Time? Negotiating the Legacy of '1968' in *The Edukators*," in Cornils and Waters, *Memories of 1968*.

¹⁴ Cf. Chris Homewood, "From Baader to Prada: Memory and Myth in Uli Edel's *The Baader Meinhof Complex* (2008)," in *New Directions in German Cinema*, ed. Paul Cooke and Chris Homewood (London: I. B. Tauris, 2011), 130–48.

¹⁵ See, for example, the "historical background" supplied by Germany's main television channel: "Die Chronik der RAF," DasErste.de, http://www.daserste.de/baadermeinhofkomplex/allround_dyn~uid,vaxvzrd24jnqw8wa~cm.asp.

¹⁶ Andres Veiel, dir., *Wer Wenn Nicht Wir*, German trailer (2011), https://www.youtube.com/watch?v=CBafuYa0qlA.

¹⁷ Thomas Kellein, ed., *1968: Die große Unschuld* (Bielefeld: DuMont, 2009). See also Abby Peterson, "Wounds That Never Heal: On Anselm Kiefer and the Moral Innocence of the West German Student Movements and the West German New Left," *Cultural Sociology* 6, no. 3 (2012): 367–85.

¹⁸ Gerhard Richter and Baader Meinhof. "Zyklus 18. Oktober 1977," https://www.gerhard-richter.com/de/art/paintings/photo-paintings/baader-meinhof-56.

¹⁹ Cf. Eric Kligerman, "Transgenerational Hauntings: Screening the Holocaust in Gerhard Richter's October 18, 1977 Paintings," in *Baader-Meinhof Returns: History and Cultural Memory of German Left-Wing Terrorism*, ed. Gerrit-Jan Berendse and Ingo Cornils, 41–63 (Amsterdam: Rodopi, 2008).

²⁰ Hagen Bonifer, "Vom Nutzen zu zweifeln," Der 2. Juni 1967, Eine anachronistische Reflektion, http://www.hagenbonifer.de/paintingshtml/paintings13.html.

21 Cf. Mia Beck, "Geschichtliche Grautöne," *Frankfurter Rundschau*, August 27, 2009, http://www.fr-online.de/rhein-main/ausstellung-geschichtliche-grautoene,1472796,3188496.html.

22 Hagen Bonifer, "Hagen Bonifer im Gespraech zu seinem Gemäldezyklus '2. Juni 1967,'" http://www.hagenbonifer.de/media.html.

23 Beate Kutschke and Barley Norton, eds. *Music and Protest in 1968* (Cambridge: Cambridge University Press, 2014).

24 Daniel Gäsche, *Born to Be Wild: Die 68er und die Musik* (Leipzig: Militzke, 2008); Timothy Scott Brown, "'The Germans meet the Underground': The Politics of Pop in the Essener Songtage of 1968," in *Musikkulturen in der Revolte: Studien zu Rock, Avantgarde und Klassik im Umfeld von "1968,"* ed. Beate Kutschke (Stuttgart: Franz Steiner Verlag, 2008), 163–73.

25 "Franz Josef Degenhardt: Vatis Argumente," (Single) Polydor 53 026, https://www.youtube.com/watch?v=a-DJfQgzGNU.

26 David Robb, "Narrative Role-Play as Communication Strategy in German Protest Song," in *Protest Song in East and West Germany since 1960*, ed. David Robb (Rochester, NY: Camden House, 2007), 67–98, here: 77–79.

27 Rainald Grebe und Die Kapelle der Versöhnung, *1968* (Hamburg: Versöhnungsrecords, 2008), http://www.youtube.com/watch?v=pliw2c9CS14.

28 Rainald Grebe, "'Massenkompatibel werd' ich nie': Kabarettist Rainald Grebe über 68," *taz*, March 31, 2008, http://www.taz.de/!15135/.

29 "1968: The Year That Changed History," *Guardian*, January 17, 2008, http://www.theguardian.com/observer/gallery/2008/jan/17/1.

30 Cf. Felicitas Schwarz, "Das Foto: Die Kommune I," http://www.arte.tv/magazine/karambolage/de/das-foto-die-kommune-1-karambolage.

31 Tom Lamont, "Baron Wolman's Woodstock Photographs: 'I Thought, There'll Never Be Anything Like This Again,'" *Guardian*, June 22, 2014, http://www.theguardian.com/music/2014/jun/22/baron-wolman-woodstock-photographs-thought-never-anything-like-this.

32 "Was ist geblieben von den Achtundsechzigern, Herr Ruetz?," *Der Tagesspiegel*, December 30, 1998, http://www.michael-ruetz.de/index.php/texte/ueber-autor-und-werk/was-ist-von-den-achtundsechzigern-geblieben.

33 The Deutsche Fotothek lists and makes available 263 photographs by Michael Ruetz: http://www.deutschefotothek.de.

34 Michael Ruetz, *Schlacht an der Spree: Ende der Unschuld*, November 4, 1968, http://www.deutschefotothek.de/documents/obj/90028299.

35 Michael Ruetz, *"Ihr müßt diesen Typen nur ins Gesicht sehen"*: *APO Berlin 1966–1969* (Frankfurt am Main: Zweitausendeins, 1980), 5.

36 Ruetz, *Sichtbare Zeit*, 250.

37 Ruetz, *1968*, 40–41.

38 Günter Zint, Pressefotos zum Download, Stiftung Haus der Geschichte der Bundesrepublik Deutschland, http://www.hdg.de/bonn/ausstellungen/wanderausstellungen/wilde-zeiten/pressefotos-zum-download/.

39 *Wilde Zeiten: Fotografien von Günter Zint*, Stiftung Haus der Geschichte der Bundesrepublik Deutschland, http://www.hdg.de/bonn/ausstellungen/wanderausstellungen/wilde-zeiten/.

40 *'68: Brennpunkt Berlin*, Ausstellung, Zeitzeugengespräche, Podien und Filme im Amerika Haus Berlin, Bundeszentrale für politische Bildung, January 18, 2008, http://www.bpb.de/presse/50471/68-brennpunkt-berlin.

41 Marco Radloff, "Politisches Statement eines Fotografen," *Bildwerk3*, February 1, 2008, http://www.bildwerk3.de/2008/02/01/politisches-statement-eines-fotografen/.

42 Astrid Proll, *Baader Meinhof: Pictures on the Run 67–77* (Zurich: Skalo, 1998).

43 Rainer Langhans and Christa Ritter, *K1: Das Bilderbuch der Kommune* (Munich: Blumenbar, 2008).

44 Gerd Koenen and Andres Veiel, *1968: Bildspur eines Jahres* (Cologne: Fackelträger, 2008), 5.

45 "Buchstäblich Wagenbach—50 Jahre: Der *unabhängige* Verlag für *wilde* Leser," Verlag Klaus Wagenbach, http://www.wagenbach.de/images/stories/50/50Jahre-Wagenbach.pdf.

46 Ulrike Anders et al., eds., *Siegfried Unseld, Chronik 1970: Mit den Chroniken Buchmesse 1967, Buchmesse 1968 und der Chronik eines Konflikts 1968* (Berlin: Suhrkamp, 2010).

Chapter Eight

1 Reinhard Mohr, *Zaungäste: Die Generation, die nach der Revolte kam* (Frankfurt am Main: Fischer, 1992).

2 Cf. Angelika Hüffell, *Schülerbewegung 1967–1977* (Gießen: Focus, 1978).

3 Sven Reichardt and Detlef Siegfried, eds., *Das Alternative Milieu: Antibürgerlicher Lebensstil und linke Politik in der Bundesrepublik Deutschland und Europa 1968–1983* (Göttingen: Wallstein, 2010).

4 Reinhard Mohr, "Zorn auf die roten Jahre," *Der Spiegel* 4/2001, January 22, 2001.

5 Reinhard Mohr, "Der diskrete Charme der Rebellion," *Spiegel Online*, February 1, 2008, http://www.spiegel.de/kultur/gesellschaft/40-jahre-68er-der-diskrete-charme-der-rebellion-a-531864.html; "Heute gibt's Dresche," *Spiegel Online*, February 2, 2008, http://www.spiegel.de/kultur/literatur/40-jahre-68er-heute-gibt-s-dresche-a-532499.html; "Ein Skandal, der die Republik veränderte," *Spiegel Online*, February 4, 2008, http://www.spiegel.de/kultur/literatur/studentenrevolte-ein-skandal-der-die-republik-veraenderte-a-532502.html.

6 Mohr, *Der diskrete Charme*, 15.

7 Reinhard Mohr, "Ein Schuss, der Deutschland verändert," *Spiegel Online*, May 22, 2009, http://www.spiegel.de/einestages/der-fall-kurras-a-948306.html.

8 Reinhard Mohr, "Schrecken aus dem braunen Sumpf," *Spiegel Online*, December 6, 2009, http://www.spiegel.de/kultur/gesellschaft/enthuellung-ueber-dutschke-attentaeter-schrecken-aus-dem-braunen-sumpf-a-665421.html.

9 Cf. Jürgen Leinemann and Gerhard Spörl, "Die Sonderwege sind zuende," *Der Spiegel*, 40/2000, October 2, 2000, http://www.spiegel.de/spiegel/print/d-17483236.html.

10 Mary Fulbrook, *Anatomy of a Dictatorship: Inside the GDR, 1949–1989* (New York: Oxford 1995), 193.

11 Timothy Scott Brown, "East Germany," in Klimke and Scharloth, *1968 in Europe*, 190.

12 Christa Wolf, "Nehmt euch in acht!," *Frankfurter Rundschau*, July 11, 2008, http://www.fr-online.de/zeitgeschichte/interview-mit-christa-wolf--nehmt-euch-in-acht-,1477344,2689666.html.

13 "Bericht der Enquete-Kommission 'Aufarbeitung von Geschichte und Folgen der SED-Diktatur in Deutschland,'" Deutscher Bundestag, Drucksache 12/7820, May 31, 1994, 90; 198–99.

14 Ulrich Bock, *Achtundsechziger: Jenaer Studenten proben den Aufstand* (Gudensberg-Gleichen: Wartberg, 2000), 128.

15 Barbara Metselaar Berthold, *Kratzen am Beton: 68er in der DDR?* (Jena: Vopelius, 2008), http://www.metselaar-berthold.de/index.php; see also the film *Wir wären so gerne Helden gewesen* (dir. Barbara Metselaar Berthold, 1996).

16 Dieter Althaus, "Und es war Sommer: Das Jahr 1968 in der DDR," in Vogel and Kutsch, *40 Jahre*, 209.

17 Stefan Wolle, *Der Traum von der Revolte: Die DDR 1968* (Berlin: Ch. Links, 2008).

18 Literally: overforeignization.

19 Anna von der Goltz, "Making Sense of East Germany's 1968: Multiple Trajectories and Contrasting Memories," *Memory Studies* 6 (2013): 53–69, here: 66.

20 Detlef Hohn, *Auch wir waren dabei: Ostern 1968 in Hamburg* (Norderstedt: Books on Demand, 2013).

21 Claus Leggewie, *Politische Zeiten: Beobachtungen von der Seitenlinie* (Gütersloh: Bertelsmann, 2015).

22 "'Ich war ein ganz schüchterner Kerl': Spiegel Gespräch mit Claus Leggewie," *Der Spiegel* 17/2015, April 18, 2015, https://magazin.spiegel.de/digital/index_SP.html#SP/2015/17/134097140.

23 See, for example, Jürgen Bevers, dir., *Kinder der 68er* (WDR/arte, 2008); Ingrid Löwer, *Die 68er im Spiegel ihrer Kinder: Eine vergleichende Untersuchung zu familienkritischen Prosatexten der jüngeren Autorengeneration* (Bremen: edition lumiere, 2011).

24 Jess Jochimsen, *Das Dosenmilch-Trauma: Bekenntnisse eines 68er-Kindes* (Munich: DTV, 2000).

25 Katharina Wulff-Bräutigam, *Bhagwan, Che und ich: Meine Kindheit in den 70ern* (Munich: Droehmer, 2005).

26 Gerhard Henschel, *Bildungsroman* (Hamburg: Hoffmann und Campe, 2014), 235.

Chapter Nine

1 Anon., "Bürgerlich bis in die Knochen," *Der Spiegel* 44/2007, October 29, 2007.

2 Margot Berghaus, *Studie der Zeitungsgruppe BILD: Die 68er Generation: Zwischen Cola und Corega-Tabs* (Hamburg: Springer Verlag, 2002).

3 Cf. Julie Friedrichs, *Wir Erben: Was Geld mit Menschen macht* (Berlin: Berlin Verlag, 2015).

4 "Schlussbericht der Enquête-Kommission 'Demographischer Wandel—Herausforderungen unserer älter werdenden Gesellschaft an den Einzelnen und die Politik,'" Deutscher Bundestag, Drucksache 14/8080, March 28, 2002, 118–19, http://dip21.bundestag.de/dip21/btd/14/088/1408800.pdf.

5 Petra Bruns, Werner Bruns, and Rainer Böhme, *Die Altersrevolution: Wie wir in Zukunft alt werden* (Berlin: Aufbau, 2007); see also Rainer Böhme, "Revolution des Alters. Die 68er gehen in Rente," March 23, 2008, http://www.bpb.de/geschichte/deutsche-geschichte/68er-bewegung/52048/68er-in-rente?p=all.

6 Peter Schneider, *Rebellion und Wahn*.

7 Anonymes Autorenkollektiv, "Gewalt in den Metropolen," *konkret* 6 (June 1968): 25–28.

8 Cf. Karrin Hanshew, "Sympathy for the Devil? The West German Left and the Challenge of Terrorism," *Contemporary European History* 21, no. 4 (2012): 511–32.

9 Cf. Matthias Matussek, "Dutschke, Goebbels und Co.," *Der Spiegel* 8/2008.

10 Peter Schneider's most recent autobiographical text, *Die Lieben meiner Mutter* (Cologne: Kiepenheuer & Witsch, 2013), continues the author's excavation of his personal history. Based on the letters his mother wrote to his father and her lover during and after World War II, he shows that emancipation and the pursuit of happiness are as much a question of individual courage as of collective ideologies. See Josef Bichler, "Peter Schneider: Die Lieben meiner Mutter" (Interview with Peter Schneider), *Der Standard*, May 10, 2013.

11 Erasmus Schöfer, *Winterdämmerung* (Berlin: Dittrich, 2008), 445–46.

12 Jochen Schimmang, *Das Beste, was wir hatten* (Hamburg: Edition Nautilus, 2008).

13 Cf. Martin Halter, "Berlin, dieser Emporkömmling," *Frankfurter Allgemeine Zeitung*, December 4, 2009, http://www.faz.net/aktuell/feuilleton/buecher/rezensionen/belletristik/jochen-schimmang-das-beste-was-wir-hatten-berlin-dieser-emporkoemmling-1893653.html.

14 The plan to attack a symbol of Germany's imperial past as a warning against a potential reawakening of its military ambitions is a plot line taken from Uwe Timm's *Rot*.

[15] E.g., Sabine Peters, "Sie fangen noch einmal an," *Frankfurter Rundschau*, January 26, 2010; Halter, "Berlin."

[16] Stephan Wackwitz, "Separatistische Lebensläufe," *taz*, September 2, 2008.

[17] Volker Hage, "Der lange Abschied von der BRD," *Der Spiegel* 5/2010, 127.

[18] Uwe Timm, *Freitisch* (Cologne: Kiepenheuer & Witsch, 2011).

[19] Cf. Julia Schöll, "Chaos und Ordnung zugleich: Zum intra- und intertextuellen Verweissystem in Uwe Timms Erzähltexten," in *(Un-)erfüllte Wirklichkeit: Neue Studien zu Uwe Timms Werk*, ed. Frank Finlay and Ingo Cornils (Würzburg: Königshausen, 2006), 127–39.

[20] Cornils, "Uwe Timm," 55–71.

[21] Peter Mohr, "Erzähler und Zuhörer: Zum 70. Geburtstag des Schriftstellers Uwe Timm," *literaturkritik.de*, no. 4 (2010).

[22] Ibid.

[23] Monika Albrecht, "Das Beispiel Kropotkin: Umsetzung von '68er Inhalten' bei Uwe Timm," in *Gegenwartsliteratur: Ein germanistisches Jahrbuch 11*, ed. Paul Michael Lützeler, Erin McGlothlin, and Jennifer Kapczynski (Tübingen: Stauffenburg, 2012), 77–102.

[24] Uwe Timm, *Vogelweide* (Cologne: Kiepenheuer & Witsch, 2013), 246.

[25] Friedrich Christian Delius, *Als die Bücher noch geholfen haben* (Berlin: Rowohlt, 2012), 78.

[26] Bernd Cailloux, *Gutgeschriebene Verluste* (Berlin: Suhrkamp, 2012), 7.

[27] Jochen Schimmang, "Mal sehen, was im Dschungel lief," *taz*, February 29, 2012.

[28] A riff on 60s TV animal conservationist Dr. Bernhard Grzimek's campaign "Serengeti darf nicht sterben."

[29] See chapter 4, "The Social Function of Literature."

[30] Hans Magnus Enzensberger, *Tumult* (Frankfurt am Main: Suhrkamp, 2014), 107.

[31] Cf. Gerd Langguth, "So harmlos war er nicht," *Cicero: Magazin für politische Kultur*, February 19, 2008, http://www.cicero.de/so-harmlos-war-er-nicht/38512.

[32] Cf. Edward Said, *On Late Style: Music and Literature against the Grain* (New York: Pantheon Books, 2006); Stuart Taberner, *The Novel in German since 1990* (Cambridge: Cambridge University Press, 2011), 9; Karen Leeder, "Figuring Lateness in Modern German Culture," *New German Critique* 42, no. 2 (2015): 1–29.

[33] Bob Dylan, the archetypal protest singer of the sixties and always ahead of his time, encapsulated this mood in his song "Not dark yet" (1997) and in the autobiographical *Chronicles* (2004). In 2012, he was given the Medal of Freedom, the highest civilian honor an American can receive, by Barack Obama, the first black American president, perhaps an indication that the times have indeed changed.

Chapter Ten

[1] Cf. Stefan Weber, "Was heißt 'Medien konstruieren Wirklichkeit'? Von einem ontologischen zu einem empirischen Verständnis von Konstruktion," *Medien-Impulse*, no. 40 (2002): 12–16, http://www.mediamanual.at/mediamanual/themen/pdf/diverse/40_Weber.pdf.

[2] Cf. Meike Sophia Baader, "Erziehung und 68," in *Dossier: Die 68er Bewegung*, Bundeszentrale für politische Bildung, May 30, 2008, http://www.bpb.de/geschichte/deutsche-geschichte/68er-bewegung/51961/erziehung-und-68.

[3] Marion Gräfin Dönhoff, "Die Rebellion der Romantiker," *Die Zeit*, January 5, 1968, http://www.zeit.de/1968/01/die-rebellion-der-romantiker/komplettansicht.

[4] Löwenthal, *Der romantische Rückfall*.

[5] Gordon A. Craig, *The Germans* (Harmondsworth, UK: Penguin, 1981).

[6] Lothar Voigt, *Aktivismus und moralischer Rigorismus: Die politische Romantik der 68er Studentenbewegung* (Wiesbaden: Deutscher Universitätsverlag, 1991), 9. Gerd Koenen talks about "the romantic-regressive desire to recreate a close 'community' in place of modern society with its irreconcilable contradictions": Koenen, *Das rote Jahrzehnt*, 56.

[7] Alois Prinz, *Der poetische Mensch im Schatten der Utopie: Zur politisch-weltanschaulichen Idee der 68er Studentenbewegung und deren Auswirkung auf die Literatur* (Würzburg: Königshausen & Neumann, 1990), 96.

[8] Kraushaar, *Achtundsechzig*, 258–68.

[9] Novalis, *Aphorismen und Fragmente 1798–1800*, http://gutenberg.spiegel.de/buch/aphorismen-5232/6.

[10] Of course, the "sanfte Revolution" of 1989 is exempt from such a verdict.

[11] Mosler, *Was wir wollten*, 80.

[12] Barbara Sichtermann, "1968 als Symbol," in *Die Früchte der Revolte: Über die Veränderung der politischen Kultur durch die Studentenbewegung*, ed. Lothar Baier et al. (Berlin: Wagenbach, 1988), 43.

[13] Jochen Schimmang, "Vom Ende des Winters," *taz*, March 18, 2008.

[14] "40 Jahre 68er Revolte," *taz special*, April 19, 2008.

[15] "I was not born to live a man's life, but to be the stuff of future memory. The fellowship was a brief beginning, a fair time that cannot be forgotten. And because it will not be forgotten, that fair time may come again. Now once more I must ride with my knights, to defend what was, and the dream of what could be." John Boorman (dir.), *Excalibur*, 1981.

[16] See my "Uwe Timm," 55–71.

[17] Herbert Marcuse, *An Essay on Liberation* (Boston: Beacon Press, 1969) (German translation: *Versuch über die Befreiung*, 30).

[18] Herbert Marcuse, "Repressive Tolerance," in *A Critique of Pure Tolerance*, ed. Robert Paul Wolff, Barrington Moore Jr., and Herbert Marcuse (Boston: Beacon Press, 1969).

[19] Francis Fukuyama, *The End of History and the Last Man* (New York: Free Press, 1992); see also Eliane Glaser, "Bring Back Ideology: Fukuyama's 'End of History' 25 Years On," *Guardian*, March 21, 2014, http://www.theguardian.com/books/2014/mar/21/bring-back-ideology-fukuyama-end-history-25-years-on.

[20] Jürgen Habermas, interview, *Frankfurter Rundschau*, March 11, 1988.

[21] See Claus Leggewie, "Der Mythos des Neuanfangs—Gründungsetappen der Bundesrepublik Deutschland 1949–1968–1989," in *Mythos und Nation: Studien zur Entwicklung des kollektiven Bewußtseins in der Neuzeit*, ed. Helmut Berding (Frankfurt am Main: Suhrkamp, 1996), 275ff.; Reinhard Mohr, "68er an die Macht," *Der Spiegel* 11/1998; Edgar Wolfrum, *Rot-Grün an der Macht: Deutschland 1998–2005* (Munich: Beck, 2013).

[22] Marwick, *Sixties*.

[23] Robert Frank, "1968: Ein Mythos? Fragen an die Vorstellung und an die Erinnerung," in *1968: Vom Ereignis zum Gegenstand der Geschichtswissenschaft*, ed. Ingrid Gilcher-Holtey, 1998, 301–7. Tellingly, the book was reissued ten years later with a new title that erased the question mark: Ingrid Gilcher-Holtey, ed., *1968: Vom Ereignis zum Mythos* (Frankfurt am Main: Suhrkamp, 2008).

[24] Wolfgang Kraushaar, *1968 als Mythos, Chiffre und Zäsur* (online book description), http://www.his-online.de/verlag/9010/programm/detailseite/publikationen/1968-als-mythos-chiffre-und-zaesur/.

[25] Ibid.

[26] Matthias Waechter, "Mythos, Version: 1.0," *Docupedia-Zeitgeschichte*, February 11, 2010, http://docupedia.de/zg/Mythos?oldid=106455. See, for example, the ZDF documentary film *1968: Mythos und Wahrheit* (dir. Peter Hartl and Jean-Christoph Caron), which was presented by Guido Knopp in the series ZDF-History on March 16, 2008, and toured by the Goethe Institute.

[27] See, for example, Thomas Steinfeld, "Herr Tur Tur und die Revolution," *Süddeutsche Zeitung*, October 27, 2007, http://www.sueddeutsche.de/kultur/mythos-herr-tur-tur-und-die-revolution-1.890191; Richard Herzinger, "1968: Wie eine Revolte zum Mythos wurde," *Welt am Sonntag*, January 7, 2008, http://www.welt.de/politik/deutschland/article1522197/1968-wie-eine-Revolte-zum-Mythos-wurde.html, or the ZDF program *Mythos 1968: Die Revolte und ihre Archäologen broadcast* (see note 69, chapter 6, above).

[28] Hubert Kleinert, "Mythos 1968," *Aus Politik und Zeitgeschichte* B 14–15 (2008), March 19, 2008, http://www.bpb.de/geschichte/deutsche-geschichte/68er-bewegung/52034/mythos-1968?p=all. Kleinert was one of the first members of the Green Party to become a Bundestagsabgeordneter and thus has a vested interest in the perpetuation of the myth.

[29] Rudi Schmidt, "1968 West und 1989 Ost: Von den Mythen jüngster deutscher Umbrüche; Was bleibt den Nachgeborenen?" *Berliner Debatte Initial* 19, no. 5 (2008): 3–13, http://www.linksnet.de/de/artikel/24441.

[30] Ibid.

[31] Varon, Foley, and McMillian, "Time Is an Ocean."

[32] Ironically, the very opposite stance to the *ideology critique* favored by the SDS.

33 Claus Leggewie, "Mythos 68er Bewegung," in *Metzler Lexikon moderner Mythen: Figuren, Konzepte, Ereignisse*, ed. Stephanie Wodianka and Juliane Ebert (Stuttgart: Metzler, 2014), 1–5, here: 4.

34 Uwe Timm, "Mythos," in *Montaignes Turm: Essays* (Cologne: Kiepenheuer & Witsch, 2015), 33–58, here: 37–38.

35 David Mitchell, *Cloud Atlas* (London: Sceptre, 2004), 408–9.

36 Martin Burckhardt, *68: Die Geschichte einer Kulturrevolution* (Berlin: Semele, 2009), dust jacket.

Conclusion

1 Thomas Etzemüller, "Virtuelle Feldschlachten: '1968' und die Macht imaginärer Bilder," in *68er Spätlese: Was bleibt von 1968?*, ed. Tobias Schaffrik and Sebastian Wienges (Berlin: Lit Verlag, 2008), 10–18, here: 18.

2 Cf. Frank Brunssen, "Das neue Selbstverständnis der Berliner Republik," *Aus Politik und Zeitgeschichte* B 1–2 (2001), http://www.bpb.de/apuz/26530/das-neue-selbstverstaendnis-der-berliner-republik?p=all.

3 Laurence A. Rickels, *Germany: A Science Fiction* (Fort Wayne, IN: Anti-Oedipus Press, 2014), 17.

4 The makers of the blockbuster movie *Der Baader Meinhof Komplex* acknowledge that their motivation was to show "die Energie, die es schon mal gegeben hatte, Gefühle, die man damals hatte." ("Bernd Eichinger über die Annäherung an den Film und die 60er und 70er Jahre," in *Der Baader Meinhof Komplex*, dir. Uli Edel, 2008, Premium Edition, Bonus DVD [ca. 15 min.]).

5 Cf. Alfred Schäfer, *1968: Die Aura des Widerstands* (Paderborn: Ferdinand Schöningh Verlag, 2015).

6 Philip Oltermann, "Jürgen Habermas's Verdict on the EU/Greece Debt Deal," *Guardian*, July 16, 2015, http://www.theguardian.com/commentisfree/2015/jul/16/jurgen-habermas-eu-greece-debt-deal.

Bibliography

THE LITERATURE ON "1968" in Germany is extensive and ever growing—confirming the argument of this book that it is in the written word that the German student movement has been preserved, remembered, constructed, and reinvented. The entries below include key historiographical, literary, and media sources on the German "1968," as well as other works cited. The figure below, which charts the publications on "1968" in Germany listed here, emphasizes one crucial point: the construction of "1968" in Germany and elsewhere is an ongoing project, with the number of books and articles on and literary representations of the movement increasing significantly since 2000. Crucially, we can see that writing about "1968" is not limited to anniversary years, though 1998 and 2008 saw a marked surge.

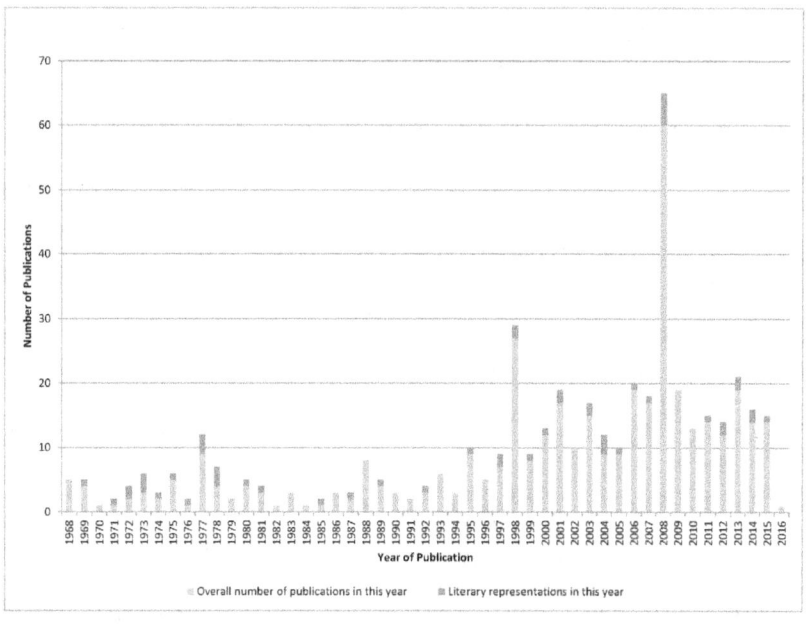

Albrecht, Monika. "Das Beispiel Kropotkin: Umsetzung von '68er Inhalten' bei Uwe Timm." In *Gegenwartsliteratur: Ein germanistisches Jahrbuch 11*, edited by Paul Michael Lützeler, Erin McGlothlin, and Jennifer Kapczynski, 77–102. Tübingen: Stauffenburg, 2012.
Alef, Rob. *Das magische Jahr*. Berlin: Rotbuch, 2008.
Ali, Tariq. *Street Fighting Years: Autobiographie eines '68ers*. Cologne: ISP, 1998.
Ali, Tariq, and Susan Watson. *1968: Marching in the Streets*. London: Bloomsbury, 1998.
Althaus, Dieter. "Und es war Sommer: Das Jahr 1968 in der DDR." In Vogel and Kutsch, *40 Jahre*, 208–22.
Altrogge, Georg. "Nur einer kann gewinnen." January 12, 2010. http://meedia.de/2010/01/12/68er-archiv-nur-einer-kann-gewinnen/.
Altvater, Elmar, Nele Hirsch, Gisela Notz, and Thomas Seibert, eds. *"Die letzte Schlacht gewinnen wir!" 40 Jahre 1968: Bilanzen und Perspektiven*. Hamburg: VSA, 2008.
Aly, Götz. *Unser Kampf 1968: Ein irritierter Blick zurück*. Frankfurt am Main: Fischer, 2008.
Anders, Ulrike, Raimund Fellinger, Katharina Karduck, Claus Kröger, Henning Marmulla, and Wolfgang Schopf, eds. *Siegfried Unseld, Chronik 1970: Mit den Chroniken Buchmesse 1967, Buchmesse 1968 und der Chronik eines Konflikts 1968*. Berlin: Suhrkamp, 2010.
Andresen, Knud, Markus Mohr, and Hartmut Rübner, eds. *Agit 883: Revolte, Underground in Westberlin 1969–1972*. Hamburg: Assoziation A, 2006.
Anonymes Autorenkollektiv. "Gewalt in den Metropolen." *konkret* 6 (June 1968): 25–28.
Anonymous. "Bürgerlich bis in die Knochen." *Der Spiegel* 44/2007, October 29, 2007.
———. "The Dentist's Chair as an Allegory in Life," *Time Magazine*, April 13, 1970.
———. "40 Jahre 68er Revolte." *taz* special, April 19, 2008.
———. "Linke Lehrer, rechte Schüler." *Der Spiegel*, January 25, 1993.
Ash, Timothy Garton. "This Tale of Two Revolutions and Two Anniversaries May Yet Have a Twist." *Guardian*, May 8, 2008.
Assmann, Aleida. *Das neue Unbehagen an der Erinnerungskultur: Eine Intervention*. Munich: C. H. Beck 2013.
Assmann, Jan. "Communicative and Cultural Memory." In *Cultural Memory Studies: An International and Interdisciplinary Handbook*, edited by Astrid Ertl and Ansgar Nünning, 109–18. Berlin: 2008.
ASTA Uni HH + Kollektiv Literaturtheorie, eds. *Literatur und Literaturwissenschaft im Zeitalter des Kapitalismus*, 69–70, Sondersammlung "Protest, Widerstand und Utopie in der Bundesrepublik Deutschland," ASTA Dokumente XV. Hamburger Institut für Sozialforschung.
Atack, Margaret. *May 68 in French Fiction and Film: Rethinking Society, Rethinking Representation*. Oxford: Oxford University Press, 1999.

Augstein, Rudolf. "Enteignen?" *Der Spiegel* 40/1967, September 25, 1967. http://www.spiegel.de/spiegel/print/d-46353340.html.
———. "Lex Springer." *Der Spiegel* 32/1966, August 1, 1966. http://www.spiegel.de/spiegel/print/d-46408143.html.
Aus Politik und Zeitgeschichte. "Die 68er-Generation." B 22–23 (2001). http://www.bpb.de/apuz/26231/die-68er-generation.
———. "1968." 14–15 (2008). http://www.bpb.de/apuz/31312/1968.
Aust, Stephan. *Der Baader-Meinhof-Komplex.* Munich: Goldmann, 1985.
Autonome L.U.P.U.S. Gruppe, eds. *Die Hunde bellen . . . Von A bis RZ: Eine Zeitreise durch die 68er Revolte und die militanten Kämpfe der 70er bis 90 Jahre.* Münster: Unrast Verlag, 2001.
Baader, Meike Sophia. "Erziehung und 68." In *Dossier: Die 68er Bewegung*, Bundeszentrale für politische Bildung, May 30, 2008. http://www.bpb.de/geschichte/deutsche-geschichte/68er-bewegung/51961/erziehung-und-68.
———. "Das Private ist politisch: Der Alltag der Geschlechter, die lebensformen und die Kinderfrage" In *"Seid realistisch,"* 153–72.
———, ed. *"Seid realistisch, verlangt das Unmögliche!": Wie 1968 die Pädagogik bewegte.* Weinheim: Beltz, 2008.
Baader, Meike Sophia, and Ullrich Hermann, eds. *68—Engagierte Jugend und Kritische Pädagogik: Impulse und Folgen eines kulturellen Umbruchs in der Geschichte der Bundesrepublik.* Weinheim: Beltz Juventa, 2011.
Baer, Willi, Carmen Bitsch, and Karl-Heinz Dellwo, eds. *Bibliothek des Widerstands.* Vol. 1, *Der 2. Juni 1967.* Hamburg: Laika Verlag, 2010.
Baier, Lothar, et al. *Die Früchte der Revolte: Über die Veränderung der politischen Kultur durch die Studentenbewegung.* Berlin: Wagenbach, 1988.
Baker, Gary L. "Aesthetics of Violence in Uwe Timm's *Rot* and Friedrich Christian Delius's *Mein Jahr als Mörder.*" *German Quarterly* 86, no. 1 (Winter 2013): 43–59.
Bartels, Gerrit. "Spürbares Bewegtsein." *taz*, September 17, 2005.
Basker, David, ed. *Uwe Timm.* Contemporary German Writers. Cardiff: University of Wales Press, 1999.
Bauer, Ingrid, and Hana Havelková, eds. "Gender & 1968." Special issue, *L'Homme: Europäische Zeitschrift für Feministische Geschichtswissenschaft* 20, no. 2 (2009).
Bauer, Karin. *Everybody Talks about the Weather . . . We Don't: The Writings of Ulrike Meinhof.* New York: Seven Stories Press, 2008.
———. "Questioning the RAF: The Politics of Culture." *Seminar: A Journal of Germanic Studies* 47, no. 1 (2011): 2–3.
Baumann, Bommi. *Wie alles anfing.* 1975; Berlin: Rotbuch, 1991.
Beck, Mia. "Geschichtliche Grautöne." *Frankfurter Rundschau*, August 27, 2009. http://www.fr-online.de/rhein-main/ausstellung-geschichtliche-grautoene,1472796,3188496.html.
Becker, Florian, Mario Candeias, Janek Niggemann, and Anne Steckner, eds. *Gramsci lessen: Einstiege in die Gefängnishefte.* Hamburg: Argument, 2013.

Becker, Hartmuth, Felix Dirsch, and Stefan Winckler, eds. *Die 68er und ihre Gegner: Der Widerstand gegen die Kulturrevolution*. Graz: Stocker, 2003.
Becker, Jullian. *Hitler's Children*. New York: Lippincott, 1977.
Becker, Thomas P., and Ute Schröder, eds. *Die Studentenproteste der 60er Jahre: Archivführer—Chronik—Bibliographie*. Cologne: Böhlau, 2000.
Behmel, Albrecht. *1968: Die Kinder der Diktatur; Der Mythos der Studentenbewegung im ideengeschichtlichen Kontext des "hysterischen Jahrhunderts" 1870 bis 1968*. Stuttgart: Ibidem, 2011.
Behre, Silja. *Bewegte Erinnerung: Deutungskämpfe um "1968" in deutsch-französischer Perspektive*. Tübingen: Mohr Siebeck, 2016.
———. "Horizont-Ende? Kämpfe um die Erinnerung der 68er-Bewegung: Eine deutsch-französische Perspektive." In Gilcher-Holtey, *"1968"— Eine Wahrnehmungsrevolution?*, 95–110.
Berendse, Gerrit-Jan, and Ingo Cornils, eds. *Baader-Meinhof Returns: History and Cultural Memory of German Left-Wing Terrorism*. Amsterdam: Rodopi, 2008.
Berger, Peter L., and Thomas Luckmann. *Die gesellschaftliche Konstruktion der Wirklichkeit: Eine Theorie der Wissenssoziologie*. 1966; Frankfurt am Main: Fischer, 1977.
Berghaus, Margot. *Studie der Zeitungsgruppe BILD: Die 68er Generation: Zwischen Cola und Corega-Tabs*. Hamburg: Springer Verlag, 2002.
Bergmann, Uwe, Rudi Dutschke, Wolfgang Levfevre, and Bernd Rabehl. *Rebellion der Studenten oder die neue Opposition*. Hamburg: Rowohlt, 1968.
Berliner Extra-Dienst 64/1967, December 29, 1967. http://www.infopartisan.net/archive/1967/266741.html.
Berliner SDS-Gruppe "Kultur und Revolution." "Kunst als Ware der Bewußtseinsindustrie." *Die Zeit*, November 29, 1968.
Berliner Zeitung. "Das ist Terror!" June 3, 1967.
Bermann, Paul. *Idealisten an der Macht: Die Passion des Joschka Fischer*. Munich: Siedler, 2006.
———. *Power and the Idealists, or The Passion of Joschka Fischer, and Its Aftermath*. Berkeley: Soft Skull Press, 2005.
Berninger, Matthias. "Die 68er im Wahljahr 1998." In Stiftung für die Rechte zukünftiger Generationen, *Die 68er*, 33–53.
Bichler, Josef. "Peter Schneider: Die Lieben meiner Mutter." Interview with Peter Schneider. *Der Standard*, May 10, 2013.
Bielby, Clare. *Violent Women in Print: Representations in the West German Print Media of the 1960s and 1970s*. Rochester, NY: Camden House, 2012.
Biermann, Wolf. *Mit Marx- und Engelszungen*. Berlin: Wagenbach, 1968.
Binder, Sepp. "Barbusig vor der Barriere: Weibliche Wunderwaffen besiegen einen Hamburger Richter." *Die Zeit*, December 20, 1968. http://pdfarchiv.zeit.de/1968/51/barbusig-vor-der-barriere.pdf.
Bissinger, Manfred, ed. *Günter Grass / Matthias Döpfner: Die Springer Kontroverse; Ein Streitgespräch über Deutschland*. Göttingen: Steidl, 2006.

Blacker, Terence. "Everything Bad in the World Today Is the Fault of the 1960s." *Independent*, August 26, 2013. http://www.independent.co.uk/voices/comment/everything-bad-in-the-world-today-is-the-fault-of-the-1960s-8784843.html.
Bock, Ulrich. *Achtundsechziger: Jenaer Studenten proben den Aufstand*. Gudensberg-Gleichen: Wartberg, 2000.
Böhme, Rainer. "Revolution des Alters: Die 68er gehen in Rente." March 23, 2008. http://www.bpb.de/geschichte/deutsche-geschichte/68er-bewegung/52048/68er-in-rente?p=all.
Bollinger, Stefan. *1968: Die unverstandene Weichenstellung*. Berlin: Dietz, 2008.
Bonifer, Hagen. "Hagen Bonifer im Gespraech zu seinem Gemäldezyklus '2. Juni 1967.'" http://www.hagenbonifer.de/media.html.
Boorman, John, dir. *Excalibur*. Film. 1981.
Born, Nicolaus. *Literaturmagazin 3: "Die Phantasie an die Macht"; Literatur als Utopie*. Reinbek: Rowohlt, 1975.
Bornhak, Achim, dir. *Das wilde Leben*. Film. 2007. Translated as *Eight Miles High*.
Bovenschen, Silvia. "Die Generation der 68er bewacht das Ereignis: Ein kritischer Rückblick." *Frankfurter Allgemeine Zeitung*, December 3, 1988.
———. "Sexuell befreite Spiesser." Interview by Heide Oestreich. *taz*, December 29, 2007. http://www.taz.de/1/archiv/digitaz/artikel/?ressort=sp&dig=2007%2F12%2F29%2Fa0048&src=GI&cHash=5443435af7.
Brandes, Volkhard, *Wie der Stein ins Rollen kam: Vom Aufbruch in die Revolte der sechziger Jahre*. Frankfurt am Main: Brandes & Apsel 1988.
Brentzel, Marianne. *Rote Fahnen Rote Lippen*. Berlin: Edition Ebersbach, 2011.
Bressen, Susanne, and Martin Jander. "Gudrun Ensslin." In Kraushaar, *Die RAF*, vol. 1, 390–429.
Briegleb, Klaus. *1968: Literatur in der antiautoritären Bewegung*. Frankfurt am Main: Suhrkamp, 1993.
Brodman, Roman, dir. *Der Polizeistaatsbesuch: Beobachtungen unter deutschen Gastgebern*. Süddeutscher Rundfunk, 1967.
Brown, Timothy Scott. "East Germany." In Klimke and Scharloth, *1968 in Europe*, 189–97.
———. "'The Germans meet the Underground': The Politics of Pop in the Essener Songtage of 1968." In Kutschke, *Musikkulturen*, 163–73.
———. "1968 in West Germany: The Anti-Authoritarian Revolt." *The Sixties: A Journal of History, Politics and Culture* 7, no. 2 (2014): 99–116.
———. *West Germany and the Global Sixties: The Antiauthoritarian Revolt, 1962–1978*. Cambridge: Cambridge University Press, 2013.
Brown, Timothy Scott, and Andrew Lison, eds. *The Global Sixties in Sound and Vision: Media, Counterculture, Revolt*. New York: Palgrave, 2014.
Broyard, Anatole. "Günter Grass Demonstrates That Fiction Is Not Only Alive but Healthier Than Ever." *New York Times*, March 29, 1970.

https://www.nytimes.com/books/99/12/19/specials/grass-local.html.

Bruns, Petra, Werner Bruns, and Rainer Böhme. *Die Altersrevolution: Wie wir in Zukunft alt werden*. Berlin: Aufbau, 2007.

Buchrucker, Armin Ernst. *Aufstand gegen Autorität und Tradition: Die Studentenbewegung von 1968 als Kulturrevolution und ihre Auswirkungen*. Oesingen: Verlag der Lutheranischen Buchhandlung, 2000.

Bude, Heinz. "Achtundsechzig." In Francois and Schulze, *Deutsche Erinnerungsorte*, 122–34.

———. *Das Altern einer Generation: Die Jahrgänge 1938–1948*. Frankfurt am Main: Suhrkamp, 1995.

Buhmann, Inga. *Ich habe mir eine Geschichte geschrieben*. Frankfurt am Main: Zweitausendeins, 1977.

Bullivant, Keith. *After the Death of Literature: West German Writing of the 1970s*. Oxford: Berg, 1989.

Bundeszentrale für politische Bildung. "Die Bedeutung von 1968 heute: Ein Streitgespräch zwischen Eberhard Diepgen und Peter Schneider." Dossier: Die 68er-Bewegung. January 30, 2008. http://www.bpb.de/geschichte/deutsche-geschichte/68er-bewegung/52052/streitgespraech?p=all.

———. Dossier: Die 68er Bewegung. http://www.bpb.de/geschichte/deutsche-geschichte/68er-bewegung/.

———. "Jahre der Rebellion." Dossier: Die 68er-Bewegung. http://www.bpb.de/geschichte/deutsche-geschichte/68er-bewegung/51790/jahre-der-rebellion.

———. "Künstler 68." Dossier: Die 68er-Bewegung. http://www.bpb.de/geschichte/deutsche-geschichte/68er-bewegung/52062/kuenstler-68.

———. "Links ins Internet." Dossier: Die 68er-Bewegung. http://www.bpb.de/geschichte/deutsche-geschichte/68er-bewegung/52115/links.

———. "Transkript: Mythos 68; Streitgespräch zwischen Gerd Langguth und Reinhard Mohr." Dossier: Die 68er-Bewegung. June 3, 2008. http://www.bpb.de/geschichte/deutsche-geschichte/68er-bewegung/52104/reinhard-mohr-gerd-langguth.

———. "Was ist unser Auftrag?" http://www.bpb.de/die-bpb/52218/was-ist-unser-auftrag.

Burkhardt, Barbara. "Eine linke Geschichte." *Theater Heute*, August/September 2002.

Burckhardt, Martin. *68: Die Geschichte einer Kulturrevolution*. Berlin: Semele, 2009.

Busch, Günther, and Uwe Wittstock, eds. "1968 Revisited: Erfahrungen mit einem Umbruch." *Neue Rundschau* 104, no. 2 (1993).

Busche, Jürgen. *Die 68er: Biographie einer Generation*. Berlin: Berlin Verlag, 2003.

Cailloux, Bernd. *Das Geschäftsjahr 1968/69*. Frankfurt am Main: Suhrkamp, 2005.

———. *Gutgeschriebene Verluste*. Berlin: Suhrkamp, 2012.

Carini, Marco. *Fritz Teufel: Wenn's der Wahrheitsfindung dient*. Hamburg: Konkret Literatur Verlag, 2008.
Caute, David. *Sixty-Eight: The Year of the Revolution*. London: Paladin, 1988.
Charim, Isolde. "Kampf um die Sehnsüchte." *taz*, April 13, 2005.
Chaussy, Ulrich. *Die drei Leben des Rudi Dutschke: Eine Biographie*. 1983; Berlin: Links, 1993.
Chotjewitz, Peter O. "Nicht versöhnt." *Der Stern*, February 18, 2004.
Cohn-Bendit, Daniel. *Forget 68*. Paris: Editions de l'Haube, 2009.
———. *Der große Basar*. Munich, 1975.
———. "Ich bin ein Held." *Frankfurter Rundschau*, April 29, 2008. http://www.fr-online.de/zeitgeschichte/daniel-cohn-bendit-ich-bin-ein-held,1477344,2795836.html.
———. *Wir haben sie so geliebt, die Revolution*. French original 1986, Berlin: Philo, 2001.
———. "Wir müssen den Geist von 1968 verteidigen." *Die Welt*, January 8, 2015. http://www.welt.de/136172915.
Cohn-Bendit, Daniel, and Rüdiger Dammann, eds. *1968: Die Revolte*. Frankfurt am Main: Fischer 2007.
Cohn-Bendit, Dany, and Reinhard Mohr. *1968: Die letzte Revolution, die noch nichts vom Ozonloch wußte*. Berlin: Wagenbach, 1988.
Colvin, Sarah. *Ulrike Meinhof and West German Terrorism: Language, Violence, and Identity*. Rochester, NY: Camden House, 2009.
Conradt, Gerd. *Starbuck—Holger Meins: Ein Portrait als Zeitbild*. Berlin: Espresso, 2001.
Cornils, Ingo. "Denkmalsturz: The German Student Movement and German Colonialism." In *German Colonialism and National Identity*, edited by Michael Perraudin and Jürgen Zimmerer, 197–212. New York: Routledge, 2010.
———. "Folgenschwere Schüsse: Die Kugeln auf Benno Ohnesorg und Rudi Dutschke im Spiegel der deutschen Literatur." *Jahrbuch für Internationale Germanistik* 35, no. 2 (2003): 55–73.
———. "The German Student Movement: Legend and Legacy." *Debatte: Review of Contemporary German Affairs* 4, no. 2 (1996): 36–62.
———. "Joined at the Hip? The Representation of the German Student Movement and Left-Wing German Terrorism in Recent Literature." In Berendse and Cornils, *Baader-Meinhof Returns*, 137–55.
———. "Literary Reflections on '68." In *Contemporary German Fiction: Writing in the Berlin Republic*, edited by Stuart Taberner, 91–107. Cambridge: Cambridge University Press, 2007.
———. "The Literary Representation of the German Student Movement." In *German Studies Towards the Millennium*, edited by Chris Hall and David Rock, 107–23. Bern: Peter Lang 2000.
———. "Long Memories: The German Student Movement in Recent Fiction." *German Life and Letters* 56, no. 1 (2003): 89–101.
———. "Looking Back: Piwitt, Rothschilds and the German Student Movement." In *Hermann Peter Piwitt*, edited by David Basker, 47–64.

Contemporary German Writers Series. Cardiff: University of Wales Press, 2000.

———. "'The Struggle Continues': Rudi Dutschke's Long March." In DeGroot, *Student Protest*, 100–114.

———. "Successful Failure? The Impact of the German Student Movement on the Federal Republic of Germany." In *Recasting German Identity: Culture, Politics and Literature in the Berlin Republic*, edited by Stuart Taberner and Frank Finlay, 105–22. Rochester, NY: Camden House, 2002.

———. "Utopian Moments: Memory Culture and Cultural Memory of the German Student Movement." In Cornils and Waters, *Memories of 1968*, 281–98.

———. "Uwe Timm, der heilige Georg und die Entsorgung der Theorie." In Finlay and Cornils, *(Un-)erfüllte Wirklichkeit*, 55–71.

———. "Writing the Revolution: The Literary Representation of the German Student Movement as Counter-Culture." In *Counter-Cultures in Germany and Central Europe: From Sturm und Drang to Baader-Meinhof*, edited by Steve Giles and Maike Oergel, 295–314. Bern: Peter Lang 2003.

Cornils, Ingo, and Sarah Waters, eds. *Memories of 1968: International Perspectives*. Vol. 1 of *Cultural History and Literary Imagination*. Bern: Peter Lang, 2010.

Craig, Gordon A. *The Germans*. Harmondsworth, UK: Penguin, 1981.

Dannenbaum, Uwe. *Berlin 1968: Die Studentenrevolte in Bildern*. Berlin: Jaron, 2015.

Dannenberg, Sophie. *Das bleiche Herz der Revolution*. Munich: DVA, 2004.

———. "Generationenkonflikt: 'Ich habe nie geglaubt, dass die 68er Antifaschisten waren.'" *Spiegel Online*, November 18, 2004. http://www.spiegel.de/kultur/literatur/generationenkonflikt-ich-habe-nie-geglaubt-dass-die-68er-antifaschisten-waren-a-327028.html.

Danquart, Pepe, dir. *Joschka und Herr Fischer: Eine Zeitreise durch 60 Jahre Deutschland*. Merzhausen: Quintefilm, 2011.

Darius, Barbara. *Die sieben Leben der Katharina Blasberg*. Cologne: Kiepenheuer & Witsch, 1997.

Dath, Dietmar, and Barbara Kirchner. *Der Implex: Sozialer Fortschritt; Geschichte und Idee*. Frankfurt am Main: Suhrkamp, 2012.

Davis, Belinda. "The Personal Is Political: Gender, Politics, and Political Activism in Modern German History." In *Gendering Modern German History: Rewriting Historiography*, edited by Jean Quataert and Karen Hagemann, 107–27. New York: Berghahn, 2007.

Davis, Belinda, Wilfried Mausbach, Martin Klimke, and Carla MacDougall, eds. *Changing the World, Changing Oneself: Political Protest and Collective Identities in West Germany and the U.S. in the 1960s and 1970s*. New York: Berghahn, 2010.

de Roulet, Daniel. *Ein Sonntag in den Bergen*. Zurich: Limmat, 2006.

DeGroot, Gerard. *The 60s Unplugged: A Kaleidoscopic History of a Disorderly Decade*. London: Macmillan, 2008.

———, ed. *Student Protest: The Sixties and After*. London: Longman, 1998.
Dehnavi, Morvarid. *Das politisierte Geschlecht: Biographische Wege zum Studentinnenprotest von "1968" und zur Neuen Frauenbewegung*. Bielefeld: Transcript, 2013.
Delius, Friedrich Christian. *Als die Bücher noch geholfen haben*. Berlin: Rowohlt, 2012.
———. *Amerikahaus und der Tanz um die Frauen*. Reinbek: Rowohlt, 1997.
———. "Anläßlich einer Ausstellungseröffnung: Gedanken beim Wiederlesen des legendären 'Kursbuch 15'." *Frankfurter Rundschau*, February 6, 1999.
———. "Ich bin eigentlich ein 66er." *Der Tagesspiegel*, December 27, 2004.
———. *Mein Jahr als Mörder*. Berlin: Rowohlt, 2004.
———. "Wie scheintot war die Literatur? Kursbuch 15 und die Folgen." www.fcdelius.de/widerreden/wider_kursbuch_15.html.
Der Spiegel. "Generation Ich: Von der Revolte zur Rendite; Die 68er regieren—und ihre Kinder gründen Unternehmen." 22/2000, May 22, 2000. http://www.spiegel.de/spiegel/print/d-21114291.html.
———. "Heiß gekocht." 44/1967, October 23, 1967. http://www.spiegel.de/spiegel/print/d-46197113.html.
———. "Ich Kobold, du Halbgott." 34/1996, August 19, 1996, and 35/1996, August 26, 1996.
———. "'Ich war ein ganz schüchterner Kerl': Spiegel Gespräch mit Claus Leggewie." 17/2015, April 18, 2015. https://magazin.spiegel.de/digital/index_SP.html#SP/2015/17/134097140.
———. "Ist Revolution unvermeidlich?" 15/1968, April 8, 1968.
———. "Der lange Marsch." 51/1967, December 11, 1967. http://www.spiegel.de/spiegel/print/d-46209544.html.
———. "Muff im Talar." 48/1967, November 20, 1967. http://www.spiegel.de/spiegel/print/d-46196225.html.
———. "Nachgefragt: Fischer soll bleiben." 3/2001, January 15, 2001. http://www.spiegel.de/spiegel/print/d-18257203.html.
———. "Titelbilder und Heftarchive 1967." http://www.spiegel.de/spiegel/print/index-1967.html.
———. "Titelbilder und Heftarchive 1968." http://www.spiegel.de/spiegel/print/index-1968.html.
———. "Und wir zeigen unsere Brüste für jeden." 51/1968, December 16, 1968. http://magazin.spiegel.de/EpubDelivery/spiegel/pdf/45865104.
———. "Vorbild Mao tse-Tung: Kunstpreisträger Peter Schneider über die Literatur in der Kulturrevolution." 15/1969, April 7, 1969.
———. "Die Wiege der Revolution." 4/2008. Under the rubric "Legenden": http://magazin.spiegel.de/EpubDelivery/spiegel/pdf/55508015.
———. "Wir Deutschen sind unberechenbar: Spiegel Streitgespräch with Springer Vorstandschef Mathias Döpfner and Literaturnobelpreisträger Günter Grass." 25/2006, 156–63.
———. "Wir fordern die Enteignung Axel Springers." July 10, 1967.

Der Tagesspiegel. "Was ist geblieben von den Achtundsechzigern, Herr Ruetz?" December 30, 1998. http://www.michael-ruetz.de/index.php/texte/ueber-autor-und-werk/was-ist-von-den-achtundsechzigern-geblieben.

Detje, Robin. "Der Teufel trug Birkenstock." *Literaturen*, no. 12 (2004).

Deutscher Bundestag. Bericht der Enquete-Kommission "Aufarbeitung von Geschichte und Folgen der SED-Diktatur in Deutschland," Drucksache 12/7820. May 31, 1994. http://dipbt.bundestag.de/dip21/btd/12/078/1207820.pdf.

———. "Schlussbericht der Enquête-Kommission 'Demographischer Wandel: Herausforderungen unserer älter werdenden Gesellschaft an den Einzelnen und die Politik.'" Drucksache 14/8080, March 28, 2002. http://dip21.bundestag.de/dip21/btd/14/088/1408800.pdf.

———. 14. Wahlperiode—142. Sitzung. Berlin, Mittwoch, den 17. Januar 2001. 13909. http://dip21.bundestag.de/dip21/btp/14/14142.pdf.

Diekmann, Kai. *Der große Selbstbetrug: Wie wir um unsere Zukunft gebracht werden.* Munich: Piper, 2007.

Dittrich, Volker, ed. *Unsichtbar lächelnd träumt er Befreiung: Erasmus Schöfer unterwegs mit Sisyfos.* Berlin: Dittrich Verlag, 2006.

Dönhoff, Marion Gräfin. "Die Rebellion der Romantiker." *Die Zeit*, January 5, 1968. http://www.zeit.de/1968/01/die-rebellion-der-romantiker/komplettansicht.

Döpfner, Mathias. "Editorial zum Medienarchiv68." http://www.medienarchiv68.de/.

———. "Sieg der Achtundsechziger." *Die Welt*, September 28, 1998.

3sat Programmarchiv. April 6, 2008. http://www.3sat.de/programm/?viewlong=viewlong&d=20080406.

Dutschke, Gretchen, ed. *Rudi Dutschke; Jeder hat sein Leben ganz zu leben: Die Tagebücher 1963–1979.* Cologne: Kiepenheuer & Witsch, 2003.

———. *Wir hatten ein barbarisches, schönes Leben; Rudi Dutschke: Eine Biographie.* Cologne: Kiepenheuer & Witsch, 1996.

Dutschke, Hosea. *Rudi und ich.* Berlin: List, 2015.

Dutschke, Rudi. *Mein langer Marsch: Reden, Schriften und Tagebücher aus zwanzig Jahren.* Edited by Gretchen Dutschke-Klotz, Hellmut Gollwitzer, and Jürgen Miermeister. Reinbek: Rowohlt, 1980.

———. *Die Revolte: Wurzeln und Spuren eines Aufbruchs.* Edited by Gretchen Dutschke-Klotz, Jürgen Miermeister, and Jürgen Treulieb. Reinbek: Rowohlt, 1983.

Dworok, Gerrit, and Christoph Weißmann, eds. *1968 und die "68er": Ereignisse, Wirkungen und Kontroversen in der Bundesrepublik.* Cologne: Böhlau, 2012.

Ebbinghaus, Angelika, ed. *Die 68er: Schlüsseltexte der globalen Revolte.* Vienna: Promedia 2008.

Eichelberg, Ingrid. *Mai '68 in der Literatur: Die Suche nach menschlichem Glück in einer besseren Gesellschaft.* Marburg: Hitzeroth, 1987.

Elder-Vass, Dave. *The Reality of Social Construction.* Cambridge: Cambridge University Press, 2012.

Ensslin, Gudrun, and Bernward Vesper. *"Notstandsgesetze von deiner Hand": Briefe 1968/1969.* Edited by Caroline Harmsen, Ulrike Seyer, and Johannes Ullmaier. Frankfurt am Main: Suhrkamp, 2009.
Enzensberger, Hans Magnus. "Erinnerungen an einen Tumult: Zu einem Tagebuch aus dem Jahr 1968." *text + kritik* 49, edited by Heinz Ludwig Arnold (January 1985): 6–9.
———. "Gemeinplätze, die Neueste Literatur betreffend." *Kursbuch* 15 (1968): 187–97.
———. *Der kurze Sommer der Anarchie: Buenaventura Durrutis Leben und Tod.* Frankfurt am Main: Suhrkamp, 1972.
———. "Die Sprache des Spiegel." *Der Spiegel* 10/1957, March 6, 1957. http://www.spiegel.de/spiegel/print/d-32092775.html.
———. *Tumult.* Frankfurt am Main: Suhrkamp, 2014.
———. *Der Untergang der Titanic: Eine Komödie.* Frankfurt am Main: Suhrkamp, 1978.
———. "The Writer and Politics." *Times Literary Supplement*, October 1967.
Enzensberger, Ulrich. *Die Jahre der Kommune I: Berlin 1967–1969.* Cologne: Kiepenheuer & Witsch, 2004.
Erdheim, Mario. *Die gesellschaftliche Produktion von Unbewußtheit: Eine Einführung in den ethnopsychoanalytischen Prozeß.* Frankfurt am Main: Suhrkamp, 1984.
Estermann, Monika, and Edgar Lersch. *Buch, Buchhandel, Rundfunk: 1968 und die Folgen.* Wiesbaden: Harrassowitz, 2003.
Etzemüller, Thomas. *1968—Ein Riss in der Geschichte? Gesellschaftlicher Umbruch und 68er-Bewegungen in Westdeutschland und Schweden.* Konstanz: UVK, 2005.
———. "Virtuelle Feldschlachten: '1968' und die Macht imaginärer Bilder." In *68er Spätlese: Was bleibt von 1968?*, edited by Tobias Schaffrik and Sebastian Wienges, 10–18. Berlin: Lit Verlag, 2008.
Faber, Richard. "Frühromantik, Surrealismus und Studentenrevolte, oder die Frage nach dem Anarchismus." In *Romantische Utopie: Utopische Romantik*, edited by Gisela Dischner and Richard Faber. 1979; Frankfurt am Main: Seifert, 2003.
Faber, Richard, and Erhard Stölting, eds. *Die Phantasie an die Macht? 1968—Versuch einer Bilanz.* Berlin: Philo, 2002.
Fahlenbrach, Kathrin. "Protestinszenierungen: Die Studentenbewegung im Spannungsfeld von Kultur-Revolution und Medien-Evolution." In Klimke and Scharloth, *1968: Handbuch zur Kultur- und Mediengeschichte*, 11–23.
———. *Protest-Inszenierungen: Visuelle Kommunikation und kollektive Identitäten in Protestbewegungen.* Wiesbaden: Westdeutscher Verlag, 2002.
———. "Zwischen Faszination, Grauen und Vereinnahmung: Die wechselvolle Resonanz der Massenmedien auf die Proteste von '68." February 6, 2008. http://www.bpb.de/geschichte/deutsche-geschichte/68er-bewegung/51830/68-und-die-medien.

Fahlenbrach, Kathrin, Martin Klimke, Joachim Scharloth, and Laura Wong, eds. *The Establishment Responds: Power, Politics, and Protest since 1945.* London: Palgrave, 2012.
Fahlenbrach, Kathrin, Erling Sivertsen, and Rolf Werenskjold, eds. *Media and Revolt: Strategies and Performances from the 1960s to the Present.* New York: Berghahn, 2014.
Farber, David. *The Sixties: From Memory to History.* Chapel Hill: University of North Carolina Press, 1994.
Fels, Gerhard. *Der Aufruhr der 68er: Zu den geistigen Grundlagen der Studentenbewegung und der RAF.* Bonn: Bouvier, 1998.
Felsch, Philipp. *Der lange Sommer der Theorie: Geschichte einer Revolte.* Munich: C. H. Beck, 2015.
Fichter, Tilman, and Siegward Lönnendonker. "Berlin: Hauptstadt der Revolte." In Ruetz, *"Ihr müßt diesen Typen nur ins Gesicht sehen,"* 160–68.
———. *Dutschkes Deutschland: Der Sozialistische Deutsche Studentenbund, die nationale Frage und die DDR-Kritik von links (Eine deutschlandpolitische Streitschrift mit Dokumenten von Michael Mauke bis Rudi Dutschke).* Essen: Klartext Verlag, 2011.
———. *Kleine Geschichte des SDS: Der Sozialistische Deutsche Studentenbund von 1946 bis zur Selbstauflösung.* Berlin: Rotbuch, 1977.
Fink, Carole, Philipp Gassert, and Detlef Junker, eds. *1968: The World Transformed.* Cambridge: Cambridge University Press, 1998.
Finlay, Frank, and Ingo Cornils, eds. *(Un-)erfüllte Wirklichkeit: Neue Studien zu Uwe Timms Werk.* Würzburg: Königshausen & Neumann, 2006.
Fischer, Erica. "Vom Tomatenwurf zum Paradiesgarten: Zu Besuch bei Sigrid Fronius in Bolivien." Radio feature, SFB RadioKultur, April 1, 2003. http://www.erica-fischer.de/texte/frauen/bolivien.html.
———. "Vorkämpferinnen der Generation 'Ally': Ein Buch über die 68erinnen füllt eine wichtige Lücke." http://www.erica-fischer.de/texte/rezensionen/68erinnen_Rezension.html.
Fischer, Gerhard. *Grips: Geschichte eines populären Theaters (1966–2000).* Munich: Iudicium, 2002.
Fischer, Joschka. "Ein magisches Jahr." *Spiegel Special* 9/1998, September 1, 1998. http://www.spiegel.de/spiegel/spiegelspecial/d-7518979.html.
Floh de Cologne. *Profitgeier und andere Vögel: Agitationstexte, Lieder, Berichte.* Berlin: Wagenbach, 1971.
Francois, Etienne, and Hagen Schulze, eds. *Deutsche Erinnerungsorte,* vol. 2. Munich: C. H. Beck, 2001.
Fraser, Ronald. *1968: A Student Generation in Revolt.* London: Chatto & Windus, 1988.
Frei, Norbert. *1968: Jugendrevolte und globaler Protest.* Munich: DTV, 2008.
Friedrichs, Julie. *Wir Erben: Was Geld mit Menschen macht.* Berlin: Berlin Verlag, 2015.
Fuchs, Anne. "F. C. Delius's *Mein Jahr als Mörder* (My Year as a Murderer)." In *The Novel in German since 1900*, edited by Stuart Taberner, 226–40. Cambridge: Cambridge University Press, 2011.

Fuchs, Anne, Mary Cosgrove, and Georg Grote, eds. *German Memory Contests: The Quest for Identity in Literature, Film, and Discourse since 1990*. Rochester, NY: Camden House, 2006.
Fuhrer, Armin. *Wer erschoss Benno Ohnesorg? Der Fall Kurras und die Stasi*. Berlin: be.bra Verlag, 2009.
Fukuyama, Francis. *The End of History and the Last Man*. New York: Free Press, 1992.
Fulbrook, Mary. *Anatomy of a Dictatorship: Inside the GDR, 1949–1989*. New York: Oxford 1995.
Fulbrook, Mary, and Martin Swales. *Representing the German Nation*. Manchester: Manchester University Press, 2000.
Füssel, Stephan, ed. *Die Politisierung des Buchmarkts: 1968 als Branchenereignis*. Wiesbaden: Harrassowitz, 2007.
Garton Ash, Timothy. "This Tale of Two Revolutions and Two Anniversaries May Yet Have a Twist." *Guardian*, May 8, 2008.
———. "The Year of Truth." In *The Revolutions of 1989*, edited by V. Tismaneanu. London: Routledge, 1999.
Gäsche, Daniel. *Born to Be wild: Die 68er und die Musik*. Leipzig: Militzke, 2008.
Gassert, Philipp. "Das kurze '1968' zwischen Geschichtswissenschaft und Erinnerungskultur: Neuere Forschungen zur Protestgeschichte der 1960er-Jahre." *H-Soz-u-Kult*, April 30, 2010. http://hsozkult.geschichte.hu-berlin.de/forum/2010-04-001.
Gassert, Philipp, and Martin Klimke, eds. *1968: Memories and Legacies of a Global Revolt*. Bulletin, Supplement 6 (2009). Washington, DC: German Historical Institute, 2009.
Gassert, Philipp, and Pavel A. Richter, eds. *1968 in West Germany: A Guide to Sources and Literature*. Washington, DC: German Historical Institute, 1998.
Geiger, Helmut, and Armin Roether, eds. *Dutschke und Bloch: Zivilgesellschaft damals und heute*. Mössingen: Talheimer, 1999.
Gerlach, Ingeborg. *Abschied von der Revolte: Studien zur deutschsprachigen Literatur der siebziger Jahre*. Würzburg: Königshausen & Neumann, 1994.
Gester, Jochen, and Willi Hajek, eds. *1968—und dann? Erfahrungen, Lernprozesse und Utopien von Bewegten der 68er-Revolte*. Bremen: Atlantik, 2002.
Getty, Gisela, Jutta Winkelmann, and Jamal Tuschik. *Die Zwillinge oder vom Versuch, Geld und Geist zu küssen*. Frankfurt am Main: Weissbooks, 2008.
Gilcher-Holtey, Ingrid. *Die 68er Bewegung: Deutschland—Westeuropa—USA*. Munich: Beck, 2001.
———. "Die APO und der Zerfall der Gruppe 47." *Aus Politik und Zeitgeschichte* 25 (2007): 19–24. http://www.bpb.de/apuz/30417/die-apo-und-der-zerfall-der-gruppe-47.
———, ed. *"1968"—Eine Wahrnehmungsrevolution? Horizont-Verschiebungen des Politischen in den 1960er und 1970 Jahren*. Munich: Oldenbourg, 2013.

———. *1968: Eine Zeitreise*. Frankfurt am Main: Suhrkamp, 2008.
———, ed. *1968: Vom Ereignis zum Gegenstand der Geschichtswissenschaft*. Göttingen: Vandenhoeck & Ruprecht, 1998.
———, ed. *1968: Vom Ereignis zum Mythos*. Frankfurt am Main: Suhrkamp, 2008.
———, ed. *A Revolution of Perception? Consequences and Echoes of 1968*. New York: Berghahn, 2014.
Gildea, Robert, James Mark, and Anette Warring, eds. *Europe's 1968: Voices of Revolt*. Oxford: Oxford University Press, 2013.
Glaser, Eliane. "Bring Back Ideology: Fukuyama's 'End of History' 25 Years On." *Guardian*, March 21, 2014. http://www.theguardian.com/books/2014/mar/21/bring-back-ideology-fukuyama-end-history-25-years-on.
Gogos, Manuel, and Andreas Pflitsch. "Die Literatur ist tot, es lebe die Literatur: Schreiben um 1968." In Schwab, Schappach, and Gogos, *Die 68er*, 373–80.
Gotto, Bernhard, Horst Möller, Jean Mondot, and Nicole Pelletier, eds. *Nach Achtundsechzig: Krisen und Krisenbewusstsein in Deutschland und Frankreich in den 1970er Jahren*. Munich: Oldenbourg, 2013.
Götze, Karl-Heinz. "Gedächtnis: Romane über die Studentenbewegung." *Das Argument* 23 (1981): 367–82.
Grass, Günter. "Die angelesene Revolution: Rede auf einer Veranstaltung des Sozialdemokratischen Hochschulbundes in Bochum." In Günter Grass, *Werkausgabe in zehn Bänden*, vol. 9, *Essays, Reden, Briefe, Kommentare*, edited by Daniela Hermes, 297–311. Darmstadt: Luchterhand, 1987.
———. *Aus dem Tagebuch einer Schnecke*. 1972; Munich: DTV, 1998.
———. *Kopfgeburten, oder Die Deutschen sterben aus*. Darmstadt: Luchterhand, 1980.
———. *örtlich betäubt*. 1969; Munich: DTV, 1995. Translated as *Local Anaesthetic* (New York: Secker & Warburg, 1970).
Grass, Günter, and Pierre Bourdieu. "The 'Progressive' Restoration: A Franco-German Dialogue." *New Left Review*, no. 14 (2002): 63–77.
Grass, Günter, and Mathias Döpfner. *Die Springer Kontroverse: Ein Streitgespräch über Deutschland*. Edited by Manfred Bissinger. Göttingen: Steidl, 2006.
Grebe, Rainald. "'Massenkompatibel werd' ich nie': Kabarettist Rainald Grebe über 68." *taz*, March 31, 2008. http://www.taz.de/!15135/.
———. *1968*. CD. Berlin: Versöhnungsrecords, 2008.
Grebe, Rainald, and Die Kapelle der Versöhnung. *1968*. Hamburg: Versöhnungsrecords, 2008. http://www.youtube.com/watch?v=p1iw2c9CS14.
Greiner, Ulrich. "Der Wiedergänger." *ZEITLiteratur* (Sonderbeilage), *Die Zeit*, October 4, 2001.
Grimberg, Steffen. "Neues aus der Wagenburg." *taz*, January 12, 2010. http://www.taz.de/!46653/.
———. "Springers 68er Archiv: Neues aus der Wagenburg." *taz*, January 12, 2010.

Große Kracht, Klaus. "'Achtundsechzig': Geschichte in der Defensive." In *Die zankende Zunft*, 69–90.
———. *Die zankende Zunft: Historische Kontroversen in Deutschland nach 1945*. Göttingen: Vandenhoeck & Ruprecht, 2011.
Guardian. "1968: The Year That Changed History." January 17, 2008. http://www.theguardian.com/observer/gallery/2008/jan/17/1.
Habermas, Jürgen. Interview. *Frankfurter Rundschau*, March 11, 1988.
———. "Der Marsch durch die Institutionen hat auch die CDU erreicht." *Frankfurter Rundschau*, March 11, 1988.
———. *Protestbewegung und Hochschulreform*. 1969; Frankfurt am Main: Suhrkamp, 2008.
———. "Die Scheinrevolution und ihre Kinder." *Frankfurter Rundschau*, June 5, 1968.
———. "Scheinrevolution unter Handlungszwang." *Der Spiegel* 24/1968, June 10, 1968. http://www.spiegel.de/spiegel/print/d-46020971.html.
Hage, Volker. "Der lange Abschied von der BRD." *Der Spiegel* 5/2010.
Hahn, Margrit. "Rudi Dutschkes Pulli hinter Glass." *Märkische Allgemeine Zeitung*, October 22, 2013. http://www.maz-online.de/Lokales/Teltow-Flaeming/Luckenwalde/Rudi-Dutschkes-Pulli-hinter-Glas.
Hahn, Ulla. *Spiel der Zeit*. Munich: Deutsche Verlags-Anstalt, 2014.
Hajek, Andrea. "Challenging Dominant Discourses of the Past: 1968 and the Value of Oral History." *Memory Studies* 6 (2013): 3–6.
Halbwachs, Maurice. *On Collective Memory*. Chicago: University of Chicago Press, 1992.
Halter, Hans. "Berlin, dieser Emporkömmling." *Frankfurter Allgemeine Zeitung*, December 4, 2009. http://www.faz.net/aktuell/feuilleton/buecher/rezensionen/belletristik/jochen-schimmang-das-beste-was-wir-hatten-berlin-dieser-emporkoemmling-1893653.html.
———. "Herz der Revolte." *Der Spiegel* 34/1996, August 19, 1996.
Hannover, Irmela, and Cordt Schnibben. *I can't get no: Ein paar 68er treffen sich und rechnen ab*. Cologne: Kiepenheuer & Witsch, 2007.
Harman, Chris. *The Fire Last Time: 1968 and After*. London: Bookmarks, 1998.
Harmsen, Caroline, Ulrike Seyer, and Johannes Ullmaier, eds. *Gudrun Ensslin / Bernward Vesper: "Notstandsgesetze von deiner Hand"; Briefe 1968/1969*. Frankfurt am Main: Suhrkamp, 2009.
Hartl, Peter, and Jean-Christoph Caron, dirs. *1968: Mythos und Wahrheit*. ZDF-History, March 16, 2008.
Hartung, Klaus. "Fehler der antiautoritären Bewegung." In Kursbuch *48: Zehn Jahre danach*, 14–43. Berlin: Rotbuch, 1977.
———. "Das große Gefühl." *Der Tagesspiegel*, April 11, 2008. http://www.tagesspiegel.de/kultur/1968-das-grosse-gefuehl/1208548.html.
———. "Selbstkritische Überlegungen und Überlegungen zur Selbstkritik nach 40 Jahren." *Ästhetik & Kommunikation* 39, no. 140–41 (2008): 95–112. http://www.aesthetikundkommunikation.de/?artikel=359.

———. "Über die langandauernde Jugend im linken Ghetto: Lebensalter und Politik—Aus der Sicht eines 38jährigen." *Kursbuch* 54 (1978): 174–88.

Hecken, Thomas. *1968: Von Texten und Theorien aus einer Zeit euphorischer Kritik.* Bielefeld: Transcript, 2008.

Heffer, Simon. "Wish You Were Living in the Sixties? You Must Be Mad. It Was a Ghastly Decade." *Daily Mail*, October 1, 2014. http://www.dailymail.co.uk/debate/article-2775837/SIMON-HEFFER-Wish-living-Sixties-You-mad-It-ghastly-decade.html.

Heider, Ulrike. *Anarchism: Left, Right and Green.* San Francisco: City Lights Books, 1994.

———. *Keine Ruhe nach dem Sturm.* Hamburg: Rogner und Bernhard bei Zweitausendeins, 2001.

———. *Vögeln ist schön: Die Sexrevolte von 1968 und was von ihr bleibt.* Berlin: Rotbuch, 2014.

Hein, Jan-Philipp. "Der Versuch einer Korrektur." *Kölner Stadt-Anzeiger*, January 28, 2010. http://www.ksta.de/medien/springer-medienarchiv-der-versuch-einer-korrektur,15189656,12772900.html.

Heinemann, Karl-Heinz, and Thomas Jaitner. *Ein langer Marsch: '68 und die Folgen.* Cologne: PapyRossa, 1993.

Heise, Helene. "Das Ende der Talare." *Spiegel Online*, November 8, 2007. http://www.spiegel.de/einestages/das-ende-der-talare-a-948827.html.

Henle, Ilse. *Lebensansichten eines alten APO-Katers.* Münster: Principal Verlag, 1998.

Henschel, Gerhard. *Bildungsroman.* Hamburg: Hoffmann und Campe, 2014.

Herzinger, Richard. "1968: Wie eine Revolte zum Mythos wurde." *Welt am Sonntag*, January 7, 2008. http://www.welt.de/politik/deutschland/article1522197/1968-wie-eine-Revolte-zum-Mythos-wurde.html.

———. "Spießer in neuem Gewand." *Die Welt*, January 14, 2007.

Herzog, Dagmar. *Sexuality in Europe: A Twentieth-Century History.* Cambridge: Cambridge University Press, 2011.

Hey, Bernd, and Volker Wittmütz, eds. *1968 und die Kirchen.* Gütersloh: Verlag für Regionalgeschichte, 2008.

Hielscher, Martin. *Uwe Timm.* Munich: DTV, 2007.

Hillgruber, Katrin. "Ein Kommunist braucht kein Deodorant." *Frankfurter Rundschau*, September 1, 2004.

Hinz-Wessels, Annette and Regina Haunhorst. "Studentenbewegung und APO." Lebendiges Museum Online, Stiftung Haus der Geschichte der Bundesrepublik Deutschland. http://www.hdg.de/lemo/kapitel/geteiltes-deutschland-modernisierung/bundesrepublik-im-wandel/studentenbewegung-und-apo.html.

Hockenos, Paul. "Germany Year 1968: Democratic Turning Point or Annus Terribilis? Germany's Debate over the Rebellious Sixties Has Everything to Do with the Present, *Logos: A Journal of Modern Society & Culture* 8, no. 1–2 (2009). http://logosjournal.com/2011/hockenos/.

———. *Joschka Fischer and the Making of the Berlin Republic: An Alternative History of Postwar Germany.* Oxford: Oxford University Press, 2008.
Hohn, Detlef. *Auch wir waren dabei: Ostern 1968 in Hamburg.* Norderstedt: Books on Demand, 2013.
Homewood, Chris. "From Baader to Prada: Memory and Myth in Uli Edel's *The Baader Meinhof Complex* (2008)." In *New Directions in German Cinema,* edited by Paul Cooke and Chris Homewood, 130–48. London: I. B. Tauris, 2011.
———. "Have the Best Ideas Stood the Test of Time? Negotiating the Legacy of '1968' in *The Edukators.*" In Cornils and Waters, *Memories of 1968.*
Horn, Gerd. *The Spirit of 68: Rebellion in Western Europe and North America, 1956–1976.* Oxford: Oxford University Press, 2007.
Horvath, Peter. *Die inszenierte Revolte: Hinter den Kulissen von 68.* Munich: Herbig, 2010.
Horx, Matthias. *Aufstand im Schlaraffenland: Selbsterkenntnisse einer rebellischen Generation.* Munich: Hanser, 1989.
Hosfeld, Rolf, and Helmut Peitsch. "Weil uns diese Aktionen innerlich verändern, sind sie politisch: Bemerkungen zu vier Romanen über die Studentenbewegung." *Basis: Jahrbuch für deutsche Gegenwartsliteratur* 8 (1978): 92–126.
Hubert, Martin. *Politisierung der Literatur—Ästhetisierung der Politik: Eine Studie zur literaturgeschichtlichen Bedeutung der 68er-Bewegung in der Bundesrepublik Deutschland.* Frankfurt am Main: Peter Lang, 1992.
Hüetlin, Thomas. "Tage der Kommune." *Der Spiegel* 27/1997, June 30, 1997. http://www.spiegel.de/spiegel/print/d-8736657.html.
Hüffell, Angelika. *Schülerbewegung 1967–1977.* Gießen: Focus, 1978.
Huffman Richard. "June 2 1967 West Berlin." http://www.baader-meinhof.com/june-2-1967-berlin/.
Jaeggi, Urs. *Brandeis.* 1978; Hamburg: Rotbuch, 1998.
Jähner, Harald. "Gudrun, jetzt muß die Knarre sprechen: Drei Romane über 1968." *Berliner Zeitung,* March 20, 2001.
Jesse, Eckhard. "Das Jahr 1968 und die Bürgerbewegung in der DDR." *Forschungsjournal NSB* 21, no. 3 (2008): 87–94.
Jochimsen, Jess. *Das Dosenmilch-Trauma: Bekenntnisse eines 68er-Kindes.* Munich: DTV, 2000.
Juchler, Ingo. *Die Studentenbewegungen in den Vereinigten Staaten und der Bundesrepublik Deutschland der sechziger Jahre: Eine Untersuchung hinsichtlich ihrer Beeinflussung durch Befreiungsbewegungen und -theorien aus der dritten Welt.* Berlin: Duncker & Humblot, 1996.
Jung, Dae Sung. *Der Kampf gegen das Presse-Imperium: Die Anti-Springer-Kampagne der 68er-Bewegung.* Bielefeld: Transcript Verlag, 2016.
Jürgens, Hanco, Jacco Pekelder, Falk Bretschneider, and Klaus Bachmann, eds. *Eine Welt zu gewinnen! Formen und Folgen der 68er Bewegung in Ost- und Westeuropa.* Leipzig: Leipziger Universitätsverlag, 2009.
Kara, Yade. *Selam Berlin.* Zurich: Diogenes, 2003.

Karl, Michaela. *Rudi Dutschke: Revolutionär ohne Revolution.* Frankfurt am Main: Neue Kritik, 2003.
Kastner, Jens, and David Mayer, eds. *Weltwende 1968? Ein Jahr aus globalgeschichtlicher Perspektive.* Vienna: Mandelbaum, 2008.
Katsiaficas, George. *The Imagination of the New Left: A Global Analysis of 1968.* Boston: South End Press, 1987.
Kätzel, Ute. *Die 68erinnen: Portrait einer rebellischen Frauengeneration.* Berlin: Rowohlt, 2002.
Kauders, Anthony D. "Drives in Dispute: The West German Student Movement, Psychoanalysis, and the Search for a New Emotional Order, 1967–1971." *Central European History* 44 (2011): 711–31.
Kellein, Thomas, ed. *1968: Die große Unschuld.* Bielefeld: DuMont, 2009.
Keller, Maren. "Golden Girls in weißer Villa." *Der Spiegel*, August 5, 2013. http://www.spiegel.de/kultur/literatur/das-buch-von-silvia-bovenschen-nur-mut-a-914575.html.
Kellerhoff, Sven Felix. "Das Archiv zur Revolte." *Die Welt*, January 18, 2010.
———. "1968 und die Medien." In Vogel and Kutsch, *40 Jahre 1968*, 86–109.
Kiesel, Helmuth. "Literatur um 1968: Politischer Protest und postmoderner Impuls." In *Protest! Literatur um 1968: Eine Ausstellung des Deutschen Literaturarchivs in Verbindung mit dem Germanistischen Seminar der Universität Heidelberg und dem Deutschen Rundfunkarchiv*, edited by Ulrich Ott and Friedrich Pfäfflin, 593–640. Marbach: Deutsche Schillergesellschaft, 1998.
Kießling, Simon. *Die antiautoritäre Revolte der 68er: Postindustrielle Konsumgesellschaft und säkulare Religionsgeschichte der Moderne.* Cologne: Böhlau, 2006.
Kimmel, Michael. *Die Studentenbewegungen der 60er Jahre: BRD, Frankreich, USA; Ein Vergleich.* Vienna: WUV, 1998.
Kinder, Hermann. *Der Schleiftrog.* Zurich: Diogenes, 1977.
Klein, Ansgar, Jupp Legrand, and Thomas Leif, eds. "1968—Alles nur Geschichte? Aktualität und Folgen eines bewegten Jahres." Special issue, *Forschungsjournal: Neue Soziale Bewegungen* 21, no. 3 (2008).
Kleinert, Hubert. "Mythos 1968." *Aus Politik und Zeitgeschichte* B 14–15 (2008), March 19, 2008. http://www.bpb.de/geschichte/deutsche-geschichte/68er-bewegung/52034/mythos-1968?p=all.
Kligerman, Eric. "Transgenerational Hauntings: Screening the Holocaust in Gerhard Richter's October 18, 1977 Paintings." In Berendse and Cornils, *Baader-Meinhof Returns*, 41–63.
Klimke, Martin. "1968 als transnationales Ereignis." *Aus Politik und Zeitgeschichte* 14–15 (2008): 22–27.
———. *The Other Alliance: Student Protest in West Germany & the United States in the Global Sixties.* Princeton, NJ: Princeton University Press, 2010.
Klimke, Martin, and Joachim Scharloth, eds. *1968: Handbuch zur Kultur- und Mediengeschichte der Studentenbewegung.* Stuttgart: Metzler, 2007.

———. *1968 in Europe: A History of Protest and Activism, 1956–1977*. New York: Palgrave, 2008.
Klinger, Cornelia. *Flucht, Trost, Revolte: Die Moderne und ihre ästhetischen Gegenwelten*. Munich: Hanser, 1995.
Klonovsky, Michael. "Demokraten wider Willen." *Focus* 31 (2005): 46–50. http://www.michael-klonovsky.de/artikel/item/91-demokraten-wider-willen.
Kluge, Alexander. *Neue Geschichten: Hefte 1–18, "Unheimlichkeit der Zeit."* Frankfurt am Main: Suhrkamp, 1977.
Knott, Unfried and Asmuth Knott. "Die Dutschke-Straße kommt." *taz*, April 21, 2008. http://www.taz.de/!16172/.
Koenen, Gerd. "Mein 1968." In Koenen and Veiel, *1968*, 6.
———. *Das rote Jahrzehnt: Unsere kleine deutsche Kulturrevolution 1967–1977*. Cologne: Kiepenheuer & Witsch, 2001.
———. *Vesper, Ensslin, Baader: Urszenen des deutschen Terrorismus*. Cologne: Kiepenheuer & Witsch, 2003.
Koenen, Gerd, and Andres Veiel. *1968: Bildspur eines Jahres*. Cologne: Fackelträger, 2008.
Komfort-Hein, Susanne. *"Flaschenposten und kein Ende des Endes"; 1968: Kritische Korrespondenzen um den Nullpunkt von Geschichte und Literatur*. Freiburg: Rombach, 2001.
Korndörfer, Lutz. *1968 im Spiegel der Presse: Die divergierenden Reaktionen deutscher und amerikanischer Printmedien auf die deutsche Protestbewegung und die Bürgerrechtsbewegung in den USA*. Münster: Lit Verlag, 2014.
Kosiek, Rolf. *Die Machtübernahme der 68er: Die Frankfurter Schule und ihre zersetzenden Auswirkungen*. Tübingen: Hohenrain, 2009.
Krause-Burger, Sibylle. *Joschka Fischer: Der Marsch durch die Illusionen*. Reinbek: Rowohlt, 2000.
Kraushaar, Wolfgang. *Achtundsechzig: Eine Bilanz*. Berlin: Propyläen, 2008.
———. *Der Aufruhr der Ausgebildeten: Vom Arabischen Frühling zur Occupy-Bewegung*. Hamburg: Hamburger Edition, 2012.
———. "Autoritärer Staat und antiautoritäre Bewegung: Zum Organisationsreferat von Rudi Dutschke und Hans-Jürgen Krahl auf der 22. Delegiertenkonferenz des SDS in Frankfurt (September 1967)." In Kraushaar, *Revolte und Reflexion*, 57–80.
———. "Denkmodelle der 68er-Bewegung." *Aus Politik und Zeitgeschichte*, no. B 22–23 (2001): 14–27.
———. "Der Eskalationsstratege." *taz*, March 8, 2005.
———. *Fischer in Frankfurt*. Hamburg: Hamburger Edition, 2001.
———, ed. *Frankfurter Schule und Studentenbewegung: Von der Flaschenpost zum Molotowcocktail 1946–1995*. Hamburg: Rogner & Bernhard, 1998.
———. "Hitler's Children? The German 1968 Movement in the Shadow of the Nazi Past." In Cornils and Waters, *Memories of 1968*, 79–102.
———. "Hitlers Kinder? Eine Antwort auf Götz Aly: Die 68er-Bewegung im Schatten der NS-Vergangenheit; Zur Analogiekonstruktion des

NS-Historikers Götz Aly." *Perlentaucher.de*, March 25, 2009. http://www.perlentaucher.de/essay/hitlers-kinder-eine-antwort-auf-goetz-aly.html.

———. *1968 als Mythos, Chiffre und Zäsur.* Hamburg: Hamburger Edition, 2000.

———. *1968: Das Jahr, das alles verändert hat.* Munich: Piper, 1998.

———. "1968 und die RAF: Ein umstrittenes Beziehungsgeflecht." *Vorgänge*, no. 3–4 (2005): 208–20.

———. "Kleinkrieg gegen einen Großverleger: Von der Anti-Springer-Kampagne der APO zu den Brand- und Bombenanschlägen der RAF." In *Die RAF*, 1075–116.

———, ed. *Die Protest-Chronik 1949–1959: Eine illustrierte Geschichte von Bewegung, Widerstand und Utopie.* Hamburg: Rogner & Bernhard, 1996.

———, ed. *Die RAF und der linke Terrorismus.* Hamburg: HIS, 2006.

———. "'Die Revolte der Lebenstriebe': Marcuse als Mentor gegenkultureller Bewegungen." In Marcuse, *Nachgelassene Schriften*, 15–25.

———. *Revolte und Reflexion: Politische Aufsätze 1976–87.* Frankfurt am Main: Neue Kritik, 1990.

———. "Rezension Gerd Koenen: Das rote Jahrzehnt." *H-Soz-u-Kult* 27 (2002). www.hsozkult.de/publicationreview/id/rezbuecher-850.

———. "Rudi Dutschke und der bewaffnete Kampf." bpb, August 20, 2007.

———. "Rudi Dutschke und der bewaffnete Kampf." In *Rudi Dutschke, Andreas Baader und die RAF*, edited by Wolfgang Kraushaar, Karin Wieland, and Jan Philipp Reemstma, 13–50. Hamburg: Hamburger Edition, 2005.

———. "Die transatlantische Protestkultur: Der zivile Ungehorsam als amerikanisches Exempel und als bundesdeutsche Adaption." In *Westbindungen: Amerika in der Bundesrepublik*, edited by Heinz Bude and Bernd Greiner, 257–84. Hamburg: Hamburger Edition, 1999.

———. "Vexierbild: Hans Magnus Enzensberger im Jahre 1968." *Mittelweg 36* 5 (2009): 52–70. http://www.eurozine.com/articles/2009-11-03-kraushaar1-de.html.

———. "Der Zeitzeuge als Feind des Historikers? Neuerscheinungen zur 68er Bewegung." *Mittelweg 36* 8, no. 6 (1999–2000): 49–72.

———. "Zur Historisierung der 68er-Bewegung." *Forschungsjournal NSB* 14, no. 2 (2001): 13–22.

Kröger, Claus. "Ausstellungs-Rezension zu Die 68er: Kurzer Sommer—lange Wirkung. 01.05.2008–02.11.2008, Historisches Museum Frankfurt am Main." *H-Soz-u-Kult*, August 2, 2008. http://hsozkult.geschichte.hu-berlin.de/rezensionen/id=65&type=rezausstellungen.

Krueger, Uwe. *Meinungsmacht: Der Einfluss von Eliten auf Leitmedien und Alpha-Journalisten—eine kritische Netzwerkanalyse.* Cologne: Van Halem, 2013.

Krüger, Horst. "Kein Geschmack für Ort und Augenblick." *Die Zeit*, August 22, 1969.

Krüger, Thomas J. A. "From the 'Death of Literature' to the 'New Subjectivity': Examining the Interaction of Utopia and Nostalgia in Peter Schneider's *Lenz*, Hans Magnus Enzensberger's *Der kurze Sommer der Anarchie*, and Bernward Vesper's *Die Reise*." PhD thesis, McGill University, Montreal, 2008. http://digitool.library.mcgill.ca/R/?func=dbin-jump-full&object_id=32407&local_base=GEN01-MCG02.

Kulish, Nicholas. "Spy Fired Shot that Changed West Germany." *New York Times*, May 26, 2009.

Kundnani, Hans. *The Paradox of German Power*. London: Hurst, 2014.

———. "Perpetrators and Victims: Germany's 1968 Generation and Collective Memory." *German Life and Letters* 64, no. 2 (2011): 272–82.

———. *Utopia or Auschwitz: Germany's 1968 Generation and the Holocaust*. New York: Columbia University Press, 2009.

Kurlansky, Mark. *1968: The Year That Rocked the World*. London: Jonathan Cape, 2004.

Kutschke, Beate. *Musikkulturen in der Revolte: Studien zu Rock, Avantgarde und Klassik im Umfeld von "1968."* Stuttgart: Franz Steiner Verlag, 2008.

Kutschke, Beate, and Barley Norton, eds. *Music and Protest in 1968*. Cambridge: Cambridge University Press, 2014.

Lamont, Tom. "Baron Wolman's Woodstock Photographs: 'I Thought, There'll Never Be Anything Like This Again.'" *Guardian*, June 22, 2014. http://www.theguardian.com/music/2014/jun/22/baron-wolman-woodstock-photographs-thought-never-anything-like-this.

Landgrebe, Christiane, and Jörg Plath, eds. *'68 und die Folgen: Ein unvollständiges Lexikon*. Berlin: Argon 1998.

Landsberg, Alison. *Prosthetic Memory: The Transformation of American Remembrance in the Age of Mass Culture*. New York: Columbia University Press, 2004.

Langguth, Gerd. *Mythos '68: Die Gewaltphilosophie von Rudi Dutschke; Ursachen und Folgen der Studentenbewegung*. Munich: Olzog, 2001.

———. *Protestbewegung: Entwicklung, Niedergang, Renaissance; Die Neue Linke seit 1968*, Cologne: Verlag Wissenschaft und Politik, 1983.

———. "So harmlos war er nicht." *Cicero: Magazin für politische Kultur*, February 19, 2008. http://www.cicero.de/so-harmlos-war-er-nicht/38512.

———. "Der verhinderte Stadguerillero." *Der Spiegel*, April 7, 2008.

Langhans, Rainer. *Ich bin's: Die ersten 68 Jahre*. Munich: Blumenbar, 2008.

Langhans, Rainer, and Christa Ritter. *K1: Das Bilderbuch der Kommune*. Munich: Blumenbar, 2008.

Langston, Richard. "Palimpsests of '68: Theorizing Labor after Adorno." In Sherman et al, *Long 1968*, 49–72.

Laudenbach, Peter. "Fröhliche Leichenschändung." *Berliner Zeitung*, May 20, 1996. http://www.berliner-zeitung.de/archiv/-rocky-dutschke--68---christoph-schlingensief-laeuft-amok-froehliche-leichenschaendung,10810590,9126794.html.

Lauermann, Manfred. "Vierzig Jahre 1968: Ein Literaturüberblick." *Berliner Debatte Initial*, elektronische Sonderausgabe 20, no. 1 (2009): 111–51.
Leeder, Karen. "Figuring Lateness in Modern German Culture." *New German Critique* 42, no. 2 (2015): 1–29.
Leggewie, Claus. "Entmystifiziert euch!" *taz*, May 3, 2005.
———. "Mythos 68er Bewegung." In *Metzler Lexikon moderner Mythen: Figuren, Konzepte, Ereignisse*, edited by Stephanie Wodianka and Juliane Ebert, 1–5. Stuttgart: Metzler, 2014.
———. "Der Mythos des Neuanfangs—Gründungsetappen der Bundesrepublik Deutschland: 1949–1968–1989." In *Mythos und Nation: Studien zur Entwicklung des kollektiven Bewußtseins in der Neuzeit*, edited by Helmut Berding, 275–302. Frankfurt am Main: Suhrkamp, 1996.
———. "1968 ist Geschichte." *Aus Politik und Zeitgeschichte* B 22–23 (2001): 3–6.
———. *Politische Zeiten: Beobachtungen von der Seitenlinie*. Gütersloh: Bertelsmann, 2015.
Leinemann, Jürgen, and Gerhard Spörl. "Die Sonderwege sind zuende." *Der Spiegel* 40/2000, October 2, 2000. http://www.spiegel.de/spiegel/print/d-17483236.html.
Lohre, Matthias. "Helmut Schmidt junior." *taz*, February 17, 2011.
Lönnendonker, Siegward, Tilman Fichter, and Jochen Staadt. *Hochschule im Umbruch; Teil V: Gewalt und Gegengewalt (1967–1969)*. Berlin: Freie Universität Berlin, 1983.
Lönnendonker, Siegward, Bernd Rabehl, and Jochen Staadt. *Die antiautoritäre Revolte: Der Sozialistische Deutsche Studentenbund nach der Trennung von der SPD*. Vol. 1, *1960–1967*. Wiesbaden: Westdeutscher Verlag, 2002.
Löw, Raimund. *Die Fantasie und die Macht: 1968 und danach*. Vienna: Czernin, 2006.
Löwenthal, Richard. *Der romantische Rückfall*. Stuttgart: Kohlhammer, 1970.
Löwer, Ingrid. *Die 68er im Spiegel ihrer Kinder: Eine vergleichende Untersuchung zu familienkritischen Prosatexten der jüngeren Autorengeneration*. Bremen: edition lumiere, 2011.
Lüdke, W. Martin. *Literatur und Studentenbewegung: Eine Zwischenbilanz*. Opladen: Westdeutscher Verlag, 1977.
———, ed. *Nach dem Protest: Literatur im Umbruch*. Frankfurt am Main: Suhrkamp, 1979.
Ludwig, Volker. *Grips Chronik*. 1969–2009. http://www.grips-theater.de/unser-haus/historie/.
Ludwig, Volker, and Detlef Michel. *Eine linke Geschichte: Textbuch*. Berlin: Grips Theater Berlin, 1992.
MacDonald, Ian. *Revolution in the Head: The Beatles' Records and the Sixties*. London: Pimlico, 1995.
Mager, Friedrich, and Ulrich Spinnarke. *Was wollen die Studenten?* Frankfurt am Main: Fischer, 1967.

Mann, Torsten. *Rot-Grüne Lebenslügen: Wie die 68er das Land an die Wand gefahren haben*. Rottenberg: Kopp Verlag, 2005.
Marcuse, Herbert. *An Essay on Liberation*. Boston: Beacon Press, 1969.
———. "Ethik und Revolution." In *Kultur und Gesellschaft 2*, 130–46. Frankfurt am Main: Suhrkamp, 1966.
———. *Kultur und Gesellschaft 1*. Frankfurt am Main: Suhrkamp, 1965.
———. *Nachgelassene Schriften*. Vol. 4, *Die Studentenbewegung und ihre Folgen*. Edited by Peter-Erwin Jansen. Springe: zu Klampen, 2004.
———. "Repressive Tolerance." In *A Critique of Pure Tolerance*, edited by Robert Paul Wolff, Barrington Moore Jr., and Herbert Marcuse, 95–137. Boston: Beacon Press, 1969.
———. *Versuch über die Befreiung*. Frankfurt am Main: Suhrkamp, 2008.
Märkische Allgemeine. "Wider die Kultur des Gehorsams: Der Schriftsteller Peter Schneider über die 68er, seinen neuen Roman und sein Leben." April 20, 2005.
Markovits, Andrei, and Philip Gorski. *The German Left: Red, Green and Beyond*. Oxford: Oxford University Press, 1993.
Marmulla, Henning. *Enzensbergers* Kursbuch: *Eine Zeitschrift um 68*. Berlin: Matthes & Seitz, 2011.
Marwick, Arthur. *The Sixties: Cultural Revolution in Britain, France, Italy, and the United States, c.1958–c.1974*. Oxford: Oxford University Press, 1998.
März, Ursula. "Archiv in der Zeitfalte." *Frankfurter Rundschau*, October 10, 2001.
———. "Immer wieder Kinderläden: Die unendliche 68-Diskussion." *Frankfurter Rundschau*, October 29, 2004.
Mason, Paul. *PostCapitalism: A Guide to Our Future*. London: Allen Lane, 2015.
Matussek, Matthias. "Dutschke, Goebbels und Co." *Der Spiegel* 8/2008.
Maurer, Susanne. "Gespaltenes Gedächtnis?" In Bauer and Havelková, "Gender," 118–28.
McManus, Susan. *Fictive Theories: Towards a Deconstructive and Utopian Political Imagination*. Basingstoke: Palgrave Macmillan, 2005.
Meier, Georg. *Alle waren in Woodstock—außer mir und den Beatles*. Berlin: Dittrich, 2008.
Meinhof, Ulrike. "Die Frauen im SDS, oder: in eigener Sache." In *Die Würde des Menschen ist antastbar: Aufsätze und Polemiken*, 149–52. Berlin: Wagenbach, 1994.
———. "Warenhausbrandstiftung." *konkret* 14 (1968): 5. http://www.infopartisan.net/archive/1967/266785.html.
Mensing, Kolja. "Auf der richtigen Seite." *taz*, June 2, 2007. http://www.taz.de/1/archiv/?id=archivseite&dig=2007/06/02/a0007.
Merkel, Angela. "60 Jahre CDU." Berlin, June 16, 2005. http://www4.dr-rath-foundation.org/THE_FOUNDATION/peoples_europe/pdf/Merkel_60_Jahre_CDU_2005_June_16.pdf .
Meschkat, Klaus. "Fantasievolle Überraschungen." *taz*, March 1, 2005.

Metselaar Berthold, Barbara. *Kratzen am Beton: 68er in der DDR?* Jena: Vopelius, 2008.
Mews, Siegfried. *Günter Grass and His Critics: From the Tin Drum to Crabwalk.* Rochester, NY: Camden House, 2009.
Meyer, Michael. "Medienhetzer und Politgammler: Springer und die 68er." *Deutschlandradio,* January 18, 2010. http://www.deutschlandfunk.de/medienhetzer-und-politgammler.724.de.html?dram:article_id=99713.
Miermeister, Jürgen. *Ernst Bloch, Rudi Dutschke.* Hamburg: EVA, 1996.
———. *Rudi Dutschke.* Reinbek: Rowohlt, 1986.
———, ed. *Rudi Dutschke, Geschichte ist machbar: Texte über das herrschende Falsche und die Radikalität des Friedens.* Berlin: Wagenbach, 1980.
Minnesota Historical Society. "The 1968 Exhibit: About the Exhibit." http://the1968exhibit.org/about-exhibit.
———. "The 1968 Exhibit: 1968 Goals and Standards." http://the1968exhibit.org/node/3240.
Mitchell, David. *Cloud Atlas.* London: Sceptre, 2004.
Mohr, Peter. "Erzähler und Zuhörer: Zum 70. Geburtstag des Schriftstellers Uwe Timm." *literaturkritik.de,* no. 4 (2010).
Mohr, Reinhard. "68er an die Macht." *Der Spiegel* 11/1998.
———. "Die Achtziger unter Kohl: Birne im Freizeitpark." *Der Spiegel,* March 26, 2010. http://www.spiegel.de/kultur/gesellschaft/die-achtziger-unter-kohl-birne-im-freizeitpark-a-685811.html.
———. *Der diskrete Charme der Rebellion.* Berlin: WJS Verlag, 2008.
———. "Heute gibt's Dresche." *Spiegel Online,* February 2, 2008. http://www.spiegel.de/kultur/literatur/40-jahre-68er-heute-gibt-s-dresche-a-532499.html.
———. "Kampf um Meinungsmacht: Springer lädt 68er zum Tribunal." *Spiegel Online,* July 2, 2009. http://www.spiegel.de/kultur/gesellschaft/kampf-um-meinungsmacht-springer-laedt-68er-zum-tribunal-a-633924.html.
———. "Schrecken aus dem braunen Sumpf." *Spiegel Online,* December 6, 2009. http://www.spiegel.de/kultur/gesellschaft/enthuellung-ueber-dutschke-attentaeter-schrecken-aus-dem-braunen-sumpf-a-665421.html.
———. "Ein Schuss, der Deutschland verändert." *Spiegel Online,* May 22, 2009. http://www.spiegel.de/einestages/der-fall-kurras-a-948306.html.
———. "Ein Skandal, der die Republik veränderte." *Spiegel Online,* February 4, 2008. http://www.spiegel.de/kultur/literatur/studentenrevolte-ein-skandal-der-die-republik-veraenderte-a-532502.html.
———. *Zaungäste: Die Generation, die nach der Revolte kam.* Frankfurt am Main: Fischer, 1992.
———. "Zorn auf die roten Jahre." *Der Spiegel* 4/2001, January 22, 2001.
Mosler, Peter. *Was wir wollten, was wir wurden: Studentenrevolte—zehn Jahre danach.* Reinbek: Rowohlt, 1977.

Müller, M. L. "Eine Waffe in den Händen der SDS-'Revolutionäre.'" *Berliner Morgenpost*, November 5, 1967. http://medienarchiv68.de/dl/203807/1374.jpg.pdf.
Müller, Michael Ludwig. *Berlin 1968: Die andere Perspektive*. Berlin: Berlin Story Verlag, 2008.
Mündemann, Tobias. *Die 68er . . . und was aus ihnen geworden ist*. Munich: Heyne, 1988.
Münkler, Herfried. *Die Deutschen und ihre Mythen*. Berlin: Rowohlt, 2009.
Naumann, Michael, and Wolfgang Kraushaar. "Wie wir uns befreiten." *Zeit Geschichte* 2/2007. http://www.zeit.de/zeit-geschichte/naumann.
Negt, Oskar. *Achtundsechzig: Politische Intellektuelle und die Macht*. Göttingen: Steidl, 1995.
———. "Demokratie als Lebensform: Mein Achtundsechzig." *Aus Politik und Zeitgeschichte* 14–15 (2008): 3–8.
Nehring, Holger. *Politics of Security: British and West German Protest Movements and the Early Cold War 1945–1970*. Oxford: Oxford University Press, 2013.
Nettelbeck, Uwe. *Prozesse: Gerichtsberichte 1967–1969*. Frankfurt am Main: Suhrkamp, 2015.
Niethammer, Lutz. "Die letzte Gemeinschaft: Über die Konstruierbarkeit von Generationen und ihre Grenzen." In Weisbrod, *Historische Beiträge*, 13–38.
Nooteboom, Cees. *Paris, Mai 1968*. Frankfurt am Main: Suhrkamp, 2003 (Dutch original 1968).
Novalis. *Aphorismen und Fragmente 1798–1800*. http://gutenberg.spiegel.de/buch/aphorismen-5232/6.
Obermaier, Uschi. "Zum Frühstück gab's bei mir Apfelsaft, Heroin und Sex." *Bild*, January 10, 2007. http://www.bild.de/leute/2007/obermaier-serie-fruehstueck-se-x-1242608.bild.html.
Offenbach, Judith. *Sonja: Eine Melancholie für Fortgeschrittene*. Frankfurt am Main: Suhrkamp, 1980.
Olick, Jeffrey K. "'Collective Memory': A Memoir and Prospect." *Memory Studies* 1 (2008): 23–29.
Olles, Werner. "Zur Rechten Gottes." In Wolfschlag, *Bye-bye '68*, 10–28.
Oltermann, Philip. "Jürgen Habermas's Verdict on the EU/Greece Debt Deal." *Guardian*, July 16, 2015. http://www.theguardian.com/commentisfree/2015/jul/16/jurgen-habermas-eu-greece-debt-deal.
ORF. "Retro spezial: 1968 Jahr des Aufstands." *Club 2*, June 13, 1978. https://www.youtube.com/watch?v=8v3bcJLaG6I.
Ott, Ullrich, and Roman Luckscheiter. *Belles Lettres / Graffiti: Soziale Phantasien und Ausdrucksformen der Achtundsechziger*. Göttingen: Wallstein Verlag, 2001.
Otto, Karl A. *Vom Ostermarsch zur APO: Geschichte der außerparlamentarischen Opposition der Bundesrepublik 1960–1970*. Frankfurt am Main: Campus, 1977.

Özdamar, Emine Sevgi. *Die Brücke vom goldenen Horn*. Cologne: Kiepenheuer & Witsch, 1998.
Paterson, Tony. "Uschi: Groupie, Addict and Heroine of the Left." *Independent*, February 2, 2007. http://www.independent.co.uk/news/world/europe/uschi-groupie-addict-and-heroine-of-the-left-434740.html.
Paulus, Julia. "Juni 1969: Die kulturelle Revolution der Frau." In Internet-Portal "Westfälische Geschichte." http://www.westfaelische-geschichte.de/web605.
Peters, Butz. *Tödlicher Irrtum: Die Geschichte der RAF*. Frankfurt am Main: Fischer, 2007.
Peters, Sabine. "Angst vor dem Chaos." *der freitag*, August 16, 2002. https://www.freitag.de/autoren/der-freitag/angst-vor-dem-chaos.
———. "Sie fangen noch einmal an." *Frankfurter Rundschau*, January 26, 2010.
Peterson, Abby. "Wounds That Never Heal: On Anselm Kiefer and the Moral Innocence of the West German Student Movements and the West German New Left." *Cultural Sociology* 6, no. 3 (2012): 367–85.
Pfeifer, Elizabeth. "1968 in German Political Culture, 1967–1993: From Experience to Myth." PhD diss., University of North Carolina at Chapel Hill, 1997.
Pieper, Werner, ed. *Alles schien möglich: 60 Sechziger über die 60er Jahre und was aus ihnen wurde*. Löhrbach: Grüne Kraft, 2007.
Pinter, Holger. *Die 68er-Verschwörung: Die Herrschaft der Unfähigen*. Siegburg: Edition Esoterick, 2010.
Piwitt, Hermann Peter. "Rückblick auf heiße Tage: Die Studentenrevolte in der Literatur." In *Literaturmagazin 4: Die Literatur nach dem Tod der Literatur; Bilanz der Politisierung*, edited by Hans-Christoph Buch, 35–46. Reinbek: Rowohlt, 1975.
Platen, Heide. "Brötchen mit Adorno." *taz*, March 5, 2002. http://www.taz.de/1/archiv/?dig=2002/03/05/a0162.
Plessen, Elisabeth. *Mitteilung an den Adel*. Zurich: Benziger, 1976.
Plowman, Andrew. "Bernward Vesper's *Die Reise*: Autobiography between the Student Movement and the Act of Self-Invention." *German Studies Review* 21, no. 3 (1998): 507–24.
———. *The Radical Subject: Social Change and the Self in Recent German Autobiography*. Bern: Peter Lang, 1998.
Plumpe, Werner. "1968 und die deutschen Unternehmen: Zur Markierung eines Forschungsfeldes." *Zeitschrift für Unternehmensgeschichte* 19 (2004): 45–66.
Preece, Julian. *Baader-Meinhof and the Novel: Narratives of the Nation / Fantasies of the Revolution, 1970–2010*. New York: Palgrave, 2012.
———. "The Lives of the RAF Revisited: The Biographical Turn." *Memory Studies* 3, no. 2 (2010): 151–63.
Prinz, Alois. *Lieber wütend als traurig: Die Lebensgeschichte der Ulrike Marie Meinhof*. Weinheim: Beltz, 2003.

———. *Der poetische Mensch im Schatten der Utopie: Zur politisch-weltanschaulichen Idee der 68er Studentenbewegung und deren Auswirkung auf die Literatur*. Würzburg: Königshausen & Neumann, 1990.
Proll, Astrid. *Baader Meinhof: Pictures on the Run 67–77*. Zurich: Skalo, 1998.
Proll, Thorwald, and Daniel Dubbe. *Wir kamen vom anderen Stern: Über 1968, Andreas Baader und ein Kaufhaus*. Hamburg: Nautilus, 2003.
Queenan, Joe. *Balsamic Dreams: A Short but Self-Important History of the Baby Boomer Generation*. London: Picador, 2006.
Raab, Klaus. "Mann von Welt." *taz*, May 7, 2008. http://www.taz.de/!16936/.
Rabehl, Bernd. *Linke Gewalt: Der kurze Weg zur RAF*. Schnellroda: Edition Antoios, 2006.
———. "Medien." In Landgrebe and Plath, *'68 und die Folgen*, 69–74.
Radloff, Marco. "Politisches Statement eines Fotografen." *Bildwerk3*, February 1, 2008. http://www.bildwerk3.de/2008/02/01/politisches-statement-eines-fotografen/.
Rathkolb, Oliver, and Friedrich Stadler, eds. *Das Jahr 1968: Ereignis, Symbol, Chiffre*. Goettingen: V&R unipress, 2010.
Reichardt, Sven. *Authentizität und Gemeinschaft: Linksalternatives Leben in den siebziger und frühen achtziger Jahren*. Berlin: Suhrkamp, 2014.
Reichardt, Sven, and Detlef Siegfried, eds. *Das Alternative Milieu: Antibürgerlicher Lebensstil und linke Politik in der Bundesrepublik Deutschland und Europa 1968–1983*. Göttingen: Wallstein, 2010.
Reich-Ranicki, Marcel. "Eine Müdeheldensoße; Zum zweitenmal: Der neue Roman von Günter Grass von Marcel Reich-Ranicki." *Die Zeit*, August 29, 1969.
———. *Mein Leben*. Munich: DTV, 2000.
Reichel, Sabine. "Uschis Märchenstunde." *Berliner Zeitung*, January 21, 2007. www.berliner-zeitung.de/archiv/nackter-diebstahl-und-ein-bisschen-verrat--wie-das-sexsymbol-obermaier-die-bewegung-der-68er-vermarktet--zur-freude-der-deutschen-uschis-maerchenstunde,10810590,10451276.html.
———. *What Did You Do in the War, Daddy? Growing Up German*. New York: Hill and Wang, 1989.
Reimann, Aribert. *Dieter Kunzelmann: Avantgardist, Protestler, Radikaler*. Kritische Studien zur Geschichtswissenschaft 188. Göttingen: Vandenhoeck & Ruprecht, 2009.
Reinders, Ralf, and Ronal Fritzsch. *Die Bewegung 2. Juni: Gespräche über Haschrebellen, Lorenzentführung, Knast*. Berlin: ID Verlag, 2003.
Reinecke. Stefan. "Kein Dämon, kein Heiliger." *taz*, December 24, 2004.
Reinicke, Helmut. *Bibliothek des Widerstands*. Vol. 12, *Rudi Dutschke: Aufrecht gehen; 1968 und der libertäre Kommunismus*. Hamburg: Laika, 2012.
Renner, Jens. *1968*. Hamburg: Rotbuch, 2001.

Rickels, Laurence A. *Germany: A Science Fiction*. Fort Wayne, IN: Anti-Oedipus Press, 2014.
Rinner, Susanne. *The German Student Movement and the Literary Imagination: Transnational Memories of Protest and Dissent*. New York: Berghahn, 2013.
Riordan, Colin, ed. *Peter Schneider. Contemporary German Writers*. Cardiff: University of Wales Press, 1995.
Robb, David. "Narrative Role-Play as Communication Strategy in German Protest Song." In *Protest Song in East and West Germany since 1960*, edited by David Robb, 67–98. Rochester, NY: Camden House, 2007.
Roediger, Henry L., and James V. Wertsch. "Creating a New Discipline of Memory Studies." *Memory Studies* 1 (2008): 9–22.
Röhl, Bettina. *So macht Kommunismus Spass! Ulrike Meinhof, Klaus Rainer Röhl und die Akte Konkret*. Hamburg: EVA, 2007.
Röhl, Klaus Rainer. *Fünf Finger sind keine Faust: Eine Abrechnung*. 1974; Munich: Universitas, 1998.
———. *Linke Lebenslügen: Eine überfällige Abrechnung*. Berlin: Ullstein, 1995.
Rosenberg, Rainer, Inge Münz-Koenen, and Petra Boden, eds. *Der Geist der Unruhe: 1968 im Vergleich; Wissenschaft—Literatur—Medien*. Berlin: Akademie, 2000.
Ross, Kristin. *May '68 and Its Afterlives*. Chicago: University of Chicago Press, 2002.
Roth, Roland, and Dieter Rucht, eds. *Neue soziale Bewegungen in der Bundesrepublik Deutschland*. Bonn: BPB, 1987.
Rothberg, Michael. *Multidirectional Memory: Remembering the Holocaust in the Age of Decolonialisation*. Stanford: Stanford University Press, 2009.
Rothschild, Thomas. *Das große Übel der Bourgeoisie*. Vienna: Promedia, 2004.
Rowbotham, Sheila. *Promise of a Dream: Remembering the Sixties*. London: Allen Lane, 2000.
Ruetz, Michael. *"Ihr müßt diesen Typen nur ins Gesicht sehen": APO Berlin 1966–1969*. Frankfurt am Main: Zweitausendeins, 1980.
———. *1968: Ein Zeitalter wird besichtigt*. Frankfurt am Main: Zweitausendeins, 1997.
———. *Sichtbare Zeit: Photographien 1965–1995*. Frankfurt am Main: Zweitausendeins, 1995.
Ruppert, Wolfgang, ed. *Um 1968: Die Repräsentation der Dinge*. Marburg: Jonas Verlag, 1998.
Rutschky, Michael. *Erfahrungshunger: Ein Essay über die siebziger Jahre*. Frankfurt am Main: Fischer, 1982.
Sabrow, Martin, ed. *Mythos "1968"?* Leipzig: Akademische Verlagsanstalt, 2009.
Said, Edward. *On Late Style: Music and Literature against the Grain*. New York: Pantheon Books, 2006.

Sander, Helke. "Rede des 'Aktionsrates zur Befreiung der Frauen' bei der 23. Delegiertenkonferenz des Sozialistischen deutschen Studentenbundes (SDS) im September 1968 in Frankfurt." In Sievers, *1968*, 372–78.
Schäfer, Alfred. *1968: Die Aura des Widerstands*. Paderborn: Ferdinand Schöningh Verlag, 2015.
Scharloth, Joachim. *1968: Eine Kommunikationsgeschichte*. Munich: Fink, 2011.
Schenk, Herrad. *In der Badewanne*. Cologne: Kiepenheuer & Witsch, 2007.
Schildt, Axel. "Eine schöne, wilde Zeit." *Die Zeit*, March 17, 2008.
———. "Überbewertet? Zur Macht objektiver Entwicklungen und zur Wirkungslosigkeit der '68er.'" In Wengst, *Reform und Revolte*, 89–102.
Schildt, Axel, and Detlef Siegfried, eds. *Between Marx and Coca-Cola: Youth Cultures in Changing European Societies, 1960–1980*. New York: Berghahn, 2006.
Schildt, Axel, Detlef Siegfried, and Karl Christian Lammers, eds. *Dynamische Zeiten: Die 60er Jahre in den beiden deutschen Gesellschaften*. Hamburg: Christians, 2000.
Schiller, Kay. "Political Militancy and Generation Conflict in West Germany during the 'Red Decade.'" *Debatte: Journal of Contemporary Central and Eastern Europe* 11 (2003): 19–38.
Schimmang, Jochen. *Das Beste, was wir hatten*. Hamburg: Edition Nautilus, 2008.
———. *Das Ende der Berührbarkeit*. Frankfurt am Main: Suhrkamp, 1981.
———. "Mal sehen, was im Dschungel lief." *taz*, February 29, 2012.
———. *Der schöne Vogel Phönix: Erinnerungen eines Dreißigjährigen*. Frankfurt am Main: Suhrkamp, 1979.
———. "Vom Ende des Winters." *taz*, March 18, 2008.
Schlager, Hilke. "Der Kongreß in Hannover." *Die Zeit*, June 16, 1967. http://www.zeit.de/1967/24/der-kongress-in-hannover/komplettansicht.
Schlak, Stephan. "Der Nicht-Anschlußfähige." *taz*, March 30, 2005.
Schlink, Bernhard. *Der Vorleser*. Zurich: Diogenes, 1995.
Schmid, Thomas. "Die 68er: Es gab kein 'rotes Jahrzehnt'." *Die Welt*, December 30, 2007.
———. "Der ganz freie Diskurs." *Die Welt*, August 22, 2009. http://www.welt.de/welt_print/politik/article4379213/Der-ganz-freie-Diskurs.html.
———. "Was Axel Springer und die '68er' gemeinsam hatten." *Die Welt*, September 22, 2015, http://www.welt.de/146679076.
Schmidt, Rudi. "1968 West und 1989 Ost: Von den Mythen jüngster deutscher Umbrüche; Was bleibt den Nachgeborenen?" *Berliner Debatte Initial* 19, no. 5 (2008): 3–13.
Schmidtke, Michael. *Der Aufbruch der jungen Intelligenz: Die 68er Jahre in der Bundesrepublik und den USA*. Frankfurt am Main: Campus, 2003.
Schneider, Franz, ed. *Dienstjubiläum einer Revolte: "1968" und 25 Jahre*. Munich: von Hase & Koehler, 1993.

Schneider, Peter. "Ausbruch aus der Käseglocke." *Der Spiegel* 21/2000, May 22, 2000. http://www.spiegel.de/spiegel/print/d-16466527.html.
———. "*Bild* macht dumm." *konkret* 3 (March 1968): 14–17.
———. *Lenz*. Berlin: Rotbuch Verlag, 1973.
———. *Die Lieben meiner Mutter*. Cologne: Kiepenheuer & Witsch, 2013.
———. "Die Phantasie im Spätkapitalismus und die Kulturrevolution." *Kursbuch* 16 (March 1969): 1–37.
———. *Rebellion und Wahn: Mein '68*. Cologne: Kiepenheuer & Witsch, 2008.
———. *Skylla*. Berlin: Rowohlt, 2005.
———. "Über den Unterschied von Literatur und Politik." In "Das Vergehen von Hören und Sehen: Aspekte der Kulturvernichtung," edited by Hermann Peter Piwitt and Peter Rühmkorf, special issue, *Literaturmagazin* 5 (1976): 188–98.
———. "Vergessen, was Manipulation ist." *Frankfurter Rundschau*, September 3, 2009.
———. "Vorbild Mao Tse-Tung." *Der Spiegel*, April 7, 1969.
———. "Wir haben Fehler gemacht." Speech held on May 5, 1967. http://www.glasnost.de/hist/apo/fehler.html.
Schnell, Ralf. *Geschichte der deutschsprachigen Literatur seit 1945*. Stuttgart: Metzler, 1993.
Schnibben, Cordt. "Vollstrecker des Weltgewissens." *Der Spiegel* 23/1967, June 2, 1967. http://www.spiegel.de/spiegel/print/d-8720253.html.
Schöfer, Erasmus. *Ein Frühling irrer Hoffnung*. Berlin: Dittrich Verlag, 2001.
———. "Der Revolutionär Dutschke hinterlässt seine Schuhe und Zehntausenden passen sie." In *Ein Frühling*, 122–33.
———. *Winterdämmerung*. Berlin: Dittrich, 2008.
———. *Zwielicht*. Berlin: Dittrich, 2004.
Schöll, Julia. "Chaos und Ordnung zugleich: Zum intra- und intertextuellen Verweissystem in Uwe Timms Erzähltexten." In Finlay and Cornils, *(Un-)erfüllte Wirklichkeit*, 127–39.
Scholz, Leander. *Rosenfest*. Munich: Hanser, 2001.
Schonfield, Ernest. "1968 and Transnational History in Emine Sevgi Özdamar's *Die Brücke vom goldenen Horn*." *German Life and Letters* 68, no. 1 (2015): 66–87.
Schrader-Klebert, Karin. "Die kulturelle Revolution der Frau." *Kursbuch 17* (1969): 1–45.
Schubert, Venanz, ed. *1968: 30 Jahre danach*. St. Ottilien: Eos Verlag, 1999.
Schulenburg, Lutz. *Das Leben ändern, die Welt verändern! 1968: Dokumente und Berichte*. Hamburg: Nautilus, 1998.
Schulz, Kristina. "Bräute der Revolution: Kollektive und individuelle Interventionen von Frauen in der 68er-Bewegung und ihre Bedeutung für die Formierung der neuen Frauenbewegung." *Westfälische Forschungen: Zeitschrift des Westfälischen Instituts für Regionalgeschichte des Landschaftsverbandes Westfalen-Lippe* 48 (1998): 97–116.

———. "Frauen in Bewegung: Mit der neuen Linken über die Linke(n) hinaus." In Klimke and Scharloth, *Handbuch*, 247–58.

———. *Der lange Atem der Provokation: Die Frauenbewegung in der Bundesrepublik und in Frankreich (1968–1976)*. Frankfurt am Main: Campus, 2002.

———. "Ohne Frauen keine Revolution: 68er und neue Frauenbewegung." http://www.bpb.de/LIBTTI.html, March 6, 2008.

Schulz-Gerstein, Christian. "Das Fräulein Tochter meutert." *Der Spiegel* 46/1976, November 8, 1976.

Schütt, Peter. "1968: Ein persönlicher und politischer Rückblick." In Wolfschlag, *Bye-bye '68*, 88–98.

Schwab, Andreas, Beate Schappach, and Manuel Gogos, eds. *Die 68er: Kurzer Sommer—lange Wirkung; Ein literarisches Lesebuch* (Begleitbuch zur Ausstellung des Historischen Museums in Frankfurt am Main). Munich: DTV, 2008.

Schwab, Waltraud. "Die letzte aus der Dutschke-WG." *taz*, March 7, 2005. http://www.taz.de/1/archiv/?dig=2005/03/07/a0247.

Schwarz, Felicitas. "Das Foto: Die Kommune I." http://www.arte.tv/magazine/karambolage/de/das-foto-die-kommune-1-karambolage.

Schwarz, Hans-Peter. *Axel Springer: Die Biographie*. Berlin: List, 2009.

———. "Die eigentlichen Helden." *Die Welt*, September 6, 1997.

Schwarzer, Alice. "Daniel Cohn-Bendit & die Kinder." *Emma*, May/June 2001. http://www.emma.de/artikel/daniel-cohn-bendit-der-vergangenheit-liegt-die-gegenwart-265010.

———. *Lebenslauf*. Cologne: Kiepenheuer & Witsch, 2011.

———. "Zur Person: Alice Schwarzer erzählt ihr Leben." October 1, 2011. http://www.aliceschwarzer.de/artikel/alice-schwarzer-erzaehlt-ihr-leben-311561.

Searle, John R. *The Construction of Social Reality*. London: Penguin, 1995.

Seiffert, Jeanette. *"Marsch durch die Institutionen?": Die 68er in der SPD*. Bonn: Bouvier, 2009.

Seitenbecher, Manuel. *Mahler, Machke und Co.: Rechtes Denken in der 68er-Bewegung?* Paderborn: Schöningh, 2013.

Senfft, Alexandra. "Kollidierende Gedächtnisse." *taz*, October 11, 2013. http://www.taz.de/!5057429/.

Seyfried, Gerhard. *Wo soll das alles enden*. 1978; Berlin: Rotbuch, 2005.

Shafi, Monika. "Talkin' 'bout My Generation: Memories of 1968 in Recent German Novels." *German Life and Letters* 59, no. 2 (2006): 201–16.

Sherman, Daniel J., Ruud van Dijk, Jasmine Alinder, and A. Aneesh, eds. *The Long 1968: Revisions and New Perspectives*. Bloomington: Indiana University Press, 2013.

Shortt, Linda. *German Narratives of Belonging: Writing Generation and Place in the Twenty-First Century*. Oxford: Legenda, 2015.

Sichtermann, Barbara. "1968 als Symbol." In Baier et al., *Die Früchte*, 43.

Siegfried, Detlef. "Furor und Wissenschaft: Vierzig Jahre nach '1968'." *Zeithistorische Forschungen / Studies in Contemporary History* 5, no. 1

(2008): 130–41, http://www.zeithistorische-forschungen.de/1-2008/id=4710.

———. *Time Is on My Side: Konsum und Politik in der westdeutschen Jugendkultur der 60er Jahre*. Göttingen: Wallstein, 2008.

———. "Die wunderbaren Jahre." In *Time Is on My Side*, 429–644.

Siepmann, Eckhard, ed. *CheSchahShit: Die sechziger Jahre zwischen Cocktail und Molotow*. Reinbek: Rowohlt, 1986.

Sievers, Rudolf, ed. *1968: Eine Enzyklopädie*. Frankfurt am Main: Suhrkamp, 2004.

Sill, Oliver. *Zerbrochene Spiegel: Studien zu Theorie und Praxis modernen autobiographischen Erzählens*. Berlin: de Gruyter, 1991.

Slobodian, Quinn. "The Axe of the Event: In and Out of the Echo Chamber of West Germany's 1968." *The Sixties: A Journal of History, Politics and Culture* 7, no. 2 (2014): 178–83.

———. *Foreign Front: Third World Politics in Sixties West Germany*. Durham, NC: Duke University Press, 2012.

Sontheimer, Michael. "High sein, frei sein." *Der Spiegel* 39/2007, September 24, 2007.

Spender, Stephen. *The Year of the Young Rebels*. London: Weidenfeld and Nicolson, 1969.

Spiegel Online. "Aktion Blanker Busen." October 16, 2007. http://www.spiegel.de/einestages/achtundsechzig-aktion-blanker-busen-a-949905.html.

———. "Springer hat die Idee einer Aussprache selbst begraben." *Spiegel Online*, August 23, 2009. http://www.spiegel.de/kultur/gesellschaft/abgesagtes-tribunal-mit-68ern-springer-hat-die-idee-einer-aussprache-selbst-begraben-a-644510.html.

———. "Springer-Tribunal fällt aus." *Spiegel Online*, August 22, 2009. http://www.spiegel.de/kultur/gesellschaft/68er-gespraech-springer-tribunal-faellt-aus-a-644461.html.

Spiegel Special. "Die wilden 68er: Die Spiegel-Serie über die Studentenrevolution." 1/1988. *http://www.spiegel.de/spiegel/spiegelspecial/index-1988-1.html*.

Staadt, Jochen, Tobias Voigt, and Stefan Wolle. *Feind-Bild Springer: Ein Verlag und seine Gegner*. Göttingen: Vandenhoeck & Ruprecht, 2009.

Stankiewitz, Karl. *München '68: Traumstadt in Bewegung*. Munich: Volk, 2008.

Stefan, Verena. *Häutungen*. Munich: Verlag Frauenoffensive, 1975.

Steinfeld, Thomas. "Herr Tur Tur und die Revolution." *Süddeutsche Zeitung*, October 27, 2007. http://www.sueddeutsche.de/kultur/mythos-herr-tur-tur-und-die-revolution-1.890191.

Stephanski, Michal. *Die 68er-Generation vor Gericht: Untersuchungen zu den Konfliktkonstruktionen in den Texten der 85er-Generation*. Frankfurt am Main: Peter Lang, 2013.

Stiftung für die Rechte zukünftiger Generationen, ed. *Die 68er: Warum wir Jungen sie nicht mehr brauchen*. Freiburg: Kore, 1998.

Struck, Karin. *Klassenliebe*. Frankfurt am Main: Suhrkamp, 1973.
Suri, Jeremi. *The Global Revolutions of 1968*. New York: Norton, 2007.
Taberner, Stuart. *The Novel in German since 1990*. Cambridge: Cambridge University Press, 2011.
taz special. "40 Jahre 68er Revolte." April 19, 2008.
Theweleit, Klaus. *Ghosts: Drei leicht inkorrekte Vorträge*. Frankfurt am Main: Stroemfeld, 1998.
Thomas, Nick. *Protest Movements in 1960s West Germany: A Social History of Dissent and Democracy*. Oxford: Berg, 2003.
Thomson, Richard Hinton, and Keith Bullivant. *Literature in Upheaval: West German Writers and the Challenge of the 1960s*. Manchester: Manchester University Press, 1974.
Timm, Uwe. *Deutsche Kolonien*, AutorenEdition (1981). Cologne: Kiepenheuer & Witsch, 2001.
———. *Freitisch*. Cologne: Kiepenheuer & Witsch, 2011.
———. *Der Freund und der Fremde*. Cologne: Kiepenheuer & Witsch, 2005.
———. *Heißer Sommer*. Munich: Bertelsmann, 1974.
———. *Kerbels Flucht*. Munich: DTV, 2000.
———. *Montaignes Turm: Essays*. Cologne: Kiepenheuer & Witsch, 2015.
———. "Mythos." In *Montaignes Turm*, 33–58.
———. *Rot*. Cologne: Kiepenheuer & Witsch, 2001.
———. "Die Rotts und die Rothschilds: Von einem, der glaubte, ohne zu arbeiten, gut leben zu können." *Deutsche Volkszeitung: Wochenzeitung für demokratischen Fortschritt*, November 30, 1972.
———. *Vogelweide*. Cologne: Kiepenheuer & Witsch, 2013.
Tolmein, Oliver. *"RAF—Das war für uns Befreiung": Ein Gespräch mit Irmgard Möller über den bewaffneten Kampf, Knast und die Linke*. Hamburg: konkret, 1997.
Tomforde, Anna. "Germans Reconsider the Lessons of 1968." *Guardian*, April 19, 1988.
Treusch, Wolf-Sören. "Ist das sowas wie Aufarbeitung: 100 Tage 'Medienarchiv 68' vom Axel Springer Verlag." *Deutschlandradio*, April 8, 2010. http://www.deutschlandradiokultur.de/ist-das-sowas-wie-aufarbeitung.1001.de.html?dram:article_id=157025.
Trinius, Stephan, ed. "War 68 eine Revolution? Kurzer Sommer, lange Wirkung—eine virtuelle Gesprächsrunde." Mediathek, Bundeszentrale für politische Bildung, 2008. http://www.bpb.de/mediathek/190170/war-68-eine-revolution.
Uesseler, Rolf. *Die 68er: "Macht kaputt, was euch kaputt macht!" APO, Marx und freie Liebe*. Munich: Heyne, 1998.
Varon, Jeremy, Michael S. Foley, and John McMillian. "Time Is an Ocean: The Past and Future of the Sixties." *The Sixties: A Journal of History, Politics and Culture* 1, no. 1 (2008): 1–7.
Vehlewald, Hans-Jörg. "Mythos Rudi Dutschke: Was ist dran am linken Helden der 68er?" *Bild-Zeitung*, April 28, 2010.

Verlag Klaus Wagenbach. "Buchstäblich Wagenbach—50 Jahre: Der *unabhängige* Verlag für *wilde* Leser." http://www.wagenbach.de/images/stories/50/50Jahre-Wagenbach.pdf.

Verlinden, Karla. *Sexualität und Beziehungen bei den "68ern": Erinnerungen ehemaliger Protagonisten und Protagonistinnen*. Bielefeld: Transcript, 2015.

Vesper, Bernward. *Die Reise: Romanessay*. Edited by Jörg Schröder. Frankfurt: März Verlag, 1977.

Viebahn, Fred. *Das Haus Che oder Jahre des Aufruhrs: Ein historisches Provisorium*. Hamburg: Merlin Verlag, 1973.

Vogel, Bernhard, and Matthias Kutsch, eds. *40 Jahre 1968: Alte und Neue Mythen—Eine Streitschrift*. Freiburg: Herder, 2008.

Vogel, Meike. *Unruhe im Fernsehen: Protestbewegung und öffentlich-rechtliche Berichterstattung in den 1960er Jahren*. Göttingen: Wallstein, 2010.

Voigt, Lothar. *Aktivismus und moralischer Rigorismus: Die politische Romantik der 68er Studentenbewegung*. Wiesbaden: Deutscher Universitätsverlag, 1991.

von Bönisch, Georg, and Klaus Wiegrefe. "Ein Abgrund von Lüge." *Der Spiegel* 38/2012, September 17, 2012. http://www.spiegel.de/spiegel/print/d-88656050.html.

von der Goltz, Anna. "Generations of 68ers: Age-Related Constructions of Identity and Germany's '1968.'" *Cultural and Social History* 8, no. 4 (2011): 473–90.

———. "Making Sense of East Germany's 1968: Multiple Trajectories and Contrasting Memories." *Memory Studies* 6 (2013): 53–69.

———, ed. *"Talkin' 'bout My Generation": Conflicts of Generation Building and Europe's "1968."* Göttingen: Wallstein, 2011.

von Dirke, Sabine. *"All Power to the Imagination!": The West German Counterculture from the Student Movement to the Greens*. Lincoln: University of Nebraska Press, 1997.

von Ditfurth, Christian. *Schatten des Wahns*. Cologne: Kiepenheuer & Witsch, 2006.

von Hodenberg, Christina. "Der Kampf um die Redaktionen: '1968' und der Wandel der westdeutschen Massenmedien." In von Hodenberg and Siegfried, *Wo "1968" liegt*, 145.

von Hodenberg, Christina, and Detlef Siegfried, eds. *Wo "1968" liegt: Reform und Revolte in der Geschichte der Bundesrepublik*. Göttingen: Vandenhoeck & Ruprecht, 2006.

von Lucke, Albrecht. *68 oder neues Biedermeier: Der Kampf um die Deutungsmacht*. Berlin: Wagenbach, 2008.

von Weizsäcker, Richard. "Ansprache beim Staatsakt zum 'Tag der deutschen Einheit.'" Berlin, October 3, 1990. http://www.bundespraesident.de/SharedDocs/Reden/DE/Richard-von-Weizsaecker/Reden/1990/10/19901003_Rede.html.

Wackwitz, Stephan. *Ein unsichtbares Land*. Frankfurt am Main: Fischer, 2003.

———. "Separatistische Lebensläufe." *taz*, September 2, 2008.

Waechter, Matthias. "Mythos, Version: 1.0," *Docupedia-Zeitgeschichte*, February 11, 2010. http://docupedia.de/zg/Mythos?oldid=106455.
Wallerstein, Immanuel. *Geopolitics and Geoculture: Essays on the Changing World-System*. Cambridge: Cambridge University Press, 1991.
———. "1968: Revolution in the World-System." *Theory and Society* 18, no. 4 (1989): 431–49.
Wallraff, Günter. *Der Aufmacher: Der Mann, der bei "Bild" Hans Esser war*. Cologne: Kiepenheuer & Witsch, 1977.
Walter, Uwe. "In Bad Boll ein Butzemann?" http://www.ev-akademie-boll.de/fileadmin/res/otg/misc/butzemann.pdf.
Waters, Sarah. "Introduction: 1968 in Memory and Place." In Cornils and Waters, *Memories of 1968*, 1–21.
Watts, Michael. "1968 and All That . . ." *Progress in Human Geography* 25, no. 2 (2001): 157–88.
Weber, Stefan. "Was heißt 'Medien konstruieren Wirklichkeit'? Von einem ontologischen zu einem empirischen Verständnis von Konstruktion." *Medien-Impulse*, no. 40 (2002): 12–16. http://www.mediamanual.at/mediamanual/themen/pdf/diverse/40_Weber.pdf.
Weiland, Severin. "Nazi-Jäger: Gauck zeichnet Beate und Serge Klarsfeld aus." *Der Spiegel*, May 13, 2015. http://www.spiegel.de/politik/deutschland/ns-aufarbeitung-gauck-zeichnet-ehepaar-klarsfeld-aus-a-1033660.html.
Weinhauer, Klaus. "Terrorismus in der Bundesrepublik der Siebzigerjahre: Aspekte einer Sozial- und Kulturgeschichte der Inneren Sicherheit," *Archiv für Sozialgeschichte* 44 (2004): 219–42.
Weisbrod, Bernd. *Historische Beiträge zur Generationenforschung*. Göttingen: Wallstein, 2009.
Weiss, Peter. *The Aesthetics of Resistance*, vol. 1. Translated by Joachim Neugroschel, with a foreword by Frederic Jameson. Durham, NC: Duke University Press, 2005.
Welzer, Harald. *Das kommunikative Gedächtnis: Eine Theorie der Erinnerung*. Munich: C. H. Beck, 2011.
Wengst, Udo, ed. *Reform und Revolte: Politischer und gesellschaftlicher Wandel in der Bundesrepublik Deutschland vor und nach 1968*. Munich: Oldenbourg, 2011.
———. Review. *sehepunkte* 9 (2009). http://www.sehepunkte.de/2009/01/14414.html.
Wesel, Uwe. *Die verspielte Revolution: 1968 und die Folgen*. Munich: Blessing, 2002.
Wetzel, Wolf. "Ein Staatsbegräbnis für '68', oder: Ihr Scheitern als Erfolgsstory." In Autonome L.U.P.U.S. Gruppe, *Die Hunde bellen*, 13–28.
Widmann, Arno. "In Frankfurt weltberühmt." *Frankfurter Rundschau*, April 30, 2008. http://www.fr-online.de/zeitgeschichte/-kurzer-sommer---lange-wirkung--in-frankfurt-weltberuehmt,1477344,2796486.html.
Wienhaus, Andrea. *Bildungswege zu "1968": Eine Kollektivbiographie des Sozialistischen Deutschen Studentenbundes*. Bielefeld: Transcript, 2014.

Willinger, Markus. *Die identitäre Generation: Eine Kriegserklärung an die 68er*. Arktos Media, 2013.
Winter, Jay. *Dreams of Peace and Freedom: Utopian Moments in the 20th Century*. New Haven, CT: Yale University Press, 2006.
Witzel, Frank. *Die Erfindung der Roten Armee Fraktion durch einen manisch-depressiven Teenager im Sommer 1969*. Berlin: Matthes & Seitz, 2015.
Wodianka, Stephanie, and Juliane Ebert, eds. *Metzler Lexikon moderner Mythen: Figuren, Konzepte, Ereignisse*. Stuttgart: Metzler, 2014.
Wolf, Christa. "Nehmt euch in acht!" *Frankfurter Rundschau*, July 11, 2008. http://www.fr-online.de/zeitgeschichte/interview-mit-christa-wolf--nehmt-euch-in-acht-,1477344,2689666.html.
Wolf, K. D. "Geschlechterrollen bei der 68ern: Kurzer Sommer, lange Wirkung—eine virtuelle Gesprächsrunde." Bundeszentrale für politische Bildung, 2008. http://www.bpb.de/mediathek/190167/geschlechterrollen-bei-den-68ern.
Wolff, Frank, and Eberhard Windaus, eds. *Studentenbewegung 1967–69: Protokolle und Materialien*. Frankfurt am Main: Roter Stern, 1977.
Wolfrum, Edgar. "Die 68er-Bewegung zwischen Protest und Gewalt." In *Die geglückte Demokratie*, 261–71.
———. "Erinnerungskultur und Geschichtspolitik als Forschungsfelder: Konzepte—Methoden—Themen." In *Reformation und Bauernkrieg: Erinnerungskultur und Geschichtspolitik im geteilten Deutschland*, ed. Jan Scheunemann, 13–47. Leipzig: EVA, 2010.
———. *Die geglückte Demokratie: Geschichte der Bundesrepublik Deutschland von ihren Anfängen bis zur Gegenwart*. Stuttgart: Klett-Cotta, 2006.
———. "'1968' in der gegenwärtigen deutschen Geschichtspolitik." *Aus Politik und Zeitgeschichte* 49, no. B 22–23 (2001): 28–36.
———. *Rot-Grün an der Macht: Deutschland 1998–2005*. Munich: Beck, 2013.
Wolfrum, Edgar, and Günther R. Mittler. "Das Jahr 1968: Vom Politikereignis zum Geschichtsereignis." *Forschungsjournal: Neue Soziale Bewegungen* 21, no. 3 (2008): 16–24.
Wolfschlag, Claus-M., ed. *Bye-bye '68 . . .: Renegaten der Linken, APO Abweichler und allerlei Querdenker berichten*. Graz: Stocker, 1998.
Wolle, Stefan. *Der Traum von der Revolte: Die DDR 1968*. Berlin: Ch. Links, 2008.
Wulff-Bräutigam, Katharina. *Bhagwan, Che und ich: Meine Kindheit in den 70ern*. Munich: Droehmer, 2005.
Zelizer, Barbara. "Why Memory's Work on Journalism Does Not Reflect Journalism's Work on Memory." *Memory Studies* 1 (2008): 79–87.

Index

3sat, 170–71
9/11, 27, 47–48, 87, 210, 225
1968 exhibit (museum exhibit), 176

Adenauer, Konrad, 50
Adorno, Theodor, 51, 79, 175, 187–88
Agit 883, 185
Ahlers, Conrad, 167
Aktionsrat zur Befreiung der Frau (Action Council for the Liberation of Women), 140, 144
Al Qaida, 54, 81
Alef, Rob, works by: *Das magische Jahr* (The Magic Year), 28
Ali, Tariq, 51
Althaus, Dieter, 191
Altrogge, Georg, 165
Aly, Götz, 86, 199. See also *Mythos 1968*
Aly, Götz, works by: *Unser Kampf 1968: Ein irritierter Blick zurück* (Our Struggle 1968: An Irritated Look Back), 2, 89–90, 136, 163, 215
Amendt, Günter, 69
American War of Independence, 221
Amerika Haus Berlin, 173, 177
Amon Düül (band), 142, 181
Angela Davis Congress, 53
Anti-Springer campaign, 36, 103, 157, 159, 161–68, 191
APO Archiv, 71
Arab Spring, 2, 57
Arbeitsgemeinschaft der Rundfunkanstalten Deutschlands (ARD), 169–70
Ash, Timothy Garton, 8
Assmann, Aleida, 13–14
Assmann, Jan, 12
Augstein, Franziska, 171
Augstein, Rudolf, 152–53, 156, 161, 167, 169
Aus Parlament und Zeitgeschichte (Politics and Contemporary History), 2, 172
Auschwitz, 142
Außerparlamentarische Opposition (Extraparliamentary Opposition), 1, 16, 23–24, 27, 45, 49, 51–53, 64, 67, 84, 87, 98, 102, 116, 131, 152, 178, 183–85, 199, 205
Aust, Stefan, 151
Aust, Stefan, works by: *Der Baader-Meinhof Komplex* (The Baader-Meinhof Complex), 34, 179
Austen, Jane, 186
AutorenEdition, 97, 102, 113

Baader, Andreas, 19–21, 33, 36, 84, 88, 120, 168
"baby boomers," 44, 151–52, 196
Bachmann, Josef, 157, 189
Bartsch, Jürgen, 86
"battle at Tegeler Weg," 46
Bauer, Karin, 12
BBC *Radio 4*, 172–73
Beat poets, 54, 62
Becker, Hartmuth, 82
Behre, Silja, 56
Benda, Erich, 40
Berger, Peter, 12
Berlin Love Parade, 169
Berlin SDS, 175
Berlin Wall, 48, 62
Berliner Extra Dienst, 156
Berliner Morgenpost, 156, 161–65
Berliner Zeitung, 156, 179

Berthold, Barbara Metselaar, 190–91
Beuys, Josef, 180
Bewegung 2. Juni, 3, 117, 197
Bichelberger, Roger, works by: *Le mai, le joli mai* (The May, the Pretty May), 95
Biermann, Wolf, 181
Bild am Sonntag, 165
Bild Berlin, 165
Bild-Zeitung, 9, 27, 40, 53, 76, 143, 153, 156, 158, 159, 165, 191, 195
Bissinger, Manfred, 166
Bisson, Terry, works by: *Any Day Now*, 95
Bittorf, Wilhelm, 168
Black September, 86
Bloch, Ernst, 26, 142 188; on constructing history, 7
Bloch, Ernst, works by: *Das Prinzip Hoffnung* (The Principle of Hope), 223
Bloch, Karola, 142
Bock, Ulrich, 190
Böll, Heinrich, 102, 158–59
Bollinger, Stefan, 67
Bonaparte, Napoleon, 107
Bonifer, Hagen, works by: *Vom Nutzen zu zweifeln 2. Juni 1967* (The Benefits of Doubt: June 2, 1967), 180, 185
Bordieu, Pierre, 56, 132
Born, Nicolas, 100
Börne, Ludwig, 101
Bornhack, Achim, works by: *Das wilde Leben*, 179
Bovenschen, Silvia, 41, 172
Bovenschen, Silvia, works by: *Die imaginierte Weiblichkeit* (The Imagined Femininity), 141; *Nur Mut* (Be Brave), 141
Boyle, T. C., works by: *Drop City*, 95
Brandt, Willy, 47, 49, 63, 130, 191
Braunschweig-Kolleg, 21
Bräute der Revolte (*brides of the revolt*) (photograph), 140
Brecht, Bertolt, 103
Briegleb, Klaus, 99

Brodman, Roman, works by: *Der Polizeistaatsbesuch* (The Policestate Visit), 171
Brown, Timothy Scott, 189
Brown, Timothy Scott, works by: *West Germany and the Global Sixties*, 61–62
Broyard, Anatole, 131
Brückner, Peter, 212
Brügge, Peter, 168
Bucerius, Gerd, 161
Buch, Hans-Christoph, 18, 104
Büchner, Georg, 106, 185
Bude, Heinz, 42–43
Buhmann, Inga, works by: *Ich habe mir eine Geschichte geschrieben* (I Have Written My Own History), 147
Bullivant, Keith, 96
Bundestag, 4, 40, 48, 65, 75
Bundeszentrale für politische Bildung (Federal Agency for Civic Education), 75, 151, 172–74, 218
Burckhardt, Barbara, 179
Burckhardt, Martin, works by: *Die Geschichte einer Kulturrevolution* (The History of a Cultural Revolution), 221

Cailloux, Bernd, works by: *Das Geschäftsjahr 1968/69* (The Business Year), 126–29, 138, 206; *Gutgeschriebene Verluste* (Credited Losses), 197, 206
Cameron, James, works by: *Avatar*, 186
Camus, Albert, works by: *L'Etranger* (The Stranger), 22
Castro, Fidel, 124
CDU (Christian Democratic Union), 4, 65, 75–77, 142
Charim, Isolde, 53
Charlie Hebdo, 6, 33
Chaussy, Ulrich, works by: *Die drei Leben des Rudi Dutschke* (The Three Lives of Rudi Dutschke), 26
Chavez, Cesar, 74
Chinese Cultural Revolution, 89

Civil Rights Movement, 1, 62
Cohn-Bendit, Daniel, on revolution, 41; founder of Revolutionärer Kampf, 90, 159; interviewed on ORF, 170; linked with Rudi Dutschke, 26, 29–33, 111, 132, 170–72; linked with Joschka Fischer, 29–33, 90, 159; linked with French May, 29–33
Cohn-Bendit, Daniel, works by: *1968: Die letzte Generation, die noch nichts von dem Ozonloch wusste* (1968: The Last Generation That Didn't Know about the Hole in the Ozone Layer), 32, 186–87; *1968: Die Revolte* (1968: The Revolt), 32; *Der Große Basar* (The Great Bazaar), 32; *Nous l'avons tant aimée, la révolution* (We Loved It So Much, the Revolution), 32
Cold War, 49, 60, 103, 152–53
Communism (fall of), 170
"continuity thesis," 3
Cosgrove, Mary, 5
Craig, Gordon A., works by: *The Germans*, 211
Cream (band), 171
Croissant, Klaus, 80
Czechoslovakia (invasion of), 1, 171, 193

Da Vinci, Leonardo, 185
Dahlem-Mafia, 157
Dannecker, Martin, 172
Dannenberg, Sophie, 194
Dannenberg, Sophie, works by: *Das bleiche Herz der Revolution* (The Pale Heart of the Revolution), 79–82, 136
Danquart, Pepe, works by: *Joschka und Herr Fischer: Eine Zeitreise durch 60 Jahre Deutschland* (Joschka and Herr Fischer: A Journey through 60 Years of Germany), 31, 197
Das Konzept Stadtguerilla (The Concept of the City Guerrilla), 35, 52

Das Philosophische Quartett (The Philosophical Quartet), 5
Das wilde Leben (The Wild Life), 143
Davis, Belinda, 146
De Carlo, Andrea, works by: *Due di due* (Two Rows of Two), 9
Degenhardt, Franz Josef, 181–82
DeGroot, Gerard, 29, 73–74
DeLillo, Don, 20
Delius, Friedrich Christian, as Lektor at Suhrkamp Verlag, 185; as commentator on revolution, 8, 14, 94, 103, 138
Delius, Friedrich Christian, works by: *Als die Bücher noch geholfen haben* (When Books Were Still Helpful), 197, 205; *Amerikahaus, oder der Tanz um die Frauen* (America House and the Dance around the Women), 117–19, 125, 136, 205; *Ein Held der Inneren Sicherheit* (A Hero of Home Security), 117; *Himmelfahrt eines Staatsfeindes* (Apotheosis of an Enemy of the State), 117; *Mein Jahr als Mörder* (My Year as Murderer), 119–20; *Mogadishu Fensterplatz* (Mogadishu Window Seat), 117; *Unsere Siemens-Welt* (Our Siemens World), 120, 205
Der Baader Meinhof Komplex (The Baader-Meinhof Complex) (film), 34, 84
Der Große Selbstbetrug (The Grand Delusion), 76
Der Spiegel, 9, 18, 24, 81, 101, 141, 151–70, 173, 187–89, 194–95, 201
Derrida, Jacques, 220
Detje, Robin, 81
Deutsche Forschungsgesellschaft (DFG), 170
Deutsche Fotothek, 183
Deutsche Historisches Museum (German Historical Museum), 3
Deutsche Kommunistische Partei (DKP, German Communist Party), 90, 113

Deutsche National-Zeitung, 158
Deutsche Welle, 151
Deutscher Herbst (German Autumn), 7, 25, 39, 47, 86, 210
Deutsch-Französisches Jugendwerk (German-French Youth Foundation), 142
Deutschlandradio, 151, 166
Diba, Farah, 33
Die Linke, 142
Die schwarzen Panther (The Black Panthers), 171
Die Welt, 90, 151, 153, 156–64
Die Welt Berlin, 165
Die Zeit, 4, 116, 131, 141, 153, 161, 166, 174, 180
Diekmann, Kai, 76–78, 195
Diepgen, Eberhard, 173
Dirsch, Felix, 82
Dittfurth, Jutta, works by: *Rudi und Ulrike: Geschichte einer Freundschaft* (Rudi and Ulrike: The Story of a Friendship), 34
Dittrich, Volker, 124
Dönhoff, Marion Gräfin, 211
Döpfner, Mathias, 158–59, 164–67
Dubček, Alexander, 190
Durruti, Buenaventura, 103
Dutschke (film), 174
Dutschke, Rudi: antinationalism, 3, 39; anti-Springer campaign, 30, 105, 110, 156, 158, 163; assassination attempt on, 1, 48, 108, 110, 120, 152, 157, 164, 189, 193; death of, 132; figurehead of German student movement, 6, 23–36, 41, 103, 110, 142, 155, 194; International Vietnam Congress, 161; legacy of, 23–36, 41, 74, 111, 191, 194; linked with Bernd Rabehl, 47, 153; Long March, 5, 215; media representations of, 158, 165–68, 170–71, 174, 179–83, 193; Nazism, 83; position on violence, 53, 70, 76, 116; RAF, 76, 215; SDS leader, 16–17, 23–29, 33, 41, 103, 110, 142, 155, 194

Dutschke-generation, 83
Dutschke-Klotz, Gretchen, 25–28, 142, 168, 172
Duwe, Freimut, 25
Dylan, Bob, 74, 181, 201

East German Stasi, 3, 16
Edel, Uli, director of *Der Baader Meinhof Komplex* (film), 84, 179
Egan, Jennifer, works by: *The Invisible Circus*, 95
Eight Miles High (English title of *Das wilde Leben*) (film), 143
Elder-Vass, Dave, 12
emergency laws, 102, 122, 129
Emma, 142
Engelmann, Bernt, 124
Enquete-Kommission, 13
Ensslin, Felix, 35
Ensslin, Gudrun, 19–21, 33, 35–36, 84, 88, 180–83
Enzensberger, Hans Magnus: editor of *Kursbuch*, 103–4, 207; "political re-education," 8; *politische Alphabetisierung der Deutschen*, 124, 138, 205; as writer on 1968, 18, 94, 101–2, 138, 154, 175
Enzensberger, Hans Magnus, works by: *Tumult* (Tumult), 197, 206–8; *Der Untergang der Titanic* (The Sinking of the Titanic), 103
Erhard, Ludwig, 52
Eschenbach, Wolfram von, 225
European Parliament, 32
European Union, 10

Fahlenbrach, Kathrin, 60, 154–55, 172–74
Federal Agency for Civic Education, 6
Federal Republic of Germany, 2, 3, 17–18, 39, 42, 46–49, 51, 54, 62–65, 76, 78, 86, 88, 91, 104, 113, 124, 133, 137, 157, 160, 169, 172, 200–201, 216
Fels, Gerhard, 66
Ferdinand, Franz, 214
Festival des politischen Liedes (Festival of the Political Song), 192

Fichter, Tilmann, 45–46, 48–49, 166
Fischer, Erika, works by: *Aimee & Jaguar*, 145–46
Fischer, Joschka, 36, 48, 65, 75, 85–86, 90, 153, 159, 187, 196, 225
"Fischer scandal," 4
Flimm, Jürgen, 173
Floh de Cologne, 181
Focus, 76, 174
Francois, Etienne, 11
Frank, Robert, 217
Frank Zappa and the Mothers of Invention, 181
Frankfurt Book Fair, 100, 130
Frankfurt Institute of Social Research, 79
Frankfurt School, 50, 82, 188
Frankfurter Allgemeine Zeitung, 174, 187
Frankfurter Rundschau, 164, 174
Frankfurter Weiberrat (Council of Frankfurt Women), 3
Franklin, Benjamin, 100
Fraser, Ronald, 69
Frauenrede, 144
Free Speech Movement, 1, 62
Frei, Norbert, 67, 70
Frei, Norbert, works by: *Jugendrevolte und globaler Protest 1968*, 172
Freie Universität Berlin (FU), 16–18, 23, 33, 45–46, 49, 74, 79, 102, 104, 141, 157
French "May," 1, 30, 73, 95, 182
French Revolution, 221
Fried, Erich, works by: *Nicht jeder ist ersetzbar* (Not Everyone is Replaceable), 25
Fronius, Sigrid, 141
Fuchs, Anne, 5
Fukushima, 224
Fulbrook, Mary, 97, 189
"Fundamentalliberalisierung" (fundamental liberalization), 6

Garibaldi, Giuseppe, 141
Gassert, Philipp, 60, 71
Gaus, Günter, 155
Gdeck, Martina, 34
Gedächtnis der Nation (Memory of the Nation), 172
"Generation Golf," 5
Gerchow, Jan, 177
Gerlach, Ingeborg, "New Subjectivity," 96–97
German Book Prize, 129
German Democratic Republic (GDR), 2, 9, 13, 17, 44, 63, 85, 156, 161, 172, 182, 189, 192, 199–201, 214, 223
German women's movement, 3, 35
Gesamtzusammenhang, 7
Gilcher-Holtey, Ingrid, 2, 217
Gilcher-Holtey, Ingrid, works by: "*1968*"—*Eine Wahrnehmungsrevolution?* ("1968"—A Revolution of Perception? Consequences and Echoes of 1968), 56; *1968: Eine Zeitreise*, 56; *1968: Vom Ereignis zum Gegenstand der Geschichtswissenschaft*, 55
Gleichschaltung, 154
Goethe, Johann Wolfgang von, 203
Goethe, Johann Wolfgang von, works by: *Farbenlehre* (Theory of Colours), 115
Gollwitzer, Hellmut, 25, 120
Göring, Hermann, 214
Gramsci, Antonio, 8
Grass, Günter, 8, 18, 159, 173; position on SDS, 129
Grass, Günter, works by: *Aus dem Tagebuch einer Schnecke* (From the Diary of a Snail), 132; *Beim Häuten der Zwiebel* (Peeling the Onion), 131; *Kopfgeburten, oder Die Deutschen sterben aus* (Headbirths, or The Germans are Dying Out), 132; *Mein Jahrhundert* (My Century), 132; *örtlich betäubt* (Local Anaesthetic), 130
Grebe, Rainald, 181
green movement, 2, 47

Green Party (Greens), 29–30, 32, 41, 47–48, 171
Greiner, Ulrich, 116
Grimberg, Steffen, 166
Grote, Georg, 5
Gruppe 47, 100, 102, 129, 205
Guevara, Che, 81, 103, 124, 130, 138, 195
Guru Guru, 181
Guthrie, Arlo, 171
Guthrie, Woody, 181

Habermas, Jürgen, 17, 39, 74, 80, 102–3, 188, 227
Haifisch-Kommune (Shark Commune), 142–43
Hair (film), 171
Hamburg Institute of Social Research, 50, 52, 71
Hamburger Abendblatt, 165
Handke, Peter, 102
Hannover, Irmela, 195
Hartung, Klaus, 41, 91–93, 154
Haus der Geschichte (House of History), 3
Hausmann, Friederike (née Dollinger), 141, 168
Havel, Vaclav, 190
Hayden, Tom, 70
Heidegger, Martin, 188
Heider, Ulrike, works by: *Anarchism: Left, Right and Green*, 148; *Keine Ruhe nach dem Sturm* (No Calm after the Storm), 148–49; *Vögeln ist schön* (Fucking Is Beautiful), 148
Heimatfilme, 175, 213
Hein, Jan-Philipp, 166
Hendrix, Jimi, 142
Henschel, Gerhard, works by: *Martin Schlosser*, 194
Henschel, Jürgen, 17, 141
Herman, Eva, 195
Hitler, Adolf, 20, 24, 30, 89
Ho Chi Minh, 124, 195
Hochschulkampf (University Struggle), 86
Hohn, Detlef, 193
Holocaust, 77, 86

Honecker, Erich, 192
Honneth, Axel, 171
Horkheimer, Max, 51
Houellebecq, Michel, works by: *Les particules élémentaires* (The Elementary Particles), 95
Hugenberg, Alfred, 157
Humboldtian ideal, 10
Humphrey, Hubert, 155

I'm a Celebrity . . . Get Me Out of Here! (television program), 11
Institute for Social Research in Frankfurt, 57
International Centre for Protest Research, 60
International Vietnam Congress, 25, 53, 59, 60, 141, 144, 163, 161, 179
Internationale Essener Songtage, 127–28, 181
Iraq War, 29
Islamic fundamentalism, 159

Jagger, Mick, 142
Jähner, Harald, 122
Jameson, Frederick, 100
Jelinek, Elfriede, works by: *Ulrike Maria Stuart*, 34
Jochimsen, Jess, works by: *Das Dosenmilch-Trauma* (The Condensed Milk Trauma), 194
Johns, Derek, works by: *Wakening*, 95
Johnson, Uwe, 129
Joplin, Janis, 195
"Joschka's wilde Jahre" (Joschka's wild years), 52
Juchler, Ingo, 59
Juni (Movement June 2), 3
Junker, Detlef, 59
Jusos, 35

Kampf dem Atomtod (Fight Against Nuclear Death), 152
Karl, Michaela, 27
Katsiaficas, George, 60
Kätzel, Ute, 144–45

Kellerhoff, Sven Felix, 162–63, 165–66
Kennedy, Douglas, works by: *State of the Union*, 95
Kennedy, Robert, 74
K-Gruppen (K-groups), 35, 46
Kiefer, Anselm, 180
Kiesinger, Kurt Georg, 142
Kimmel, Michael, 59
Kinderladen, 144
Klarsfeld, Beate, 142, 172
Klarsfeld, Serge, 142
Kleinert, Hubert, 218
Klimke, Martin, works by: *The Other Alliance*, 60–61
Klinger, Cornelia, 98
Klonovsky, Michael, 76
Kluge, Alexander, 68
Koenen, Gerd: as coeditor of *1968: Bildspur eines Jahres*, 184; as critic of 1968, 86–89, 172, 198–99; linked with "red decade," 2, 180
Koenen, Gerd, works by: *Das rote Jahrzent: Unsere kleine deutsche Kulturrevolution 1967–1977* (The Red Decade: Our Little German Cultural Revolution 1967–1977), 86–88, 149; *Vesper, Ensslin, Baader: Urszenen des deutschen Terrorismus* (primal scenes of terrorism), 215
Koenigs, Tom, 171
Kohl, Helmut, 25, 30, 63, 200
Köhler, Horst, 75
Kölner Stadt-Anzeiger, 166
Kommando 2. Juni (Command June 2), 158
Kommune I (Commune I), 3, 16, 36, 45, 57, 79, 129, 142, 155, 162, 169, 178, 191, 207, 226
Kommunistischer Bund Westdeutschland (KBW, Communist League of West Germany), 86
konkret, 9, 33, 84–85, 144, 152, 157, 185, 198
Kosiek, Rolf, 82–83
Köster, Barbara, 172
Krahl, Hans-Jürgen, 50, 144

Kraushaar, Wolfgang, as leading scholar on 1968, 1, 8, 10, 31, 50–62, 70, 88–90, 94, 172, 179–80; on Götz Aly, 89–90; on Dutchke and violence, 70, 76, 88; linked with Joschka Fischer, 31; on Peter Schneider, 104
Kraushaar, Wolfgang, works by: *1968 als Mythos, Chiffre und Zäsur* (1968 as Myth, Cypher and Caesura), 52, 217; *Achtundsechzig: Eine Bilanz* (Sixty-Eight: An Assessment), 54, 212–13; *Die Bombe im jüdischen Gemeindehaus* (The Bomb in the Jewish Community Center), 3; *Fischer in Frankfurt*, 52, 149; *Frankfurter Schule und Studentenbewegung* (Frankfurt School and Student Movement), 50; *Protest-Chronik* (Chronicle of Protest), 152
Kröger, Claus, 177
Kromher, Stefan, director of *Dutschke*, 142, 180
Krüger, Horst, 131
Krüger, Thomas, 107
Kulturzeit extra: Mythos 1968; Die Revolte und ihre Archäologen (The Revolt and Its Archaeologists), 171
Kundnani, Hans, works by: *Utopia or Auschwitz: Germany's 1968 Generation and the Holocaust*, 67–68
Kunkel, Annegret, 81
Kunzelmann, Dieter, 36, 142
Kunzru, Hari, works by: *My Revolutions*, 95
Kurlansky, Mark, 1, 51
Kurras, Karl-Heinz, 16, 49, 189
Kursbuch, 41, 91, 101, 103–4, 105, 144

Lafontaine, Oscar, 48
Langguth, Gerd, 75–76, 166, 172–73
Langhans, Rainer, 11, 36, 142–43, 168, 195
Langston, Richard, 68

le Carré, John, works by: *Absolute Friends*, 95
Leggewie, Claus, 2, 53, 219
Leggewie, Claus, works by: *Politische Zeiten: Beobachtungen von der Seitenlinie* (Political Times: Observations from the Sidelines), 193–94
LEMO (Lebendiges Museum Online), 172
Lenin, Vladimir, 195
Lennon, John, 195
Lettau, Reinhard, 18
L'Homme: Europäische Zeitschrift für Feministische Geschichtswissenschaft, 146
Long March, 67, 97, 103, 106, 110, 123, 171, 178, 200, 215, 224
Lönnendonker, Siegward, 18, 45–46, 48–49
Löwenthal, Richard, 74–75, 211
Luckmann, Thomas, 12
Lüdke, Martin, 96, 137
Ludwig, Volker, 173, 177
Luxemburg, Rosa, 101

Mahler, Horst, 3, 36, 79
Manheim, Ralph, 131
Mann, Torsten, 82
Maoism, 106, 112, 141, 200, 206
Marcuse, Herbert, as "mentor" of German student movement, 7, 26, 51–52, 56, 101, 110, 113, 126, 188, 216, 220
Marcuse, Herbert, works by: *Das Ende der Utopie* (The End of Utopia), 111; *Eros and Civilisation* (*Triebstruktur und Gesellschaft*), 121; *Versuch über die Befreiung* (An Essay on Liberation), 117; *Vietnam: Analyse eines Exempels* (Vietnam: Analysis of an Example), 111
Marmulla, Henning, 103–4
Martin Luther King Jr., 152
Marwick, Arthur, 59, 217
Marx, Karl, 129, 175, 195
Marxism, 46, 63–64, 74, 106, 202

März, Ursula, 81, 116–17
Maurer, Susanne, 146
McManus, Susan, 7
Medienarchiv68, 165–69
Meinhoff, Ulrike, 3, 9, 33–37, 84–86, 124, 144, 152, 168, 179
Meins, Holger, 36, 116
Merkel, Angela, 4, 65, 75–76, 226–27
Meschkat, Klaus, 53
Meyer, Michael, 166
Michel, Detlef, 178–79, 197
Miermeister, Jürgen, 25–26
Mitchell, David, 220
Mohr, Peter, 203
Mohr, Reinhard, 164, 173
Mohr, Reinhard, works by: *1968: Die letzte Revolution, die noch nichts vom Ozonloch wußte*, 186–87; *Der diskrete Charme der Rebellion* (The Discrete Charm of the Rebellion), 187–89
Möller, Irmgard, 141
Mosler, Peter, 213
Mosler, Peter, works by: *Was wir wollten, was wir wurden* (What We Desired, What Became of Us), 39, 50
Müller, Michael, 161–62
Münkler, Herfried, 219
Mythos 1968, 171, 216–22

Nafisi, Iran Azar, works by: *Reading Lolita in Tehran*, 95
National Socialism (NS), 2, 24, 38, 49, 51, 54, 60, 63–64, 67, 83, 86–87, 89, 110–11, 119–20, 124, 129–30, 142, 146, 149, 163, 166, 169, 172, 213–14, 223–24
Nationalepos (National Epic), 214
Nautilus, 153
Nazi generation, 14, 80 169, 180–82
Negt, Oskar, 6, 53, 66–68, 88, 103
Nenning, Günter, 170
New Criticism, 97
New Left, 55, 59, 75, 84, 122, 124
New York Times, 131
Nibelungenlied, 214–15
Niethammer, Lutz, 43

Nietzsche, Friedrich, works by: "Vom Nutzen und Nachteil der Historie für das Leben," (On the Use and Abuse of History for Life), 63
Nirumand, Bahran, 84, 172
Noack, Hans-Joachim, 168
Nora, Pierre, 42
Noteboom, Cees, 95
Novalis, 213

Obermaier, Uschi, 142–43, 147, 168, 171, 179
Occupy movement, 2, 23, 57, 225
Offenbach, Judith, works by: *Sonja: Eine Melancholie für Fortgeschrittene* (Sonja: A Melancholia for Advanced Readers), 147
Ohnesorg, Benno, as martyr, 17–18; images of, 17, 141, 168, 182; legacy of, 16–23, 39, 191, 219; linked with Friederike Hausmann, 141; linked with Uwe Timm, 110, 117, 136, 141, 215; literary representations of, 18–19, 21, 23, 36, 117, 136, 215; shooting of, 2, 16–23, 33, 36, 46, 86, 109–10, 117, 129, 141, 152–53, 156, 165, 168, 189, 219
Old Left, 59
Olles, Werner, 90
Olympic Games (Munich, 1972), 86
ORF (Österreichischer Rundfunk), 170
Organisation und Bedingungen des Widerstands (Organization of and conditions for resistance), 17
Osterunruhen (Easter riots), 1
Ostpolitik, 5, 49, 63, 191
Özdamar, Emine Sevgi, works by: *Die Brücke vom goldenen Horn* (The Bridge of the Golden Horn), 148

pardon (magazine), 142
peace movement, 2
Peters, Butz, 35
Pflasterstrand, 153, 187
Philosophisches Quartett, 196

Pikulik, Lothar, 213
Pinter, Holger, 83
Piwitt, Hermann Peter, 98, 138
Plessen, Elisabeth, works by: *Mitteilung an den Adel* (Notes for the Nobility), 146–47
Plowman, Andrew, 8, 96
Polenz, Ruprecht, 78
Port Huron Statement, 71
Powers, Richard, works by: *The Time of our Singing*, 95
Prague Spring, 62, 191
Preece, Julian, 137
Prinz, Alois, 212
Prinz, Alois, works by: *Lieber wütend als traurig* (Rather Angry Than Sad), 34
Protestarchiv, 71
Pynchon, Thomas, works by: *Vineland*, 95

Queenan, Joe, 73

Rabehl, Bernd, 3, 18, 27, 48, 103, 153
RCDS, 173
"red decade," 2, 87–89, 149, 180
red-green coalition government, 4, 6, 29–30, 51, 54, 67, 79, 153, 169, 179, 225
"red-green project," 4, 7
Reemtsma, Jan Phillip, 50
Regner, Sven, works by: *Herr Lehmann* (Mr. Lehmann), 194; *Der Kleine Bruder* (The Little Brother), 194; *Neue Vahr Süd*, 194
Reichardt, Sven, 58
Reichel, Sabine, works by: *What Did You Do in the War, Daddy?*, 147
Reich-Ranicki, Marcel, 131
Reidemeister, Helga, works by: *Rudi Dutschke: Spuren*, 142
Reinecke, Stefan, 53
Reinicke, Helmut, 27
Reitz, Edgar, 173
"Republican Club," 36
Revolutionärer Kampf (Revolutionary Struggle), 90

Rhineland-Palatinate, 78
RIAS Berlin, 166
Richards, Keith, 142
Richter, Gerhard, 180–81
Richter, Hans Werner, 18
Rickels, Laurence, 224
Rietzler, Rolf, 168
Ring Christlich-Demokratischer Studenten (RCDS), 44–46, 75–78
Rinner, Susanne, 134–35
Röhl, Bettina, 3–4, 85–86, 194
Röhl, Klaus Rainer, 9, 84–85, 144, 179
Rolin, Olivier, works by: *Tigre en papier* (Paper Tiger), 95
Rolling Stones (band), 86
Rosenthal, Kurt, 171
Ross, Kristin, 11, 44, 73
Ross, Kristin, works by: *May '68 and Its Afterlives*, 65–66
Rotbuch Verlag, 106, 205
Rote Armee Fraktion (Red Army Faction, RAF), 2–3, 12, 19, 27, 29, 34–36, 43, 48, 52–53, 64, 76, 81, 84, 86, 89, 114, 117, 123–24, 136–37, 141, 158, 179–80, 187, 206, 215, 226
Rote Hilfe (Red Aid), 86
Rote Sonne (Red Sun), 171
Rowbotham, Sheila, works by: *Promise of a Dream*, 140
Rudi-Dutschke-Straße, 11, 27
Ruetz, Michael, 24, 140, 182–83
Rüger, Sigrid, 144
Rumsfeld, Donald, 29
Russell, Bertrand, 157

Safranski, Rüdiger, 5, 196
Salvatore, Gaston, 84, 168, 183
Sander, Helke, 144
Sarrazin, Thilo, 82
Sartre, Jean-Paul, 22, 26
Scharloth, Joachim, 70
Schildt, Axel, 43, 172
Schimmang, Jochen, as major writer on 1968, 14, 94, 133, 138, 206, 214
Schimmang, Jochen, works by: *Das Beste, was wir hatten* (The Best We Had), 197, 200–202; *Der schöne Vogel Phönix* (The Beautiful Bird Phoenix), 27, 125–26, 138, 200
Schlacht am Tegeler Weg (Battle of Tegeler Weg), 120
Schlegel, 213
Schlingensief, Christoph, works by: *Rocky Dutschke*, 179
Schmid, Thomas, 2, 90, 151, 159, 160, 163–64, 166–67
Schmidt, Andreas Christoph, 170
Schmidt, Helmut, 49
Schmidt, Rudi, 218–19
Schmitt, Carl, 200
Schneider, Franz, 75–76
Schneider, Peter, literary representations of 1968, 201; gives famous speech, 33, 102, 169; as major writer on 1968, 8, 14, 85, 94, 104–5, 111, 132, 138, 149, 169, 173, 215; as organizer of anti-Springer campaign, 157, 164, 166–67
Schneider, Peter, works by: *Eduards Heimkehr* (Eduard's Return), 107; *Lenz*, 106, 110, 125, 133, 205; *Rebellion und Wahn* (Rebellion and Delusion), 197–99, 207; *Skylla*, 107–9, 117, 138, 197
Schnell, Ralf, 96
Schnibben, Cordt, 168
Schnurre, Wolfdietrich, 18
Schöfer, Erasmus, as major writer on 1968, 14, 94, 133; linked with Werkkreis Literatur der Arbeitswelt, 102
Schöfer, Erasmus, works by: *Ein Frühling irrer Hoffnung* (A Spring of Crazy Hope), 27, 120, 123, 136, 138; *Die Kinder des Sisyfos* (The Children of Sisyphus), 120–25, 199–200; *Winterdämmerung* (The Twilight of Winter), 197, 199–201, 215; *Zwielicht* (Twilight), 122–25

Scholz, Leander, works by: *Rosenfest* (Celebration of Roses), 19–20, 136
Schönbohm, Wulf, 78
Schortmann, Cècile, 171
Schrader-Klebert, Karin, 144
Schulz, Kristina, 146, 172
Schulze, Hagen, 219
Schulz-Gerstein, Christian, 147
Schütt, Peter, 90
Schwanitz, Dietrich, works by: *Der Campus* (The Campus), 80
Schwarz, Hans Peter, 158, 162, 163
Schwarzer, Alice, 142
Searle, John R., 12
Second Iraq War, 224
Second World War, 82
Seminar: A Journal of Germanic Studies, 12
Semler, Christian, 84, 103, 151, 164, 196
Sender Freies Berlin, 170
Seppel, Ursula, 141
Seyfried, Gerhard, 185
Shafi, Monika, 132–34, 153
Shah of Persia (Iran), 1, 16, 33, 10, 141, 179
Shortt, Linda, 45
Sichtermann, Barbara, 213
Siegfried, Detlef, 71, 172
Siegfried, Detlef, works by: *Time Is on My Side: Konsum und Politik in der westdeutschen Jugendkultur der 60er Jahre* (Time Is On My Side: Consumption and Politics in the West German Youth Culture in the Sixties), 57–58
Sill, Oliver, 106
Silver Generation, 152
Slobodian, Quinn, 154
Sloterdijk, Peter, 5, 69, 196
Social Democratic Party (SPD), 47–49, 63, 65, 87, 130, 178
Sontheimer, Kurt, 26, 170–71
Soviet Union, 85
Sozialdemokratischer Hochschulbund (SHB), 45, 130, 155
Sozialistischer Deutscher Studentenbund (SDS, Socialist German Student League), 3, 16–17, 21, 23, 26–27 33, 45–49, 57–59, 76–80, 86–87, 90, 103, 110–12, 129–30, 141–45, 148, 157, 159, 161, 180, 186, 192, 206
Spender, Stephen, 95
Spiegel Special, 30
Spiegel Special no. 1, 168
Springer, Axel, 26, 105, 155–58, 161–66, 167, 170–71, 198
Springer press, 1, 5, 11, 18, 24–25, 27, 36, 44, 46, 90, 120, 129, 151, 153, 155–61, 167–69, 173–74
Springer Tribunal 2.0, 189
St. George, 30
Staadt, Jochen, 18, 46, 166–67
Stalinism, 66
Stasi, 2, 13, 49, 165, 189, 191–92, 223
Stasi Records Agency, 13
Stenzel, Hans-Joachim, 157, 166
Stern, 155, 166, 174
Strauss, Franz Josef, 167
Stunde Null, 221
Süddeutsche Zeitung, 174
Südwestdeutscher Rundfunk (SWR), 170
Suhrkamp Verlag, 103
"summer of love," 1, 74, 152, 182
Swales, Martin, 97

Tagesschau, 195
Taibo, Paco Ignacio, works by: '68, 95
Tangerine Dream (band), 181
taz, 151, 153, 166, 174, 182, 187, 195–96
Teufel, Fritz, 16, 36, 141, 181, 195–96
The City Preachers (band), 181
The Educators (English title of *Die fetten Jahre sind vorbei*), 179
The Grateful Dead (band), 181
The Rolling Stones (band), 224
The Sixties: A Journal of History, Politics and Culture, 69, 219
Theweleit, Klaus, 170–71
Third Reich, 2, 147, 154, 162, 169
Thomas, Nick, 8

Time, 131
Times Literary Supplement, 101
Timm, Uwe, as major writer on 1968, 8, 14, 94, 132, 138, 219–20; linked with AutorenEdition, 102; linked with Jürgen Henschel, 141
Timm, Uwe, works by: *Am Beispiel meines Bruders* (In My Brother's Shadow), 21, 117; *Deutsche Kolonien* (German Colonies), 113–14; *Freitisch* (Free Meals), 197, 202–3; *Der Freund und der Fremde* (The Friend and the Stranger), 21–23, 117, 138, 203 215; *Heißer Sommer* (Hot Summer), 18–19, 27, 80, 110–12, 114–16, 125, 133, 135–36; *Kerbels Flucht* (Kerbel's Escape), 114; *Morenga*, 113–14; *Rot* (Red), 28, 113–17, 126, 137–38, 202–3, 215; *Vogelweide* (Bird Meadow), 197, 203–4, 215
Todesnacht (death night), 36, 141
Tomatenwurf (tomato-throw), 140, 142
Treusch, Wolf-Sören, 166–67

Uccello, Paolo, works by: *St. George and the Dragons*, 215
Ulbricht, Walter, 192
Ullstein Verlag, 156
United Nations, 171
Unseld, Siegfried, 185

Veiel, Andres, 171
Veiel, Andres, works by: *1968: Bildspur eines Jahres*, 184; *Wer, wenn nicht wir?*, 180
Vesper, Bernward, works by: *Die Reise* (The Trip), 88, 147
Vesper, Will, 88
Vietcong, 17, 180
Vietnam War, 1, 17, 23, 30, 46, 53, 84, 101, 115, 117–19, 130–31, 149, 152, 156–57, 171, 178, 182
Vogel, Bernhard, 78
Vogel, Meike, 170
Vogelweide, Walter von der, 21, 215
Voigt, Lothar, 212

von der Goltz, Anna, 44, 192–93
von Dirke, Sabine, 57
von Lucke, Albrecht, 6
von Weizsäcker, Richard, 3, 42, 64
Vostell, Wolf, works by: *Nur Die 1*, 180

Waader, Hannes, 181
Wackwitz, Stephan, works by: *Ein unsichtbares Land* (An Invisible Country), 45
Waechter, Matthias, 217
Wagenbach Verlag, 153, 205
Wagner, Richard, works by: *Götterdämmerung* (Twilight of the Gods), 200; *Ring Cycle*, 213, 215
Walden, Matthias, 26, 170–71
Wallerstein, Immanuel, 60
Wallraff, Günter, 102, 158
War Crimes Tribunal on Vietnam, 157
Warsaw Pact, 1, 171, 191–93
Was war links?, 170
Watson, Susan, 51
Watts, Michael, 67
Weimar Republic, 157
Weingartner, Hans, works by: *Die fetten Jahre sind vorbei* (The Years of Plenty are Over), 179
Weiss, Peter, 103
Weiss, Peter, works by: *Die Ästhetik des Widerstands* (Aesthetics of Resistance), 8, 100; *Viet Nam Diskurs* (Viet Nam Discourse), 102
Welt am Sonntag, 165
Welzer, Harald, 12
Werkkreis Literatur der Arbeitswelt, (Cooperative Literature of the World of Work), 102, 120, 124
Wesel, Uwe, 18, 79
West German Greens, 48
Wetzel, Wolf, 78
White, T. H., 214
Wieser, Harald, 168
Wilde Zeiten, 184
Wildmann, Arno, 177
Wilhelm II, 214
Willinger, Markus, 83
Windaus, Eberhard, 40, 45

Winkler, Heinrich August, 189
Winkler, Stefan, 82
Winter, Jay, 38
Wirtschaftswunder (economic miracle), 5
Wissenschaftskritik, 10
Wissmann statue, 112, 114
Wodianka, Stephanie, 219
Wolf, Christa, works by: *Nachdenken über Christa T.*, 189
Wolfe, Tom, works by: *The Electric Kool-Aid Acid Test*, 95
Wolff, Frank, 40, 45
Wolff, K. D. 172
Wolfrum, Edgar, 62–65
Wolle, Stefan, 172, 192

Women's Liberation movement, 140
Woodstock Festival, 152, 182
"Woodstock generation," 44
World War II, 1
Wulff-Bräutigam, Katharina, works by: *Bhagwan, Che und ich: meine Kindheit in den 70ern* (Bhagwan, Che and I: My Childhood in the 70s), 194

Zahl, Peter Paul, 133, 185, 196
Zaungäste, 14, 45, 186
Zedong, Mao, 175, 195
Zint, Günter, 168–69, 183
Zweites Deutsches Fernsehen (ZDF), 27, 151, 169, 170

www.ingramcontent.com/pod-product-compliance
Lightning Source LLC
Chambersburg PA
CBHW051600230426
43668CB00013B/1917